Caribbean

SEA OF THE NEW WORLD

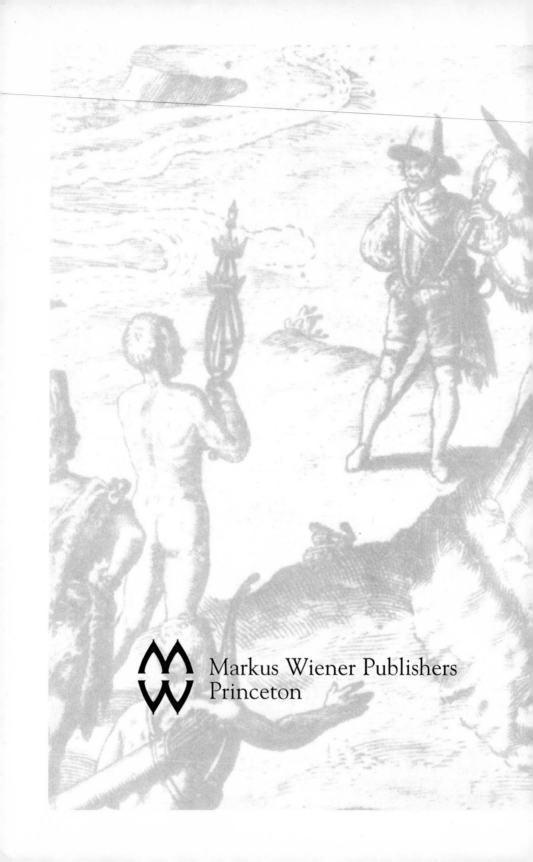

Markus Wiener Publishers
Princeton

Caribbean
Sea of the New World

Germán Arciniegas

Translated from the Spanish by Harriet de Onís

First Markus Wiener Publishers edition, 2003
Second printing, 2011

Published by arrangement with Alfred A. Knopf, a division of
    Random House, Inc.
Copyright © 1946 by Alfred A. Knopf, Inc. for the main text
Copyright © 2003 by Norman Girvan for the Foreword
Copyright © 2003 by Markus Wiener Publishers for the
    bibliographical update

Cover illustration: View of Havana by Alain Manesson Mallet
    (Paris, 1683), from Description de l'Univers. Collection of
    Luis Martinez-Fernández.
Cover design by Maria Madonna Davidoff

For information write to:
Markus Wiener Publishers, 231 Nassau St., Princeton, NJ 08542
www.markuswiener.com

Library of Congress Cataloging-in-Publication Data
Arciniegas, Germán, 1900–
        [Biografía del Caribe. English]
        Caribbean, sea of the New World / Germán Arciniegas.
        Includes bibliographical references and index.
        Contents: bk. 1. The Golden Age — bk. 2. The Silver Age — bk.
        3. The Age of Enlightenment —bk. 4. The Age of Liberty.
        ISBN-13: 978-1-55876-312-8 (alk. paper)
        ISBN-10: 1-55876-312-0 (alk. paper)
        1. Caribbean Area—History. I. Title.
F2175.A713 2003
972.9—dc21   2003049650

Markus Wiener Publishers books are printed in the United States
of America on acid-free paper, and meet the guidelines for permanence
and durability of the Committee on Production Guidelines for Book
Longevity of the Council on Library Resources.

CONTENTS

v

CONTENTS

ACKNOWLEDGMENTS

Despite the length of this book, which I would have wished briefer and less involved, it does not go beyond the beginning of the twentieth century. The events that have taken place in the Caribbean since then would afford material for another book which would be as fantastic and dramatic as the account set forth. I have not entered upon this second part lest the tale become interminable, and because it has seemed to me that it required more detailed handling. Moreover, I have wanted to keep a perspective that should preserve the charm inherent in the remembrance of things past. A book on the Caribbean covering the last thirty years would involve a complete study of the politics of the period in order to determine the responsibilities incurred by foreigners and natives alike in permitting this frontier zone of America to become the prey of soulless commercial enterprises and the private domain of base dictators. Manifestly, this would result in a work of a quite different nature.

I have had the plan of this book in mind for years, but its realization became possible through the unusual opportunity afforded me during my visiting professorships, in the years 1943 and 1944, at the University of Chicago, Mills College, and the University of California. In these institutions, and principally at the University of California, thanks to its splendid library of Latin American History, I found advice, material impossible to come by anywhere else, and the time needed to complete the work. I wish to take this opportunity to thank these institutions for having invited me to occupy a chair in them, and my associates for their competent aid. Among my many friends there, I owe special gratitude to Robert Redfield, J. Fred Rippy, Herbert E. Bolton, S. Griswold Morley, Rudolph Schevill, and Leonard Olschki, from all of whom I received valuable suggestions regarding my work.

I also wish to express my gratitude to the Guggenheim and the Rockefeller foundations for their contribution to the maintenance of my chairs in Chicago and Berkeley, and to Mr. Henry Allen Moe and Professor William Berrien of the aforesaid foundations for their interest in my work.

Finally, but no less gratefully, I owe to my excellent translator, Harriet de Onís, whose work exceeds all praise, timely suggestions throughout which have been of inestimable help to me.

All this encouragement and advice would have been as nothing but for the unfailing moral support of my wife to whom this book, like my others, is dedicated as a tribute of my devotion.

Bogotá, August 1945

FOREWORD

The Making of the
Greater Caribbean

GERMÁN Arciniegas' *Caribbean: Sea of the New World* was first published in 1946, one year after the Spanish original *Biografía del Caribe*.[1] It is a breathtaking and magisterial work, encompassing four centuries of history of the Caribbean basin in its broad sweep, told in a compelling narrative style. Of course the Antilles, Greater and Lesser, are there; but so too are Central America, the Isthmus, the land of *Nueva Granada* (now Colombia and Venezuela), and the three Guianas. For Arciniegas, the Caribbean Sea was the Mediterranean of the New World, "a place of fertile and dramatic encounter of peoples, races, religions, and cultures."[2] Today we know that region as the Greater Caribbean, *El Gran Caribe*. Arciniegas' account of its history was one of the first of its kind by a native scholar.

That the book marked a turning point in Caribbean historiography is now widely acknowledged. Dr. Bridget Brereton, Professor of History at the University of the West Indies, declares in an authoritative essay published as part of UNESCO's *General History of the Caribbean* that Arciniegas was one of "two authors writing in the 1940s [who] departed significantly from the imperial tradition in their approach to the region's past."[3] According to Professor Gustavo Bell of his native Colombia, Arciniegas broke with the traditional nationalist perspectives of Hispanic American historians by "incorporating this part of the world into the long history of the West, presenting the Caribbean as the equivalent of the Mediterranean; an integral part of the violent expansion of the Judeo-Christian world that began with the arrival of Columbus at the shores of Hispaniola."[4]

As such, *Caribbean: Sea of the New World* takes its place as one of the earliest expressions of a Pan-Caribbean intellectual and political consciousness; a product of the stirrings in the 1930s and 1940s that also produced C.L.R. James' timeless account of the Haitian Revolution (quoted by Arciniegas),[5] Eric Williams' thesis on capitalism and slavery in the West Indies,[6] and W. Adolphe Roberts's history of the Caribbean.[7] Such was the boldness of Arciniegas' intellectual enterprise that a quarter of a century was to pass before Eric Williams and Juan Bosch, following in his footsteps, were both to publish histories of the region presented as a *locus classicus* of imperial conquest and rivalry.[8] Nearly a full half-century elapsed before the Association of Caribbean States would give institutional expression to his conception of the Caribbean as the entire zone of Middle America centered on the Sea.[9]

It was Arciniegas' special gift to combine broad thematic conceptions with complete mastery of detail, woven into the narrative with the skill of a born storyteller reminiscent of that other great Colombian writer, Gabriel Garcia Marquez. There are four "Books" in this book, corresponding roughly to the four centuries from the arrival of Columbus to the construction of the Panama Canal. Their titles tell the themes: the Golden Age, the Silver Age, the Age of Enlightenment and the Age of Liberty. The chapter headings hint at the human drama underlying the broad brushstrokes. Columbus' saga that ends in his lonely death is "The Tale of Christopher the Frustrated"; the reign of Elizabeth I is the story of "The Queen of England and her Forty Thieves"; Jamaica after the English conquest is "The Land of Cromwell the Protector and of Morgan the Pirate"; Venezuela's first war of independence is the adventure of "Miranda, Liberty's Knight Errant."

For Arciniegas, the detail does not get in the way of the story: the detail *is* the story. And the story is told from the standpoint of those who lived it. Consider his account of the building of the Citadel of Henri Christophe:

> The problem confronting Haiti was Napoleon's second campaign against the island. To those who had achieved their independence after such a desperate

x

struggle, it was a question of life or death. The king put everybody to work, even old men, women, and children, day and night, in the forests and in the towns, setting up brick kilns, quarrying stone from the mountainsides, bringing in logs, and carrying cannon up the steep slopes to build a fortress. This fortress—the Citadel—was big enough to hold a large part of his people and was planned to withstand a siege of months or years, so strategically located on the heights and with walls so thick that it could be neither destroyed nor captured. The Citadel came to be considered the eighth wonder of the world. Yet, compared with the human factors that went into its construction, the gigantic structure is but a trifling testimony to the sacred fire that animated those impassioned lovers of liberty. There is no exaggeration in calling it the world's eighth wonder. Perhaps one could go further and call it the first wonder of liberty. On the summit of La Ferrière for centuries the Citadel would be visible, like a prolongation of the mountain, its walls rising sheer above the abyss, two hundred meters long, one hundred and fifty meters thick, and eighty-seven meters high.

. . . . . On a mountain-top of Haiti his clenched stone fist, the Citadel, stands defying time, a symbol of the Negroes' impassioned fight for freedom. (pp. 347, 349)

Here, the author captures a twofold meaning, historical and contemporary; the meaning of the Citadel to those who were *there* and its meaning to those who are *here*.

It is a style that runs throughout the book. This is not dry history or predictable political polemic. It is what present-day reviewers call "a good read." We share Columbus' growing terror as his first voyage stretches on and on, seemingly without end. We are part of the intrigue and double-dealing of the court of

Ferdinand and Isabella. We scheme with Balboa as he outsmarts his king to ensure that he is the first to "discover" the Pacific (to which he was led, of course, by the indigenous people). We travel with Morgan on his swashbuckling and bloodthirsty rampage through Cuba and the Isthmus. We shiver in a carriage crossing the frozen river Dnieper as Francisco de Miranda regales the Russian prince, Gregory Potemkin, with tales of his military exploits. All this and much more, Arciniegas brings to life.

From the standpoint of contemporary scholarship, to be sure, the book has many gaps. The machinations of all the European powers are amply treated, but within the region the coverage is primarily Hispanic: the English, French, and Dutch islands between them receive at most four of the 26 chapters. Conspicuously absent is a treatment of the subjects of slavery and the plantation system that have been the central preoccupations of Anglophone Caribbean historians. Indentureship and the East Indian experience are nowhere to be found. Neither are the role of women and the experience of gender. Regrettably, the English edition lacks detailed source references that would assist the modern scholar. And the account stops at the end of the 19th century.

On this last limitation, the author was as blunt as he was unapologetic: to deal with the last 30 years "would involve a complete study of the politics of the period in order to determine the responsibilities incurred by foreigners and natives alike in permitting this frontier zone of America to become the prey of soulless commercial enterprises and the private domain of base dictators" (p. vii).

But the gaps in coverage noted above are subjects that have since been treated at length by many others. The value of this book lies in the story that is told and in the manner and time of its telling. It helped to lay the intellectual foundation to the conception of the Greater Caribbean as a zone of shared historical experience. And the story of the republication of the English edition is itself a minor tale of serendipity, worthy of Arciniegas' telling.

In early 2000, while packing my household effects to move to Port of Spain to take up my assignment with the Association of

Caribbean States, I stumbled upon a decaying copy of the 1946 edition of Arciniegas' book. It came via my mother, salvaged from the library of my late father. I knew nothing of the book or of its author; but the title and the chapter headings held a certain interest. I placed it, along with several hundred others, in the shipment to Trinidad. Thereupon I promptly forgot about it.

A year later, while preparing the John Clifford Sealy Memorial Lecture,[10] I read Professor Brereton's article which mentioned Arciniegas' book and made reference to it in the lecture. It was several weeks after the lecture, however, that it came to me in a "flashback" that I actually had a copy of the original English edition in my collection, courtesy of the insatiable interest of my late father in the history of Latin America and my own annoying habit of not throwing away any publication that might be of interest in the future.

The next event in this remarkable sequence was the arrival at the ACS Secretariat, in mid-2001, of the gift of several copies of the new Spanish edition from vice-president Gustavo Bell Lemus of the government of Colombia. The republication had been undertaken in 2000 to mark the centenary of Arciniegas' birth. From this, I learnt that the book was a classic of Colombian historiography, that its erudite and prolific author had produced an average of nearly one book per year over a 65-year period and had become a cultural icon in his native land, dying only two years before at the age of 99. From that time on, I knew that the English edition, too, would have to be republished as a contribution to the intellectual history of the idea of *El Gran Caribe*, the subject of my Sealy Memorial Lecture and the *raison d'être* of the ACS.

The opportunity soon came with the formation in October 2001 of CAPNET, the Caribbean Publisher's Network, with a membership embracing the Greater Caribbean. My proposal to CAPNET was to establish a special window for the publication of translations of outstanding Caribbean works to make them available to readers in other Caribbean languages. A start could be made with Arciniegas' book; and my own aging copy of the original English edition could be the template.[11]

Our hope is that through this and other publications of translated Caribbean works the rich intellectual heritage of the region will be made more widely available to its scholars, thereby helping to fertilize the growth of the Pan-Caribbean consciousness so ably pioneered by Arciniegas and others of his generation.

Norman Girvan
Secretary General, Association of Caribbean States
Port of Spain

NOTES

1. Germán Arciniegas, *Caribbean: Sea of the New World*, translated by Harriet de Onís (New York: A.A. Knopf, 1946); *Biografía del Caribe* (Buenos Aires: Editorial Sudamericana, 1945; Bogotá, Colombia: Editorial Planeta, 2000).

2. Gustavo Bell Lemus, Prologue to the 2000 Spanish edition, p. xii (my translation).

3. Bridget Brereton, "Regional Histories," in *General History of the Caribbean*, vol. 6: *Methodology and Historiography of the Caribbean*, edited by B.W. Higman (London and Oxford: UNESCO Publishing/Macmillan Education, 2000), p. 315. The other author to whom Brereton refers is W. Adolphe Roberts of Jamaica (see note 7 below).

4. Gustavo Bell Lemus, Prologue to the 2000 Spanish edition, p. xii (my translation).

5. C.L.R. James, *The Black Jacobins: Toussaint L'Ouverture and the San Domingo Revolution* (London: Secker and Warburg, 2nd rev. ed. 1963; first published 1938). Arciniegas quotes James on p. 331 of the present edition, p. 367 of the 2000 Spanish edition.

6. Eric Williams, *Capitalism and Slavery* (Chapel Hill: University of North Carolina Press, 1944).

7. W. Adolphe Roberts, *The Caribbean: The Story of Our Sea of Destiny* (New York: The Bobbs-Merill Company, 1940).

8. Eric Williams, *From Columbus to Castro: The History of the Caribbean* (London: André Deutsch, 1970); Juan Bosch, *De Cristóbal Colon a Fidel Castro: el Caribe, Frontera Imperial* (Santo Domingo, 1999; first published 1970).

9. The ACS was launched in 1994.

10. El Gran Caribe, available on the ACS website in English, Spanish and French; at <http://www.acs-aec.org/SG/cliffordsealy_eng.htm>.

11. CAPNET, and in particular its President Ian Randle, were more than enthusiastic. A letter to Vice-President Bell produced immediate endorsement from the government of Colombia and led to ready permission being granted from Editorial Planeta of Bogotá, publishers of the 2000 Spanish edition, and from the Arciniegas family. Jane Gregory Rubin of the Reed Foundation generously arranged financing to subsidize the cost of the Caribbean edition (Kingston, Jamaica: Ian Randle Publishers, 2003). To all these collaborators and stakeholders, the ACS is hugely indebted.

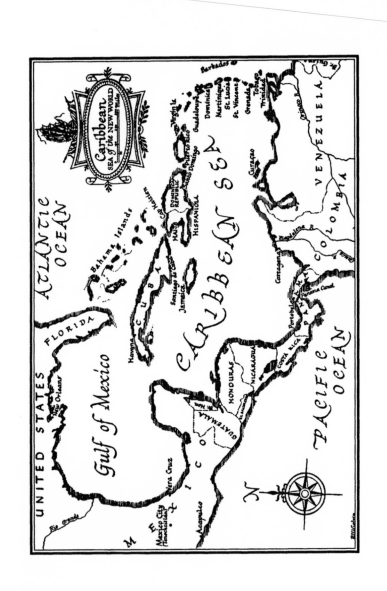

BOOK I

THE GOLDEN AGE

TO THE MEMORY OF ALBERTO ARANGE URIBE

I

FROM THE GRAECO-LATIN SEA
TO THE SEA OF THE CARIBEES

Our Mediterranean, or better, our hero, is a lake.
EMIL LUDWIG

We may say that the Antilles was the cockpit where the struggle for the dominion of the seas was fought out.
WALDEMAR WESTERGAARD

IT IS true that the sixteenth century was the golden age of Spain, but this is not the whole truth. For the sixteenth century was golden not only for Spain, but for England, for France. It was the century of Cervantes, of Shakespeare, of Rabelais. In the three kingdoms letters had never before reached such heights of splendor. Nor kings either. Charles V, Philip II, Elizabeth, Francis I were golden monarchs with whom history adorned itself. But the matter goes deeper still. With the discovery of America, life acquired a new dimension; it was the change from plane to solid geometry. Before 1500, men's movements had been within small areas; they had been confined to a barn-lot, had sailed upon lakes. From 1500 on, the continents and the ocean-seas emerge. It was like the passing from the third to the fourth day in the first chapter of Genesis.

All this drama was lived, as much as or more than in any other spot on the globe, in the Caribbean Sea. There the discovery took place, there the conquest began, there the academies for adventurers came into being. The violence with which the horizons were being widened launched men upon paths of the most daredevil temerity. There was not a peasant or knight of the day, a page or king, a poet or monk, who did not have a streak of the adventurer in him. Columbus and Vespucci, Cortés and Pizarro, Drake and Hawkins, Charles V and Queen Elizabeth,

3

Cervantes and Shakespeare, Father Las Casas and Ignatius Loyola, were all marked with the same brand. The whole thing seemed an epic, a romance of roguery. Elizabeth was in prison when she was about to become Queen of England, just as was Francis when he was King of France, and Cervantes and Columbus.

All that was great in Europe at this time was in one way or another linked to the focal adventure of the Caribbean. There were kings in the background of all the discoveries, conquest, plunder. Columbus speaks in the name of Their Catholic Majesties; Balboa takes possession of the Pacific Ocean and Cortés of Mexico in the name of the Emperor Charles V; Hawkins and Drake raid the Caribbean ports flying the standard of Queen Elizabeth; the Florentine pirate Giovanni da Verrazano works in partnership with Francis I of France. The struggle between England and Spain begins in the Caribbean. The day the viceroy of Mexico smashed an English pirate fleet to smithereens in the port of San Juan de Ulua marked a change of direction in European politics. The Caribbean, in the sixteenth century, was like a gaming table, where the crowns of the kings of Europe were the stakes and the pirates rolled the dice. It was there that English sailors attained their flag-rank.

During the Middle Ages the struggles between kings had been in the nature of family quarrels. By marriage, by inheritance, empires grew or shrank like bellows manipulated by capricious royal hands. Naples was tossed back and forth between the kings of France and of Spain like a ball. At times Portugal had a king of its own, at times it was under the crown of Castile. The same thing was true of Flanders. On the head of Charles V rested the crowns of Spain and of Germany. But underneath all this ran powerful subterranean forces, the restless energies of the people seeking an outlet, the rising power of the middle classes. Of these the modern States were born, the fruit of this anonymous sap in Spain, in France, in England. Serfs, peasants, fishermen, highwaymen, merchants, students carried out the conquest, manned the pirate ships, forced the

4

hands of the kings and involved them in wars they had not sought.

The people had their hates, their loves, their prejudices, their superstitions — in a word, their faith. As always, they embodied the vision of the past and the vision of the future. Tradition and hope, history and adventure. They provided the impulse, the gambler's instinct, with life and death as stakes, that kept the drama at a pitch of intensity that made it possible in a quarter of a century to have gazed upon all the seas, and in another quarter of a century to have explored the farthest corners of the New Continents. It was men of the people who circumnavigated the seas on a couple of planks, with a rag for a sail, and who with hatchets in their hands cleared a path to the heart of the Amazon or scaled the heights of the Andes. Thus in the sixteenth century the map of the world was drawn with a rag, a few boards, a knife. These three things form the real coat-of-arms of the Caribbean.

The people had their religion. Passions ran so high that wars seemed religious wars in the name of kings not of this earth. Spain had its own Church. It is strange that no one has ever alluded to the Spanish Catholic Apostolic Church, as one speaks of the Roman, the Greek, the Russian, or the Anglican Church. Each of these has its own coloring so distinctive as to be unmistakable. In the sixteenth century, which is the century of Luther and Calvin, Spain organized the ranks of its church with the militia of St. Ignatius Loyola, strengthened the defenses of the dogmas with Cardinal Cisneros, reaffirmed its faith by garbing Charles V in a monk's habit and burning heretics — Lutherans, Huguenots, Jews — at the stake whose flames Torquemada fed with a pallid fervor. In the waters of the Caribbean, Drake was neither an Englishman nor a pirate: he was a heretic. And to Drake the governor of Cartagena or Santo Domingo was the representative not of the King of Spain, but of someone much worse: of the Pope, the enemy of the Church of England.

So the Golden Age was also the age of violence, fire, sword, passion, in which the most divergent types clasped hands like good companions. They had all been swept up in this seething

tide of stirring masses. Rabelais wrote the fantastic voyages of
Pantagruel, perhaps the most magnificent of his books, inspired
by the voyages of the pirate Juan Florentin. Cervantes could not
make up his mind whether to write *Don Quixote* or sail for the
Caribbean, to Cartagena, to Guatemala, to the kingdom of New
Granada — a refuge, as he himself says, for rogues and thieves.
Shakespeare filled his dramas with scenes taken from Ralegh's
trip to Guiana. Lope de Vega composed his *Dragontea* on the
life of Francis Drake, whom the Spanish called The Dragon.
If one were to draw the literary map of the Caribbean there
would be found on it all the names of the poets, the novelists,
the dramatists, as though they had dreamed of setting up their
republic of letters alongside the tents of the buccaneers or the
watch-fires of the freebooters.

In the beginning was the Mediterranean. Everything that fell
within its sphere of influence received the impress of its blue
hands; all that remained outside that sphere lay murky and fearsome. The interior of Africa was the dark continent; but to the
north, from Alexandria to Ceuta, the shore line was brilliant with
its schools of philosophers and nests of white houses. Asia, turgid
and mysterious, lay sealed within the vast kingdoms of China,
of India; where it approached the luminous body of water it
became "Asia Minor," poetical and musical in the names of
Smyrna, Tyre, Damascus, Sidon, that still echo in the *Song of
Songs*. From the lacework of sculptured marble that adorned
the throat of Athens to the Spanish ports that resounded with
the raucous chatter of the Arabs, Europe was gay and diaphanous. Facing the sea, the blue coast of France. Inland, from the
Alps to the fog-shrouded North, the world of the barbarians, the
Black Forest.

History books speak of the Occident; of the countries of the
Orient; of the ancient world. Mere words, fragments of a sentence devoid of subject or verb. For the subject is "the sea," or
more precisely, the Mediterranean; and the verb is "to sail."
This sea was not only the sole historic reality, but the poetic
image by which all the struggles, efforts, and dreams of centuries

6

were expressed. There was a time when political geography rested
not on the mainland, but on the ocean wave. Each little corner
had its own name, proclaimed its sovereignty as though it were
a kingdom. The pennons of kings floated from the mastheads.
The quarterings of nobles were emblazoned on the sides of the
ships. The castles were floating ones, of wood; the armies, sailors whose oars cut the waters. In the old maps, and even today,
one reads: Marmoran Sea, Candian Sea, Aegean Sea, Adriatic
Sea, Ionian Sea, Tyrrhenian or Tuscan Sea, Carthaginian Sea,
Iberian Sea. Behind each of these names there is often nothing
but a city, or a lighthouse. Their history is poetry because nations
in their infancy do not write their history: they sing it. In the
little Aegean Sea, the egg from which the Mediterranean was to
come, Homer led his people to immortality. He was a mighty
captain. It is as though his rhapsodies had sired poetry.

From the three directions the world then possessed, men
moved toward the Mediterranean. Behind them they left the
plains of Siberia, the mountains of India, seas which, when not
silent, were dead, the sands of the Sahara. People of every sort,
eager to see, hear and talk with one another followed the paths
to this common sea, talkative, bustling, international, the focus
of the news of the world. They all struggled to find a place in its
transparent confines. Only some of the barbarians from the center of Europe were so dazzled by its gleaming light that they
plunged back into their forests. But for many centuries three
continents gazed upon one another across its waters. From one
shore to the other, men of east and west, north and south, con-
versed. It was here that their divergent souls intermingled and
even came to understand one another. More than four thousand, five hundred years ago the Egyptians descended the Nile,
and Alexandria, at its mouth, linked its sacred barges to the seafaring world. Step by step, all along the coast there sprang up
cities whose names are unforgettable: Athens, Carthage, Rome,
Genoa, Marseille, Barcelona, Seville, Tunis, Venice. . . . What
a necklace all their names make! The eternal skies, the suns that
burnished the tresses of Titian's women, the stars Salammbô
counted on the last night of Carthage, lay the same over the

7

Acropolis of Athens, the vineyards of Italy, and the orange groves of Valencia. Pirates and thieves of Greece, soldiers of Julius Caesar, Phoenician traders, philosophers, apostles, saints, freemen, galley-slaves — they were all to be found here. The shepherds descended from the pastures to bathe, to gather shells. Praxiteles caught its foam in marble. Some poems speak of it as the "White" sea. And other seas that branch off from it like the fingers of a hand were known as the "Red" sea, the "Black" sea. . . .

Today statues are often found amidst the sands, or in the fields, or near the site of the ancient cities. They probably rolled from their altars some fifteen hundred or two thousand years ago. In the Aegean there is a tiny island that was once the refuge of bandits and poets. Perhaps it was also the site of those somewhat dubious meetings between Greek maidens and gods which gave birth to mythology. The little island is of volcanic origin. In the pockets of earth between its barren rocks grow the olive and the vine. One day a peasant in pulling up a tree uncovered the entrance to a cave, and inside the cave lay hidden the Venus with the broken arms. The peasant shouted: "Behold!" And the world answered: "A miracle." The little island of Melos became famous. At least one city, Venice, left the land to sink its foundations in the water. Venice has been compared to a lamp; but, in reality, the lamp was the sea itself. As far as its powerful light spread, gleaming forth without any shade to dim it, so far reached the world.

There came a day, as everyone knows, when this small, bright hemisphere of the world grew dark. Europe felt that superstitious terror which lays hold of savages when an eclipse comes. It was the Middle Ages. Some call it the Dark Ages; others, the Mystic Night. Everything was enveloped in shadows for several centuries. Men withdrew to the forests.

It began with a cataclysm: the invasion of the barbarians. With the dying away of the hoarse voice of Attila — that bearded giant who could neither read nor write — the monasteries came into being, the naves of the Gothic churches with their roses

8

of glass shining through the darkness. Writers argue whether an epoch in which mysticism achieved moments of the most sublime elevation, in which man attempted to storm the dwelling-place of God by force of saintliness, can properly be called a clouding-over of life. This is beside the point. It is obvious that when the world withdrew from the Mediterranean into the forests it turned its back upon the brightness of the sun. The marvelous old lamp was blacked out by the funereal shadows of the pines.

The contrast must have been violent. On the eve of the change, Rome was at the height of its splendor. Crowds stood waiting in line for hours to enter the Circus where dancers from Spain, fighters from Africa, entertainers from all over the world brought surcease from the petty problems of daily living. For a copper one could spend the day in the baths. The warm water left the body pleasantly relaxed; the muddy waters of gossip comforted the soul with the news of neighbors' misfortunes. And for all there were benches where one could while the time away, gazing at statues of marble or the moving, flexible bodies of women playing ball. Rome had a population of over a million. It was sprawling and easy-going, with its palaces resting firmly on century-old stones, its bustling life of politics and sports, where the names of the old patrician families, like the stones of the Forum, seemed the center of the universe. But the barbarians were coming. Alaric's horn resounded, and the hoofs of the Goths came thundering down like an onrushing herd of cattle. To the Romans this seemed an unspeakable act of insolence, stupidity, folly. The people continued going to the Circus, the Senate, the Forum, the baths. Alaric gave the screw another turn, and hunger began its work. The granaries of the rich were emptied. It was not enough: pestilence made its appearance. There was no room to bury the piles of dead, nor anyone to shovel the dirt into the trenches where the bodies of the dying mingled in horrible promiscuousness with the rotting corpses of the dead. There was no power to withstand the onslaught of those stone-headed ruffians. An appeal to the invader's clemency was decided upon.

To Basil, a Spanish senator, was entrusted the difficult mission of interceding with the King of the Goths. He was accompanied by a tribune who was skilled in negotiations and had friends among the Goths. Putting up a bold front, they presented themselves before the prince in his tent, and with a blustering air not at all in keeping with the real situation, they said to him: "We have come, sir, to offer you an honorable peace. If this is not accepted, we will sound the trumpets and the people will rise as a man to fight for their rights with the courage of their despair." The barbarian replied: "The thicker the hay, the easier the mowing." Further parley was useless. "What is the King's demand?" "All the gold and silver of the city; all chattel goods; all the slaves!" "If these are your demands, O King, what, then, do you leave us?" "Your lives." It was no mean generosity, and the answer admitted of no reply. He threw it into their faces as one throws a bare bone to a dog.

And this was only one scene of the first act. Rome fell slowly. Finally its palaces sank buried in layers of dust. The Empire was wiped from the map. The world forgot the Mediterranean Sea. The reign of the Black Forest had begun.

Centuries passed. Once more the lamp began to glow with light. It was the emergence anew of the Graeco-Latin Sea. At the beginning, with the sputtering of the Crusades, it seemed but a flickering mystic flame in a rough vessel, fed by the oil of the Italian olives. But from that beginning the light began to dissipate the webs of darkness and advanced like a fire, lighting up the heavens once more, penetrating the earth, revealing the naked beauty of woman with the riotous enthusiasm of a bacchanal. Out of the reborn cities fluttered flocks of white: lateen sails on their way to the conquest of Jerusalem, first; then to bring back cloves, pepper, silk, carpets, daggers. Little by little came the sound of noisy words re-echoing through the old amphitheater: Genoa, Pisa, Naples, Venice.

Nobody else has painted the scene so faithfully as Sandro Botticelli. To him all this was the return of the Greek Venus to the coasts of Italy. The naked goddess, serene, resting on the perfection of her own beauty, advances. Here, once again, is the soul of the old poems. The warm air envelops her and turns her hair to gold. The breeze ripples through the plumage of the trees that let their flowers fall like birds. She is still in the sea; her feet rest on the curve of a shell that seems a rose-colored wave. One more step, and her feet will touch the shore of Italy. Her hands play with two doves, all animation and grace, that are on the point of rising and taking off in flight. Botticelli (or those who gave the picture the name of "The Birth of Venus") made a mistake. It is simply "The Renaissance."

The painting of this vision of the Mediterranean coincides with the discovery of America, or, to be more exact, of the Caribbean Sea. The last act of one drama was taking place in Italy; here, the curtain was just rising. In the very year of the death of Lorenzo the Magnificent, 1492, Columbus reached Guanahaní. What did his men see from the bridges of the three caravels? Copper-colored Indian girls who peered fearfully out through the tangled jungle. The Caribbean Venus walked naked, as God had sent her into the world. Her jet-black hair hung down her back like brush-strokes of tar. The children, poised in the tops of the trees, were one with the monkeys and chattered with the parrots. As their surprise wore off, the Indians began to lose their fear. They wanted to see the hairy-faced Europeans. They leaped over the waves, riding their ponies of hollowed-out tree-trunks. On their broad, savage faces laughter gleamed from white, even teeth, from sly, black eyes.

These Caribees had ideas of their own. In their wars, an enemy who fell in battle was meat for their larder. From their cabins human legs hung like smoked hams. Under the eaves of their palm-thatched huts, protected from the fierce rays of the sun, the old men squatted to smoke; in braziers of fired clay they burned dry leaves, inhaling the smoke and then blowing it out through the nose. In their festivals they adorned their heads with feathers and painted their bodies red with annatto. They hung collars of bones, teeth, nails of wild beasts, snails, about their necks. They ate worms and other disgusting things. They were free and unabashed.

"Carib" means "wild Indian." It was a word of war that spread over the American scene like the poison in which the tips of the Indians' arrows were dipped. And the same was the sea. Hurricane winds raised waves like living mountains, and then shattered them against the beach and swept them inland, shivering the trees to splinters. After a storm, the broken limbs of the forest drifted about upon the whirling waters like the spars of a wrecked ship.

In the sea there were sharks. In the swamps the alligators basked in the mud. In their huts the Indians fattened animals several handspans long, half-lizard, half-snake: iguanas. Gold and sand were intermingled in the river-beds. The natives traded gold for pieces of glass. They went mad over a bell, a mirror. They seemed so savage that the Spaniards brought back the most fantastic reports about them: one tribe had tails like dogs, another ears so long that they dragged on the ground. . . .

On this side of the world there had been in times gone by, and still were when the Spaniards arrived, densely populated cities, with great temples and palaces. They were nearly all inland, on the crest of the mountains. For the Greeks, Carthaginians, and Romans the sea was everything; for the Aztecs, Incas, or Chibchas, the mountains. Not one of our great native peoples had a port or knew a fleet; the eyes of their kings never followed a billowing sail in dreamy contemplation. Inland lay gentle, fertile, open savannas. The coast of the Caribbean was torrid, hurricane-swept. In the highlands the fields had to be industriously tended to yield their crops of grain: there husbandry came into being and flourished. Down in the islands it was enough to cast a hook into the sea, gather the fruit that dropped from the tree, light up the leaves of tobacco. . . .

Our old nations lived within the confines of their castles of crags. They sprang up, grew, even died without knowing of one another. The people that carved the huge monoliths of Tiahuanaco along the shores of Lake Titicaca, almost touching the clouds, never knew that in another corner of the hemisphere the Mayas were similarly engaged in raising aloft their pyramids.

The Incas communed with the sun. The Aztecs communed with the sun. But there was no common sea to facilitate the meeting of these two peoples. There was no opportunity for an interchange of ideas, for any of those encounters that have been so rich and fecund for mankind and opened new horizons to the intelligence. When the population on the islands became too dense, their inhabitants set out on their wooden ponies until they found land at the mouths of the rivers, the paths that led to the inland valleys, to the mountains. They never returned. Whole tribes forsook the Antilles and the sea.

When Columbus arrived with his ships the Caribbean suddenly became the point of intersection of all routes. For the first time the people of this hemisphere saw one another's faces. And they were seen by the whole world. Men came from Europe to write about them, to launch to the wind a new poetry. The Caribbean acquired new dimensions, became the sea of the New World.

This was the last great adventure of the mariners of the Mediterranean. They came to discover from Genoa and Florence, from Cádiz, even from Greece, for there was room for them all in the caravels. The early pages of this history are dotted with Italian names: Columbus, Vespucci, Verrazano, Caboto. It was Toscanelli who pricked on Columbus's curiosity. Agents of the Medici or Juanoto Berardi supplied the boats in Cádiz with stores of hardtack, flour, garlic, oil, onions, and wine. Those men, whose veins the Renaissance had filled with quicksilver, ultimately realized that by the route that led to Asia Minor the Mediterranean was a closed sea. The open door was through the Pillars of Hercules, over the Atlantic; and the captive boats came flying out.

And so this wild sea, with its coconut palms and its Indians who ate the roots of yucca and smoked tobacco, came to be looked upon as the storehouse of fantastic treasures. The young adventurers of the Old World went mad. The pathways leading to El Dorado began in the islands, they believed. The shores were strewn with nuggets of gold; the floor of the gulfs, with pearls. The forests were perfumed with cinnamon. Columbus thought to see the city with the marble bridges described by Marco Polo. Here was the site of the Garden of Eden. It was a feverish comedy of errors.

Thus the Mediterranean and the Caribbean were brought face to face for the first time in their history. Two magic mirrors, one reflecting the image of the past, the other of the future. It is a curious thing that this unique moment should have been immortalized in the name of a Florentine family. It was one of those families of courtiers that produced diplomats, seafarers, merchants, clerics, all people to the manner born. They had a love of art and adventure, and a kind of unharnessed genius. Some were rich, some poor, but all were quick to poke their heads through any window opening on anything new or strange. They were the Vespucci. It is impossible to travel any road in the life of Florence without coming upon a Vespucci. Wherever any great enterprise was taking place, wherever there was some outstanding figure, there they were. And they had their charm. They were talkative. They seemed gifted. Everybody was their friend. Ghirlandajo decorated the family chapel. Savonarola received Giorgio Antonio in his convent, and commissioned him to translate tales from the Greek into Latin. Amerigo played with Piero de' Medici, the son of Lorenzo the Magnificent. And as the family had been born under a lucky star, it was more natural than miraculous that the winds of fortune of the day should have been caught fast in their family tree.

Up to this moment the Mediterranean had ruled the world. Afterwards Europe freed itself, began to make its own history, became a continent. But as we have already said, the last and most perfect image of this sea was Botticelli's painting. And who was this nude Venus, in whose blue veins, beneath the rose-hued skin, runs the poetry of twenty or thirty centuries? Where did Botticelli get his inspiration? Who was she? Simonetta Vespucci. And as for the Caribbean, how did the news of the New World reach Europe, apart from Spain? Who wrote the first account that was read in all tongues and all lands? Amerigo Vespucci.

Amerigo and Simonetta were young and almost of an age; to be exact, Simonetta was two years older than Amerigo. He was the son of Anastasio Vespucci; Simonetta, the wife of Marco Vespucci. They both lived in the manor-house of the Vespucci, in the Santa Lucia di Ognissanti quarter. A few steps away was the house of Sandro Botticelli. Through the spacious drawing-rooms the alert eyes of Amerigo and Simonetta watched the moving procession: Vespucci, Medici, Savonarola, Leonardo da Vinci, Ghirlandajo, Botticelli, Piero di Cosimo. . . . The grand prize of the lottery was won by Simonetta and Amerigo. Stefan Zweig wrote an enchanting little book about Amerigo's luck entitled *Amerigo, a Comedy of Errors in History.* Simonetta's life affords material for a no less amazing study. I am at a loss to understand why no one, so far, has studied them together in a single novel.

Simonetta was from Genoa. She was fifteen years old when she entered through the gates of Florence, and Florence became illuminated through her presence. Never had such beauty been seen. She was one of those women whose life is fleeting, who hardly seem to touch the earth in passing, and who for centuries afterward are the subjects of poetry, painting, legend, novel — in a word, of history. A year later Florence celebrated its most splendid festival, of which the Medici were patrons. It was during the rule of Lorenzo. He was already the Magnificent though he was only twenty-six. Giuliano, his brother, the more handsome and attractive, was only twenty-two. The plaza of Santa Croce was decked in silk and flowers. The shields that Lorenzo and Giuliano carried had been designed by Verrocchio. Giuliano's costume, with its silver armor, had cost eight thousand florins. When Simonetta appeared, the shouts, the music, the songs of the rich, of the populace, of men, women, that echoed beyond the walls of the city grew hushed. There she stood in the calm beauty of her sixteen summers, hardly ruffled by a quiver of triumph. Florence hailed her as "Queen of Beauty." All the poets, from Politian who recorded the tournament in verse, crowned her with song. Giuliano gazed lovingly upon her. Lorenzo sang her youth:

15

Quant'è bella giovinezza,
Che si fugge tuttavia.
Chi vuol essere lieto sia —
Di doman non è certezza.[1]

This quatrain became the leitmotiv of the memory of the most brilliant day Florence ever knew. It is like the music that, four centuries later, Rubén Darío, sprung from the cradle of the Caribbean, was to put in his verses:

Juventud, divino tesoro,
ya te vas, para no volver.[2]

The lovely Simonetta had entered the home of the Vespucci. On her portrait painted by Piero di Cosimo this inscription can be read: SIMONETTA LANVENSIS VESPUCCIA. The letters are large, as though designed for the medallion of a queen. But no one painted so many portraits of her as did Botticelli. She plaited and unplaited her golden hair — it was the favorite device of his brush — in pictures that were to make him immortal. Simonetta was his inspiration. She was the Spring of his "Primavera," the Venus of his "Venus and Mars"; and, above all, the Venus of "The Birth of Venus," of the Renaissance. It makes an interesting study to compare in Botticelli's work his portraits of Giuliano de' Medici and of Simonetta Vespucci. Giuliano, with lips tightly drawn and thin as sword-blades, is always looking down, eyelids lowered — something shames or embarrasses him. Simonetta, on the contrary, seems the mistress of Giuliano and of all the Florentine world, with her noble brow, her calm, wide-open eyes. She is good, she is sweet, but, above all, she is a queen.

Simonetta died when she was twenty-three years old. She was carried to her grave with her face uncovered. All Florence

[1] How beautiful is youth,
Fleeting with each passing hour.
Take your happiness while you may —
There is no promise of tomorrow.
[2] Youth, the gods' own treasure,
Departing, never to return.

16

wanted to look one last time on that incomparable brow, on those lips where the most exquisite smiles had hovered. They all followed her, poets, artists, the whole city, gazing upon her. And among the ecstatic crowd walked Leonardo da Vinci, a friend of Amerigo Vespucci. Lorenzo de' Medici, who was in Pisa at the time, received the news at night. It was a clear starry night. He was conversing with his friends in the garden. There was an unusually bright star in the sky which no one had observed before. Without hesitation Lorenzo remarked: "That is Simonetta." A short time afterwards Giuliano fell, victim of an assassin in the horrible conspiracy of Pazzi. The Magnificent, to perpetuate his memory, engaged Botticelli to paint the episodes of the festival in which Simonetta had been the Queen of Beauty. This order gave rise to the painter's immortal works.

At about the same time that Simonetta died, Amerigo Vespucci left Florence. The plague had broken out there. Some tragic destiny seemed to hover over the gay, sumptuous city. The rule of Lorenzo marked its high-water point. Lorenzo's father was "the Gouty." His son was to be Piero the Unlucky. Shortly after the death of the Magnificent, the Medici had to flee. The fickle Florentines looted their palaces. In his ascetic fury, Savonarola hurled into the flames everything he could lay his hands on until the judges of the city finally burned him on the fires of his own kindling. This was the normal course of events in those cities and those times.

As for the Vespucci, they were roaming the face of the world. They were now three brothers. Antonio had entered the University of Pisa. Jeronimo went to Palestine to try his fortune and lost his last florin. Amerigo went to Spain, where he had found a post in one of the establishments of the Medici, who even more than artists or statesmen were merchants, bankers. Their agents were to be found in all the markets of Europe. And now that Piero, with whom Amerigo had played when they were children in Florence, was the head of the house, Amerigo was assigned to their branch in Seville. It was through this door that he entered the world that was to bear his name.

Amerigo was a fool for luck. He was the same age as Columbus. They were born the same year, the one in Genoa, the other in Florence. But while Columbus, irritable, tragic, haughty, self-pitying, aged and bowed by misfortunes, was sending petitions filled with laments to his sovereigns, Vespucci, care-free, untrammeled, light-hearted, was spinning his pleasant tales.

The gigantic enterprise was Columbus's brain-child. His was the initiative, he solved the mystery of what the world was like. His tenacity got him the command of the three caravels, and he made the discovery. But Fate willed that neither his tongue nor his pen should tell the world what he had found. Of his letters and diaries — which the Catholic Kings kept carefully concealed — the only parts published during his lifetime were the account of the first voyage, in the letter addressed to Rafael Sánchez in which he tells of the Indian islands he had discovered above the Ganges; and the letter from Jamaica — a series of heart-rending complaints that might fittingly have been uttered beside the Wailing Wall. "Up to now," he says, "I have wept for others: now may Heaven have pity and let the earth weep for me." This was what he had to show for his life. The Spaniards distrusted him. He was a foreigner and suspect. From Admiral of the Ocean Sea he became a supplicant. The bright world he had discovered was hidden from view by his own trembling, imploring hands.

At this point Amerigo appeared, and dissipated this beclouded confusion with the clarity and charm of his wit. He made three or four trips to America — the number does not matter — and out of his experiences he composed a number of magnificent letters, designed to entertain Piero de' Medici, the Unlucky, and Piero Soderini, another friend of his childhood, now gonfalonier of the Florentine Republic. Piero de' Medici was in France, driven into exile by his compatriots, forming alliances in the hope of recovering his lost grandeur. His struggle was a web of disappointments, bitterness, disillusionment. Amerigo, whom we might now call Amerigo the Magnificent, was like a light in the night to him. He gave Piero the best of news: the emergence of a new world. Amerigo was the first person to make such a statement. Those islands that Columbus had seen on the Ganges — Amerigo makes them into a continent, a new world. Such is the magic of his pen. And to Piero Soderini, wearied with the cares of politics and government, he says: "Lay aside your burdens and listen to this marvelous tale." Vespucci speaks of Dante and Petrarch, but he brings to mind Boccaccio. His tale is a chapter of the picaresque novel laid against the magic background of uncharted islands and a continent that is coming into being. He draws an unforgettable picture of the Caribbean. He is the Botticelli of the new sea opening before his eyes. A wild sea, peopled by savages. It is Vespucci who for the first time puts his hand to our folklore and paints our typical American scene to delight a grandee of Florence. "*Anchora que vostra Mag. stia del continuo occupta ne publici negotii, alchuna hora piglierete discanso di consumare un poco di tempo nelle cose ridicule o dilectevoli.*" [3] And he adds: "For after the care and thought your affairs demand, my letter may afford you some little pleasure, just as fennel gives a better flavor to the food one has eaten and helps digestion."

Of all that he beheld, it was the women that appealed most to Vespucci, the Venuses of the Caribbean, somewhat more naked than those of Botticelli, with their reddish skin, their handsome, graceful, well-formed bodies. If they were dressed, they would look as white as our own. They swim better than their European sisters, they can run miles without tiring. Neither wrinkles nor fat mar their beauty. The men are not jealous; the women, voluptuous and unflagging in their desire. "We greatly took their fancy."

Next to the women, the hammock. How pleasant he found those nets, swaying in the breeze, where one can sleep far better than in the stuffy beds of Europe. The talkative Florentine had discovered the delights of the siesta. To be sure, as he says, these people do seem barbarians; they use neither napkins nor knives and forks and they eat all the time, without the order and

[3] Although Your Magnificence is continually occupied with affairs of state, it might amuse you in an hour of leisure to spend a little time on trivial or entertaining matters.

plan of civilized nations. But what a pleasure to sleep in a hammock!

Vespucci and his men established close relations with the Indians. At times they frightened them with the roar of their cannon; at times they won them over with mirrors and trinkets. With some of the tribes they made war; with others they made friends. They discovered villages of fishermen who lived in houses that stood on poles above the water, and inland settlements that were separated from the coast by mountains and rivers. One day Vespucci, who had made friends here as everywhere else, went inland to explore. The Indians had so many times begged him to go that he could no longer refuse them. Vespucci and about twenty others made a trip that took them nine days. Every village they came to received them with delight. The natives touched, they caressed, they fêted their visitors. The best food, the finest woven hammocks, the most luscious girls of each settlement were put at their disposal. When they returned to their ships the savages bore them in triumph. If any of the visitors seemed to weary, the Indians carried him in a hammock so he would be more comfortable than on a litter. And they brought hammockfuls of gifts: bows, arrows, feathers, parrots. The earliest chronicles of the New World are bright with the colors of countless parrots.

Vespucci was the first person to describe the New World in terms that fired the enthusiasm of the men of the Renaissance. His letters were passed from hand to hand. They were translated into every tongue, published everywhere. In this period, in which an entertaining writer was held in greater esteem than a navigator who had devoted his whole soul to his vast undertaking, it may be said that the first prize for the novel was awarded to Amerigo Vespucci, the Florentine. Someone, swept away by enthusiasm, went even further and said: if these new lands described for the first time by Vespucci are to have a name, let us not select some such effeminate word as Europe or Asia; let us call them by his name, the land of Amerigo. And thus the New World received its baptismal name, though Vespucci himself did not live to know it.

History is full of sharp contrasts. While Vespucci was writing his letters, and the first was being published, Columbus was addressing his sovereigns from Jamaica. Vespucci was sounding the clarion call of triumph; Columbus, imploring pity. Then came Vespucci's second letter. One sees him in it, from the first to the last line, floating upon the sea of fortune. Why did he cross the Atlantic this time? At the request of the King of Portugal. Vespucci did not want to go; he was busy with commissions that had been assigned him by the monarchs of Castile. But the King of Portugal insisted. "And so the king Dom Manuel, knowing that I could not go to his court at that time, sent Julián Bartolomé Iocondo, who was then living in Lisbon, to me with orders that he bring me back with him. With his coming, and as a result of his entreaties, I had no choice but to set out for that court, although everyone who knew me disapproved of my decision. And so I left Castile where I had received many honors and where the King himself had a high regard for me; and the worst of all was that I left without saying good-bye to anybody." This was how he departed. And how did he return? "We entered the port of Cádiz once more, with 222 captives." And what was Columbus doing at this same time? Requesting King Ferdinand's permission to ride a mule to the court. The use of mules as saddle animals was reserved for people of rank, and it entailed no small effort to secure this permission. To his son Don Diego he confided his tribulations: "If without pressing the matter too much I were granted a permit to travel by mule, I would try to start out for there after January, and this I will do even without it. . . ."

II

THE TALE OF CHRISTOPHER
THE FRUSTRATED

Never did eyes behold the sea so high, so menacing, all foam.
COLUMBUS

THERE had been a day when Columbus was the happiest man
the world had ever seen. This was the day on which for the first
time his eyes beheld and his hands touched the land of the New
World. Up to the previous evening many had considered him a
madman; now they saw that he was a man of wisdom. And he
who until then had maintained himself serene and steadfast
now went mad with joy. The strange thing in that uneasily
balanced life is that at the very moment when the basis of his
theory was being proved right — that sailing west one can reach
the East — he became submerged in a sea of confusion. His
youth was over. He finally came to deny his own science and, in
his hours of despair, threw himself into the arms of fable. There
had been only one ray of light in his life: October 12, 1492.

That is the point at which we stand. Behind lay his disappointments and tribulations. Even the Queen was hard of
heart: with one hand she raised up the Christians, with the other
she chastised the Jews. As Columbus sailed from Spain the land
resounded with the lament of the Jews. But the atmosphere of
the three little caravels was not much better. Again and again
the wings of death brushed Columbus's unbowed head. His life
hung in the balance, and more than once when it seemed as
though they would never get anywhere. There were those among
the terrified crew who thought: "How much better to throw this
old fool overboard, or hang him from a yardarm, and sail safely
back to Spain!" There came a day when this evil thought almost
became a deed. Mutiny was gathering among his men. Columbus discussed the situation with Martín Alonso Pinzón. Martín

was a man of greater age and experience, and he knew how to handle men. He answered unhesitatingly: "Sir, let your honor hang half a dozen of them, or throw them overboard; and if you don't venture to, my brothers and I will board you and do it; a fleet that has set out under the orders of such great princes does not turn back without good news." Columbus was horrified by the advice. "Martín," he answered, "let's keep on good terms with these hidalgos, and sail on for a few days more, and if during the time we don't find land, we shall take further counsel as to what we should do." When poor Columbus buried himself in his own thoughts — which was what he most frequently did — and felt his flesh and saw his wings, he must have thought: "I am part eagle and part chicken."

The name by which Columbus's caravel was familiarly known was *La Gallega*. But he, zealous to show himself a good Christion — though perhaps of recent vintage — always called it the *Santa María*. He let the other two be known by their nicknames, *La Pinta, La Niña. La Niña* was the trimmest and swiftest of all; few other ships of her tonnage ever crossed the ocean so many times. This time she was carrying twenty-four aboard. It is worth giving a thought to these two dozen men, singing the *Salve*, gnawing at their hardtack, drinking wine and chewing garlic, in the midst of an ocean never before furrowed by a ship, and following a dream that was not their own. *La Niña* — officially the *Santa Clara* — had always been lucky. But the *Santa María* was another story. She was bigger, and ill fortune dogged her. There were forty men aboard. On her forecastle, which was only about seventy feet long, among sailors thirty and forty years old there were boys whose beards had not yet begun to sprout. When it fell calm, these latter jumped overboard and went swimming around the ship as though coming to discover a world were a kind of vacation. Jests and oaths flew across from ship to ship. With a stone they were carrying for the cannon one of the boys killed a pelican.

The presence of the New World began to manifest itself in the air, the waters, the clouds. From the 7th to the 11th of October, though no land was visible, yet it could be felt, foretold. On the 7th *La Niña*, which naturally was in the lead, ran up a flag and fired off a gun, the signal for land ahead. But it was a mistake: it was a cloud, not land. No matter. All were on the alert, and up at dawn. The Admiral speaks of the fragrance in the air. This was the smell of verdure that can be noticed on approaching these islands of ours. On Monday, the 8th, they saw flocks of land birds; on Tuesday, the 9th, they could hear the birds passing overhead all night; Wednesday, the 10th, the tension was almost unbearable; Thursday, the 11th, a reed, a stick, a land plant, and a board. All took heart again. But as yet there was no land to be seen.

What an experience! They were seeing a new world being born, like morning when it emerges from behind the mountains. And it was a world that was only in the smell of the air, in a land bird, in a reed. But that night the cabin-boy chanted the call for dinner more gaily: "To table, to table, Sir Captain. Long live the King of Castile by land and sea! Who makes war on him, off with his head; who says not amen, no drink for him. Now to table; who doesn't come won't eat." Dinner was over. Night was closing in. Then came the *Salve*, "which the sailors sing after their fashion." Columbus had promised those on watch "a silken doublet for the one who first sights land." The sovereigns had offered a reward of ten thousand maravedis.

From the sterncastle Columbus strained his eyes peering into the shadowy horizon. It seemed to him that he saw a light. But he said nothing, lest they think him a visionary. But he took Pedro Gutiérrez, a steward, by the arm and asked him: "Do you see a light?" Pedro thought he did. Then he called Rodrigo Sánchez, the comptroller: "Do you see the light?" Rodrigo saw nothing. At two that morning a shout came from *La Pinta*. Rodrigo de Triana, the lookout on the forecastle, had sighted land. Now no one slept. The sails were lowered. There lay the New World. The ninety who shared in the adventure watched the dome of the East become suffused with rosy light.

The man Columbus had his odd little ways. He bilked young Rodrigo out of his reward. Fernando Columbus, in his biography of his father, offers this ingenious explanation of the episode: "*La Pinta* gave the signal for land sighted, which was first seen by Rodrigo de Triana, a sailor, when it was two leagues off; but the reward went to the Admiral . . . for it was he who first saw the light in the darkness of the night, which was symbolic of the spiritual light he was bringing into the darkness."

Columbus's log-book is no longer a mere navigator's record, with entries of winds, dialogues with the North Star, the compass, and the quadrant. Now he paints trees, relates the miracle of how under his hands the islands multiply and are offered up to him by the Caribbean. He speaks of strange men, catches the sound of words never heard before. He is writing poetry. It is the first song to America, and a beautiful song it is, though it never enjoyed the popularity Vespucci's letters were to have, and it came within a trice of not being published at all. It became known long years after his death, and in a badly preserved, tattered form. Perhaps it is better so; it brings out better the contrast with his feverish pen that goes leaping from island to island in that archipelago wrested from the night of centuries. But it was he, Christopher Columbus and none other, who set down the first words, who sketched the first profile of one of our islands. Centuries after these days there fell by chance into the hands of a wealthy lady of Spain a little notebook, bound in vellum, most of its pages destroyed. It was the journal in which Columbus had set down his personal notes. There is the first sketch of Hispaniola. It is a map, and quite an accurate one, too; but it is more than a map. It has its touches of passion, of man's adventure.

In this diary one beholds not only the birth of the New World. It is, besides, the first page of Spanish American literature. For the first time the language of Castile was employed in the painting of these lands. Shortly afterwards there was to pour forth a veritable avalanche of chronicles, novels, verses that would occupy a province of their own in the republic of letters. Hernán Cortés, Bernal Díaz del Castillo, Fernández de Oviedo, Las Casas, Fray Pedro Aguado, Álvar Núñez Cabeza de Vaca. . . .

Their books paint real, not imaginary, adventures. The scene is that which they themselves have discovered with their lances. The wars take place in lands previously unheard of, scaling one of the greatest mountain ranges in all the world, crossing swamps, jungles, and deserts, and they are captained by their own temerity. But the first cell of all this already exists in Columbus's little book. A little book that can be read in an hour, in a streetcar. It is the first dialogue between Europe and America.

There is in it already the legend of the Amazon women, and he speaks with great conviction of the island where these warlike women live alone. And the first tales of monstrous peoples, with tails or muzzles like dogs'. It seems to him that these people who gaze in wonder on his beard believe him sent from Heaven, and he suggests ways in which this may be turned to advantage to enslave them. Even before he took ship Columbus was thinking of gold and slaves. He came to know those two great products of the Caribbean: tobacco and the hammock. He did not understand the use of tobacco, which was to become so widespread in the world, but he did introduce the benefits of the hammock into navigation, and from then on sailors no longer had to sleep on boards, but swung pleasurably in nets of cotton.

The first thing that the Admiral encountered was the parrot. It would seem to be the heraldic bird of this hemisphere. While the caravels were still on the high seas, on the 7th of October, Martín Alonso Pinzón saw parrots that afternoon. And then macaws. On the 12th of October, Indian women came swimming out to the boats "and they brought us parrots." That day Columbus closed his journal with these words: "No animal did we see at all, only parrots." And when Columbus returned to Spain he entered with parrots and macaws as his advertising posters. For hundreds of years this was to be the bird of the Western continent.

Columbus was not of the stuff of which conquerors are made. He lacked the lightninglike, ruthless decision of the soldiers who were to follow him. But he was the forerunner of the gold-hunters. From the moment he signed the articles of agreement

26

with the Catholic Kings he promised them gold. He was obsessed by the idea. He had not yet seen it, and he was already on the trail of it. On the 12th of October there appeared on the strand Indians whose only adornment was black and red paint. And the next day: "I watched carefully and tried to find out if there was gold." Finally one arrived with a piece of it hanging in his nose, and Columbus immediately decided to search for it there. It is to the southwest, he said, as though he were seeing it. And he wrote: "This is the birthplace of gold." Two days later he was already on another island "to learn whether there is gold there." And the next day on another because "as far as I can gather, there is a gold mine there." As far as he could gather — and he had only arrived from Europe on the 12th! And so in the account of his first ten days in the islands the word *gold* appears twenty-one times. Sometimes there are passages like this: "And it is gold, I cannot be mistaken; with the help of God I will find it wherever it is." Each mystical outburst is followed by a plea for gold. Perhaps he had a presentiment of how fleeting his grandeur was to be, grew increasingly aware of the power of money, that key which opens many doors for him who has a country as well as for him who has none. Gold — the word slipped out, Heaven only knows how — gold, which can even get souls out of Purgatory. . . .

But the fact is that Columbus was in his glory. He saw everything in the light of his stroke of good fortune. Even adversity was interpreted as an act of Providence, as though God Himself were leading him by the hand. On one occasion the *Santa María* ran aground on a coral reef and was pounded to pieces by the swell. There was barely time to bring the cargo ashore and get the crew off. It was the flagship, but what did that matter? He did not realize that he would have to return with only two ships; he seemed indifferent to the fact that he would have to leave thirty men on the island; he did not even complain, he who was an expert in complaining. He saw it all as an indication that God wanted him to stop there for a few days to explore the island. As this happened on the 24th of December, it came as a

Christmas present. He decided to build a fort that should be the basis of a settlement. This was how La Navidad came to be founded, with its garrison of thirty men.

The first island he had seen was Guanahaní, which means Island of the Iguanas. He named it San Salvador. Then, in deference to the sovereigns, he named the next three islands for them: Isabela, Fernandina, Juana — this last for the ill-fated heir, Don Juan. After this he went along sprinkling the map with joyousness: Cabo Hermoso, Cabo Lindo, Cabo de la Estrella, Cabo de la Campana, Río de la Luna, Valle del Paraíso, Isla de la Amiga. This is no longer geography — this is poetry, a poem in which everything is clothed in beauty. The fish were like bright roosters, multicolored in hue; from the hills the breezes came laden with the sweet odor of flowers or trees; the wind "blew gently once more, filling all the sails of the ship, the main course, the two bonnets, the spritsail, mizzen, topsail, and the boat's sail on the poop. . . ."

Thus the journal is like a tapestry of the West Indies that might be hung as a backdrop on the stage of our history, against which later will pass conquistadors, friars, viceroys, madmen, bandits, and saints. When its pages were read in Spain, Spain began to feed upon the image of America. The chroniclers of the King, the historians, found inspiration in them. There was to come the day when Cervantes and Lope de Vega drew upon them for their novels, their plays, their verses. A priest and chaplain of the Archbishop of Seville used Columbus's own words to paint one of the most delightful pictures we have of those beguiling islands: "The lands lie high, and through them run lofty mountain ranges with towering peaks, beautiful and of a thousand configurations, all accessible and covered with trees of a thousand different kinds and shapes, so tall that they seem to reach the sky. They never seem to lose their leaves, as far as one can judge, for it was in the time when it is winter here and all the trees lose their leaves, and they were the same as here in the month of May. And they were covered with flowers and with fruits and pods. And amongst the trees the nightingale sang, and other birds in the mountains in the month of November as they do here in May; there are six or seven varieties of palm there, and the diversity of them arouses admiration; the fruits, trees, plants that grow on the island are wonderful to behold; there are pine groves, meadows, fields of great size; the trees and fruits are not like those we have here; there are mines of gold. . . ."

Columbus was on his way back. A storm had driven him on to the coast of Portugal. To anyone remiss in greeting him with the deference due him, he haughtily observed: "Have a care not to interfere with me, for I am traveling on business of the sovereigns of Castile." So many people were anxious to see him that the sea was dotted with ships and skiffs. The King of Portugal ordered the courtiers to go to receive him, and showered attentions upon him. Then his entry into Spain. The streets and roads were black with curious crowds, and in Barcelona the whole city turned out. Ferdinand and Isabella, seated in brocade-canopied chairs, placed him beside them. When the King rode out on horseback, Columbus rode on one side, the heir to the throne on the other. Titles were heaped upon him. He displayed his parrots and his Indians, the gold nose rings and nuggets. . . .

Seventeen ships! Twelve hundred fighting men! All under the orders of that Italian charlatan at whom the learned doctors of Salamanca had laughed, right in his face, not so many months before. And now he was going on this second voyage as Admiral, Viceroy, and Governor. He might now use Don before his name, and foot-soldiers and knights accompanied him. The knights rode aboard ship on their horses. They had shipped ten mares, three mules, boars, sows, calves, goats, cows, and sheep. In addition to the ship's crew there were farmers and workmen, and friars, who had not been on the first trip, and who now celebrated mass upon deck. And there were cosmographers like Juan de la Cosa, and future discoverers like Ponce de León and Alonso de Hojeda, and the Italian Michele de Cuneo, and the physician and surgeon Doctor Chanca, and the Admiral's brother Diego. In Seville it was a real struggle to hold back the wave of hidalgos and adventurers who tried to come aboard. Nothing so impressive had ever been seen before. The Queen, who was already thinking in terms of empire and colonies, sent him cuttings of sugar cane and grape roots. The flagship was a new *Santa María*, nicknamed by the sailors *Marigalante*. They set out on September 24, 1493.

It was a happy crossing. The islands they discovered as they approached their destination were baptized with beautiful and pious names: Deseada, Marigalante, Guadalupe, San Cristóbal: the archipelago of the Eleven Thousand Virgins of the Sea. But the Caribs received them at arrow's point. One sailor was transfixed as though he were a butterfly, and Michele de Cuneo was almost scratched to pieces by a girl who did not take kindly to his advances. All this seemed to bode no good.

Columbus was anxious to find the men he had left in the fortress of La Navidad, and to learn how his first colony had prospered. It would be good to embrace those brave fellows who were eagerly awaiting his return. The gallant fleet of seventeen ships was now off Hispaniola, but there was no sign of the Spaniards. Finally a party that had gone ashore to explore the banks of a river, came upon two corpses, one with a rope tied around his neck, another at his ankles. Could they be, peradventure, the bodies of Christians? Then they found two more, one with a bearded face. There was no room for doubt. These Indians — the gentlest souls in the world, Columbus had written — had not left one Spaniard alive. The houses were burned to the ground. The keg that was to have been filled with gold stood there empty. This was what Columbus had to show to the hopeful Spaniards who had embarked under the banner of his dream. His star had begun to decline. He was in the midst of a hostile land, and he did not know what to do with the twelve hundred fighting men who had sailed with him, or how to face the problem of governing people and territories, he who knew only ships and the sea.

What followed was the prelude to the final drama. He founded the city of Isabela, as the permanent site of the Hispaniola colony, in a spot that could hardly have been more unsuitable, for there was no harbor. He sent an army inland in search of gold. Gold, gold, gold. That was what he needed to revive failing hopes and to make his star shine bright once more. Tearfully he pleaded for it in his prayers. But there was no gold on the island. After much searching, the exploring party returned with a few handfuls. And Columbus had expected tons. Seeing the storm that was brewing, he tried to rid himself of as many men as he could. Many had fallen ill; dissatisfaction was rife. If he did not send several hundred of them back to Spain, they would wind up mutinying and hanging him. So he loaded twelve of the ships with such products as he could come by, and dispatched them to Cádiz. Instead of gold they carried letters to the sovereigns giving a list of the colonists' needs. There must have been gloomy faces in Cádiz when they saw so many ships returning so soon and without treasure.

But Columbus felt better. There he was, free again from so much responsibility, and with his five ships, and a world to the north, south, and west to be discovered. With the most adventurous of the party he put out to sea, leaving the colony in the hands of his brother Diego and Pedro Margarit, the Catalan. He sailed halfway around the coast of Cuba, believing it a part of India, and he discovered Jamaica. Several months were spent wandering about on the seas. But his age had begun to show on his face when he returned to Isabela. He was tormented by gout. His hair was graying. And, worst of all — as was to happen so often from then on — he came back with empty hands. He could see in the greedy eyes of the settlers that what they wanted was not land but gold.

There was a drama going on in the soul of the Admiral; there was a drama in Isabela. The Spaniards were getting fed up with the one tribe they were coming to dislike above all others: the Columbus tribe. By this time it was not just Christopher and Diego. There were three of them now, for as soon as Bartholomew, who had been wandering about England and France, heard of Christopher's discovery, he managed to get a hundred crowns from the King of France to take him to Castile, and in Castile, permission from the Queen to come out to the Caribbean and share its delights with his brother Christopher. The first of the colonists to take offense and make trouble were the Catalans, headed by Margarit and Fray Buil. They took the three caravels Bartholomew had come out with, and sailed for Spain, with the faction of malcontents, to spread the news of the failure of the Antilles enterprise through Castile. Fray Buil, a Benedictine, with the patience characteristic of his order dedicated himself to slandering Columbus.

Meanwhile in Isabela things were going from bad to worse. There were so many sick that the settlers did not know what to do with them. The "French disease" was rotting the blood of the gluttonous Spaniards, who slaked their lust on the wild, hot-blooded Indian women. The Caribs were being enslaved. Columbus, as he saw his dream of gold receding like a mirage, invented the system of tribute: every three months each Indian must bring in a Flanders hawk bell full of gold dust. As a receipt for his delivery, he would receive a tin medal to hang around his neck. The order was ridiculous, because in Hispaniola there was only a little gold dust to be found in the river-beds. Since it was impossible for the natives to fulfill the dreams of avarice, they were brutally tortured.

The Queen of Castile had lent an ear to the malcontents. She sent out a judge to investigate what was going on. She still treated the Admiral with affection and respect, but justice had been sought from her, and she was not one to refuse it. Christopher sent his brother Diego to defend him. Columbus did not want him to appear with empty hands, and so he was to carry back Indian captives in the four ships that were being fitted out. Fifteen hundred had been rounded up on the island. The five hundred handsomest were selected and put aboard. But, as the caravels were unable to carry so heavy a human cargo, two hundred of them died in the crossing. They were thrown into the sea, and the caravels left behind them a wake of brown Carib flesh.

In the settlement fortune continued adverse. Now it was the wind. In the clutch of the hurricane the world trembled like a frightened bird. What a terrifying noise that of the leaves shaken by its violent hands! The twisted fronds of the palm trees were lashing not the sand, but the sea foam. The waves advanced into the heart of the forest. The frail huts of the Spaniards shivered and collapsed at the impact of the uprooted trees, and the whole desolate scene was lighted up by blinding flashes of lightning. The pleasant brooks became torrents of mud, corpses, sticks, rubbish, and their filth covered the tops of the tallest trees. The sea pounded the ships anchored in the harbor with such fury that the hulls split asunder, the bridges were torn off, and the masts gave way. Of the four ships left to Columbus, three were shivered to kindling wood. When the wind finally died down, the sun came out, the sea grew calm beneath the perfect blue of a serene tropical day, it was a sad sight that met Columbus's eyes: muddied trees, fallen branches choking the paths, and the riven ships. The friars murmured of the wrath of God. And the worst of it was that they were speaking the truth. Terror had set its stamp on everyone's face.

The Admiral decided to build a caravel with the planks they managed to salvage from the disaster. It would be the first caravel built in the New World to cross the Atlantic. The idea seemed absurd, but they began the work. Everyone put his shoulder to the wheel, and the little colony hummed with the ring of hammer and the sound of saw, with the oaths and all the buzz of a diminutive shipyard. The same hope cheered the hearts of all: this ship would carry them back to Spain. And so *La India* came into being. Naturally, *Niña* rode out the storm; and, as though clasping each other's hands, *Niña* and *India* set out for Spain.

Three years and three months earlier, on March 15th, 1493, Columbus had returned to Spain to receive a crown of glory. Parrots like gay circus posters announced his passing through the streets of Seville. His companions were not sailors, they were discoverers. And like his namesake, Saint Christopher, on his shoulders he bore a new world. His joy was so great that he wrote to Santángel, the Queen's treasurer, a letter that concluded with these words: "Let processions be held, and solemn feasts; adorn the churches with palms and flowers; let Christ rejoice on earth as in heaven over the salvation which is at hand of so many nations lost in darkness until now. Let us rejoice both at the triumph of our faith and at the increase of temporal goods, by which not only Spain but all Christendom shall benefit."

It was a sad, dejected Columbus who returned this time. The two small ships that made the crossing brought two hundred and twenty-five Christians, and those who survived of thirty prisoners. How this number of people ever managed to crowd into two ships the size of the *Niña*, on which only two dozen sailors had traveled before, is a mystery that can be explained only by their frantic desire to leave that hell of the Indies at all costs. These people had set out for the paradise Columbus had described. The priest, Andrés Bernáldez, under whose roof the Admiral, Viceroy, and Governor rested from his fatigues saw him arrive "wearing clothes the color of the habit of Saint Francis, and fashioned more or less like a habit, and with the cord of Saint Francis, in sign of devotion." When he went to visit the King and Queen, he had the Indians march ahead of him. He had brought with him a chain that weighed six hundred castellanos, and when about to enter a city he would hang it about the neck of one of the Indians. With this display of merchandise he had brought back with him, Columbus seemed a peddler rather than an admiral and viceroy.

The King and Queen still believed in Columbus, but he had lost the people's backing. This time there would be no fine fleet of seventeen ships for the trip back to the Caribbean; with difficulty he managed to fit out six. Gentlemen and peasants were not crowding the wharf begging to be taken on in any capacity. Nobody wanted to ship. It was necessary to appeal to the prison inmates. They were offered the choice of serving out their sentences in jail or embarking on the New World venture. After all, law-breakers are dreamers, and many of them accepted the proposition. There was nothing novel about this solution from the penal point of view; the galleys were traditionally floating prisons, and, in time, France would hit upon the plan of sending her "lifers" to these very lands Columbus was to discover. The strange thing was that the Catholic Kings should have upheld such a policy. To them the conquest of the Indies was above all a spiritual undertaking, to carry the benign light of the Scriptures to the heathen. The Pope had given them authority to take possession of the lands discovered in their name because they were engaged in a crusade for the faith. But in whose hands were the monarchs going to place this pious and edifying labor? The text of the pardon offered to the criminals answers the question with biting irony: "We, to provide for this, and not only make possible the aforesaid conversion and settlement, but to show clemency and pity to our subjects as well, desire and order any and all males, and such of our subjects and inhabitants as up to the day of the promulgation of this our letter have committed any murder or assault, or any other crimes of whatsoever nature, except heresy or lèse-majesté or treason, premeditated murder, arson, counterfeiting, or sodomy, or taking gold or silver or money or other prohibited things out of our kingdoms, to go and serve in Hispaniola" — for which end they will be released from prison and sent aboard the ships. Plainly speaking, it was as though the Catholic Kings had set the Devil to baking holy wafers.

Thus it was that on May 30, 1498, Columbus embarked on his third voyage, on which he was really to discover the continent. Until then all he had touched upon was that chain of green islands which, running from Guanahaní in the north to Marigalante and Dominica in the south, separates the Caribbean from the Atlantic. But on the other side of the islands (though nobody knew it yet) lay the continent, the mainland, the great America of the Andes, the Mississippi, the Amazon, the Plate. The first to set foot here, too, would be Columbus. But a Columbus with fatigue in his eyes, abstruse, embittered, speaking with the accents of a prophet who has ceased to be a historical figure and has become a character in a tragedy. With his crew of cutthroats and adventurers, his blood-shot eyes, his long graying locks disheveled by the wind, he stands on the bridge like a strange figurehead of madness.

He had never been one to make friends easily. There was a lack of warmth in his soul that impeded cordial fellowship with other men. The spirit of Christopher the Frustrated did not frequent those humble paths of the heart where good companions foregather in the pleasant shade of friendship. Columbus had never had friends, but only associates. Whether destiny had so willed it, or whether through community of blood those who had been his advocates at the court, those who had first heard the account of his discoveries — even before the Queen herself — had been the outstanding figures among the converted Jews in Spain: Luis de Santángel, the Queen's treasurer, and Gabriel Sánchez, the treasurer of Aragón. It was a miracle that these two should have saved their skins when the flames of the Inquisition were glutting themselves upon other Santángels and Sánchezs, their close relatives, whose names fill the pages of the *Libro Verde de Aragón*.[1] Naturally, these two men who thought in terms of figures were his partners rather than his friends. And partners were the members of his family and the Genoese whom he tried to link to his undertaking for reasons that are not clear. Among the Spaniards who were the flesh of the discovery, the timber of the caravels, the nerves of this huge body struggling to make itself the master of the New World, he did not make friends, either with those of humble rank, because he had acquired delusions of grandeur, or with those higher in the scale, because his distrust and reserve kept him aloof from his captains. There was a complete absence of simple cordiality.

The one who felt this void most of all was he himself. He knew that the Queen would not be with him in the struggle that was dividing the enterprise into two factions — Columbus on one side, the Spaniards on the other. To whom could he turn his eyes? To God. But it was with a despairing, supersti-

---

[1] The "Green Book" was a kind of *Who's Who* of the converted Jews of the kingdom of Aragón, complied by some anonymous author, probably an official of the Inquisition. It began to circulate in manuscript form in the reign of Philip IV, and caused a great hue and cry because it proved that many an aristocratic family in Spain had some Jewish ancestor, thus invalidating its claim to being "Old Christians" and of "clean blood." The Inquisition forbade the circulation of the pamphlet.

tious passion, somewhat artificial, of the head, not the heart, expressed in a jargon of Biblical phrases. He tried to be more Catholic than Isabella the Catholic. And Isabella, who was a woman of good common sense, realized that the man was losing his mind. This is the Aeschylean background against which Columbus's third voyage was carried out, the voyage on which he was to discover the continent.

All that was visible of the first land they sighted on this trip — on August 1, 1498 — was the peaks of three hills against the horizon. A miracle: There was the symbol of the Holy Trinity! And the island was named Trinidad. Those they discovered after this he dedicated to the Virgin: Asunción, Concepción. But the marvelous thing was that this time his ships really reached the continent, the coast of Venezuela. At last, the mainland! But was it the mainland? Among the Church Fathers a favorite theme of speculation had been the exact location of the Garden of Eden. And now Columbus had found it. Proof was almost unnecessary, the fact was self-evident. The hand of God had been guiding him. And he was able to testify that its form was not that of a jagged mountain, as some theologians had believed, but of a hill shaped like the stem end of a pear.

Because of such statements (which nobody, beginning with the Queen, believed), the letter that might have served to accredit Columbus as the discoverer of the New World in the eyes of the learned men of Europe, the letter in which he spoke of the "great continent," was regarded as the maunderings of a fool. Peter Martyr dismissed it as "tales on which one need waste no time." Ferdinand, the Admiral's son, with filial devotion kept it to himself. By one of Fate's ironies, that very spot which Columbus took to be the Garden of Eden was to be the background four centuries later of episodes that a writer with a great sense of reality put into a book entitled *The Devil's Paradise*. It was the jungle to which we give the name of "Green Hell."

And Columbus returned to Hispaniola. This time he did not go to Isabela, which no longer existed. He went to Santo Domingo, which had been founded by another. What he found there was afterwards related in few words by his son: "The whole island was seething with discontent and rebellion. Many of those he had left there were dead, and only about 160 men were left, and they were suffering from syphilis."

The history of this spectacular failure is, in part, the history of another Columbus: Bartholomew. His governorship of Hispaniola had been a disaster. There was a great difference between Bartholomew and Christopher. The former had found his Garden of Eden on Hispaniola, in the company of a certain *cacica*. This idyl furnished material for subsequent writers, who described at length the rollicking scenes of naked brown girls dancing with garlands of flowers. But these delights were rudely interrupted by the stern realities of government. Hunger was threatening the colonists, and Francisco Roldán, a cross-grained, ambitious hidalgo, in the name of the "commune," began the first revolution of the people in America, this time against the dictatorship of the Columbuses. By the time Christopher reached Santo Domingo, Roldán and his followers had set up a separate republic. Christopher did not know what to do. He tried to come to terms with Roldán. He gave in to him. And as a result of this concession an institution came into being that was later to form the basis of colonial policy in America: the *repartimiento*. Grants of land with the Indians living on it were made to Roldán's rebels so that they might live in ease on the work of others. After making this agreement — a form of appeasement — Columbus turned severe, and began to squelch every sign of insubordination on the gallows. And it was not he alone; it was the three Columbus brothers who took solace and comfort from the gibbets at both ends of the city, each with its grisly fruit dangling from it.

The sight that greeted Bobadilla as he sailed into the harbor was two freshly hanged corpses. He was the judge who had been sent out by the Queen and endowed with full powers to bring the Columbus brothers to heel. This was to be the way the third voyage ended. The three of them — Christopher, Bartholomew, and Diego — after a brief struggle had to bow their necks and submit to Bobadilla's authority. And as Spanish justice was carried out with iron and blood, the sometime Viceroy, Governor, and Admiral now sat in chains in prison. Bobadilla had found not only the two gallows with their complement, but also seventeen Spaniards in a dungeon whom the Admiral had destined to the slip-noose. But this was nothing; the whole settlement lodged complaints against Columbus and his brothers, and to these lesser charges was added a more serious one: that Columbus had plotted with the Genoese to hand over to them the world he had discovered.

A series of coincidences lent weight to this generally held suspicion. There was not a single voyage in which Columbus did not bring Italians with him. On the first, Giacomo the Rich of Genoa, Anton de Calabria, and Giovanni de Venezia; on the second, Michele de Cuneo of Genoa, an old childhood friend; and on the third, the Genoese Giovanni Antonio Colombo, the son of Christopher's uncle Antonio, who had been sent to Spain by his brothers in Genoa and had come out to Santo Domingo as captain of one of the ships. The house of Centurione of Genoa had acted as agent to supply him with the money to make the third voyage. In Genoa, Pantaleón Italian and Centurione had sold the wheat belonging to the Order of Calatrava, and had sent Columbus drafts against these funds to fit out his ships. And Columbus himself, when he sailed from Spain, had stipulated in his will that a certain percentage of his income was to be paid into the bank of St. George in Genoa, where it was to form a capital fund to ease the tax burdens of the Genoese and to keep up the house of the Columbus family in that city. As Castile seemed to be slipping from his hands, Columbus turned his eyes once more to the homeland of his early years.

How serious a charge was preferred against Columbus on the basis of the malcontents' insinuations is something that will never be known. The record of Bobadilla's investigation has disappeared. The priest Bernáldez says that some accused him of concealing gold he was receiving; others of wanting to give the island to the Genoese. The Hieronymite friars wrote that the ills of the island dated from the time of Admiral Columbus, who discovered it "in keeping with an agreement he had made with the Genoese." Be this as it may, the Queen's investigator shipped Columbus back to Spain in chains. He had to wait six weeks before the royal order came to strike them off. The captain of the caravel had offered to remove them before, but Columbus — who took a certain pleasure in playing the victim — "would not consent to this; he did not want anybody but their Royal Majesties themselves to act in the matter as they saw fit; he was determined to keep the shackles as relics and remembrance of the reward he had received for his great services, and so he did [relates his son], for I saw them always in his chamber and he wanted them buried with him."

On the shores of the island of Jamaica lived a group of castaways. The majority of them were boys of thirteen and fourteen. They lived on cassava, chicha, and cornbread, which the Indians traded in return for glass beads and bells. These were the hundred and sixteen survivors of Columbus's last adventure, of the fourth voyage he began to dream of as soon as he was free of his irons. It was a year, three months, and four days since they had sailed down the Guadalquivir from Seville. Since then they had known only hunger, tempests, war. They had set out in four ships; two had reached this coast. These two were "rotten, worm-eaten, full of holes." All that could be done with them was to beach them and turn them into living quarters. There was no chance of any expedition's coming that way. After thinking the matter over they came to the conclusion that if there were some man brave enough to set out to sea in a canoe and cross over to Hispaniola, perhaps the governor's heart of stone would soften and he would extend them a helping hand. They all remembered that when they were coming from Seville they had wanted to put in to that island when the storm overtook them, but the governor had refused them even this. Columbus had no right to set foot on the lands he had placed in the hands of his sovereigns. He never knew whether the packet of letters he sent imploring aid had even been opened.

Columbus, there in the midst of this group of his misery-

ridden followers, wandered through his own soul and gave vent
to his emotions in a monologue that at times brought flashes of
haughty anger to his eyes, at times flooded them with tears. A
year and a half he had spent at court, following the King and
Queen like a dog — pleading, exhorting, promising — until he
managed to kindle a last hope in the Queen, who always ended
by believing him. Columbus had been like a cabbalistic prophet,
and finally nobody could say how many of the universe's secrets
he knew, and to what extent he was a sleep-walker inspired by
his own dreams. He no longer talked of discovering a new world;
this was already done. Now it was something even more extraordinary: discovering the strait that must lead to the other
sea, which was to be the goal of many nations for four centuries
until one day it was opened by the hand of man in Panama, at
the very spot where Columbus had gone to look for it. And on
the strength of this illusion ships were armed with cannon and
manned by old men and boys. On May 9, 1502, one hundred
and forty had set out from Seville. How different the four voyages had been! On the first, Columbus had set out with the
boldest sailors; on the second, with men of rank; on the third,
with jailbirds; on the fourth, with young boys. The rumor of his
agreements with the Italians must have been cleared up at court,
for no fewer than seven Genoese and one Milanese sailed with
him on this voyage. If there had been any truth in the charges,
they would not have been allowed aboard. Thus equipped, Columbus reached the lands of Veragua and Panama. In four hours
he found more gold than had been seen in Hispaniola in four
years. And he lost his ships. Let him speak for himself of his
tribulations:

"For eighty-eight days of terrible tempest I did not see the sun
nor the stars of the sea; the ships were leaking, the sails split, anchors,
spars, lifeboats, and supplies lost. My men were sick. All were con-
trite; many promised to take the habit of a religious order, and were
making confessions to one another. There was my son Ferdinand,
only thirteen years old. It wrenched my soul asunder to look at him.
I was sick; I had a cabin built on deck so that I could guide the helm.
And to think how little my twenty years of service have availed me!

I have not a roof tile in Castile. If I want to eat or sleep, at times I have not the money to pay my reckoning at the inn. And another grief tore out my heart from the back: Diego, my son, whom I had left in Spain, bereft of honor and property. . . .

"Cariay, Veragua! The gold mines, the province where there is unlimited gold, where the people use it to adorn their feet and arms and to line and trim chests and tables! The women wear collars of it that reach from their neck to their waist. Ten days' journey off is the Ganges. It is no farther from Cariay to Veragua than from Pisa to Venice. I knew all this, from Ptolemy and from the Scriptures, and I told it to the Queen, and the site of the Garden of Eden. . . . How weary I was! And the ships, and the men.

"My old wound has opened up; for nine days I gave up hope of life. Never did eyes behold the sea so high, so menacing, all foam. The ocean was like blood, seething like a cauldron on a roaring fire. Never did the sky look so fearful; all one day and night it blazed like a furnace, and each time the lightning flamed out I looked to see if it had carried off my masts and sails. . . .

"Christmas Day: the sea lashing in fury at the wild coast. Epiphany: rain that never stopped. January 24: the high, swift river broke my cables. I sent men inland; they found many mines. There was gold everywhere. In four hours all had secured gold. As my crew were seafaring men, and most of them young boys, nobody had seen mines, and very few gold. . . . The Indians came to kill us. We had to fight them. The sea rose and grew rough. I was alone in one of the ships off shore, and with fever. With great difficulty I climbed up to the highest part of the ship, calling and weeping to the mariners, to the four winds, for help; but none made me answer. Wearied, I fell asleep moaning. I heard a compassionate voice say:

" 'O thou foolish and remiss one in trusting and serving thy God! Took He more thought for Moses or David, his servant? From the time thou wast born He has watched over thee. He has made thy name marvelously known throughout the land. He gave thee the Indies for thine own; thou hast distributed them as thou hast seen fit, and He gave thee power to do so. He gave thee the keys to the Ocean-Sea which was locked with heavy chains. What more did He for the chosen people of Israel when He brought them out of Egypt? Or for David, the shepherd boy whom He made king of Judea? Turn back to Him, and recognize the error of thy ways. His mercy is boundless; thine old age shall not prevent thee from accomplishing great works; His heritages are vast. Abraham was more than a hundred years old when he engendered Isaac. And was Sarah a young girl? . . .'

"Half-dead I heard all this. And whoever it was that was speaking concluded, saying: 'Have no fear. Be of good heart. All these tribulations are written on tablets of marble, and there is a reason for them.'

"I arose, and in nine days the weather turned fair. In the name of the Blessed Trinity I set out on Christmas Eve with my ships rotten, worm-eaten and unseaworthy. I left one at Belén, another at Belpuerto. I set out for Hispaniola. The wild sea buffeted me. I turned back with my sails gone. I had lost my rigging. The ships were so riddled by the worms that they were like a honeycomb. The men were dispirited. And here I am. Nobody knows where these lands I have seen lie, the lands of gold. They can only bear witness that they have seen gold, that in this land of Veragua they have seen more gold in two days than in four years in Hispaniola. The land could not be more beautiful nor better tilled, nor the natives more cowardly, nor the harbor better, nor the river fairer.

"Your Majesties are the lords of this, the same as of Xérez or Toledo. Here you will secure gold. The gold is of finest quality; who has it has a treasure, and can do what he wishes in the world, even help souls into Paradise. Of the gold of Veragua they brought 666 quintals to Solomon. Of this gold he fashioned 300 lances and 200 shields, and the rack for them of gold, and many vessels of great size and rich with precious stones. David in his will left 3000 quintals of gold of the Indies to Solomon to help with the construction of the Temple, and according to Josephus it was from these same lands. Jerusalem and Mount Zion will be rebuilt by the hands of Christians. The one who shall do this will come out of Spain: the prophet foretold this to Abbot Joaquin. And who will offer himself for this task? If Our Lord takes me back to Spain, I pledge myself to do it. . . .

"I do not think it right to rob the Quibian of Veragua of his gold; good policy will avoid scandal and a bad name, and will bring it about that all of it will come to the treasury, to the last grain. . . . This is not a child to be raised by a stepmother. It is not just that those who have opposed this undertaking should benefit from it, nor their children. Those who left the Indies, fleeing the hardships, and maligning them and me, returned with official appointments. It was the fear of this that induced me to request, before I came, that I be allowed to govern them in Your Majesties' names. . . . For seven years I followed the court, and everyone to whom I spoke of this enterprise regarded it as a joke; now, even the tailors beg to be allowed to make discoveries. . . .

"I was arrested and put aboard a boat with my two brothers, loaded down with chains, and naked. There is not a hair on my head now that is not white, and I am ill. The restoration of my honor and the punishment of those who brought me to such a state will redound to the credit of your royal nobility. It is impossible to keep silent in the face of such an affront; I beg Your Majesties to forgive me. Up to now I have wept for others; now let there be mercy for me in Heaven and let the earth weep for me. . . ."

These are the very words of Columbus's soliloquy, which he set down on paper and sent to the sovereigns in a letter. It was not madness to think these things; but it was madness to write them — and madder still to address them to the monarchs, with nothing but the planks of a wrecked ship under his feet. But this was Columbus. And at his side there was another madman, Diego Méndez. Diego Méndez was to carry the letter. He nailed a pole to a big canoe, tied a piece of cloth to it, and so put out to sea on the Caribbean as though he were sailing a sheltered lake in the snuggest sailboat. This was not the first exploit of this extraordinary personage, whose life deserves not one book but many. An even rasher deed was to go by himself to the tent of a cacique in Panama, when the Indians were threatening to attack, to find out what his secret intentions were. Méndez was not a soldier nor a sailor; he was a philosopher. He read Erasmus. The only treasure his children found when he died was a shelf of books, almost all of them by the author of *The Praise of Folly*. This was the man the shipwrecked crew saw set out with a few Indians as oarsmen. At last, on the brink of the grave, Columbus had found a friend, and this friend reached Hispaniola. For seven months the governor, Ovando, solacing himself with the thought of Columbus's mishaps, kept Méndez a prisoner. In Jamaica, Columbus and his men wondered if he had been lost. No — he had not died, and he had not forgotten. Eventually released from prison, he spent the weeks and months scanning the horizon, until one day he saw some ships coming from Spain. Through Diego Méndez's efforts, it was on one of these ships that Columbus returned to Spain.

Just two more words about this Diego Méndez, because he is typical of many others who were to follow him, leaving pieces of their life in these lands. Like Columbus, he returned to Spain, and Columbus commended him to his son Diego. The years went by. Diego became governor of the Indies, not so much by reason of being his father's son as by clinging to the skirts of a lady-in-waiting of the court whom he married. He became the lord of Hispaniola. And with the exquisite politeness of the accomplished courtier he turned his back upon Diego Méndez, leaving him with outstretched hand. . . . Méndez died forgotten. In his will he asked only that a stone be placed upon his grave, on it to be carved a canoe under which in very clear letters was to be inscribed: CANOA. . . .

To return to Columbus. Back in Spain he was borne up by the hope of seeing his Queen again. She would make everything right, he knew; she would reinstate him in his rightful possessions and punish his enemies. Probably the first questions he asked as he stepped ashore were: "And where is the Queen? Where is the court now?" "The Queen is dying." Isabella lay on her deathbed, and this madman could not be allowed to importune her. He was never to see her again. Now he would have to deal with Ferdinand of Aragón. His gout was troubling him again, and he did not know how to get to the court. He thought of hiring from the cathedral of Seville the magnificent catafalque that had been used at the funeral of the Duke of the Infantado. My lord the Admiral could not have chosen a finer carriage. But then he descended to a humbler level and requested the King's permission to ride a mule. But only bishops used mules as mounts; time went by and the permit had not arrived. The Admiral felt his end drawing near. He spent his time writing letters about the mule, about his sons, about his rights and claims. In one of them, ironically enough in the light of later events, he recommends Amerigo Vespucci to his son. The Admiral wanted to help this Italian friend, such a nice fellow, whose services deserved better pay than he had received. . . .

As a matter of fact, at that moment King Ferdinand was taken up with a very important piece of business, namely, his marriage to a lively eighteen-year-old girl who should make his widowerhood more endurable. This was Germaine de Foix, who had been brought up at the court of France, where life was a pleasant affair. Spain at the moment was a cockpit; intrigue and deception were the order of the day. Philip the Fair had entered the country, contrary to the pledges he had given, to take control of the kingdom of Castile in the name of his wife, Joanna, who was completely mad. Ferdinand could not stand his son-in-law, and the latter reciprocated his feelings. Philip refused to allow the King to embrace his own daughter. Every courtier of Castile concealed a possible traitor. Under these circumstances, it was no small concession that Ferdinand ultimately granted one thing to Columbus: permission to ride a mule. In the midst of the question of the mule, the suffering caused by the gout, the marriage of old Ferdinand and the young girl, the plottings of Philip the Fair, the aberrations of the melancholy Joanna, and the latest news from America — which in the hands of others more brutal and less self-pitying than Columbus was beginning to pour treasure into Spain — Christopher Columbus died obscurely, not in want but without friends, on May 20, 1506. Accompanied by four or five persons, he was carried quietly to the grave, which closed to give final rest to this restless mariner. This was his fifth voyage, his real voyage to Paradise. One little ship, manned by a single sailor, and four or five comrades who murmured gently from the shore: Farewell, my Captain!

III

SANTO DOMINGO, NEW WORLD
A–BORNING

I know full well that all comparisons are odious to some of those listening to what they would prefer not to hear; and this is what will happen to certain Sicilian and English readers with this book of mine, especially when they see this chapter, in which I repeat what I have said and written on other occasions: that if a prince had no other domain than this single island [Hispaniola], in a short time it would surpass such other islands as Sicily and England; for what is disregarded here would make other regions very rich.

FERNÁNDEZ DE OVIEDO

FORTUNATELY, the New World was not as Columbus had described it in his last letter. There was more to it than lamentations and Biblical outbursts. Life was sensuous, and at times gay and easy. Combat and fatigue were followed by certain compensations quite different from shipwrecks and the Admiral's gloomy frenzy. Thus, by a strange quirk of Fate, the only unattractive description of the New World is that left by its discoverer; it completely lacks sex appeal. And the strange thing is that this was not because he lacked the gift for this kind of writing, for at times certain lines creep into his letters . . . God save us! Nor because he lacked the materials for the descriptions that titillated Amerigo Vespucci's readers. Samuel Eliot Morison, who has followed the Admiral's footsteps with painstaking exactitude, says: "There must have been considerable sporting between the seamen and the Indian girls, for the habits of the Tainos were completely promiscuous." But he adds: "Columbus said nothing of that, since his Journal was intended for the eyes of a modest queen." This is the important point. Moreover, in the literature of the discovery of the New World, Columbus represents not that Spain which was light-heartedly awakening, but the Spain that was buried with Queen Isabella:

47

the Spain without sinful Renaissances, without liberty or license, the crusading Spain in which the echo of a chorus of friars is always audible. Columbus, on guard against saying anything that might brand him as unorthodox, anticipated the formula of Gracian Dantisco upon the art of spinning tales for Spanish consumption: "Let the gentleman who proposes to relate a tale or fable see to it that there are no lascivious or immodest words, or of an indecency that may disgust those who hear them; for things can be said in a roundabout way, employing decent, modest terms, never clearly mentioning certain things, especially if there are women among the listeners."

To put the matter in a nutshell: Spain was not at that time what Columbus thought it, nor was the New World what he painted it. And life and history can be presented without so much hedging and beating around the bush as he employed.

After the death of Queen Isabella, after the death of Columbus, Spain began to come apart at the seams. When Isabella cast her eye upon Ferdinand and married him, she worked a miracle: she sewed together the scraps of kingdoms that composed Spain to make a great nation. Before her day the history of Spain was the separate histories of Castile, Navarre, Aragón, and Granada. All these the Queen wove together as a girdle for her gown. But when she breathed her last and was laid to rest, what ambitions sprang up, what slightest pretext was employed to break up the Spanish nation! Upon what had been austere, penurious Castile there descended a flock of birds of prey — the Hapsburg eagles; and even a little warbling bird from France who sang the sweetest melodies in the ear of old Don Ferdinand the Catholic. The cities of Spain took on an unwonted international quality. The youths read Erasmus, and many strange foreign tongues were heard at the court.

Nothing gives a better idea of this interlude in the Spanish drama than the interview between Ferdinand the Catholic and his son-in-law, Philip the Fair. It took place in Sanabria. Ferdinand had acted as regent of Castile after the death of the Queen; but the heirs to the throne were Joanna, their daughter, who was mad, and Philip her husband, who was fair to see. The Castilians had been urging Philip and Joanna to come and take over the government of Castile. They were fed up with the regency of Ferdinand, the Aragonese, and they felt that there might be good pickings for the clever in a new set-up. Philip needed no urging. He could hardly wait to see himself crowned. And flouting a treaty, promises, and words of honor, he arrived armed to the teeth to take possession of the kingdom. He had come from Flanders. The courtiers of Castile fell over themselves to surround him with attentions. Ferdinand, who with Isabella had raised Spain to the position it occupied, now watched his friends fall away to fawn upon the new arrival.

Beyond a doubt a new world was coming into being in Spain. For the moment nobody could tell which was to have the upper hand, the spirit of the interlopers or that of the native sons. Across the sea another world was being brought forth, too. The change of rulers in Spain had produced a state of nervous tension there. It is necessary to have lived under the threat of that mystery known as "court favor" to understand many chapters in the history of the Caribbean. But life is stronger than politics. The Caribbean was opening out, its contours were being revealed by the light kindled by the violence of the intrepid conquistadors. The island of Santo Domingo, Hispaniola, was a model of all Spain's future colonies in America. In miniature, it embodied the whole drama. Anyone who knows the inside history of Santo Domingo during the first fifty years has, so to speak, a condensed view of the life of Colonial America.

Santo Domingo was the first permanent city founded by Europeans in America. It was the seat of the first government, of the court, one might say. The governor, who was soon known as the viceroy, lived in his "palace." Ferdinand Columbus relates that the governor Bobadilla had the insolence to establish himself in the "palace" of his uncle. The governor made peace treaties with the "kings" or "queens" of native peoples, or warred upon them. (Subsequent readers have found these terms somewhat misleading. A "queen" was in reality a *cacica* — a tribal lead-

49

er. A "palace" was a hut. A "city" was a place where one or two hundred Spaniards lived with their Indian servants or their Negro slaves.) A hurricane came along, tore off the straw thatch of the roofs, pulled out the poles that supported the walls, and carried off the city Bartholomew Columbus had founded. Ovando, the new governor, rebuilt it. This time the houses were of stone — no more castles in the air. He laid out straight streets. The essential outlines of a city in the Spanish manner took shape: church, fort, hospital, jail. Cathedral and university would come later. In all these words, which can be accepted only with reservations, one sees the ingenuous pride of the founders who, threatened by hurricane and hostile arrows, were shaping new republics with their hands. They looked upon them and rejoiced in them. The faith of their creative will disarms the disdainful commentary.

Fernández de Oviedo, who first described the city, wrote: "As for its buildings, in proportion, no city of Spain — not even Barcelona, which I have seen many times — excels it. All the houses of Santo Domingo are of stone, like those of Barcelona; or their walls are of strong and beautiful mud-and-wattle that resembles fine mortar. And the location is better than that of Barcelona, for the streets are broader, straighter, and more level."

Along these streets the three colors of the flag of the New World were beginning to be seen: the color of the Indian, of the Spaniard, and of the African. The Indians were the color of "light parrots." They went clad in air and sun. In their combats, their bucklers were their bellies. The Spaniards were soldiers, but every day more hidalgos were arriving. Hidalgo (*hijo de algo*), strictly speaking, means the son of a known father, to differentiate him from one who is little better than a bastard. But the kings, out of the kindness of their hearts, had ordered that persons who had committed serious crimes not carrying the death penalty be exiled to Hispaniola, where they might live in freedom and peace. The only stipulation made was that no Moors, heretics, Jews, repentant backsliders, or persons newly converted to the Holy Faith "except Negro or other slaves" be allowed to enter Hispaniola. Every Spaniard sailing for Hispaniola was allowed, at the beginning, to take along one slave;

later the number was increased to twenty. All wanted to have slaves, which was very natural. Father Las Casas was an ardent supporter of the idea. The Hieronymite friars suggested sending out armed expeditions to Cape Verde or Guinea to catch them. Fray Bernardino de Manzedo wrote: "All the inhabitants of Hispaniola beseech Your Majesty to authorize them to take along Negroes; it seemed to all of us that it would be a very good thing, provided there was the same number of females as males, and that they were recently imported and not raised in Castile, for these latter are inclined to turn out mean."

Things were getting organized. Nicolás de Ovando, no one can deny it, was a governor who knew his business. Any Spaniard who showed trouble-making tendencies was politely summoned to his presence, conducted aboard a ship, and returned to Spain. Monasteries were opened for the friars who were beginning to arrive. Ovando laid the foundations for the hospital. The lands, with their Indians, were divided up among the Castilians; some received fifty Indians, some one hundred. The Indians were made to work until they dropped. The results were not bad. Great fields of sugar cane raised their green shoots; the air echoed with the shouts of overseers urging on the horses turning the sugar mills that ground out the sweet syrup that became great loaves of sugar. A fair amount of gold was washed. The wives of the gentlemen, some white, some the color of light parrots, decked themselves out in gay finery. Gold refineries were set up, and jewelers were allowed to make chains and other ornaments — hand-hammered, not soldered — so that everyone might adorn himself as befitted his quality. The hidalgos led a delightful existence, ravishing Indian girls, playing cards, drawing their knives on any pretext, and — mounted on their blooded Andalusian sorrels — fencing with long spears. Great numbers of horses, dogs, pigs, goats, and chickens had been brought over. Even the friars found fields white for the harvest. They had allotments of Indians, like the gentlemen, and they performed marriages, baptized, preached. The Franciscans thundered sermons against the Dominicans, and the Dominicans against the Franciscans; so vehement did the antagonism become that each order sent a delegate to the court requesting the King to make the other group hold its tongue.

The Indian women were gentle and uninhibited. The "queen" Anacaona organized a feast for the governor at which three hundred maidens sang and danced the *areyto*, one of the most delightful pastimes imaginable. Anacaona was "gracious and regal in her speech and manners and gestures, and a great friend of the Christians." The *areytos* were dances accompanied by song. Sometimes holding hands, sometimes with arms interlocked, the girls, in a chain or group, repeated the movements of their leader, in a kind of contredanse, all very studied, singing now soft, now loud, while the drums beat an accompaniment. Their songs told of tribal exploits or legends, and they performed so well that the Spaniards observed: "They remind us of the songs and dances of the peasants when, in certain regions of Spain, during the summer, men and women amuse themselves to the sound of the tambourine."

The younger Spaniards, and even those not so young, found the limits of the city too narrow, and set out to measure new lands with their lances. In Spain they had been nobodies; here they grew into great figures of history, whose heads touched the stars. One of these lads was Juan Ponce de León, who was to conquer the island of San Juan (Puerto Rico) and to discover Florida. Another was that ranking conquistador of lasses in Spain, soon to become the greatest conquistador of the Indies, Hernán Cortés. So with all of them. Juan de la Cosa came here — Vespucci — Alonso de Hojeda, with the tale that he had discovered the Island of the Giants — Vicente Yáñez Pinzón, who saw the Amazon where it flows into the ocean — Bastidas, who sailed along the coast from Venezuela to Panama, where Columbus had not touched. From Santo Domingo, Balboa set out to discover the Pacific; Pizarro to conquer Peru; Herédia to found Cartagena; Díaz de Solís to discover the Plate estuary and to die on the River Plate; Sebastián del Campo and Diego Velásquez to explore Cuba, find it to be an island, and rule over it. For all of these men Santo Domingo was university, newspaper, tavern buzzing with rumor and "inside information," and gathering place where exciting news made everyone's heart beat faster. Here they received their baptism of fire, killed their first Indians, found and gambled away their first gold. Daggers often ripped through the air; more often, oaths.

One day Alonso Niño and Cristóbal Guerra came to the city. A marvelous book could be written about their extraordinary voyage. With thirty-one men, in a single boat, they had set out from Spain. One of Columbus's letters had mentioned the pearls of Venezuela, and they had set out to find them. And they did. The treasure they brought back was enough to make a man lose his senses. The people in Santo Domingo gazed upon it with awe: some of the pearls were the size of hazelnuts. Niño and Guerra sailed back to Spain. They disembarked at a port of Galicia with fifty-five marks of pearls to show their countrymen. Says one historian: "They came ashore loaded with pearls as though they were hay." The voyage of this single caravel, which lasted only sixty-one days, proved more effective than all of Columbus's letters.

There was nobody in Santo Domingo who did not set out to look for pearls. Even the Dominicans and Franciscans crossed the sea, to remain in Venezuela. When their colleagues, the Hieronymite friars, came later to pay them a visit in the name of the King, they found them established and prepared to set their house in fitting order. "The Franciscan fathers have requested certain things for their vestry which they say they need in these lands, and both they and the Dominicans have asked us for cannon, powder, and others arms. . . ."

While the Spaniards were finding this New World their oyster, the Indians were growing more and more resentful. The newcomers would not let the Indians' women alone. The men were sent off to the mines for a "stay" — which meant eight months of hard work — and the women were left behind. When the men returned they found their homes in ruins. The women, rather than raise children to be slaves, killed them at birth.

Hundreds of Indians died at this forced labor. Others committed suicide. One Indian called upon his comrades to rise against the invaders because when he went to the judge to complain that a Spaniard had taken advantage of his wife, the judge answered him with a kick. One Spaniard, to amuse himself, set his dog upon a cacique; in a few seconds the dog had torn out the chief's bowels. The chief's men rose against the Spaniard. The Dominicans, defending the Indians, made a terrible fuss over the matter. The Franciscans took the side of the Spaniards. "God forgive me if I think evil," murmured Father Las Casas, "but the Franciscans had a *repartimiento*. . . ." And so they raised a whirlwind of sermons to which the voices of the overseers formed a contrapuntal chorus. Santo Domingo was a center of physical education and of spiritual exercises.

The governor wanted neither scandals nor disturbances. He had come out to see that things were done according to rule. After duly pondering what had taken place, and considering appropriate measures, he decided that the place to begin was at the top. He announced a festival in honor of "queen" Anacaona and her tribal chieftains. He promised there would be a great celebration in the Spanish manner, with equestrian feats, including fencing on horseback, to be held before the "palace" of the queen. The Indians were delighted. The queen and her chieftains, festively painted with black and red, gathered to see the gallant tournament. The Spaniards were waiting only for the governor's sign. There were greetings and smiles, and the horses curveted impressively. Ovando laid his hand on his breast, upon the cross of Calatrava — this was the signal. The Spanish horsemen rushed into the palace and slaughtered all the chieftains. Only Anacaona was spared. More fittingly to honor her, she was hanged in the square. The punishment so terrified the Indians that from then on they walked the chalk mark, and in commemoration of this event the governor founded the town called Sancta María de la Vera Paz. Fernández de Oviedo says: "The governor was very devout and a great Christian, and very charitable and generous to the poor; soft-spoken with all. He greatly befriended the Indians and all the Spaniards; he was like a father

to all of them, and he set them all an example of right living;
he was a religious and very prudent gentleman, and he ruled
the land in peace and tranquility."

Things of this sort were inevitable. Bring together Indians
and white men, serfs and masters, slaves from Africa, in a new
society, and there are bound to be brushes. The Indians declined in number, but new ones were brought in from the Bahamas. Every day the city improved in appearance, and up the
fine river that stretched in front of it came ships from Spain
bringing gunpowder, garlic, and oil, and carrying back sugar,
gold, and pearls. At times the King grew provoked with the
news brought him by the Dominicans, but he always rejoiced to'
receive bars of gold and marks of pearls. The island was not too
rich in mines, but by dint of working the natives to the bone
the Spaniards got gold out of them. The treasurer of Santo Domingo became so rich that he lost his mind: one day he gave a
banquet and instead of salt he put gold dust in the salt cellars.

One day a larger fleet than usual sailed in. It was bearing
something of great importance, a viceroy. Diego Columbus had
finally achieved his ambition. His wife was Doña María de Toledo, of one of the great families of Spain. Doña María came
with all the retinue of a vicereine: ladies-in-waiting, maids-of-
honor, secretaries. The viceroy was handsome, tall, and of fine
presence; the vicereine, energetic and with a good head on her
shoulders. Now all would see what a court was — the hidalgos
and picaroons who had come out from Spain, and the Negroes
and the Indians maids who still remained to dance and sing
areytos. The viceroys at first took up their quarters in the fortress, but later they built themselves a "palace." This time it was
the real thing; four centuries have passed over its stones, and
there the stones stand to bear witness. It was described to the
King by one who had seen it: "I know of no house so fine in
Spain, all of stone, with its many and spacious rooms, and the
most beautiful view of the land and the sea that can be imagined. Your Majesty could be lodged there as well as in the
finest house in Castile."

55

This was as it should be. The son of the discoverer of these lands had at last received his due, had been honored, and he felt himself a king. He was a small-scale reproduction of the ruler of Castile and Aragón. The vicereine married off her maids-of-honor to the richest of the land-grant holders. These first little genealogical trees she planted with her own hand, watered, pruned, and watched grow with real maternal solicitude. The viceroy had lands, slaves, sugar-mills; the juice of the cane was the first sweetness life had offered him.

Don Diego was a man of determination and character, and he made enemies. It irked him that anyone should embark on a voyage of discovery without his permission; once in Castile he had got into a quarrel with Ferdinand Magellan, who was equipping an expedition with the King's authorization. Here in Santo Domingo his pride had become still more overweening. The King watched the growing insolence of the young whelp who as a child had been his page. One day he pulled him up short: "I am amazed," he wrote, "that you should take offense because I write to you and the other officials conjointly concerning matters of government, for all those I have seen engaged in such tasks usually welcome advice. You are well aware of the fact that when the Queen — may she be in Glory — and I sent Commander Ovando out as governor of this island because of the bad account your father gave of himself in this post you now hold, he found everything in a lamentable state of confusion and disorder. Let me urge upon you that henceforth you conduct yourself in such a manner that it will not be necessary for me to write you letters of this sort."

Under the heavy hand of the new masters, peace was being established. The measures taken by Governor Ovando could not have been more efficacious. With the memory of Queen Anacaona's body swaying in the air, the Indians bowed their heads. If occasionally they tried running away to the hills, the dogs brought them out in pieces. But Don Diego Columbus had to face a new problem: the revolt of the Negroes, which began with the twenty slaves of his own sugar plantation. On

56

the day after Christmas, which is a time of hope and rejoicing, these Negroes ran away and plotted with others on neighboring plantations. Although the idea of freedom was still too new for the world, they attempted it. From plantation to plantation the rebellion spread. The first Spaniards who attempted to oppose them were killed. When Don Diego received the news, he mounted his horse and set out with all his knights and hidalgos. The expedition had the appearance of a boar hunt. The dogs ran about, sniffing, barking, wagging their tails. The horses neighed and pranced. And, as in an English hunting print, the vicereine watched them set out with the air of the lady of the manor wishing the party "Good hunting." The Indians looked on in silence. The Negroes had taken to the hills.

Nine Spaniards had been killed. Melchior de Castro's ranch had been sacked. They had threatened to cut the throats of all the whites in the town of Azua. Don Diego and his men would have wished their horses had wings to fly to punish such impudence. Melchior de Castro could endure no more. His blood was pounding in his ears, and there was a bellowing in his breast as of all the cows of his ranch. He outdistanced Don Diego and organized and conducted the battle. Fernández de Oviedo describes it in a page that is like a Gobelin tapestry of the most perfect medieval design:

"At the hour when the morning star appears on the horizon they caught up with the Negroes. Eagerly they set upon them, shields firmly clasped and lances fixed for the charge, calling upon God and Saint James the Apostle, the twelve riders forming a squadron, few in number but bold-hearted men. Stirrup to stirrup, loose-reined, they charged into the midst of all those Negroes, who were stoutly awaiting the attack of the Christians; but the horsemen broke through them to the other side. In this first charge some slaves fell, but they quickly formed ranks again, hurling stones, lances, and darts; yelling louder than before, they awaited the second charge of the Christian knights. This was not long in coming; for, in spite of the many wooden lances hurled by the slaves, the horsemen attacked again, invoking once more the name of Saint James and finding their mark in

57

many of them, and scattered the rebels anew as they rode through them. When the Negroes found themselves so suddenly separated from each other and so boldly attacked and scattered by so few and such bold knights, they were afraid to stand against the third charge that was coming. And they turned and fled to the hills and crags that were near the spot where the encounter took place, and the field and the victory was to the Spaniards. Six Negroes were left dead, and many others were wounded; the aforesaid Melchior de Castro was wounded in the left arm by a spear. And the victors remained on the field until day came because, as it was night and very dark, and the terrain was rough and thickly wooded in spots, they could not see those who fled."

The viceroy was satisfied. His knights harried the defeated through hills and ravines. One by one the Negroes fell, and their bodies dangled from many gallows that were set up along the road. Don Diego returned to the city. Doña María de Toledo threw her strong arms about him. The knights stroked their silky black beards. This viceroy, observes the chronicler, had served God and Their Majesties well. The rebellious Negroes had been punished, and the others were terrified and taught a lesson.

Not long afterwards the Hieronymite friars arrived in Santo Domingo, with wide powers. As Spain was ruled now by Ferdinand, now by Philip, then by Cardinal Cisneros, followed by Charles V, and always by some minister who was more powerful than the sovereigns themselves, there kept arriving in Santo Domingo people of the most varied sorts. The appearance of a new governor — the victorious enemy of his predecessor — indicated a change of wind at court that blew up a hurricane in the Antilles. Now it was Bartolomé de Las Casas who was calling the tune in Castile. Thanks to his overwhelming gift of gab, his vehement passions, and his touching accounts of the unhappy Indians tortured by Spanish butchers, he succeeded in having these friars sent out to the island and in getting a plan drawn up in Castile for an ideal republic, a Utopia that served the Jesuits as a model when they established their communistic state in Paraguay. The friars had instructions to take a general census of the Indians and to assemble them in villages of three hundred souls that were to be founded where there was good water, abundant woodland, and green pastures. Each family was to have a big house, land on which to plant yucca and corn, and twelve hens and a rooster. There was to be a church in each village, a hospital, and a house for the cacique. Everyone was to wear clothing and sleep in beds, and there was to be no eating on the floor. Everyone was to be satisfied with his own wife. Each village was to have community property, commons for the stock to graze, and ten or twelve mares, fifty cows, five hundred pigs, and a hundred sows. The Indians were to attend mass and be seated in orderly fashion, the men separate from the women.

There is nothing more agreeable and edifying than to draw up a republic on paper. And on paper it remained.

Notwithstanding all this violence and the ebb and flow of events, twenty-five years after the Spaniards' arrival Santo Domingo was a different island. Everything, even the landscape, had changed. The Indians had made the acquaintance of horses, iron, gunpowder, friars, the Spanish tongue, the name of Jesus Christ, glass, velvet, bells, gallows, caravels, pigs, chickens, donkeys, mules, sugar, wine, wheat, Negroes from Africa, men with beards, shoes, and paper and writing — or, as they believed, white leaves that spoke to the ear. The children began to talk a language never before heard. The fields were covered with sugar cane; the mines were being worked. Where once there had been forest, the noisy clamor of a sugar-mill now filled the air. Never had a single generation witnessed such sweeping, violent changes. The caciques hung shriveled from the gallows. A stone city had come into being. There was a viceroy. And carpenters, tailors, shoemakers. And a bell calling people to mass. The Indians watched the doughty hidalgos bend the knee and bow the head before the elevation of the Host. The island had become a New World for the Indians. Newer for them than for the Spaniards themselves. Those who survived the first rude encounter and their own bewilderment observed that their very skin was changing color, and the Indian women gazed with tenderness on the fruit of their blood and that of the new arrivals, the first half-breeds, wailing in their cradles of straw.

The Spaniards, too, were making the acquaintance of new things. Cassava bread, corn, corn liquor, tobacco, syphilis, hammocks, yucca, canoes, arrows, pearl beds, wars, alligators, seas, and forests where every tree was different from those they knew in Spain, where every bird sang a new song, every dawn revealed a mountain never seen before, every struggle was a breath-taking experience, more breath-taking than the gold they had never before seen and which they now held in the hollow of their trembling hands.

IV

THE PACIFIC, OR WHAT THE COMMON MAN DISCOVERED

He saluted the Austral Sea and gave infinite thanks to God and all the saints in heaven for having reserved the glory of such a reward for him who was not a man of great wit or learning or high-born.

PETER MARTYR

HERE are the islands. Across from them, the mainland. The continent to be explored, from which will emerge Mexico and Peru, with cities of stone and kings clad in gold, and the green chain of the Andes with its diadem of snow, and the Orinoco, the Amazon, the Paraná, and silver-boweled Potosí, and emerald-veined Muzo. Here are rivers, mountains, cities, mines, kings unknown but dreamed-of. From the hammocks of Santo Domingo, at the hour of the siesta in the breathless tropical heat, castles rise in the air.

As a matter of fact, the outlines of the continent had already been seen. Its profile was being sketched with daring strokes by those who knew nothing of geography. We know that the pearl coast was explored by Alonso Niño and Cristóbal Guerra in a single boat. With four boats, Vicente Yáñez discovered the Amazon. With two, Diego de Lepe penetrated farther south than anyone before. These pathfinders either were common seamen, or came from humble peasant families who did not even know what a ship looked like. They had not had the advantages of education, or the favor of kings, or money. The fathers of our America were the sons of nobody. And yet America is the offspring of men whose like are rarely to be found in the annals of the world.

On one of his voyages Columbus had explored the coast of Guiana and Venezuela, almost touching upon the pearl banks; on another, Central America as far as Veragua, where he saw the first gold of the mainland. Now these two points on the map had to be joined, and this piece of land explored that the imagination of the Spaniards saw set in a brooch of pearls with chains of gold. The visions of the *Thousand and One Nights* did not surpass theirs.

There dwelt in the outskirts of Seville a notary who when he heard talk of such things was unable to go on with his work; his pen slipped from his fingers. He was going out to conquer this coast. His name was Rodrigo de Bastidas. He fastened his ink-horn to his belt, along with his sword, and sent out a call for volunteers to join him. Given that natural propensity of the Spaniards to undertake the impossible, he had no lack of followers, and his two ships were quickly manned. This time the pen-pusher would do no writing; he was going to make history. And he did. He saw that whole strip of the coast that Columbus missed: Darien. And this fragment was America's only tribute to the memory of the Admiral; it became known as Colombia.

As so frequently happened, the notary's ships were lost in a storm. By a miracle the shipwrecked men reached Santo Domingo. But Bastidas had seen gold. In spite of the wreck, he arrived with two chests full of it. He tried to hide it, but it was an open secret. It was a great piece of good luck that under these circumstances he ever managed to get out of the jail into which the governor clapped him, as was the custom of the day. But, in the meantime, people began to plan and even undertake expeditions. Darien was now the word that fired the imagination. Four or five years of search and exploration gave rise to the conviction that the man who made himself governor of Darien would hold in his hands the key to all future discoveries. For Darien was not merely the gold Bastidas had brought back in his chests; it was the route of the great conquests of America.

Darien was the point where Central America and South America come together. From the first moment, the poor devils in Santo Domingo saw that this was the pivotal point of the world that was coming into being. The same thing holds true today, four hundred years later: whoever has control of this nexus of land holds the mastery of the world. For the moment it was nothing but a lair of jaguars and wild Indians, a morass of swamps. The gulf of Uraba, which the Spaniards had reached, was so inhospitable a dwelling place for man that the Indians had to live in huts built like big nests in the tops of the trees. Below lay an oozy swamp writhing with snakes. Women, children, and gaffers climbed like monkeys on long ladders of withes. Although no one would think it, this was the mainland, and here the Spaniards were to found the first cities. From the human point of view, it was absurd; from the geographic point of view, absolutely right.

And who had their eyes on the governorship? In the bright nights of Santo Domingo this was the topic of conversation of men of the most varied sort. There was Juan de la Cosa, the cosmographer, who had accompanied Columbus and Bastidas, and had then become master of his own ship. He was one of the few who knew the sea. His name has been remembered as that of the first man to make a map of the New World. One of his companions was the swineherd Francisco Pizarro, who had found it simpler to cross the sea than to face the owner of the drove of pigs he had allowed to wander off. Another was Hernán Cortés, who had already made a name for himself in Spain as a conqueror, though not of lands. There was also one Bachelor Enciso, a lawyer who had grown wealthy on the island with his profession. In Santo Domingo everyone gambled, blasphemed, got into debt, and took to the law, and no lawyer in Spain had such a sphere of activity as in Santo Domingo. Moreover, Enciso had his literary ambitions, and he left a book.

But among all this distinguished company, with their admirable antecedents, there were perhaps none to be compared with Alonso de Hojeda and Diego de Nicuesa. Hojeda had made a reputation for himself on the island from the days of Columbus, when he had introduced the praiseworthy custom of cutting off the Indians' ears or noses to teach them how wrong it is to take the property of another without his consent. Queen Isabella was very fond of him because he was a man who performed great acrobatic feats and because he had a rare wit. Slight of figure, handsome of face, with very large eyes, he was one of those Spaniards who can delight a tavern and captivate a court. Once when the Queen went up to the tower of the cathedral of Seville (relates Las Casas) from whose height the people below look like dwarfs, Hojeda walked out on the beam that projects twenty feet beyond the tower, as swiftly as though he were on the pavement, and when he came to the end of it he pirouetted on one foot, turned around, and walked back just as fast. But the feat that most endeared him to the Queen was an exploit he performed in Santo Domingo which combined acrobatics with wit. One day he went to call upon a cacique whom he planned to take prisoner. With great courtesy he invited him to come with him to the river for a swim, where he would show him the kind of bracelets the kings in Europe wore. These were a pair of hand-cuffs that he put on the ingenuous cacique, and when he had snapped them shut, he swung him on his horse and carried him off to jail. This exploit caused great merriment when it was related at court. The cacique was hanged.

Diego de Nicuesa was a good running mate for Hojeda. He, too, was slight of stature, but so agile and strong that when he fenced with a lance on horseback he could break his adversary's bones with the impact of the lance against the other's shield — so it was said. He aroused great admiration among the Indians of the island, and even among the Spaniards, by reason of the circuslike feats he performed with his Andalusian mare. He had been a courtier, and he probably owed his popularity there to his musical accomplishments; for centuries he was remembered as "a great player of the lute."

So the matter of completing the discovery and conquest of the New World was in the hands of this small group: a musician, an acrobat, a map-maker, a lawyer, a swineherd, a Don Juan, and others of the same kind who lived in Santo Domingo on cassava bread and hopes. In Spain matters of a different nature were under discussion: the cost of the radishes consumed by Queen Germaine and her gay friends at a banquet; the death — so opportune — of young Philip the Fair, which some said came from drinking a glass of water while he was overheated, others attributing it to an attack of indigestion; the return of Don Ferdinand as regent of Castile in the name of his daughter, Joanna the Mad, and so on. Everyone knew that the real Council of the Indies was the one made up of these adventurers of Santo Domingo, and that the conquest was the work of America rather than of Spain, of the people rather than the King. It was the America of the people, white and half-breed, that was beginning to take form in the Caribbean; the King put his stamp of approval on it afterwards. And when the moment came to select a governor for the province of Darien, which had been discovered by a notary of Seville, he conferred joint authority upon the acrobat and the musician, Alonso de Hojeda and Diego de Nicuesa.

Hojeda set out first, with his ships. He was accompanied by the map-maker, the swineherd, the notary, and no one knows how many others, or how obscure and unknown. Nicuesa followed later with the rest. At the last minute Hernán Cortés, the Conquistador, was forced to remain on the island because of sickness. The first city that was founded bore the symbolic name of San Sebastián. It was the creation of Hojeda, who had in mind the image of the saint who was martyred by arrows. The reason is evident. In Hojeda's first brush with the Indians several Spaniards were killed, among them the map-maker, Juan de la Cosa, who looked like a porcupine when they had finished with him. Hojeda had to watch his colony dwindle away under the onslaught of hunger, fever, and the Indians. It is said that when he and Nicuesa met he burst into tears. One day he received an arrow in his leg. He called the surgeon and said to him: "Run a white-hot iron through the wound." The surgeon hesitated. Hojeda shouted: "If you don't obey me instantly, get ready for the gallows." There was a smell of burning flesh; the governor had a limp, but he lived. Hunger was becoming unbearable. Enciso, the lawyer, had promised to send out help from Santo Domingo, but it did not arrive. Hojeda decided to put Francisco Pizarro, the swineherd, in charge of the colony and go himself to bring succor from Santo Domingo. This is the last we shall see of him.

When he reached the city he was in such a bad way that he took the habit of a Franciscan monk and died without a cent in his pocket. As he bowed his wasted head, all passion spent, he seemed a kindly man. It was a far cry from this limping, pale, suffering man to the merry acrobat of Seville who had pirouetted in the air on the Giralda Tower.

While Hojeda in Santo Domingo was making ready for his trip to the other world, the people he had left in San Sebastián decided to abandon the site and to found a city somewhere else under the leadership of the lawyer Enciso, who finally brought aid. They chose the opposite side of the gulf, and the new city was named Santa María la Antigua de Darien, because Enciso, when on the verge of being shipwrecked, had made a vow to Santa María la Antigua of Seville: "If you save us, Blessed Virgin, I will consecrate my first foundation to you." And he did not keep her waiting long. While the white men and Indians were raising the houses of Antigua, in San Sebastián the grass was creeping back and new trees were springing up in the streets and squares Hojeda had laid out.

The soldiers sized up the situation. Hojeda was not coming back. The King had made no appointment. Nobody could stand Enciso and his legal quibbling. Pizarro still seemed the swineherd of Extremadura. It was evident that it was the men themselves who were in command — that is to say, the people, the commons. The thing to do was to name one of themselves leader, and the choice was unanimous: Vasco Núñez de Balboa!

And where had this Balboa come from? He was the perfect Sir Nobody. He was not even a lute-player or a musician, and still less a map-maker or lawyer. Concerning his emergence on the horizon of American history two schools of thought have sprung up, and their proponents defend their respective positions with great zeal. One group claims that he first appeared crawling from a barrel, the other that he came out of a furled sail. This was not acrobatics, but prestidigitation. What really happened was this: there in Santo Domingo, like so many others, Balboa had lost his shirt gambling. He had come out to America ten years before, and now in Santo Domingo, as in Spain, he found himself beset by creditors on all sides. It was idle to hope that he might join one of the expeditions, for the island was his jail. But he knew about the mainland and the riches to be found there, since he had seen them when he came out from Spain with Bastidas. So, with the mainland as his objective, he decided to make a bold try for it and flee hidden on the ship that would seem the most unlikely — that of the lawyer Enciso, which was setting its sails for Darien. It is at this point that the historians lock horns, one set determined to pull him out of a barrel, the other to extricate him from the folds of a sail. Either operation must have been complicated by the fact that Balboa did not stow away by himself; he had his dog with him. When they were well out at sea, and Balboa appeared on deck, the rage of the lawyer knew no bounds. He was on the point of anchoring off the first island they passed and casting the stowaway ashore for the Caribs to devour. You don't play fast and loose with the law, Balboa. But the crew, who were birds of the same feather as Balboa, finally managed to calm the lawyer, and by the time the ship reached the coast it was plain to anyone that it was no longer Enciso who was in command, but Balboa. It was Balboa who suggested founding Antigua where Enciso founded it. It was he who put into the men's minds the idea that it would be a good thing to appoint him leader. He was the first to pick up an ax to clear the forest, to tend the sick soldier, to plan the raids on the Indians to get their corn and gold, and to order that the gold be divided up among those who had earned it by the sweat of their brow and not among those who had spent their time scribbling in comfortable chairs in Antigua. Before anyone rightly knew what was happening, Balboa had made himself master. The map-maker and the acrobat being dead, he put the lute-player — who came out to give them orders — aboard a leaky ship, which foundered at sea, and Nicuesa was devoured by sharks. He clapped the lawyer in jail on charges of conspiracy, and instead of hanging him sent him back to Santo Domingo to be tried. The only one he kept beside him in a post of authority was Pizarro, the swineherd.

The truth of the matter was that the only person capable of making a colony out of these two settlements ravaged by hunger, death, and suffering was the captain of the commons, Vasco Núñez de Balboa.

At the time this was taking place, Diego Columbus was the governor of Santo Domingo. The idea of Balboa's continuing as captain did not displease him, and he confirmed him in his command. The King, to whom Balboa had already written, seconded Don Diego's action. Meanwhile, Balboa let no grass grow under his feet. Everyone, he said, must show fitting respect for the captain selected by the people. A priest, Balboa's own confessor, on failing to remove his bonnet when greeting him was put in prison for his oversight. A group of men who had studied at the university plotted against the captain; he put them in a cage. He made alliances with the native tribes, set the Indians to planting corn for his soldiers, and gathered gold in one place and another. He took for his concubine a cacique's daughter who had been presented to him by her father, a singularly attractive girl who fell passionately in love with him. Balboa began to have as many parrot-colored friends as white ones. Once when an Indian tribe had prepared a secret attack, an Indian girl who was in love with him warned him of it, and through her the colony was saved. The son of a cacique who had seen the Spaniards quarreling over the division of gold said to Balboa: "I can't understand why men fight over something anybody can have; if what you want is gold, why don't you cross these forests and on the other side you will find all you want, and the other sea, and rich, prosperous nations?"

This was all Balboa needed for discovering the Pacific. Immediately he dashed off an excited letter to the King, running over with his happiness, his plans, and the information of the Indians. It is one of the finest documents of those days. God had willed that he, who is nothing (wrote Balboa), should discover those marvelous lands. His breast swelled with happiness and joy. But he knew that God helps those that help themselves. He had no intention of being one of those governors who lie abed, giving orders. He had been and would ever be in the front ranks, making his way through forests and swamps, elbow to elbow with his soldiers. And he talked of gold: There are caciques to whom the Indians bring it in baskets strapped to their backs. In Davaive there are two ways of gathering it — to wait until the rivers rise, and then, when the floods subside, gather up the nuggets that have lodged between the rocks and that are as big as oranges or a man's fist; the other, to set fire to the woods and, when the trees have been burned out, just pick up the lumps of gold. There are caciques who barter nuggets of gold for children; these Indians are very fond of the meat of children, and they serve them like roast suckling pigs. One cacique has a gold mill in which a hundred men work. There are places where gold is stored in sheds, like corn. . . . The second part of the letter is even more attractive. Balboa speaks of the other sea, which is not tempestuous like the Caribbean, but smooth, deep, and calm. Bigger pearls are found near its islands. The boats of other kingdoms furrow its waters. "If the King authorizes me, and sends me a thousand men, I will discover all this." A thousand men from Santo Domingo, because men from Spain won't do — they are not used to the climate. Here Balboa speaks for the first time as the Spaniard who feels himself an American, as against the one who has never left Castile and knows only the things of the peninsula. Here, in embryo, we see the beginning of the independence of America. As guarantee of his good faith, Balboa offers the only thing that is really his to pledge, his head.

One final detail, which speaks for itself: "May it please your Majesty to order that no bachelor of law come to these lands, under threat of severe penalties, because there is not a one who has come who is not a devil, leading the life of a devil, and not only are they bad themselves, but they get everyone involved in suits and trouble. . . ."

When the King read this letter, he lost his head. The news ran through Hispaniola first, and then all over Spain. People invited one another to go to find gold, as though it were a fishing trip. Now everything became clear to the King; that scamp of a Diego Columbus had not helped either Hojeda or Nicuesa so that he himself should be able to conquer the mainland and the sea that led to the Orient, to Cipango. He had been more than right in sending him that letter in which he had not minced words: "And to serve me, in the future do not give occasion for anyone to say that you do not carry out my orders because you can see what a bad impression this makes, and how difficult it is to correct."

Ferdinand, His Most Catholic Majesty, believed that he could now undertake an enterprise that would eclipse those of his late wife, Isabella. Under his regency, the other half of the world would be discovered. No longer would people speak of these lands as Darien or Uraba, but as Golden Castile. This was the name he began to give them in his letters. Of course — and this is very human — the first thing Ferdinand did, like the true king he was, was to knife the captain of the people's choice in the back, conferring the governorship on one of his courtiers so that all the glory should remain in the circle of his favorites. A nice how-d'ye-do it would be if a captain of the ranks were to discover the other ocean! And to forestall such a contingency the new governor carried among his papers a specific order to throw Balboa into prison as soon as the mainland should be reached, and to "send him to our court under arrest."

It was a fine thing to see Ferdinand, rejuvenated by the youth of his new queen, taking a hand in everything, dickering with the officials of the Clearing House of Seville because they considered 15,000 arrobas of flour and 3,000 quintals of hardtack too much. Didn't they realize, he asked scornfully, the importance of this undertaking? And didn't they know that the better bolted the flour, the less danger of its spoiling? No further arguments; all this was to be included in the stores, and plenty of kegs of oil and vinegar, and 1,500 arrobas of wine, an abundance of beans and chick-peas and sardines and fish for the trip. Ferdinand spoke with a chief steward's head for detail and a king's generosity. This is the way things are done when discoveries are made under royal patronage.

When Columbus had already made his discoveries and had been named Viceroy and Admiral, he had been authorized to take with him, when he embarked for Hispaniola, three sheets, four pillows, one thin spread, six towels, two silver goblets, two pitchers, one salt-cellar, twelve spoons, two kitchen forks, four frying-pans — two large and two small — two saucepans, one large copper pot and one small one, and other things in proportion. But the courtier who was coming out to rob Balboa of his discovery was to be stinted in nothing. The decree restricting the use of silk did not hold for him, and he was allowed to take all he wanted, including brocade, so that the Indians might see "that Our ways are much more ceremonious than theirs." The armada was completely stocked with tools and a thousand other things, including some whose purpose was unmistakable: two hundred troughs for washing gold. The governor was accompanied by a doctor, a surgeon, a druggist, and Ruy Díaz, expert in gems, who was to be the appraiser of all the pearls, diamonds, rubies, and other precious stones that might be found. . . .

And who was this favored courtier who had been appointed governor? Not an acrobat or a musician, this time, but a great jouster. His name was Pedrárias Dávila. He was seventy years old, and not long before this he had almost been buried by mistake. He had been believed dead, and the nuns of the convent of Torrejón had kept a death watch over him all one night. The next day as they were about to lower him into the grave, a faithful servant threw his arms about the coffin and heard something moving inside. They raised the lid; Pedrárias was breathing. In commemoration of this miracle, he ordered a requiem mass said for himself each year in the church where he was to have been buried, a mass to which he listened from the grave that had been dug for him. When he traveled, he always carried his coffin with him, and it was the first thing that met the eye of visitors entering his room. Notwithstanding, he was a severe, energetic old man. And gallant and courtly. And the best jouster of the realm. Once when the King of Portugal presented him with two salvers of gold coin and jewels as the winner of a tournament, he said to the bearers: "Present them to the Queen's ladies-in-waiting, and let them divide them among themselves."

Pedrárias did not belong to the old nobility; he was the grandson of a converted Jew who had made a fortune. But such things mattered little to the King now. Pedrárias had a matchless coat-of-arms: his wife, Isabel de Bobadilla, the niece of the Marquesa de Moya. The days it took Pedrárias to get ready to leave seemed centuries to Ferdinand. But at last one day he set sail. Twenty-two ships! Two thousand men! Complete with everything, garments of silk and brocade, cannon, culverins, pennons, the niece of the Marquesa, the sardines, the kegs of wine, the hardtack, the coffin, the well-bolted flour, the warrant to arrest Balboa, the doctor, the surgeon, the gem expert, the lawyers. . . . Never had a more impressive fleet weighed anchor. And, in the flagship, old Pedrárias, like a figurehead, setting out to discover the ocean and its environs.

In Antigua a few months before this, Vasco Núñez de Balboa had embarked his hundred and ninety Spaniards in nine canoes and a brigantine. A horde of Indians followed them. He had heard in time about the Pedrárias business and, while King and jouster were involved in matters of brocade, silk, and hardtack, had judged it advisable to steal a march on them and do things as God intended.

So, with their faces steadily fixed westward, Núñez de Balboa and Francisco Pizarro — prototypes of the Unknown Soldier — set out to work a miracle: with the survivors of that pesthole of a settlement they discovered the Pacific Ocean, first, and then half of South America. It was the first time the representatives of the people had undertaken an enterprise of such scope, and they carried it out in their own manner and with their own methods. The account of the exploit reads like a novel.

They landed at the port of Acla. There Balboa left the majority of the Spaniards to look after the boat and canoes, and he set out with a small group. With them they carried a few handfuls of parched corn and their knives — the first to stay the pangs of hunger, the second to hack their way through the jungle. They were so sure of finding their sea that nothing could stop them, neither the torrents of the rivers nor the strange Indians nor the snakes. Never had paths been cleared with such eagerness, faith, and vigor. They seemed lads of twenty. The Indians were infected with their enthusiasm. Many died in the severe ordeal; they were left along the way — victims of occupational hazards. The rest pushed on. The Indians brought the news: "You can see it from the top of that hill." Balboa ordered his men — there were sixty-seven left — to wait on the slope; he was going up alone. The only noise to be heard was the sound of the captain's strides. Quiet, like statues, the sixty-seven watched him ascend. Every twig that snapped, every stone he dislodged, filled the great silence and re-echoed in the men's breasts with the beating of their hearts. There it was. The sea. The wide, blue, limitless plain barely ruffled by the wind. It was ten o'clock on the morning of September 29, 1513. The air was diaphanous. The distant strand was fringed with lacy waves. Balboa fell to his knees, and raised his hands to heaven. The prayer that fell from his lips was drowned in his own tears and the clamor of the sixty-seven men who, startled out of their momentary awe, rushed like madmen to gaze upon the dream come true. Thalassa! The sea! The sea, they cried like the Greeks of old as though they, these uncouth adventurers, held its blue in their souls, in their hands, in their words. They cut down a tree, made a cross, and with the point of their knives cut the name of King Ferdinand upon it. A priest chanted the *Te Deum laudamus*. The notary drew up the legal certificate of the discovery, and set down the sixty-seven names. There they stand, immortalized: Baracallo, the carpenter; León, the silversmith; Olano, the Negro; Beas, the parrot-colored; the priest Pedro Sánchez (who never once held mass for the men); Lentin, the Sicilian; García, the seaman; Pizarro, the swineherd. . . .

Four days later Balboa reached the shore. With twenty-three Spaniards he went forward to take possession of the Ocean. It was the vesper hour. He advanced into the water until it reached his knees, bearing the royal banner on high, and began to walk back and forth, saying in a loud, hoarse voice:

"Long live the mighty and powerful sovereigns Don Ferdinand and Doña Joanna, in whose name, and for the royal crown of Castile, I take possession of these waters and lands and coasts and harbors and austral islands. And if there be any prince or captain, Christian or infidel, or of any faith, sect, or quality who claims power over these lands or waters, I stand ready and prepared to oppose him in the name of the monarchs of Castile."

The men of Castile listened in silence; the Indians, in bewilderment — never had they seen so strange a sight. The notary's pen flew over the paper. And in this manner Vasco Núñez de Balboa, the leader of the commons, placed the Pacific Ocean in King Ferdinand's hands.

When Balboa and his men returned to the settlement they were greeted with wild enthusiasm. It was the triumph of the common man. Balboa at once wrote the King a complete account of the exploit. Everyone worked hard to build up the city, which seemed to grow each day under the stimulus of triumph and hope.

When His Serene Majesty received the news, Pedrárias was already on the way to Castile the Golden. Before long the courtly jouster could discern the low-lying coast. America! His eyes gleamed with satisfaction. The ships stood offshore. The merry rabble gathered about the harbor to greet him with noisy cheers. Knowing the importance of first impressions, Pedrárias prepared to make a triumphal entrance. The ships were decked out in banners and embroidered waistcloths, and he and Doña Isabel de Bobadilla, in silk and brocade. The eyes of the spectators on shore watched eagerly to see whom they knew among those coming ashore. A bishop, bless my soul! Courtiers by the dozen. Women. And who was that fellow with the bright, restless eyes? If it wasn't Enciso the lawyer again! Pedrárias touched his pocket to feel the crackle of the warrant he was carrying for Balboa's arrest. But Balboa smiled, and about the lips of all those gathered on shore there was a suspicion of a grin that filled Pedrárias with an unpleasant foreboding. He held out his hand to Isabel, and they descended like royalty. They had hardly set foot on land when they were given the news: the other ocean had been discovered, the King had been notified.

Not many days had elapsed when letters arrived from the King. There was one for Balboa that Pedrárias tried to extract and keep from reaching him. But the news leaked out, and the bishop flew into a rage. Pedrárias had no choice but to eat crow and hand over the letter. It contained the King's expression of his gratitude to Balboa for his services, in token of which he appointed him Adelantado of the Southern Sea. The words of the King dripped honey: "By this same mail I am writing the governor to give you all help and favor in your affairs and to treat you as a person to whom I wish to show special regard, who has served me well and will continue to do so, and I am sure he will. And you, the better to serve me, help him and advise him regarding what should be done, and even if he does not consult you on all matters, be sure to counsel and assist him."

For the moment Pedrárias had to forgo the idea of putting Balboa in the calaboose; the bishop would not have countenanced it. All Pedrárias could do was to put him on trial to render an accounting of his administration, thus restricting his liberty of movement. He eventually stripped him of all he owned. Eighty-five years later a grandson of Pedrárias, the illustrious Count of Puñonrostro, would write: "The most serious charge that can be brought against my grandfather is of not having cut off his [Balboa's] head when he brought him to trial." But the King had given Balboa power over the coast of the Pacific, and it was his ambition to discover these lands, perhaps as far as Peru, an idea that was probably already kindling Pizarro's imagination. One day he planned to make his getaway. Everything had been prepared in secret. He had arranged for some support from Santo Domingo, and his comrades were ready to follow him. As soon as Pedrárias learned of this he saw his chance. "Treason," he shouted, and clapped Balboa into jail. There were riots among the men, the bishop took a hand in the affair, and finally a diplomatic solution to the difficulty was hit upon: Balboa was to marry Pedrárias's daughter, who was in Spain, and everything would remain in the family. The agreement was subscribed to with great solemnity. Pedrárias had done the very same thing as the cacique of Darien, who had also given his daughter to Balboa, and everybody was happy. And in this they were merely following the precedent of the royal houses of Europe. With this understanding, Balboa, accompanied by a group of his men, set out for the mountains to build the ships they would need for the exploration and conquest of the Pacific.

Naturally, Pedrárias did not intend to bring out his daughter or permit Balboa to proceed with his discoveries. As soon as the boats were ready he would put them under the command of another. The treachery was perfectly planned. It was his revenge. It may be that Balboa suspected this, but he did not care; he had great faith in his undertaking. He divided his men into crews, and they began to cut down trees, saw them into planks, and carry them on their backs over the mountains that looked down on the new sea. It was a marvel to behold these men building the first two ships that were to sail the Pacific. For over a year all of them, from Balboa down to the last peon, the last Indian, had put all they had into the endeavor; their untrained hands had shaped the hulls, had set up the masts, had sewed the sails, had calked the seams, until at last they saw their wooden castles floating down an unknown river.

And, while Balboa was engaged in this, Pedrárias's fine colony was wasting away under his very eyes. The people were dying in the streets, moaning "Bread, bread!" Brocade was bartered for corn. A crimson doublet was worth a pound of bread. One person of high rank, relates the chronicler of the events, ran through the street shrieking that he was dying of hunger; he stumbled, fell to the ground, and "his soul departed from him." The Indians were no longer on friendly terms with them. With every raid the Spaniards made into the interior they only sowed terror and invited reprisals. Herrera tells that Pedrárias's captains roasted the Indians alive, set the dogs upon them, ran them through with their lances, killed them for their fat with which they cured their wounds, kept haunches of Indians hanging on hooks to feed their hunting dogs. In Pedrárias's home wild gambling went on; one night, at chess, he lost a hundred slaves. But the old man was as tough as hickory. It was all they could do to keep him from setting out on a voyage of discovery himself.

The King tried to find an explanation for this dismal failure

76

of the most ambitious expedition his government had ever launched. He had only Pedrárias's letters to go on: it was all Balboa's fault — he had misinformed the governor. And so all his wrath was concentrated against Balboa. He wrote him that he wondered how he had dared to write such lies. The King sent the letter to Balboa in care of Pedrárias with instructions to give it to him only when he had him under arrest. In this incident the King and Pedrárias saw eye to eye, joined like the links of a cuff-button.

Balboa's arrest came about in a simple and unforeseen manner. It was evident that Pedrárias was going to be removed from office, and that a new governor would be appointed. Balboa got wind of this, and he conceived the hope that the choice might fall on him. He sent one of his comrades to see what he could find out from those close to Pedrárias; but the governor discovered the spy and ordered Balboa arrested. From Pedrárias's point of view this smelled of sedition. Francisco Pizarro arrested Balboa. Without a moment's delay he was put on trial, and sentenced to have his head cut off. There was no appeal; the governor's order was final. And this was the end of the captain of the commons, Don Vasco Núñez de Balboa, the discoverer of the Pacific Ocean. He came off worse than Columbus.

Two last details.

No sooner had Pedrárias seen Balboa's head fall like a coconut, than he set out to take possession of the Ocean as though all that Balboa had done had never been. One might have died laughing to see the old fellow on the shore, with a notary at his elbow, shouting that in the name of Their Majesties he was taking possession of the waters and the lands, "from the pebbles of the rivers to the leaves of the forests." And then, with the water up to his knees, repeating the scene of the banner.

But the legend that Balboa had left an immense fortune refused to die in Spain. Years went by, and even the Emperor Charles V believed it, to the point of sending Fernández de Oviedo out to Castile the Golden to represent him in the matter, and divide up the treasure. Fernández de Oviedo did not find it because it did not exist. But the curious thing was the use to which the treasure was to be put, and the reason for the determined search: one of that horde of hungry Flemings who had come into Spain in the suite of Charles V and were sucking its life-blood away, Charles de Puper, Lord of Laxao, was to receive one-fifth of Balboa's fortune. . . .

V

DEMOCRATIC STIRRINGS UNDER CHARLES, THE MELANCHOLY

It is customary in all the nations of the world to want to cover the live coals with their own ashes.

PRUDENCIO DE SANDOVAL

T<small>HE</small> C<small>ASTILIANS</small> had carried the body of Ferdinand the Catholic to Seville, and had put it in its place beside that of his wife Isabella. Prince Charles was in Flanders, learning how to rule. He was fifteen years old. Along with the news of his grandfather's death the envoys had brought him the King's testament; the boy had been left the kingdoms of Castile and León. From then on, crowns and more crowns would accumulate upon his head. At the moment he was still a pretty-faced, beardless youth, weak of character, halting in speech, guided by his teachers. He did not know a word of Spanish. Flanders had been his school and Flemings his masters. There his real guardian, his other grandfather, the German Emperor, had directed his training. He had had two tutors; one had tried to bend his inclinations toward books, the other toward horses. Charles preferred horses. He would never be able to express himself well in Latin, but he was considered a good rider. And one day this man of melancholy humor would leave the horses, and so many other things, to retire to a convent. This was the way of the sixteenth century.

In Spain the people awaited Charles's arrival with misgivings. He is a German, they said; how can he understand the affairs of Spain? Ferdinand would have liked to see the crown on the head of Prince Ferdinand, Charles's younger brother, who had grown up in Spain, but his counselors advised against any such move. Speculation on this possibility was rife, and about the bed where the King lay, trying to make his peace with God, hovered the curiosity of the courtiers. Among them was Adrian, the Vice-

Chancellor of Louvain, later Pope Adrian VI, Charles's teacher and now his ambassador to the King. Adrian wanted to pay his respects to the King. "He only wants to see if I am dying; tell him to go away; don't let him in," answered the sick man. With these words he gave vent to the irritation the presence of the Germans and Flemings aroused in him. But he died, and there descended on Castile the German eagles. To the people they seemed to have not only two heads, but many more claws than appear in the heraldic devices.

In Brussels the funeral services decreed by Charles were befitting the occasion. A double line of palings erected from his palace to the cathedral blazed with cressets. Two hundred paupers dressed in mourning carried lighted tapers in their hands. The church was hung with black, and on the altars six thousand candles burned. Above the catafalque, draped with the arms of Castile and Aragón on brocade, myriad tapers cast their flickering light over the pale faces of priests, friars, canons, bishops, and abbots garbed in copes, and over the severe faces of the nobles. In the streets it seemed as though the houses must tumble down under the weight of the people clustered in doorways and windows, darkening the cornices and roofs to see the three Kings-of-Arms go by, the powerful charger caparisoned in brown-and-green damask, and the standards of the Catholic Kings and the banners of all the seigniories they had won from the Moors. Resting upon a pillow borne by a horse with purple velvet housings came the golden crown guarded by six knights. Then the heir, on a mule trapped in black to its hoofs. On one side rode the Pope's emissary; on the other, the Emperor's, followed by the royal ambassadors, Knights of the Golden Fleece, and a throng of pedestrians.

Bishop Manrique chanted the mass and the responsories. Then the royal arms were flung upon the floor, and three times, with a loud and solemn voice that re-echoed from the vaulted roof, the bishop called out: "King Don Ferdinand! King Don Ferdinand! King Don Ferdinand!" A deep bass voice that seemed to come from beyond the tomb answered: "He has died." This was the signal. A sigh of relief escaped from every breast, and a wave of copes, silk, brocade, and lace rose to break gently at the feet of young Charles. It was the nobles and dignitaries accepting him as their king. He withdrew to a kind of tent that had been raised at one side, removed the black hood he had been wearing, and emerged with a smile that was reflected on every lip, in every eye of the vast gathering. Long live the King!

Charles made his entrance into Castile. He was swept along, a fragile flower, on the roaring flood of Flemish courtiers that accompanied him. A tide of resentment at these rapacious intruders rose in the breast of the suspicious peasant, the nobles who feared for their time-honored privileges, and the Spanish Catholic Apostolic Church. Competence played no part in the distribution of offices; they went to the highest bidder. The court was no longer a drawing-room, but a market place. At the King's request the Pope issued a bull allowing him to deduct a tenth of the Church's rents for his privy purse. The protests rent the welkin. "M. de Chièvres is not satisfied with the money he has stolen from the kingdom, from rich and poor; now he wants to lay hands on the treasures of the Church." The Cortes refused to vote obediently the subsidies asked by the King when they took the oath of fealty to him. Charles was becoming acquainted with the people he had come to govern and with the growing ambitions of the nobles. The first hairs began to sprout on that pretty face. Suddenly his other grandfather, Maximilian, died, which meant that he was to receive the crown of the Empire also. Rarely was a grandson more blessed by fortune. And in addition to the crowns of Spain and the Empire he was soon to receive another and unexpected one, that of the empire of Mexico.

When Charles became ruler of Castile, America was but an outline on the map. The continent had only one profile, its Atlantic shore. Nobody knew what lay along the sea Balboa had discovered. Only half of the Caribbean itself had been explored; the whole coast from Florida to Yucatan was still unknown. During the forty years of Charles's reign all this was to be explored and seen; these forty years transformed the world. It was Charles who launched the ships of Magellan that circled the globe; viceroyalties and governments were set up; all the capitals of America, except Santo Domingo and Havana, were built. Explorers entered through the Pacific, crossed the Andes, and came sailing out on the other coast through the mouths of the Amazon, the Orinoco, the Plate. Cities were founded from the sea coast, like Buenos Aires, to the summit of the mountains, like La Paz, Quito, Bogotá. Valdívia and his armies reached Chile in the south, and Coronado reached California in the north.

With Cross, horses, and dogs the conquistadors covered distances in America equivalent to many times the length and breadth of Europe. Cortés, Pizarro, Valdívia, Jiménez de Quesada, Mendoza, De Soto, Irala, Alvarado, Belalcázar, Federmann, entered Mexico, Peru, Chile, New Granada, the Plate, the Mississippi, Paraguay, Guatemala, Quito, Venezuela, slaughtering the Indians in the name of Saint James the Apostle, and subjecting them in the name of Charles V.

Charles had come to Spain to be crowned. He reached Tordesillas sweating and fuming. The Cortes of Barcelona had turned his honey to vinegar with their haggling and pennypinching. Now he had to face those of Castile, which were in no better frame of mind. The people began to voice loud protests over the presence of Germans in Spain. The shoemaker and the peasant, the blacksmith and the baker were not interested in the Fleming nobles, or in the crown of Aix-la-Chapelle, or in the bankers of Germany, but in their land, their bread, their hides, and their forges. The air was heavy with resentment. Between the sessions of the Cortes of Barcelona and those of the Cortes of Castile, Charles stopped at Tordesillas, thus adding a note of sadness to his wounded pride. His demented mother was there, and he halted to press a kiss of filial devotion on that poor mad brow. There he sat, in his leather armchair, when an importunate group of young men burst in upon him. They had come from Seville as fast as they could travel, stubborn, vexatious, after wringing a reluctant consent from the Council for the Indies and bribing the King's ministers. They knelt at the royal feet. They had not come merely from Seville, they explained, but from the other side of the sea, from the Indies. Crowded in one little old boat, rigged with dirty, patched rags for sails, they had crossed the Atlantic carrying a cargo of gold. They pronounced a new word, "Mexico," and handed the King a huge disk of gold, another of silver, a helmet full of gold nuggets, handfuls of jewels. The courtiers looked on in amazement. "This has been sent you by Hernán Cortés, a humble servant of Your Majesty, who has the pleasure of bringing you an empire in the New World, greater than those of Europe. Here are his letters, and the letters of the men who went with him."

And so into the King's lap there dropped first Mexico, then Peru, then Quito, New Granada, Chile, all America, as though by magic. While the knights of Flanders and Castile, the bankers of Germany, the friars of Toledo, banqueted him, danced attendance upon him, took advantage of him, and used him to further their own ends, in the camps of the Caribbean the adventurers planned and carried out their conquests. Most of them, if not all, were rebels who, behind the back of the authorities and against their opposition, were following in Balboa's footsteps, and even seemed to have come out of the same barrel, out of the same sail fold as he. Meanwhile the other monarchs of Europe looked on in envy. That beardless youth who had left Flanders to take possession of the brown plains of Castile was turning into a lord of mighty ambitions, the horseman of Titian's canvas. The kings of France and England considered how best to lay a snare for him, to clip his wings, whether in Italy or in Flanders or in the Caribbean. For this reason one day the Caribbean was to be the scene of the struggle for naval supremacy in Europe.

The Caribbean and the Gulf of Mexico come together in a figure 8 with the strait of Yucatan forming the waist between the upper and the lower halves. Below the strait, on the lower curve of the 8, everything had been discovered and explored; this had been carried out from Santo Domingo. Now through the port of Yucatan the Gulf of Mexico was to be explored. This was still an unknown sea, which spread out like a broad amphitheater and was to be the background against which the history of Mexico, North America, and Florida was to be written. What Santo Domingo had been for the lower half, the island of Cuba, the second rallying point of adventurers, would be for the northern.

Cuba — Fernandina, as Columbus had called it — began to re-echo to the tramp of Spanish feet when, twenty years after its discovery, Diego Velásquez arrived as governor. Santiago, Havana, and Matanzas were founded. The fields became transformed into green plantations of sugar cane. The captains hunted Indians in the near-by islands. A few Negroes and fewer horses had been brought in. Not many years later the island had become one of the great horse-breeding centers and one of the greatest camps of Negro slave labor. For the moment it was just a camp of soldiers and vagabonds. There were no stone houses. There was no viceregal court. Its settlers were men who had been unable to get hold of lands or Indians in Santo Domingo, who were in the black books of the law, or who were in search of new adventures. There were also many who had come from Darien, fed-up with the struggle between Pedrárias and Balboa. Fate willed that these men were not to flounder about in the jungles and swamps of Darien, but to discover the halls and temples of Moctezuma. As in Santo Domingo, it was an enterprise of the common people. The story opens with these words of a soldier: "We decided to get together, one hundred and ten of those of us who had come from the mainland and those in Cuba who had no Indians, and we arranged with a hidalgo by the name of Francisco Hernández de Córdoba, who was a rich man, to be our leader." They were all have-nots. The boats in which they set out had been bought on credit. The rich man, Hernández de Córdoba, was just a stalking-horse. Nobody knew exactly where they were bound for, and their one idea seemed to be to capture Indians on neighboring islands and sell them for money in the Cuban market. The captain cherished the idea that they might come upon some rich territory of which he could take possession and become governor. And so a few puffs of wind, a few turns of the steering wheel, a little luck, and the ships had reached the island of Cozumel, off the coast of Yucatan, at the very door of the Aztec empire. .

It was not swamps they saw here, nor huts nesting in tree-tops. The coast was hard and dry. The houses were of stone, and the temples of masonry. In the latter the priest, robed in cotton and armed with a flint knife sharpened to a razor's edge, slit open the breast of the sacrificial victim as though he were a chicken, and tore out the heart still beating. The Indians wore gold ornaments in their noses, in their ears. This did not seem an island, but a continent. Hernández de Córdoba returned to Cuba with these tales. Fortunately for the governor of the island, he had no more than told the story of his discovery when he died. So now the governor prepared the ships, himself. And to keep everything in the family, he put his nephew, Juan de Grijalva, in command of the expedition.

Grijalva not only filled in the details of the picture of Yucatan, "land of yuccas," but he talked with Moctezuma's ambassadors. They came out to receive him bearing many white flags. On that coast where the sun blazes down and coats of mail are unbearable, Indians and Spaniards gathered under the shade of the ceiba trees. Moctezuma's emissaries presented Grijalva's men with pineapples and sapodilla plums. These were the fairest delights of the conquest, better than gold, these fruits of the New World, which refresh both rich and poor and whose flesh is the most exquisite of delicacies.

The soldier Bernal Díaz del Castillo had been with Pedrárias in Darien and had then gone to Santo Domingo and Cuba; he had set out first with Hernández de Córdoba, now accompanied Grijalva, and later shared in the conquest of Mexico and Guatemala with Cortés and Alvarado. He was a curious character. When approaching eighty he laid down his sword and took up his pen to write one of the most delightful books of history that have ever been set down. Even now, while Grijalva's soldiers, and he too, were hunting nuggets of gold, he sowed some orange seeds. And thus he achieved a twofold immortality, that of his connection with the conquest of Mexico, and that due him for the perfume, gold, and sweetness of the oranges he sowed.

Grijalva went as far as the little island of San Juan de Ulua which lies outside Vera Cruz and is the key to the conquest of Mexico. When he returned to Cuba he brought back not only the news of Moctezuma but the memory of the savor of the sapodilla plums, many jewels of gold, and copper axes — which were believed to be of gold; and the dream of Mexico became reality. The governor scolded his nephew for not having carried on with the conquest. But evidently he belonged to those Spaniards Balboa spoke of whose conquests were made in bed, and it was necessary to look for a new captain for the third expedition. And here Hernán Cortés makes his appearance.

Of all the Spaniards in Cuba, Hernán Cortés was perhaps the only one who had not made a career of arms. He had spent fifteen years in the islands, and, just as in Spain, his conquests had been women, not lands. He had not gone with any of the expeditions to the mainland. He was on the point of embarking for Darien, but some ailment made it impossible. "His friends said it was syphilis, because the Indian women, much more than the Spanish, infect those who have relations with them." His latest adventure had set the tongues of the whole colony wagging. The heroine was Catalina Suárez, "La Marcaida." She was one of the four Suárez sisters, beauties all of them, and the toast of the island. Diego Velásquez, the governor, was mad about one of them "who was no better than she should be." Cortés monopolized La Marcaida, though he never came to the point of leading her to the altar. There was gossip, then threats, and finally an ultimatum from the governor. But Cortés was not being ordered about. There was to be no shotgun marriage for him with La Marcaida. The governor put him in the stocks; Cortés managed to get away and took sanctuary in the church. There nobody could lay a finger on him. But he got bored shut up in the church, and went out — and the authorities laid hold of him. This time they threatened to hang him. He got away again. But he came back when he got good and ready, and one night, fully armed, unexpectedly walked into the governor's house. He had come to arrange matters on a friendly basis. All right, he would marry Catalina. And he arranged matters so satisfactorily with the governor that, according to Gomara, "they shook hands, and after talking for a long time they went to sleep in the same bed, where Diego de Orellana found them the next morning."

Thus it happened that Cortés, who had made no name for himself either as a soldier or as an explorer was known to everybody on the island. He had worked in mines and on plantations. He was nineteen years old when he came out to Santo Domingo, and he had left Spain because it was too small to hold him. He was so poor that, for a while, he and two other friends shared a single cape. When with the passage of time Cortés's history is written and properly judged, it will be clearly seen that the man who at this moment seemed nothing but a cheap adventurer in Cuba can be compared only to Alexander the Great or Julius Caesar. Before proceeding further it would be well to read the pen-portrait that López de Gomara has left of him:

"Fernando Cortés was of goodly stature, stoutly built and with a broad chest; of ashy complexion, fair beard, and long hair. He was very strong, very brave, and skilled in the use of arms. As a boy he was wild, but he became settled when a man; and so he made a name for himself in the wars, and, in peace, he became the mayor of Santiago de Barucoa, which was and is considered the greatest honor by its residents. There he acquired the reputation for what he later became. He had a great weakness for women, and always indulged it. The same was true of gaming, and he was a wonderful dice-player, skillful and good-natured. He was very fond of eating, but temperate in his drinking, though he had plenty. He could endure hunger without complaining when he had to, as he showed on the road to Higueras and on the sea that bears his name. He was strong and stubborn, and he had more quarrels than was becoming in a man of his position. He spent unstintingly on war, women, friends, and to satisfy his whims, but was tight-fisted in certain things, which made some call him an upstart. In dress he was elegant but not ostentatious, and he was very neat of person. He liked dwelling in a fine house and being surrounded by his family, having plate of silver and good service. He lived like a fine gentleman, with so much poise and judgment that he annoyed no one and seemed to the manner born. It was said that when he was a boy he had been told that he would win great estates and be a great lord. He was jealous in his own home and forward in the home of others, the earmark of a whoring man. He was devout, a great prayer, and he knew many prayers and psalms; he was a great giver of alms, and when he was dying he charged his son never to forget charity, saying that with this his sins would be atoned for. His silver and arms bore this device: JUDICIUM DOMINI APREHENDIT EOS, ET FORTITUDO EJUS CORROBORAVIT BRACHIUM MEUM, a motto which befitted the conquest. Thus, as you have heard it, was Cortés, the conqueror of New Spain."

In his domestic conquests Cortés had learned one thing that captains and soldiers generally ignore: diplomacy, the art of deceiving and governing men and seducing women. The most delicate spring in that whole brutal machinery which was America in the first half of the sixteenth century was Hernán Cortés. His career was not a clash of arms, but a work of art. It is hard to understand why Velásquez put him in command of the fleet. There was his nephew, Grijalva, who had begun the discovery and whom the soldiers respected. There were rich men and captains seasoned in combat. As for Cortés, he was continually in debt, mixed up in the worst scrapes. The governor himself had put him in the stocks, had threatened him with the gallows, and yet they wound up sharing bed and board. Those in the know wondered enviously at Cortés's luck. And he laughed, for laughing was one of the things he enjoyed most. Cortés had pulled his wires with the greatest astuteness to get himself appointed captain of the armada. He did nothing himself, but he had his friends suggest his name to the governor, and when the moment came Velásquez sent for him. As might have been expected, Cortés did not have a penny to bless himself with. But the next day his house was decorated with banners and the table decked out on borrowed money. He strolled the streets in a plumed helmet, medals and chain of gold, and velvet raiment with inserts of gold; at his side walked Catalina Suárez, La Marcaida, equally fine. In the square the public crier was announcing the coming expedition at the top of his lungs, and in the house of Cortés, in a confidential voice, his friends were being invited to come and make their fortune. Some madman blurted out the truth to the governor, that Cortés would make himself the master of the lands he conquered. Others — not mad — had already warned him of this in secret. That broad breast of Cortés, covered with lace and jewels, advanced proudly through this stormy sea. The governor began to have his doubts and misgivings; he tried to hit on some way to hold Cortés back, imprison him if necessary. Cortés advanced. Nothing could stop him, shrewd fellow that he was. The boats were being loaded. There were already five thousand flitches of bacon stored in them, six thousand measures of corn, yucca, chickens, oil, chick-peas. Cortés had bought out a whole store of beads for barter with the Indians, and such horses and mares as he could lay his hands on, since their cost had soared sky-high in Cuba. There were eleven ships. The members of the expedition were five hundred and eighty soldiers, one hundred and nine sailors, and two priests. The port of embarkation for the conquest of Mexico was not Seville, but Havana, just as in the case of Peru it was to be Panama.

Down the slope that led to the harbor came the governor on his mule. The ships were ready to weigh anchor, waiting only for Cortés to come aboard the flagship. The governor was pale with rage, though he tried to cover it up. "My son," he shouted to Cortés, "what are you doing? Why are you starting out without bread and meat for your trip?" "Sir," answered the other with a smile, "I kiss Your Excellency's hands; the ships are well provisioned, and where I am going my men will lack for nothing. God be with Your Excellency, for I am going to serve God and my King, and to seek my fortune with my comrades." A cannon boomed out the signal for departure. Sailors, soldiers, all went busily to work. The sails began to swell in the wind. On board there were shouts, boisterous laughter, tears of the soldiers (who always cry). "May God and the Blessed Virgin of Seville watch over you and bring you safely back!" called the women on shore, with moist eyes. A malicious smile might have been detected under Cortés's blond beard.

The gentleman on the mule turned back up the slope toward

89

the government house. He rode slowly, retracing his steps, turning his back on the finest adventure of the New World.

With a gentle but firm hand Cortés was taking the measure of the domain he was entering upon. His hearty laugh bridged the gulf between himself and his men. But at the same time he made his authority felt. There was to be no plundering or terrorizing of the Indians. He saw clearly that he was entering the mainland, not islands. In Tabasco he established his first alliance with the Indians, and they brought him four diadems, some lizards, two figures resembling dogs, earrings, and five ducks, all of gold. They hung a wreath of flowers about his neck. "And all this was nothing compared with the twenty women they gave us, one of whom was very fine and was known as Doña Marina." Cortés received the gifts very graciously, but in the case of the women he refused to accept them unless they became Christians and were baptized. When this formality had been observed, he divided them up among his captains; Doña Marina, the cleverest and most uninhibited of the lot, went to Alonso Puerto Carrero, a cousin of the Count of Medellín. She was to become Cortés's mistress and the mother of his son Martín. Cortés destroyed the idols and set up the cross. He talked to the chiefs about Our Lord Jesus Christ, and about a mighty and powerful king, Charles of Castile.

From Tabasco the fleet proceeded to Vera Cruz, where in March 1519 the camp, the city, was founded. The commission that Velásquez had given Cortés was to explore and trade with the Indians. What the soldiers saw before them was a continent, and what was needed was a different thing: a government of their own, a republic. Cortés called the men together, set up a town council, appointed mayors and aldermen, handed the wand of justice over to the mayors, and said with great solemnity: "The power is now in your hands; from this moment I resign my authority as captain-general in favor of the mayors and aldermen, and they are at liberty to appoint whomever they think most fit to the post of captain-general." And with these words he coolly withdrew, annulling at one stroke the authority of the governor of Cuba. He declared his independence and turned everything over to the people, just as Balboa had done and as all the great captains of the Conquest were to do in the future. At this first meeting, the mayors, who knew what was expected of them, discussed "many matters bearing upon the well-being of the republic, and decided to elect for their leader and captain Hernán Cortés; and, to give the election greater validity, they called all the people into assembly." The soldiers gathered in high spirits, laughing as boisterously as they had in the face of the governor of Cuba. One of the mayors made a speech in the name of the republic which was a panegyric of Cortés. But the commonalty must choose, let them speak. "Cortés! Cortés!" shouted the people. And the surging crowd went to find him. Cortés received them with signs of deep emotion. This was a surprise he had not expected. "They had to entreat him for a long time; as the proverb runs, you coax me, and I want it." The delegate who offered him the captaincy employed the time-honored formulas for the occasion: "We have come to beg and request, and, if necessary, demand that Your Excellency accept this post of captain-general, for the people are determined to have no other, and it is fitting that Your Excellency should heed the wishes of those who so esteem him."

With this, the last faint image of that rider ascending the slope on mule-back in Havana faded away.

They reached the site of Vera Cruz during Holy Week. A friar who was famed for his voice conducted mass. Cortés himself helped to drive the stakes and turn the ground to begin building the city. It was then that Moctezuma's ambassadors arrived. They spread straw mats out on the ground and laid upon them those treasures we have already seen: the great disk of gold and the other of silver, the handfuls of jewels, which Cortés sent to King Charles. Cortés was no less generous; he sent Moctezuma a carved chair, a string of beads, a velvet cap adorned with a medal of Saint George killing the dragon. To the Indians of the vicinity he presented two shirts, two caps, beads, hawks' bells; in return they brought him a helmet full of gold nuggets, which went to Spain, too, along with letters from the town

council describing the beauties of the New World, insulting
Governor Velásquez, and asking to have Hernán Cortés appointed their captain. Incidentally we might mention that when
Charles received these jewels and documents in Tordesillas he
put them away in his coffers. With imperial loftiness, he did
not even bother to thank Cortés or answer the letter. The gold
nuggets went to Germany. Centuries later, Cortés's letters turned
up in the archives of Vienna.

But to return to Cortés and his republic. He had made up his
mind to go to the heart of Mexico, there where the emperor
who had sent him the jewels, the mountains crowned with
snow, the broad green valleys, and the city of stone were. But
to accomplish this he had to remove from his men the temptation to turn back — in other words, destroy the ships. But all
this with a great show of legality, discussing the matter in a
meeting of the town council, at which the pilots had been instructed to say that the ships were so worm-eaten as to be unseaworthy so that it would seem that Cortés was only bowing
to the inevitable. A few minutes later the hulls were being
scuttled, the masts stripped off, and sails, rigging, and ironwork
were being carried off to the settlement. Those without backbone or ambition could go on thinking about Cuba. Those who
wanted land, gold, adventure, and glory had only to keep their
eyes fixed ahead, on the mountains of snow and gold. Under the
cruel blaze of the sun and the fierce onslaughts of the mosquitoes, oozing sweat from every pore, but busily wielding shovel
and ax, carpenters, soldiers, friars, and peons raised their voices
in one cry: On to Mexico! It was the voice of Hernán Cortés
that re-echoed in five hundred Spanish throats. Marina's heart
fluttered in her breast like that of a bird.

And as soon as the soldiers had left the seashore for the slopes
of the mountains, the city began to move, too. Cortés had christened it Villa Rica de la Vera Cruz; he should have added "the
Restless." Only a few weeks after he had founded it, on the
very strand where he came ashore, the cabins were being torn
down to be rebuilt a few miles inland. Two years later the city
must have decided that it had gone too far, for it returned, with

its streets, its square, its church, and its town hall, to be closer to the island of San Juan de Ulua, which seemed its beacon and its bulwark. Years went by; yellow fever came and threatened to carry off all its inhabitants, white, black, and parrot-hued, and the viceroy said, "Let's get out of here," — and the city again carried its streets and its square, the church and the town hall some miles to the south. The mud-and-wattle huts with which Cortés's Bohemian city had begun its existence were supplanted by fortresses, thick walls, and stone castles with mounted cannon to defend Mexico against the French and the English, as well as the Spanish themselves. The island of San Juan de Ulua would one day witness a battle that was to change the course of European policy, and range England and Spain opposite each other in the struggle for empire. But for the moment Vera Cruz was the scene of one of Cortés's smaller master strokes of ingenuity: after making himself the captain of the commonalty, he brought about the greatest Indian revolution, and became first the Indians' leader and then their master.

Not far from Vera Cruz lived the Cempoals, one of the great nations that had fallen under the dominion of the Aztecs. At the time that Cortés was sending friendly messages to Moctezuma, he was secretly stirring up the Cempoals, and they finally rose in open revolt. On the arrival of Moctezuma's tax-collectors, who had formerly struck terror into their hearts, they took them prisoner. Protected by Cortés's army, they refused to pay tribute to the king of the Aztecs any longer. There were dances and feasting, enlivened with war whoops, the beating of drums, and the shrilling of flutes. Cortés was the idol of the Cempoals. And Cortés was the hope and comfort of Moctezuma's emissaries because he liberated them secretly and sent them to the king to tell him that he was indignant over the insolence of the Cempoals and that he would leave Moctezuma a free hand to deal with them as he saw fit.

In Cortés's own camp there were still friends of Governor Velásquez who were plotting against him. One day they managed to get hold of a boat that would carry them back to Cuba, and they secretly manned it, with their arms and belongings.

Cortés surprised them, tried them, and had them sentenced by his judges. Pedro Escudero and Juan Cermeño were hanged; the pilot Gonzalo had his feet cut off; the Peñate brothers, sailors, received two hundred lashes. "Would that I did not know how to write," lamented Cortés as he signed the sentences, "that I would not have to send men to their death." Bernal Díaz del Castillo comments: "It seems to me that this expression is frequent among judges when they are sentencing people to death." ·

Cortés was now ready to start inland. He had fewer than five hundred soldiers with him, only thirty-two crossbows and thirteen muskets, and but fifteen horses. A count in Spain used more arms and horses on a deer hunt, and Moctezuma was known to have an army of over forty thousand warriors. This conquest was to be carried out with swords, bits of bright glass, and sweet words. The city of Mexico, carved out in the middle of lakes, with its great stone towers, its highways through the lake, its canals where merchants displayed their wares, its huge temple, its square larger than that of Salamanca, and the palace of Moctezuma, was the wonder of the American world. But Cortés made his way to the heart of the city, laid hold of Moctezuma with his velvet-gloved iron fist, and began to make himself master of his conquest. Without even a dozen and a half horses! And while he was performing this hazardous feat he learned through Moctezuma, who had been informed by his messengers, that the governor of Cuba was making plans to destroy Cortés. Velásquez had assembled a huge fleet — nineteen ships, nine hundred men, cannon, crossbows, muskets, lances, eighty horses — under the command of Pánfilo de Narváez, to overthrow Cortés and bring the conquest under its rightful master, Governor Velásquez. Cortés left Moctezuma in charge of Pedro de Alvarado and a hundred men, and with the rest of his party set out to meet Don Pánfilo. Just as he was beginning to bring the Indians under control he was faced by a conflict with the Spaniards, and it looked as though he were going to have more trouble with Don Pánfilo than with the king of the Aztecs. As he marched to meet Velásquez's army, Cortés had only one third as many men as Narváez commanded. But he employed the strategy of the fifth column: he began to bore from within. He managed to get bars of gold into the hands and fair words into the ears of the captains of the opposing force. His promises had a pleasanter sound to many than the harsh orders of Don Pánfilo. When it came time to do battle, the victory was already Cortés's. He made a surprise attack at break of day. Each of his captains had a special mission to carry out: one was to capture the artillery; another was to take Salvatierra, the toughest and most dangerous of their adversaries; a third, Don Pánfilo de Narváez. The whole thing was over in an hour or less, and the casualties were fewer than twenty. When the little blood that had been shed began to dry under the scorching sun, Don Pánfilo had been disarmed and taken prisoner, and Cortés had nine hundred recruits, eighty horses, powder, ammunition, and bacon. A farewell gift from the governor of Cuba!

Probably Cortés had not been too hard-working a student in the two years he spent at the University of Salamanca. But what he had picked up there helped him in his second *Relation* to Charles V, now not merely King of Spain, but also Emperor of the Holy Roman Empire. And more than this: Emperor of the New World, because the lands Cortés was laying at his royal feet were better, richer, and farther-flung than those in Europe. "They are so vast and so many, as I wrote you in my other *Relation*, that you may well call yourself emperor of them, and no less fittingly than of Germany, which, by the grace of God, Your Majesty holds." This letter, like the other, was accompanied by a rich present of gold and jewels from Moctezuma's treasures.

The letter sent off, Cortés returned to his soldiering. There was still a war. Messages came from the city of Mexico that the Indians had risen against Alvarado and had him encircled. Cortés and his men would have to enter at the point of their lances. All of them, the veterans and the new recruits, were taking part in this campaign under the command of the captain of the people. Boats had to be built so that if their advance by road was blocked they would be able to reach the city by water. Fortunately, there were now plenty of carpenters and blacksmiths, as well as sails and cordage from the boats Don Pánfilo had brought over to build them, to the greater glory of Cortés.

The fight was a savage one. Cortés suffered defeat — the shame of it! — at the hands of the Indians led by Cuauhtémoc, that indomitable chieftain who had emerged from the people to seize the reins from Moctezuma's weak hands. Cortés's troops had to flee Mexico City by night, throwing hastily improvised bridges across the canals, and leaving behind them in the water cannon, mangled horses, comrades, while the Indian arrows pursued them, filling the air with their sinister whine. This was Cortés's "sad night." The empire he had been carving out with strokes of daring and luck seemed to be slipping through his fingers. How vain sounded his boasts of the triumphs he had described in his letter to the Emperor! How profitless and insignificant his victory over Pánfilo de Narváez! These contemptible Indians, this insolent Cuauhtémoc had humbled the Spanish arms. There was not a black thought that did not nest in the soul of Cortés that grim night.

But with the dawn Cortés rose like an ancient god of battle from the blood of his own wounds and those of all his men. He reorganized his troops, and the Indians with whom he had fought the first war supported him. Little groups of Spaniards came trickling in from the coast, attracted by the enchanted tale of his fortune and conquests. They knew what this conquest would mean in riches and glory.

While Hernán Cortés in Mexico was fighting the Spaniards of official standing and defeating them, in Spain Charles V had to fight those of the lower ranks until he crushed them. There were democratic stirrings among the people on both sides of the Atlantic. Here, as in Spain, the voice of the commons, of the captains of the people, had been raised. But whereas the nobles of Castile had finally stamped out the uprising of the *comuneros*, and the court favorites flourished in the Emperor's shadow, here in America no one could stop the Cortéses, the Balboas, the Pizarros, the Belalcázares, in spite of the efforts of impotent governors to block them.

Charles V's coronation at Aix-la-Chapelle was a solemn affair, with all the rites and ceremonies the occasion demanded. But while this was taking place, the *comuneros* of Spain were arousing the people, proclaiming war, because they did not want any more Germans coming into Spain, or a King of Castile living and ruling outside of Spain, or the people's money (and that coming in from America) being siphoned off into the hands of foreign bankers. And they had the insolence to tell him all this, point by point, in a long letter that a shameless scoundrel delivered into the imperial hands. They went further: they demanded that when he had to absent himself from Castile the person to whom he delegated authority as head of the government must be a native of Castile or León. They wanted no more Flemings, or foreigners of any kind. The *comuneros* put up a desperate fight. They besieged and captured towns and cities, they named Joanna the Mad their champion. They fought even with poisoned arrows, whose use they may have learned from the American Indians. They set fire to warehouses containing merchandise worth thousands and thousands of ducats. The Emperor was beside himself with rage. He ordered the bearer of the letter punished for having been party to such a piece of insolence. All the machinery of the Empire was gradually set in motion until finally the last voice of the commonalty was silenced. This voice was that of Juan Bravo, one of the great leaders of the revolt. As he was being led to the block he indignantly interrupted the crier who was proclaiming: "This is the justice His Majesty . . . has ordered meted out to these gentlemen. He has ordered them beheaded as traitors and disturbers of the peace and usurpers . . ." with: "You lie, and so does he who orders you to say this. Not traitors, but watchers over the public weal and defenders of the liberties of the nation." And Charles V re-entered Spain with his retinue of Germans and men of Castile. But perhaps he had learned something; at any rate he knew that under his mailed fist lay a Spain of granite. And the Emperor was a man of melancholy nature.

As Charles sat in the banquet-hall at Aix-la-Chapelle, Cortés, in Vera Cruz, was writing his letter of *Relation*. It reached the Emperor at the same time as the letter the *comuneros* had writ-

ten him from Castile. Cortés's letter bore the promise of gold;
that of Castile was all complaints and demands. These two
great documents of the people reveal their aspirations, their courage, their misfortunes, their ingenuous faith, and the works of
their hearts and arms. The Emperor's reply to the letter of his
subjects in Castile was written in powder and chains. That of
Hernán Cortés he graciously turned over to Jacob Cromberger,
the German printer of Seville, because by this time the Germans
had a finger in every pie in Spain. And Cromberger brought it
out in a fine edition, in Gothic folio, as was the fashion of the
day.

Charles now had no choice but to accept the accomplished
fact of Cortés's greatness. He who had seemed defeated for good
on that sad night when the arrows of Cuauhtémoc whistled
over his head and his soul returned to take the city of Mexico,
starving it into surrender, destroying the aqueduct of Chapultepec, and making even Cuauhtémoc submit to him. Charles V
rewarded him by making him captain and governor of New
Spain. And as captain and governor, Cortés embarked upon new
conquests, organized the colony, and improved his own estate.
He was as much a king in New Spain as was Charles V in Old
Castile. When Cuauhtémoc, the great rebel, seemed to him a
possible menace, he had him hanged from a tree. With the
noose around his neck the Indian said to him: "Why do you
kill without justice? God will call you to an accounting!" Cortés
was unmoved by these considerations. The conquest had taught
him many things, and he did not intend to let the Mexican
eagle escape his firm hand again. To him it seemed that he had
added still another head to the double Hapsburg eagle, and
such a triumph was not to be endangered by a moment of hesitation or weakness.

VI

EL DORADO AND THE FOUNTAIN
OF ETERNAL YOUTH

It is believed, and devout Christians affirm it, and experience bears them out, that after the Blessed Sacrament had been placed in the churches of this island, the hurricanes stopped. And no one should wonder at this, because as soon as the Devil had ceased to be master of this land, and God had brought it back under Him, there would naturally be a difference in the weather, and in the tempests and storms, and everything else.

FERNÁNDEZ DE OVIEDO

Everyone may believe what he pleases; I think that nature can do great things.

PETER MARTYR

T HE SPANIARD of the fifteenth and sixteenth centuries was not the lord of creation, but only one of God's creatures. He had no science to defend himself against nature. How wonderful it would have been to have a rod to catch the lightning when there was a storm, or a machine to fly safely over the jungle, or a little white tablet that would take away the pain when a toothache came. But such flights of fancy had not been invented. When the winds howled and the storm broke, all a man could do was commend himself to God. The doctors were sorcerers. Man had to choose between the way of God and the way of the Devil. With this choice the sinner was confronted at every turn, and it was the theme and the drama of his life. The man of the six-teenth century was not the rational animal philosophers speak of, but an imaginative soul. For centuries, when the census of a city was taken, the report never said: "Toledo has so many inhabitants," but "Toledo, a city of so many souls." The natu-ral man who could contemplate without fear, even with a cer-tain pride, his place in the order of things had not yet been

99

born. The Spaniard of the conquest was at the mercy of the four elements — air, fire, water, earth — and his defense lay in the supernatural. For him everything revolved within the orbit of the superstitious, the mystic, the divine, the miraculous, the providential, the magical. The greater the disproportion between the insignificance of man and the infinite mercy of God, between the defenselessness of the sinner and the power of the Devil, the better one understands this world. The weapon of defense was the miracle. And the more absurd the miracle, the more impressive.

To the host of peasants, carpenters, blacksmiths, bakers, and shepherds whose lives were circumscribed by the village square and the priest's sermons, the donkeys that carried their jars of olives, the casks in which the wine aged, the ovens where the bread was baked, the church where they received the baptismal waters, and the cemetery where they slept in peace, it was a miracle, this business of crossing the salt sea, where for weeks and weeks there was nothing to see but waters that changed color. If one managed to reach the other side it was by the mercy of God. Columbus himself realized that his ideas could make headway only on the basis of their supernatural connotations. "Neither books nor maps were of help to me," he said in an almost frenzied outburst; "but there was fulfilled in me that which the prophet Isaiah had foretold." On another occasion he wrote to the Queen: "Your Majesty, I have just reached the Garden of Eden." He wrote this the way one sends a postcard from a town one happens to pass through. During the later years of his life the Admiral drew up an inventory of prophecies. The thing that gave Columbus the reputation of being crazy was not that he made prophecies, but the use to which he put them. His application of them was always in his own favor. This was what did him harm.

As far as the Spaniard was concerned, the difference between his imagination, which spurred him on, and his reasoning faculties, which did not function, is evident. With charts and compass nobody could have persuaded him to leave the land he knew to venture into an unexplored world; on the wings of fancy he allowed himself to be taken from one side of the ocean to the other, from one end of the earth to the other. Any exploit smacking of the heroic aroused his enthusiasm because it fitted in with his theories of contrast. As I said above, the more absurd the miracle, the more impressive. Thanks to this, it was possible for Cristóbal Guerra to set out in a little boat with thirty companions and cross the Atlantic and discover the coast of Venezuela; for Diego Méndez to cross the Caribbean in a canoe to deliver a letter for Columbus.

Geography and history were expressed in colored images. They took on the nature of art. America appeared clad in gold, pearls, silver, and emeralds; her forests were scented with cinnamon and inhabited by giants, dwarfs, and Amazons, her seas by sirens. The more they learned about this land, the surer the conquistadors were that everything in it was prodigious. Here, Plato's imaginings were fulfilled. What had seemed the inventions of the Greek or the Latin poet proved to be prophecies of what they were seeing. That mysterious island of Antilla, which appeared and disappeared on fanciful maps, was right there. The existence of the Atlantida was proved beyond the shadow of a doubt. There were conquistadors who sought with lynx-keen eyes and a blind faith the footprints of the Apostles who had dwelt in the New World. Columbus was seeking the cities with the marble bridges that Marco Polo had described. There was no one who did not inquire about the land of the Great Khan. Peasants whose only dealings heretofore had been with their donkeys now talked about the pearls of Ophir and the temples of Solomon. The conquistador's model of action was Amadis of Gaul.

The maps are the maps of a *chanson de geste:* The waters are alive with horrendous monsters; in the ornamental borders one sees Indians roasting haunches of Spaniards on the spit. But perhaps the most fanciful of all is the shape of the newly discovered lands. Seas and rivers stretched to unbelievable dimensions. Everything was on a reckless scale, and small wonder; the conquistador for whom the ten miles he has walked become a hundred in the telling ends by believing himself.

And let him who does not believe in fairy tales cast the first stone. The Italians were worse than the Spaniards. They rounded each other out. Oviedo quotes Boccaccio as an authority. And was it not Columbus, the Genoese, who first began looking for monsters on the islands, and repeating the tale of the Amazons that he had read in Marco Polo? Vespucci talked about giants. And Peter Martyr stated that in a black sea some hundred leagues from Panama dolphins had been seen that sang in harmony like the sirens and lulled their hearers to sleep in the same manner. Sebastian Cabot told of men with legs like ostriches.

Nor did the Germans take a back seat, nurtured as they were in medieval sagas. In Venezuela, Ehinger claimed to have discovered the Amazons, and Nicholas Federmann, a nation of pigmies. In the Plate region Ulrich Schmidl became one of the legion seeking the silver caves where the White King dwelt. And the English added their contribution. There is no more vivid description of the giants of Patagonia than that of Francis Fletcher, who accompanied Drake on his trip around the world. But at the head of them all stands Sir Walter Ralegh with his El Dorado and his fabulous Guianas.

In no other climate of America did these fantastic legends thrive more vigorously than in the Caribbean. There were the island of the Amazons reported by Grijalva, that of the giants of Vespucci, and Columbus's monsters. But of all the legends, the two that were most widely accepted, that inspired the maddest, most heroic exploits, were El Dorado and the Fountain of Eternal Youth. For many years the explorers of North America were following the will-o'-the-wisp of the fountain that made old men young. Those who explored the South were looking for the chief whose subjects threw handfuls of gold dust over him until he glittered like the sun. Thus what was later to be denominated North America and South America were at that time known as La Florida and El Dorado. Into these two adventures Spaniards, Germans, and Englishmen flung themselves, mounted on the wild horses of their own folly. And if one stops to think who it was that launched them on their mad career, it was none other than Christopher Columbus, the first apostle of these mad dreams.

The adventure of the Fountain of Eternal Youth began in this way: there was a certain Ponce de León who had spent some twenty or twenty-five years in different parts of these islands. Each day new islands appeared before his eyes, and tempting Indian girls who could make young fellows just out from Spain lose their senses by the way they sang and danced their *areytos*. He never forgot those first years in America with Columbus when — strong, venturesome, happy, in the flower of his thirty-three years — he drank to the full of the pleasures life could offer. Later he was with Ovando; it was still pleasant to go on a tear and have all the Indian girls he wanted in the sultry tropical nights. "He was a poor squire when he came through here" — poor but happy, witty, and a lord within his own domains. He had been made captain of the island of Borinquen, which is the poetic name of San Juan de Puerto Rico. During an Easter week in the month of April 1513 — April Easter, happy year, the people say — he landed upon a verdant coast and baptized it Florida.

Years had gone by. Ponce de León was approaching sixty. The authorities of Santo Domingo had attempted to humiliate him by removing him from the governorship of Borinquen. These were machinations of the Columbus family. But the old man was stubborn, adventurous, and a dreamer, and refused to bow his proud head. He played with the idea — the deceptive dream — of recovering those days of amorous triumphs, youthful enterprises, and heroic adventures, of being as he was when he first set out with Columbus. Lord of La Florida, by the grace of His Majesty, the King. . . . So, following the star of a myth, he set out to discover the Fountain of Eternal Youth.

The Indians, who could read the desire in his eyes, fanned the flame. There, over that way, back there — they told him — is the fountain. . . . Ponce de León was like a man possessed. It was not only the tales of the Indians that urged him on, but the stirrings of his own subconscious. The fountain of life and of youth

existed, for he had seen old engravings that showed its bubbling
waters, leaping, shimmering in a spring landscape. And always,
in the background, a significant detail: a love scene. This was
the first graphic expression of what psychoanalysts today term
wishful thinking. And now the picture was coming to life. The
knight who stooped to drink of the life-giving waters was Juan
Ponce de León, and the Venus in the background was an Indian
girl.

Why should anyone think it impossible to find the enchanted
fountain in this new world so rich in prodigies? Columbus had
started the ball rolling with his tale of the Garden of Eden he
had discovered. He had described the Tree of Life and the four
great rivers of the world flowing from the enchanted rocks. These
were the rivers mentioned by Pierre d'Ailly in his *Ymago Mundi*,
an allegorical geography that had fired the Admiral's imagination. The rocks were the peak of Adam, which marked the
limits of the Orient according to the savants of the Middle Ages.
And that tree of the American rivers was the most beautiful
tree the waters of the world had ever formed, where the golden
rays of the sun were reflected from fountains of a thousand
colors. There were black rivers that gushed from rocks of ebony,
others white as milk, golden as honey, red as wine, or crimson
as an oath of Seville. Some were frozen, others boiled. In Guana-
cavelica in Peru was the river of death; its waters, according to
Father Acosta, turned into rock, and whoever drank of them died
because they congealed into stone in his stomach. The counterpoint to this was the Fountain of Youth, which turned old men
into lads again. It was the fountain told of in the book of the
wonders of Asia: "I, Prester John de Mandeville, saw this fountain and drank three times of its waters, and since I drank I
am hale, because those who drink of its waters are always
young. . . ."

And so the discovery and exploration of North America began at the point of a fable. On the strength of it Ponce de León
mobilized an army of men whose ingenuousness ill befitted their
years. There was not a river or brook in all Florida whose waters
they did not drink, nor a swamp or lake in which they did not

bathe. (And bathing in itself was quite an adventure for the hidalgos of those days.) But all they proved, as Oviedo ironically observed, was that their sexual vitality was waning, and that they were as gullible as callow youths. "And one of these was Johan Ponce himself, who was foolish enough to believe all that nonsense the Indians told him."

Not that the Spaniards did not find youth in Florida, but it was not the kind they were seeking. It was in the Indian bowmen who were the handsomest and strongest they had ever seen. The most powerful European could not bend the bows they drew. The arrows they shot went into a horse on one side and came out on the other; they could pierce a coat of armor. Nothing of the sort had ever been seen in the Antilles. Ponce de León received proof of their prowess in his own flesh, and he returned to the islands with an arrow wound in his leg, as a consequence of which he died.

The same thing happens with a myth as with a lie of any sort; once the story gets started nobody can stop it. After a few months nobody remembered Ponce de León's misadventures; but there floated in the air an idea that there was an enchanted land in Florida. If one man had not been lucky enough to find it, another would. Had not the same thing happened in Mexico? Mexico was a word to conjure with, a word that spurred men on and made them forget their failures. The same year that Ponce de León died of his arrow wound, Cortés entered the City of Mexico in triumph. Might there not be another Mexico behind those green curtains Ponce de León was unable to penetrate? Where there is a continent there are bound to be wondrous things. Florida was a continent. Everyone dreamed of conquering it, but there was one who desired it more than anyone else. It was one who wanted to equal Hernán Cortés, that Don Pánfilo who, having set out to bring him to book, had been defeated by him and made a laughing-stock, and had lost an eye into the bargain. There might be another Mexico — thought Don Pánfilo to himself — in that land of eternal youth. Another Mexico, and I would be another Hernán Cortés. And so he set out to make himself master of Florida, authorized by the Emperor and full of hope.

He did not set out from the Antilles in modest fashion, like Ponce de León, but from Spain itself. His ships carried six hundred men. Hope had filled them with mettle. One hundred and sixty soldiers, new recruits perhaps, deserted in Santo Domingo. He replaced them with veterans from Cuba. Nothing could stop him. He was caught in a hurricane and rode it out. Such mishaps were nothing new to him — ships split asunder, men drowned. Finally they reached Florida. It was on Good Friday of 1528, that day of the year when men's minds turn to thoughts of repentance and the abyss of eternity and meditate upon Christ's sufferings and man's sinfulness. The only consolation they can find is God's infinite mercy and, on the third day, the glorious resurrection. The memory of the joyous bells of Seville pealing their tidings of cheer and hope echoed in their hearts.

The shores of Florida bore no resemblance to those of Mexico. In Mexico they were of stone and gold; here they were trees and rivers. It was an expedition into the vegetable kingdom. In the Indian villages all they found was thatched huts and fields of corn. They had to make their way fording rivers, lakes, and canals. Each day's journey brought them to new curtains of hanging green moss. The gold must be farther inland, in the land of the Appalachians. The men of Castile by this time were frightened and disillusioned, and if they went on risking their lives it was because of the one quality that never fails the Castilian: his honor. At last they reached the village of the Appalachians. The same old story: forty huts, corn fields, insignificant bits of gold. Perhaps the treasure was in another village, Aute. Nine days more through forests and swamps. Each day was like a lesson in natural history: birds, deer, rabbits, bears, and panthers. In Aute, nothing. Corn.

There is a book that tells of Don Pánfilo's expedition in Florida, *The Shipwrecks*, by Alvar Núñez Cabeza de Vaca, who was one of the party. The title speaks for itself. There were shipwrecks on land and on sea, armies that were swallowed up by quagmires, ships shattered to bits against the keys. Of the six hundred soldiers that set out, four survived to tell the tale. Don Pánfilo kept pushing farther and farther inland without knowing where he was going. Oviedo had warned him before he left Spain not to be covetous or rash, neither credulous nor hot-spurred, to be content with what he had and the improvement in his fortunes brought about by his wife — who knew more about conquests than he did — and not to expose himself to further stones (one had knocked his eye out in Mexico). But Don Pánfilo's arrogance was stronger than all these arguments, and here he was lost. Nobody knew where the ships had been left. Those who had horses fled. Somehow they made their way back to the sea, but when they finally reached the shore, there was no way to go ahead or turn back. Whereupon Don Pánfilo took the only course possible under such circumstances: he called a council of his men. The soldiers decided upon a step that in boldness outstrips anything recorded in the annals of the conquest — to build ships *there* in which to cross the sea. They had neither tools, iron, forge, oakum, tar, rigging, shipwrights, nor food to keep themselves alive while they were at work. And yet, in forty days, with one carpenter, they built five ships, and the remains of the army embarked in these. The horses were killed one by one to supply them with food. Some brought in corn from the Indian villages, others cut down trees, others pieced together sails. From the iron of their stirrups, spurs, and crossbows they made axes, saws, and nails; out of deerskin and the wooden cannon, the bellows for a forge. The horses' manes were twisted into rigging; the soldiers' shirts became sails. Stones were used for anchors, resin of the pine trees for pitch. Water skins were made from the horses' hides. When the soldiers went aboard, the ships almost foundered under their weight. The men were crowded in so tightly that they looked like bunches of bananas.

And, after all this, on September 22, 1528, came the final defeat: shipwreck. Pánfilo de Narváez could make only one answer to the despairing cries of his soldiers: each man for himself. One of those who managed to save himself was Cabeza de Vaca. His adventures took him from the heart of Florida to Paraguay, at the other end of America; during years and years of hair-raising experiences, he stands out as one of the stoutest-hearted and noblest of the conquistadors. He was taken prisoner by the Indians, and they made him a slave. But, as he was a man "of sagacity and infinite resource," he always managed to save his skin. He became known as a doctor, a miracle-healer. He cured the sick, he revived the dead, and his fame spread from Florida to the border of Mexico. From tribe to tribe he traveled, Doctor Cabeza de Vaca, the Wizard Cabeza de Vaca, farther and farther west until finally one day he reached New Spain, the empire that Cortés had built up. And with all the freshness, simplicity, and ingenuousness that characterize the epoch he set down in his memoirs the miracles he had performed. As, during this first half of the sixteenth century all you had to do to cure a sick person or bring one who had died back from the other world was to breathe in his face, adding to the breath a few words of the *Hail, Mary* and a little faith, Cabeza de Vaca's book makes convincing and delightful reading.

There was an interlude in Cabeza de Vaca's life, the days he spent in Spain after the shipwreck in Florida and before he set out on his adventures in Paraguay. In the relation of his voyages, he says: "Here I have set down only my misfortunes; but there is something else I shall tell no one but the King." The Spaniards in Spain were more credulous than the Indians of Florida. The story began to spread from table to table, from inn to inn: Cabeza de Vaca knows about treasures in Florida that he won't tell to anyone but the King. The story acquired the snowball growth that might have been expected: he knows about fabulous riches in Florida. A fig for Mexico and Peru! The real treasures are those of Florida, which Vaca won't tell about to anyone but the King.

Just as Don Pánfilo dreamed of repeating Cortés's exploits, there was at court then one of Pizarro's lieutenants who hoped to find another Peru in Florida. This was Hernando de Soto. He had gone out to America with nothing but his shield and his sword. He accompanied Pizarro to Peru, and won as much fame there as the Marquis himself, no less for his uprightness than for his bravery. He was among those who took Atahuallpa prisoner — he himself trying courageously but vainly to save the captive's life; his share of the spoils was large; he came back to the court with 180,000 ducats and lived in great style. He had come up in the world; his wife was a daughter of Pedrárias Dávila, and he reflected in his own person the glory that had been won in Peru. The treasures that had been taken from Atahuallpa so surpassed those of Mexico that nobody remembered Cortés any longer. People were saying: if Hernando de Soto plans to go to Florida then Florida must be another and richer Peru. How the soap bubble Cabeza de Vaca had tossed into the air glistened and gleamed! Hidalgos sold houses, vineyards, olive groves, annuities to join Hernando de Soto. Soldiers came from Portugal begging for a chance to go with him, and in May of 1539 they set out.

Hernando de Soto was gallant, tactful, and noble. As for his bravery, his lance was said to have been the second in the conquest of America. Magnanimous, he had always been an advocate of gentleness rather than ruthlessness. In Florida he always tried to make peace with the Indians. But if they prepared an ambush for him, before they could shoot an arrow he was in the thick of them, striking off their heads with his sword, lancing them, riding them down. Thus he advanced deeper and deeper into this world of broad savannas and deep rivers, determined to discover what it was that Cabeza de Vaca would confide only to the King. It was one of the great epics of the Spanish conquest, painted in crimson against the brilliant green of North America. Not one handful of gold did they find. But they accomplished other things: there is the vivid relation of a Portuguese knight of Elvas; the heroic legend of Hernando de Soto, "the inland Columbus of Florida," which was recounted by the Inca Garcilaso de la Vega in one of the most beautiful books of the sixteenth century; and, summing up all that had been written and experienced, a map probably drawn by one of the soldiers. It looks like a comb of rivers running parallel to each other on their way to the Gulf of Mexico. Rivers and more rivers were what they had seen, had crossed, sometimes with the water to their armpits, or so high they had to swim them or cross on bridges improvised, "worked out by geometry," by the engineer Francisco, a Genoese. The names they gave the rivers revealed their fatigue, their hopes, the trials they were undergoing, the moments of despair when it was necessary to invoke the saints. Reading the list of the rivers that appear on this map, with a little imagination one gets a good idea of what Hernando de Soto's expedition was like: River of Peace, River of the Canoes, River of the Cross, River of the Nativity, River of the Sand-banks, River of Snow, River of Flowers, River of the Angels, Low River, River of the Holy Ghost, River of the Mountains, River of Gold, River of the Fishermen, River of the Magdalene, River of the Palms. Others had discovered what was known as *tierra firme,* the mainland. Hernando de Soto had discovered the land of moving waters, the pathway to the Mississippi, whose tributaries form that great tree which holds North America in its branches. In South America, in Mexico, others had scaled mountains. In Florida, which came into being because of the myth of a fountain, the symbol was a river that cut through the plains. From then on the Spaniards, who were men of the land and were seeking gold, turned their backs upon Florida. In 1542 Hernando de Soto left his mortal remains in the river where his life ended and his fame began.

One day he felt death coming, in the form it so often takes in the lands of the Caribbean. Two fiery hands seemed to be crushing his temples; his fever-ridden body trembled. He sent for the priest and confessed his sins, commending his soul to God. Then he called his captains one by one, to bid them farewell, and then the soldiers, in groups. He did not want to leave any of them without a parting word of comradeship and gratitude. The raging fever died down and Death threw its icy sheet over his exhausted body. The eyes of de Soto's rude companions were full of tears. Late at night, so that the Indians might not see or know or hear what had happened, the captains and soldiers carried the body of Hernando de Soto, tied to the trunk of an oak, down to the river. Even the sounds of the men's sobs were hushed. Murmuring gently, the water flowed between its green banks. Smoothly Hernando de Soto's solitary boat slipped into the swift, deep waters of the Mississippi. All the Spaniards could see in the wake that followed it was the glitter of the stars overhead, like a double row of swords to honor the passing of the soldier.

While in the north Ponce de León, Don Pánfilo, and Hernando de Soto had been suffering these rude buffets of fortune in their search for the Fountain of Youth, to the south there was not a single camp of Spaniards that was not thinking of the other myth: El Dorado — the Golden King. For these men, habitual gamblers, life was a game in which one waited to be dealt the winning card. The Indians kept pointing inland, toward the peaks of the mountains, saying: "There's where he is." It would be safe to say that for ten years men set out from all the hot coastal settlements for the icy mountains, navigated all the rivers, covered the map of South America looking for the Golden King.

The main centers of the conquest were about the broad base of the Andes. Along the coast of the Caribbean and the Pacific there were little cities, scattered here and there, at which new groups of adventurers arrived every month. Coro had been founded in Venezuela, Santa Marta in Colombia, Panama in Golden Castile, Quito in Ecuador, and Lima in Peru. From all these places one could see the mountains in the background. First the word *El Dorado* had been a secret of the soldiers, a word to be whispered in the ear, a magic formula, an Open Sesame. Then it became the cry of the crowds, avid of glory and riches, who wanted to set out in search of them.

Without knowing about each other, three covetous armies were on the march at the same time. One moved over the sweltering plains of Venezuela under the command of a German, Nicholas Federmann, who had gone beyond the boundaries of the territory he governed, lured by the green of farther pastures. Another was coming along the slope of the mountains; this one had set out from Ecuador, and at its head was Sebastián de Belalcázar, who had shaken off Pizarro's overlordship to make himself master of the lands he had conquered. The third, pushing through the jungles of the valley of the Magdalena, in Colombia, was climbing the steep Andes; it was led by Jiménez de Quesada, who, as soon as he was at a safe distance from his legitimate governor, called a meeting of his soldiers and advised them to elect him captain. The men enthusiastically fell in with the idea, as in the case of Balboa and Cortés.

They were all headed for the same spot, the same bleak plateau. These were not marches of weeks or of months, but of years. Several thousand men were reduced to several hundred. They crossed swamps, jungles, deserts, frosty sierras, and steaming valleys, suffering hunger, war, death, and encounters with Indians, jaguars, and crocodiles; they left the tropical coast to scale mountains ten thousand feet high, where the sleet froze on their beards. Finally, in 1538, they reached the uplands. It was a plain broken by mirrorlike lakes where Indians, wrapped in blankets of cotton, huddled in some protected spot to fashion their clay utensils and where the timid deer bounded through thickets of myrtle. Fishing rafts woven of withes slid lazily along the river to the music of deep-throated frogs and the flight of little ducks known as *tinguas*. In the afternoon everything turned to gold: the clouds that hung over the circle of mountains surrounding the plateau, the water of the quiet pools, even the air that enveloped the hills. At night everything turned to ice: the Milky Way that foretold the hoar-frost of the morning, the wind that numbed the fingers, the water that froze in the clay vessels and the wooden troughs. In the morning everything became rosy-hued: the cheeks of the dawn, the drops of dew, and the wind that blew perfumed from the hills. This was El Dorado: a bit of sky, a little water, the air that changed color as it caressed the quiet plains. The first to understand this and to take advantage of these things were the animals of the conquistadors — the dogs that leaped into the water after a duck and shook themselves with delight after their immersion; the chickens that Federmann had brought with him, who cackled with enthusiasm every time they laid an egg; and Belalcázar's pigs, grunting with satisfaction as they wallowed in the mud.

Jiménez de Quesada stripped the Indian rulers of their jewels and of the little golden flags at the entrance to the fenced-in enclosures that gave forth a muted chime as the wind stirred them. The pile of booty — as high as a man seated on his horse — was divided up, but that was all there was. Of the large army he set out with, only one hundred and sixty reached the plateau with Jiménez de Quesada. This was the exact number of Belalcázar's men, and of Federmann's. It would seem as though destiny had planned it that this highland should be the abode of balance, of equilibrium. The leaders did not reach for their swords, because these cool, poetic uplands seem to check bellicose tendencies. They exchanged speeches and then set out for the court so that their liege lord, Charles V, might decide which had the better claim. Federmann believed the choice would fall on him as a German; Belalcázar based his hopes on his military career, which had shared the brilliance of the Pizarros; Jiménez de Quesada put his faith in the persuasive powers of his tongue.

As the three descended the mountains and sailed down the river and out upon the open sea on their way back to Spain, the men who had remained behind searched high and low for gold. They found a mine of emeralds, a hill that contained salt, and iridescent butterflies of pearly blue — but no gold. Jiménez de Quesada, however, was a dreamer, and he refused to give up his dream. He was to return. And that same year he kept talking in Spain about the mythical El Dorado as though it really existed. Hernando de Soto was sailing the waters of death on his boat made of a solitary tree trunk.

VII

FIRST ROUND: FRENCH PIRATES
AND GERMAN SHARPERS

*After all, what I wanted to find out, my dear Machiavelli, was who
my friends are and who my enemies.*

LOUIS XII

IN THE early years of the sixteenth century Europe was like a
gaily colored picture book. The thrones of England, France, and
Spain, were occupied by three youths, the King of Spain being
the youngest. His two rivals, who had viewed his coronation
with fatherly condescension, were beginning to regard him with
astonishment, suspicion, and envy. The confines of his realm
were growing by leaps and bounds without any effort on his part.
Henry VIII of England was his senior by eight years, Francis I
of France, by six. These two admired and wooed each other.
When Francis decided to let his beard grow, so did Henry. When
Francis shaved his off, Henry followed suit. Francis had the
reputation of being one of the handsomest princes who had ever
graced a throne. Charles began to reign at the age of sixteen,
Henry at eighteen, Francis at twenty-one. Henry and Francis
were gay and luxury-loving, great talkers. Charles was taciturn.

The rivalry began between Francis and Charles. They represented two diametrically opposed attitudes toward life. Francis
was the Renaissance. He had grown up among poets, musicians,
and courtesans. When it was a choice between morals and politics, he never hesitated. With the same ease that he pledged
his word he broke it. Louis XI had left him as a legacy this wise
counsel: Never promise anything you intend to do. Francis was
the first to surround himself with a truly regal court. When he
traveled from one end of his kingdom to the other, never spending two weeks in the same castle, he moved with hundreds of
lackeys, nobles, knights and ladies, musicians, singers, pages,

horses, dogs, litters, table services of gold and silver, robes, armor, and hangings — everything except his wife. She stayed at home keeping house. It was like a huge theatrical company offering the people a show that cost them a great deal, but in which every act was a top billing. The dances, banquets, jousts, and fireworks were worth to the peasant what it cost him to keep up the court, and this was why Francis did not have the problem of the commoners' haggling with the King over the taxes. Everyone was content to pay his share, and when the nobles got drunk, so did the people.

Some of the differences between the two men may have been due to the mothers who bore them. Charles's mother was mad. Francis's mother, Louise of Savoy, was not only sane, but as shrewd as a fox. A charming widow at eighteen, she set her sights on the throne. If Louis XII had no male offspring, her son would be the heir. Of no avail was the bull that Louis XII had obtained from the Pope annulling his marriage so that he might take a more agreeable spouse who would give him a son. Each time the new queen announced a blessed event it was always a girl. Once there was a son; Louise trembled. But the infant died, and Louise's hopes rose again. After all, her fears were groundless; had not Saint Francis of Paul prophesied that Francis would be king?

Francis initiated his reign with the war on Milan. He won the battle of Marignano, the plume of his cap fluttering amidst sheaves of lances, and destroyed his enemies as one crushes an eggshell. It was a magnificent tourney. And the king returned with the finest of trophies: Leonardo da Vinci, who joined the court of the conqueror. Francis lavished honors upon him and bought his finest paintings, which formed the nucleus of the treasures of the Louvre. France became dotted with castles. Italian gardeners turned fields into gardens, created fantasies in cascades and fountains. And, in the background, was the genius of da Vinci.

Thus things went along until the moment when Francis of France and Charles of Spain matched forces for the crown of the Holy Roman Empire. The electors were seven. How much would they cost? Before Charles even laid his plans, Francis had begun negotiations. The Archbishop of Trèves, one of the electors, had set his price at 150,000 écus and a pension of 4,000 pounds; besides which, Francis was to let him have eight-year-old Renée, the second daughter of King Louis XII, as wife for the Duke of Brandenburg. The Archbishop of Mainz wanted so many écus, so much as a pension, and a cardinal's hat. And so on down the line. The price of the votes was agreed upon, the terms drawn up and signed, and sworn to by God and the saints. Francis had a majority. But the electors went on bargaining. The Archbishop of Mainz changed sides six times, raising his figure each time. If necessary, said Francis, I am prepared to spend three million ducats.

Francis had begun jockeying two years before the death of the Emperor Maximilian. To strengthen his case he had drawn up a boastful document outlining his patent superiority over Charles. Charles, he said, was a callow youth, whereas *he* had triumphed in war over Milan and had proved his prowess at arms and his experience in worldly affairs. His court was the most brilliant, his kingdom the oldest in all Europe and the first to be converted to Christianity — "four times the size of England," wrote the English chancellor, "with four times its population, four times as rich, and with better credit than all the rest." Compared with France, Italy was a patchwork that the kings of Europe and the popes used as a battlefield. Spain was barely coming into being; a generation before, it had been nothing but a collection of petty kingdoms. England was a fog-bound island. Henry VIII, who also would have liked to buy the electors, and sent his ambassadors to make a deal, saw plainly that he could not compete with either Francis or Charles. The Pope, who was a Medici, arrayed himself on France's side, and Francis was now able to raise his bids with the offer of cardinals' hats.

The delegates of the King of Spain arrived late. But old Maximilian, who was watching over his grandson's interests, took matters into his own hands; with money he demanded from Charles he planned and he plotted until, when the moment came for him to yield his soul to his Maker, he had undone nearly all Francis's work. The Germans preferred Charles because he was of their own blood. But the deciding factor was the league of bankers that supported Charles. It was the gold of the Fuggers and the Welsers that defeated Francis, and it took every penny Charles could scrape together. On June 18 of 1519 the electors met in the church of St. Bartholomew in Frankfort. After mass, during which the guidance of the Holy Ghost was invoked to assist them, they took their oath, one by one, on the first page of the Gospel according to Saint John: "By the faith that joins me to God and to the Holy Roman Empire, I swear that I shall make my choice to the best of my understanding and ability, and shall vote as my conscience guides me, free from all pacts, all bribery, pledge, or compromise of any kind. . . . May God and all the saints assist me!" Then the sessions began. There were still some last-minute offers. But, in the end, Charles won by a unanimous vote. To be sure, he was in debt up to his eyelashes, but he was Emperor. Francis, shrewd and self-possessed, declared that he was satisfied with the outcome. But in his heart he vowed war against the black-garbed callow youth who had defeated him.

Fate had been unkind to Francis. The Pope, who had offered him cardinals' hats for the electors, had changed sides at the last minute. Henry of England, whose guest he had been at that magnificent festival on the Field of the Cloth of Gold, had become an intimate friend of Charles. Charles had gone to pay him a visit, and the evenings spent at Windsor Castle were delightful family reunions. Charles found his aunt Catherine, the Queen, charming. When he left, Henry accompanied him on board ship "and they embraced one another fondly because of the great love they bore each other." Then the two of them joined forces against France. The first skirmishes began. It was a jolly war. "The English, by the terms of the treaty, built a large fleet and went out to harry all the coast of Brittany and stole much cattle and took many Bretons prisoner, and sacked many towns, burned many villages, and on the day of the Magdalene they sacked a fine town called St. Pol de Lyon, where it was said the booty amounted to over four hundred thousand ducats, and in all this they found neither danger on the sea nor resistance on the land; and on the 25th of August a great army of Spaniards, Germans, English, and Flemings gathered in Flanders and entered the lands of the King of France, sacking, pillaging, burning all the villages through which they passed, and this they continued all through the months of September and October, until the winter set in and the rains and snow made them break camp, and the King of France recovered in a few days all he had lost. . . ."

This was the way wars were fought in those days: no declarations of war, just pirate raids. Francis was bent on revenge. So were the fishermen of Brittany, pirates in the making. Francis's eyes turned toward the Caribbean. It was from America that Charles got the gold for his European enterprises. Those nuggets sent by Cortés tipped the scales in the elections, and were now helping him pay off his debts. By what right did Charles enjoy the sole usufruct of those lands? Pope Alexander VI had promulgated a bull authorizing the Kings of Spain and Portugal to divide the New World between them. But had he the right to do this? Did those lands belong to him?

To Francis of France, Alexander was a Spanish pope, a Borja rather than a Borgia, and in this case he was favoring his own. The ambassadors from Spain addressed him in Spanish — something unheard-of. The Catholic Kings had sent him the first fruits of the earliest gold from America, and Alexander had used it for the embellishment of his own church, Santa María de las Nieves, as it was known in Spanish, or Santa Maria Maggiore. All this had the air of a family affair to Francis. He was not bound by the bull. And with a burst of Pantagruelian laughter, he exclaimed: "The sun shines on me just the same as on the other, and I should like to see the clause in Adam's will that cuts me out of my share in the New World!"

And so the bull was drowned out in this peal of laughter, which was echoed, with the same words, by the pirates when they raided the islands of the Caribbean.

Just as the man makes the occasion, the occasion makes the

man. At this very moment the pirate appeared. He was called
Giovanni da Verrazano and, though he was from Florence, it
was as a French pirate that he waylaid the ships of Spain. The
Spaniards sometimes called him Juan Florentin, others The
Frenchman. In those days wars were waged by mercenaries —
an excellent arrangement, since it safeguarded women, children,
peasants tilling their soil, and the peace-loving citizenry, and left
the fighting to those whose turbulent inclinations and natural
belligerence made them excellent soldiers. Juan Florentin's crew
was made up of Frenchmen skilled equally in the use of knife
and of sail. Verrazano, or Florentin, was regarded as an ornament of his profession. As a young man he had been in Syria
and Cairo, trafficking in silks and spices. It seems that he had
accompanied the Portuguese on their voyages to the Orient and
the Spaniards on their explorations of the Caribbean. He was
a man who knew much secret lore. And he was a great navigator;
he could chart the position of a ship with such accuracy that
his brother Hieronymus, on the basis of information received
from him, in 1529 drew up one of the most exact and complete
maps of the world.

Verrazano's great exploit, the one that made him famous and
feared, was his assault on the boats carrying the priceless treasures Cortés had taken in the city of Mexico after the death of
Moctezuma. Gold, pearls, emeralds, exquisitely carved objects,
masks encrusted with colored stones, rich cloaks ornamented
with figures of birds and flowers worked in feathers of a thousand
colors, live pumas — everything was included in the fabulous
booty Cortés was sending to Charles V with a letter of relation
that was the apogee of his conquest. The boats set out confi-
dently from Vera Cruz. Everything went along smoothly, the
monotony of the thirty days' voyage lightened by divers trifling
incidents. Captain Quiñones had his head laid open by a sword
slash in a fight over a woman, died, and was tossed overboard.
In a storm one of the pumas got out of the cage; some of the
soldiers climbed into the rigging, where, from their safe perch,
they teased the enraged animal; others rushed for lances and
swords. When the affair was over, the puma and one soldier were

dead and four men were wounded. But suddenly a pirate craft was sighted. It was Verrazano, who fell upon the rich prize, captured two of the boats carrying the treasure, and with this splendid booty sailed triumphantly into the port of La Rochelle. Oviedo calculated the treasure at 150,000 ducats. The pearls alone weighed six hundred and eighty pounds. The pirate loyally informed King Francis at once of his feat, and handed over to him his share of the booty.

In no time the sea was infested with pirates. In Spain everyone from the Emperor to the humblest subject was burning with indignation. The Cortes demanded that these French freebooters be punished. The Emperor declared war upon them, offering a generous reward for the capture of Juan Florentin. Francis was happy. Verrazano had not discovered a continent, but he had invented a new type of warfare.

While King Francis was engaged in his disastrous campaign in Italy, that second war which ended in his defeat and capture at Pavia by the Spaniards, Verrazano continued with his pirate activities. The King, returned from his imprisonment in Spain, commissioned him as a privateer, and Verrazano wrote him letters describing his adventures. The bankers of Lyon put up the money for him to fit out his ships. In Dieppe the name of Verrazano was a rallying standard. The corsair, touched at many points of the American coast, discovered New York harbor, in about 1523, and his name is linked with those of the great discoverers. He was one of the great navigators. To the Spaniards who felt his ripping claws time after time, he was nothing but a pirate thief, and finally, in a naval battle, they captured him. The account by Charles V's chronicler is like a page from a child's chap-book:

"In those days there was a famous French pirate by the name of Juan Florin who for eighteen years had been roving the seas plundering Spaniards and Venetians and Italians and all the enemies of the King of France, who in one year had given him 4,000 crowns to arm his ships and make war on his enemies; and on the 3rd of October six Basque galleons encountered the pirate Juan Florin off Cape St.

Vincent, and when they recognized the fleet of the aforesaid pirate
they decided to attack and do battle with him, and they came alongside and grappled the boats, and such a fierce and hard-fought battle
took place that it lasted from eight o'clock in the morning until two
in the afternoon, and the pirate Juan Florin attacked and defended
himself stoutly; but in the end, as his hour of misfortune had come,
they sank the galleon he was on and took him prisoner. He was put
in prison and confessed that he had robbed and sunk 150 ships and
galleys and galleons, and schooners and brigantines, and that once
he had captured a ship of the Emperor's that was coming from the
Indies with more than 30,000 gold pesos. . . . When the Emperor
was notified of his capture he ordered him executed, and as his
captors were already bringing him in they met the messenger His
Majesty had sent out with the order in Colmenar de Arenas, and for
this reason he was beheaded in the square of that town. And as they
read him the sentence he spoke these words: 'O God, how have you
permitted such a thing to happen? O Fortune, how have you brought
me to such a pass? Is it possible that I, who have killed so many,
must die at the hands of one man alone?' He offered 30,000 ducats
as ransom for his life, but the good Emperor preferred to bring the
miscreant's evildoings to an end rather than have his money."

They laid Verrazano's head in the dust, but his fame, the
wealth he had won, and the curiosity his discoveries had aroused
spread throughout France among seafaring, adventure-loving
men. The greatest enthusiasm was in Dieppe. This was the old
port that had formed the bold seamen and greedy merchants
who carried on their piracy and other enterprises around the
English Channel. Dieppe in France, with Normandy and Brittany in the background, and Plymouth in England, with Devon
at its back, were the two great naval academies. Pillaging each
other, falling upon the inhabitants, they had learned the arts
of boarding, running up the Jolly Roger, sacking, and looting.

Juan Terrier who was one of the first to raid the ships in the
Caribbean, was from Dieppe, as were the d'Angos. Jean d'Ango
was a real celebrity. He was a viscount, of a family of rich
burghers, a favorite of Marguerite d' Angoulême, Francis's sister.
When Francis traveled through Normandy, he stayed at d'Ango's
house. A banker, d'Ango was finally ruined as a consequence of

huge loans to a poor creditor: the King. His house was a center for sailors, geographers, artists, nobles, pirates, and merchants. Jean d'Ango had inherited his taste for adventure, for his father had armed the first privateers who sailed for the Caribbean. Jean carried his audacity to the point of sending his fleet up the Tagus to besiege the King of Portugal. His expeditions in America ranged from the Antilles to Canada. The King not only commissioned him a privateer, but authorized him to form a company. By the terms of the charter, one tenth of the booty taken from the enemies of the King and of the Holy Catholic Faith was to go to the King. One raid on a fleet arriving from the Caribbean netted them 280,000,000 maravedis. Thus Dieppe was the cradle of the adventures that linked France to the troubled destinies of the Caribbean.

Life in the islands of the Caribbean had taken on a new aspect. In the ports the talk was all of pirates and freebooters. The cities were little fortresses that the enemies attacked and burned at will. Every Spaniard constituted himself a sentinel, but often he cried "To arms" for no reason at all, and again, when he tried to give the alarm, a French knife was already at his throat. At times the Castilian ships — this happened to Hernando de Soto in Santiago de Cuba — found the ports closed against them because they were mistaken for Verrazano's ruffians. The encounters were fierce but picturesque.

But of all the maritime adventures of the French during this period there was one that was to achieve immortality. It was animated by the spirit of a daring, satirical doctor who voyaged in a boat of paper. Everything in it is imaginary, and everything in it is real. The islands he discovered were in a novel, but a historical novel. The cannon balls fired at Charles V were words invented by his impudent pen, but sarcasm can be a crueler weapon than a lombard. If Vespucci and Columbus could paint on their maps monsters they had never seen, paradises their fancy feigned in the lands of America, why was it not licit for this witty scamp to think up an archipelago in the

Antilles and people it with the lords of the earth in a literary carnival? Of all that took place during the reign of Francis I, this new fashion of making discoveries was most in keeping with the humor of the Renaissance. Here art met no obstacles, and as the author was a gifted navigator who knew how to avoid the reefs of the court and the shoals of the friars, who laughed at the Sorbonne savants until the tears came, who outdid Erasmus himself in calling things by their right names, his marvelous voyages were published and all the world delighted in them, despite the blasts of the Inquisition and without the author's being roasted at the stake as might have been expected.

Among the circumstances that favored the author was the pleasure that Francis took in the book. Francis is the hero of the novel, and under the protection of his favor Rabelais let fire at Charles V or the Pope with a gusto that may have come from mirth or anger, or both. No Frenchman could ever forgive Charles for having taken Francis prisoner and confined him in a tower with a single window from which to gaze upon the sun, the birds, and the monotonous passing of the clouds.

Our account of the Caribbean should, of course, limit itself to actual voyages and leave the imaginary to one side, even though they are among the most amusing and entertaining. But it would have been unforgivable not to mention this literary result of the explorations in the Caribbean. If our sea had been nothing more than a backdrop for François Rabelais's book, this alone would have assured its immortality.

At the time the French were raiding the Caribbean, sometimes as pirates, sometimes as corsairs — in either case with the approval of their King — the Germans were making their entry under the standard of Charles V and with benefit of the law. These Germans were bankers who got whatever they wanted out of Charles, not only because they had lent him the money to set the crown of the Holy Roman Empire upon his brow, but because he had to turn to them every time he needed funds — which was three hundred and sixty-five days a year.

The King of France and Charles were both spendthrifts.

Francis threw his money away on palaces, concerts, courtesans, festivals, and finery, Charles on wars and coronations. In point of bookkeeping, the result was the same. Francis had spent the dowry of his betrothed years before they were married. Later he ruined his friend Jean d'Ango, who lived to see thistles growing in the courtyard of his castle, once the pride of Normandy. He confiscated the property of the Duke of Bourbon. To get themselves out of difficulties, kings sometimes resort to measures that would land a poor man on the gallows, as when in paying off his ransom money to Charles V, Francis mixed in a large number of counterfeit coins.

And Charles V ran him a close second. He arranged for his own marriage twice with daughters of the King of France, and once with the English princess — and then, as might have been expected, he married someone else. When the King of England challenged him to a duel, one of the grievances he alleged was that he had lent Charles 500,000 écus, which Charles refused to pay back, although four years had elapsed since the date set for payment. Charles borrowed money from anyone who had it to lend, even his worst enemy. And he pledged any security asked for. He pawned the Moluccas to the King of Portugal for 350,000 ducats. So it is not to be wondered at that he handed over the province of Venezuela to the Welsers, and to the Fuggers the right to conquer and settle Chile.

Thus, for twenty or thirty years, the Caribbean swarmed with agents of the German bankers. They were in Hispaniola trading glass beads for gold. They got hold of silver mines in Mexico. But, because they were gullible enough to believe in El Dorado and other fables, the goal of their ambitions was Venezuela. For twenty years a series of German governors appointed by the Welsers had the exclusive control of this colony. It did not go against the grain for Charles to make this concession: the Welsers had been very generous with their loans, and, besides, Charles was not only King of Spain but also German Emperor. He was a Hapsburg, and bound by ties of blood to the inhabitants of the farther bank of the Rhine.

The casual reader is startled when in the accounts of the

Spanish conquest of this period he comes upon names such as Seiler, Ehinger, Hohermuth, Federmann, Von Hutten, and Seisenhoffer, which have a strange ring in the history of Venezuela. But if we are going to be sticklers, we should have to admit that it was equally strange that the King of Spain should be named Hapsburg rather than Pérez or Villadiego. What is worth pointing out is that, at about the time Charles V became one of those typically Spanish gentleman who wore nothing but black and at the end of his days retired to a monastery, the jungle swallowed up the Welsers and their agents. The Germans had spared no effort. They set fire to the native villages, had every Spaniard on their books as a debtor, and enslaved the Indians. But the Germans failed; they did not found a single city nor establish one colony. The gold evaded them, the mass of the Spaniards refused to co-operate with them, and at times — as in the case of Ambrosius Ehinger, who died choking with helpless rage — the Indians managed to put a poisoned arrow into them.

After years of vain struggle, this empire of money the bankers had tried to build up crumbled to nothing. The King finally refused to pay them. Some of them wound up in a prison cell, and others — the more fortunate, like Ulrich Schmidl and Federmann — found their way back to Europe each with a parrot on his shoulder and a notebook of impressions under his arm. The experience was so drastic that for many years the Germans wanted no part of the conquest. Much, much later one of the branches of the Hohenzollerns — none other — invested money in a slave-running venture. But this belongs to another century, and, for the moment, has nothing to do with this rambling tale.

VIII

THE QUEEN OF ENGLAND AND HER FORTY THIEVES

Drake was lavish of his presents. He presented the Queen with a diamond cross and a coronet set with splendid emeralds. He gave Bromley, the Lord Chancellor, 800 dollars' worth of silver plate, and as much more to the other members of the Council. The Queen wore her coronet on New Year's Day; the Chancellor was content to decorate his side-board at the cost of the Catholic King. Burghley and Sussex declined the splendid temptation; they said they could accept no such precious gifts from a man whose fortune had been made by plunder.

JAMES ANTHONY FROUDE

The Queen bestowed upon him
A stick-pin for his tie. . . .
VALLE-INCLAN

AT THE beginning of the sixteenth century England's weight in the scale of world affairs was that of a stalk of tobacco. To give Europeans an idea of Santo Domingo in the Caribbean, the comparison both Oviedo and Father Las Casas hit upon was England. Of course, they both added, Santo Domingo was far more valuable. From the point of view of natural wealth, the two islands could not be named in the same breath. And, as far as the natives were concerned, those Indians who painted themselves black and red, and decked themselves out in feathers and skins, recalled, in detail after detail, Julius Caesar's description of the English in his account of the Roman conquest.

The judgment of the English writers themselves is no less cogent. Geoffrey Callender, in his excellent study of the naval history of England, says: "Phoenicians, Romans, Angles, Saxons, Jutes, Danes, Normans; and Julius Caesar, Aulus Plautius, Julius Agricola, Hengist, Horsa, Canute, Hardrada, William I, Henry Plantagenet, Bolingbroke. Warwick the Kingmaker, Edward VI there you have the list of some of the invaders and conquerors of England: and the catalogue could be extended without difficulty."

The events we have just examined bear this out. When Henry VIII tried to put in a bid for the crown of the Holy Roman Empire, his commissioners realized at once that he was in no position to compete with his cousins, the Kings of France and Spain. He had neither army nor money nor credit worth mentioning. His fleet was just coming into being, and the rest of Europe had hardly a suspicion of what this was to amount to. The Old World had known only two seas, the Mediterranean to the south, and the Baltic to the north. The Mediterranean fleet was the Venetian; that of the Baltic was the Hanseatic League's. London, Plymouth . . . whistle-stops. What has our fleet been, the Englishman of that day might ask himself. And his answer would be: Some fishing smacks that sail to Iceland when the cod is running, or to Kinsale in the sardine season; and a few merchants and pirates or corsairs who go on from the coast of Devon to Bordeaux, Cadiz or Lisbon, or out of the Thames estuary to Antwerp.

Henry VII had made a start in the time of Their Catholic Majesties. It was he who gave the merchant marine its first impulse, and he would have liked to have a share in the transatlantic crossings. But his realm was not in a position to spread its sails freely. Columbus sought his support, but in vain; had he been successful, the fate of the world would have been very different. When Columbus's fleet returned to Spain, Henry's conscience must have given him some bad moments. Then a Venetian, Sebastian Cabot, appeared on the scene, and urged the King to make up for lost time. Cabot, who sometimes worked for Castile and sometimes for England, explored the coast of North America under the flag of Henry VII. Henry paid him a little under ten pounds sterling for his discoveries. This was something. Spain, fearful, and rightly so, saw enemies behind every bush, and this single detail aroused her suspicion of the English. Their Catholic Majesties hurriedly ordered Hojeda to take possession of the coast of Darien before the English pirates could do so in Henry's name. Nothing could have been farther from Henry's thoughts; but in the fishing ports the fishermen (the burghers, that is to say), the corsairs, and the pirates grasped the situation clearly. In England, just as in France or in Spain, the monarchs were far behind the commoners, to whom fighting was a catch-as-catch-can procedure. It was not long before English pirates were competing with the French.

Henry VII was not interested in warships. He had no idea of taking the offensive, and he was among those who believed the island's best defense was its ramparts of good, green water. Henry VIII had other ideas, and history has proved him right. Walls of timber were necessary. And in spite of the love labors that so beset his life, Henry VIII found time to build warships armed with heavy cannon. When he died there were eighty-five of these ships, a great achievement for those days. He gave little thought to the merchant marine, but it was not necessary; the pirates were doing the work for him. They discovered that rich lode which in the sixteenth century was more valuable than all the coal veins — coal-colored human flesh. The procedure was very simple: they caught the Negroes in Sierra Leone and sold them in Santo Domingo. Thus that little island of England, which Father Las Casas and the historian Oviedo had dismissed in such an offhand manner, began to grow. Behind the wall of spars and canvas, through the fog that shrouded London and Plymouth, the lights were burning bright in the forecastles — but only a few people understood the message these winking lights were signaling.

One day an astounding thing took place at the court of Henry VIII. William Hawkins, a wealthy burgher of Plymouth, who was engaged in smuggling blacks into the Antilles from Guinea, brought a live Indian from Brazil and exhibited him in White-hall. "This was the first savage chieftain brought to England," and he was a nine days' wonder. The inhabitants of the city gazed in amazement at his pierced cheeks and lower lips in which were hung little jewels like those the Englishwomen wore in their ears. William Hawkins was duly rewarded for his achievements — was twice made mayor of Plymouth, later was elected to Parliament, and became the richest man in the city.

Paraphrasing the book of Genesis, the history of the relations between England and Spain, in the days of Henry VIII and Charles V, would read like this: In the beginning there were the women. In the waxworks museum in London, one whole room is needed for Henry and his six wives. A superficial glance would suggest that these successive marriages were due to the fickle fancy of a capricious monarch; but nothing could be farther from the truth. Never before had a king had to change queens in order to change ladies. No; poor Henry was the personification of a king in search of a male heir. It was unthinkable that the crown of England should rest on the empty head of a woman. In the four and a half centuries prior to Henry, there had been only one queen in England — Matilda, of unhappy memory. Philosophers, statesmen, and preachers throughout the island raised their voices in protest at the thought of going through such an experience again. And Henry saw that nothing more could be hoped for from his wife, Catherine. The three sons she had borne had died almost at birth; only the daughter Mary, born in 1516, thrived. It seemed like a malediction of God. The doctors had informed Henry that his wife, Catherine of Aragón, would bear no more children. Henry, realizing that there was no time to be lost, had already fixed his fancy on Anne Boleyn, and had sent ambassadors to Rome to induce His Holiness to annul the marriage. In all Europe there was no better Catholic than Henry VIII, "Defender of the Faith." When Charles V's soldiers sacked Rome in 1527 and made the Pope prisoner, Henry challenged Charles to a duel; such an offense was not to be tolerated. Now he told his ambassadors to remind the Pope of his services and to bring all pressure to bear to secure the annulment. Time was of the essence, for Henry had already married Anne secretly, and an heir was on the way.

As far as Queen Catherine was concerned — "my Aunt Catherine," as Charles V called her — England, like the rest of Europe, was becoming uneasy over Spain's growing power. Henry had been well disposed at first. Even on the occasion of the victory at Pavia, he had ordered celebrations in London; barrels of wine were set up in the public squares, and the drinks were on the King; there were Te Deums in the churches and fireworks at night. It is a pleasant thing to see a rival in prison. But it is not so pleasant, he quickly reflected, to see another rival mount so high. The arms of Spain extended over half of Europe. America was Castile's preserve. The Pope himself was afraid of Charles. All this began to go to Charles's head. He wanted nothing more to do with Henry VIII. Those days when they had outdone each other in mutual attentions were but a memory by this time. He had agreed to marry Henry's daughter, true; but now he demanded that she be sent to him immediately — she was barely nine years old — with a dowry of 600,000 ducats. It was obvious that he was trying to go back on his bargain, and Henry sent neither the daughter nor the ducats. Charles at once married Isabel of Portugal, a beautiful woman who brought him a million ducats. His troops received their pay.

The Pope was not so indulgent with Henry VIII as he had been with Louis XII. He refused to grant the annulment, and the Church of England was born. Then Anne Boleyn gave birth — to a daughter! It was the last straw. Henry realized that he could not spend ten years in experiments with Anne as he had with Catherine, so Anne was sent to the Tower. There followed one of the basest trials that royal history records, and Anne lost her head.

After the death of Edward VI — that ardently desired son who finally arrived, but who reigned for only six years — came the queens, Mary and Elizabeth. Spain cherished the dream of dominating this troublesome English kingdom; it was pleasant not only to dream of it as another jewel in the crown of Castile, but also to see it Catholic, Apostolic, Roman again. By English law the crown went first to Mary, Henry VIII's elder daughter, whom Catherine had brought up in the Spanish manner. She was a Catholic to the marrow of her bones. More than that, she was the wife of the prince who, two years later, was to be crowned King of Spain as Philip II. In London, mass was again being said. The philosophers viewed the succession with horror, shuddered at the thought that the kingdom was in the hands of a woman. The rich, who earlier — under Henry — had shared in the expropriated wealth of the Church, blenched at the threat to what they held dearest: their property. In London the people were sick of the sight of the Spaniards who darkened the streets; for every Englishman, there were four Spaniards, "making life unbearable to the English nation," to quote a historian.

Queen Mary felt only one serious obligation, besides that of restoring the true faith: to have a son. She became so obsessed by the idea that several times she persuaded herself that her hopes were to be realized; preparations were made, the bells pealed, but each time it proved to have been only wishful thinking. And if there was no son, the crown would pass to the daughter of Anne Boleyn, Elizabeth — who in Mary's eyes was nothing but a Protestant bastard. The son never came, Mary died, and in 1558 Elizabeth came to the throne. England, despite the philosophers' fears, became an island of queens. They were to fill the new centuries of her history. Steered by their hands, the nation sailed out of its harbors dark with fog and soot to become the flagship of the seas of the world. And the one who first worked this miracle was Elizabeth the cautious, the wily, the prudent, the stingy, the learned, the Virgin Queen, with William Shakespeare on her one hand and Sir Francis Drake on the other.

One thought filled the mind of Elizabeth's subjects: whom would she marry? Year after year Parliament pleaded with her. "Your Majesty," groaned that august body, "it is time that you married and bore a child." And the Queen, ever shrewd and witty, replied: "But who has a greater interest in this matter than I?" And suitors crowded the court, and the air buzzed with rumors, and she let herself be wooed, but cautiously, always evading the issue when the moment of decision came. Queen Mary was not yet cold in her grave when Philip II sent a special mission to negotiate a marriage with the new sovereign. But the Queen of the Sea, as history has called her, was as slippery as a fish, and slid through his fingers.

She knew where she was going — a thing not infrequent among the English — and luck was on her side. Just as Spain, in a sense, was the creation of Isabella the Catholic, so England was the creation of Elizabeth the Protestant. War with Spain was her destiny. Gradually her power grew until one day in 1588 she had the satisfaction of seeing the Invincible Armada of Philip II lie splintered at the approaches to her harbors. But the real field of battle was the Caribbean. In this remote corner of the wild seas was fought the daily and unrelenting — and the most telling — combat. Here on the coast of Mexico, in Cartagena with its stone fortresses, in the Gulf of Darien, off the Guianas, at the tip of Florida, the future admirals of England were schooled. And it was as pirates that they served their apprenticeship. If centuries later it could be said that the battle of Waterloo was won on the playing fields of Eton, there is more reason to maintain that England's navy and its empire were formed in the not so aristocratic school of piracy. The Queen found freebooters delightful, and allowed the grace of her favor to shine upon their weather-beaten faces.

The name with which history has christened these corsairs and pirates of the Queen is very expressive: "sea dogs." The county of Devon was full of them. This was the home of the Hawkinses and the Drakes and the Raleghs. There they had learned to hate Philip II's Spaniards, there they had learned the routes to Africa, Brazil, North America, and the Caribbean. William Hawkins of Plymouth had shown them the way. John, his son, followed in his footsteps, and outshone him. In the Spanish histories, John is known as the pirate Juan de Achines. But it is an exaggeration to call him a pirate. His real profession was that of smuggler, and his associates in these ventures were the cream of London society. The pirate was a horse of a different color; the pirate was Sir Francis Drake.

The venture John Hawkins proposed to his rich associates was to form a company for the purpose of catching Negroes in Guinea to sell in Santo Domingo. It is perfectly clear that slave-trading was considered one of the most honorable of professions. Spain was issuing licenses to its own subjects for the sale of slaves, and that most Christian and humanitarian of friars, Bartolomé de las Casas, recommended their introduction to the Antilles. Why, then, had not the English the same right to do business as the Spaniards? In Africa the natives made slaves of defeated tribes, so all the slave-trader had to do was to buy up the prisoners from the conquerors. Really, said the English, it was an act of mercy, because however badly off the Negroes might be in the Antilles, their fate as prisoners of other Negroes in Africa was still worse. But considerations of this sort were for the future. At the moment there were no protests. Hawkins's proposal was enthusiastically received. Lord Pembroke and the Earl of Leicester bought shares in the company, as did Sir Thomas Lodge, Lord Mayor of London. The Spanish Ambassador protested, not in the name of any Christian sentiment, but in defense of the monopoly set up by His Catholic Majesty. Queen Elizabeth kept Hawkins in port until the storm had blown over. Then, up with the sails, and a good voyage!

Getting hold of Negroes was no problem. Nor reaching the Antilles, either. Hawkins knew the way, and understood the business. The difficulty was selling them. All the gentlemen in Santo Domingo, Venezuela, Cartagena wanted to buy Negroes, but none wished to break the laws of Castile. Hawkins, in turn, was prudent and wily, and he wanted to do things properly and leave a good impression. At times he threatened to bombard the ports; again, he pretended he had got off his course, and asked for shelter in the harbor. In one way or another, he managed to establish contact with the governor, the hidalgo, with anyone who had money, and in this way he disposed of his merchandise, filled his pockets, and departed. More than once he was given a certificate of good conduct signed by the governor. He was looking not for trouble, but only for a market. Once in Santo Domingo, after he had sold two hundred Negroes, he left a hundred and twenty-five in trust, in case there were any charges outstanding against him. It is safe to assume that John Hawkins never expected to get a pound for these slaves. What he had done was a perfect piece of slave-running, but there was in him that same mixture of good faith and sharp business sense characteristic of all England's economic enterprises; not one penny gets away. The Spaniards were amazed at the considerate fashion in which the English extended credit, and then at the serious way they took their role of creditors. They did not realize that, to Hawkins, business law was more sacred than the common law, and that for this reason smuggling, carried on in an honorable manner, was not bound by the King's restrictions. Especially if he happened to be only the King of Spain. At any rate, Hawkins reached Santo Domingo with three ships and sailed away with five loaded with gold, sugar, and hides. He had so many hides, and was so ingenuously impudent, that he sent two ships of this merchandise to be sold in Cádiz! It goes without saying that the King of Spain seized the hides and the Negroes that Hawkins had left in Santo Domingo. Mr. Hawkins was outraged. He made a great hue and cry. He wrote to King Philip himself, saying with easy familiarity: "How can Your Majesty do such things to an old gentleman who was the first to welcome Your Majesty when he came to England to marry the late Queen Mary, God rest her soul? Doesn't Your Majesty remember that I was then a member of the council of Plymouth, and that we spent three hundred pounds on the banquet we gave in your honor? How can you now confiscate my hides and my Negroes? . . ." The Queen herself interceded for John Hawkins. She wrote Philip a little note asking him to be clement. Philip's reply was brief and biting: he would not return one hide, and any Englishman who showed his face in the Caribbean would be treated like Hawkins. This was the law of Spain.

Hawkins turned over in his mind the manner of getting around the difficulty. Sir William Cecil advised the Queen not to encourage these dubious enterprises. But the Queen had a clearer vision of things than Sir William. She not only permitted Hawkins to set out again, but she bought shares in his company herself and gave him two of her own ships. Hawkins was the hero of the day. The Queen received him at the palace, the shareholders received a sixty-percent return on their investment. All the inhabitants of Plymouth wanted to share in his enterprises. On this new expedition a young man who had already been in the region of the Caribbean offered his services. He would soon be England's greatest hero, Francis Drake. Naturally, Shakespeare had listened with interest to the tales of these men. In *Henry IV* he speaks of the crocodiles that Hawkins saw in the Hacha River:

> ". . . *As the mournful crocodile*
> *With sorrow snares relenting passengers.*"

And here begins the tale of the pirate, Sir Francis Drake.

The boys of England had invented a game, war between Englishmen and Spaniards. One took the part of Philip II. He always lost, and the others pretended to hang him. Philip II represented the interloper. It was he who wanted to bring back mass, the Pope, the Catholic Church. When his ambassador arrived, the boys pelted him with snowballs. Thus Francis Drake grew up in an atmosphere of political and religious warfare. The Pope had awarded Spain the sole rights over America. Why? The King of Spain had decreed that only Spaniards could sell Negroes in the Antilles. Why? The religious orders, stripped of their holdings by the Protestants, were stirring up trouble in Devon. All the calamities that befell the island, they told the peasants, were due to the King's having broken away from the Church. And their indignation knew no limits on the day the ministers of the Crown ordered that, beginning on Easter Sunday, the Bible would be read in the churches in English, in the Edward VI version. Monks and peasants rose in rebellion. In threatening numbers they marched through the countryside until they reached Plymouth, forcing open the city gates. Those who were for the King, the Bible of Edward VI, the new Church of England, had to flee. Among these were Edmund Drake and his sons, who lost or abandoned to the Catholics all they had. The Protestants made the island of St. Nicholas their stronghold. This island, which became a symbol, is known as Drake's Island. The Drakes were born to be leaders. Warfare passed from the land to the sea. Francis Drake had grown into a stripling who spent more time on the water than he did on shore.

There was not an inch of the coast he and his father did not know — every reef, every inlet, every cove, every hiding place, every bank, every shoal. The boy was one of those lively gromets, thoroughly at home among the masts and rigging, who know how to turn a puff of wind to good use, how to weather a storm and trim a sail. His keen eye scanned the distant horizons by day and pierced the thick darkness of the night. But aboard ship there was one thing that was more precious than the boy, the sails, or the anchors; it was a little mound of paper: the Edward VI Bible. At mealtime, the boys stood with bowed head, listening in silence that was part humility and part pride, piety, and defiance, while Edmund Drake read aloud from the Holy Book. Once Elizabeth was seated on the throne, their prospects grew brighter; the Protestants could breathe freely again. Edmund Drake returned to land, as rector of a church. Francis stayed at sea.

In the villages of Devonshire, accounts were heard every day of how Englishmen had fallen into the clutches of the Inquisition in Seville, how their ears and noses were cut off and they were roasted over the fires. Every new report that the old wives repeated, seasoning it to their taste with each telling, was a new stimulus to piracy. It is true that the Inquisition was untiring in its persecution of Luther's followers. The most damning thing that could be asked about a person was: "Who knows but that he is a Lutheran?" The English people left the affairs of Europe in the Queen's hands. Elizabeth would decide whether she was or was not at war with Spain. But on this side of the line, that arbitrary meridian which Pope Alexander VI had set up, there was no peace. Drake was not thinking in terms of the sly smuggling that made the Hawkinses vulgar merchants. This young man was filled with thoughts of pirateering in the French manner. The business of slave-running was not for him. He would make straight for the gold of the galleons, the pearls of Río Hacha, the silver of Potosí, the treasures of the Perus. . . . He would fall upon the cities and put them to the torch, bathe his knife in blood to the hilt, humble the Spanish pride to ashes, and watch the terrified nuns run, the priests of the Pope of

136

Rome tremble. When he was twenty-one his name was already known in the Caribbean. He had been exploring the coast, looking for places where his ships could hide and discovering how the ports could best be attacked. This was the world where he would win eternal fame, and whose waters hold his remains. The Caribbean was the sea of the robber captain, Francisco Draque. Or, if you prefer, of Admiral Sir Francis Drake.

When, one day in October 1567, six ships set sail from Plymouth toward the Caribbean, nobody suspected that their fortunes would alter the relations between England and Spain for good. Until that time there had been popular grievances, and the two nations had indulged in small and frequent mutual annoyances, like the pinches of nuns who hate each other sweetly. Up to then the diplomatic exchanges of the two nations had been of velvet. After this voyage they became of mail. The person who least suspected and least desired and least benefited from this state of affairs was the gentleman who captained the expedition, John Hawkins. His policy was one of honest smuggling and everybody friends. He believed in a business war, a white war. Drake thought differently; for him, the *business* was *war*. But John Hawkins, a man of experience, was the captain; and Drake, twenty-two years old, was in command of only one little ship, the *Judith*.

Queen Elizabeth had sent two of her own ships with the expedition, the *Jesus of Lübeck*, which was the flagship, and the *Minion*. Among the crew there were many gentlemen, some of the best people of London. Also some Frenchmen, Huguenots like Captain Bland of La Rochelle. Hawkins had a page to serve him, and was attired like a prince. Before they reached Cabo Blanco, the six ships had become seven, having seized a Portuguese caravel, which Hawkins put under Drake's command. The hypocrites piously christened it *Grace of God*. In Sierra Leone they fell upon some other Portuguese ships, and took hundreds of Negroes. From there they crossed to America. In spite of the opposition of the Spaniards, the ships anchored in Santo Domingo, Margarita, Borburata. "We skirted the coast from one settlement to another, doing business with the Spaniards as best we could," wrote Hawkins; "the matter was a little difficult because the King had given his governors orders that under no circumstances were they to countenance dealings of any sort with us; nevertheless, we did a good business, and we enjoyed ourselves."

At Río Hacha, Drake, who had outdistanced Hawkins, followed his own methods. The first cannon ball tore a hole in the house of the treasurer. Drake had put all his pride into this shot, for the year before he had come off the loser at Río Hacha. To round matters off, he also shelled a ship of the viceroy's that was entering port. When Hawkins arrived and saw what Drake had done, any doubts he may have had about the fledgling he was hovering under his wing were dispelled. From Río Hacha they proceeded to Santa Marta. From there to Cartagena. These cities marked the points along the coast of the mainland where Spain had concentrated her strength. Cartagena was the key to the door of South America. Hawkins went along selling his slaves like any peddler going from door to door. At Margarita he received pearls in payment, at Río Hacha bars of silver, at Cartagena gold. The business finished, it was time to turn home.

He set his course through the strait of Yucatan; from there he would proceed through the channel of the Bahamas before the hurricanes set in. But the hurricanes arrived ahead of schedule. The sky turned black, and for four days the storm blew relentlessly. The vessels groaned and began to ship water; Hawkins was a very unhappy man because, if it did not clear, the pearls would be at the bottom of the sea again. The storm finally blew itself out, but the ships were in need of repairs. There was nothing for it but to put into the port of Vera Cruz. Hawkins, sly old fox that he was, knew that if he approached flying his own flag, he would be blown to bits, so he hoisted the pennon of Castile. In the harbor, where the King's fleet was momentarily expected, the people began to wave to them gaily. But, strangely, those on board did not answer with the usual shouts and gestures. When the ships finally dropped anchor off shore, and the

people began to swarm aboard — God save us! It was the English, the Lutherans, the Huguenots, the pirates! Hawkins and his
crew lost no time, and the port was quickly in their hands. Faithful to his business ethics, Hawkins proposed an arrangement
and dispatched a messenger to the capital. He was to be allowed
to repair his ships unmolested. Meanwhile, he sold Negroes,
laid in provisions, made himself master of the artillery, and
trained the cannon on the entrance to the bay. The King's fleet
was due at any time, and he had to be ready.

And the King's fleet did arrive, bringing none other than the
new viceroy of Mexico. A gale was blowing, and the thirteen
ships of the viceroy had to take refuge in the bay or be splintered
against the rocks. Hawkins sent a ball from "his" cannon across
the flagship's bows. If the viceroy — he notified him — did not
agree to terms and offer him guarantees, he would bombard him.
The suggestion was fantastic. England was not at war with Spain;
this was a Spanish port; and I — said the viceroy — am the viceroy. That you are, answered Hawkins, of your King Don Philip,
but I am likewise the viceroy of my Queen Elizabeth of England, and if you have soldiers on your ships, I have the advantage
of "my" cannon. The viceroy had no choice but to accept Hawkins's proposal. Whereupon Hawkins once more became the
affable, talkative merchant who gave the impression of standing behind the counter of a shop rather than on the bridge of a
ship. They drew up an explicit agreement and, as a mutual
guarantee, exchanged a dozen of the most important persons on
each side. When the twelve Spanish gentlemen were in his
hands, Hawkins graciously opened the port to the viceroy, as
who should say: "Come in and make yourself at home."

Nothing was further from the viceroy's plans than to keep his
word. We have already seen that this is not merely a gentleman's code of honor; it is true of kings as well. Hawkins's mind
did not work that way because he was only a burgher of Plymouth. Instead of the twelve gentlemen he was to send as hostages,
the viceroy had dressed up twelve peasants. The Spaniards
could hardly keep their faces straight when they saw Hawkins,

who had sent the cream of his crew, receiving the twelve hostages as befitted their presumed station, bowing and seating them at his table. And thus two, three, four days went by. The Spaniards were getting ready to spring the trap, with complete assurance, for there is no better protection than to work in the shadow of a broken word of honor.

In his garments trimmed with gold buttons and pearls, Hawkins must have cut a finer figure than the viceroy himself. Seated in his cabin on the *Jesus of Lübeck*, the Queen's ship, he had asked his page for a drink of ale, which was brought him in a silver tankard. As he was quaffing it, he heard a noise on deck. He had suspected something, but he was reluctant to believe his own thoughts. The Spaniards were already boarding him. Behind the hills, on the shore the Spanish troops were drawn up. Within the narrow confine of the bay, Hawkins's little fleet was unable to defend itself or attack. Slowly Hawkins finished his ale, like a gentleman, and set the tankard on the sideboard. It had no more than left his hand when a culverin ball knocked it off. Outside there were heard shouts in Spanish, shouts in English, all employing the vocabulary of combat. A Spanish boat, loaded with powder, exploded. Drake slipped his moorings and managed to get out of the port before anyone else. He did not even stop to find out how things were going with his leader. Hawkins had to abandon the Queen's flagship, which was sinking, and board the *Minion*. There all who had managed to save their skins took refuge, and this was the second ship that put out to sea. But so many had crowded aboard that at the first place they could put in, Hawkins was obliged to set a hundred ashore. And with the survivors he managed to reach England to relate his misfortunes. In the port of San Juan de Ulua he had lost the pearls — four hundredweight of pearls — the bars of silver, some Negroes, many gentlemen, the Queen's ship, the silver tankard. . . . The hundred men he had put ashore had to endure the attacks of the Indians, the fevers, and hunger, until finally those left alive fell into the hands of the Spaniards. Or, to be more exact, of the Inquisition, which proceeded to try them, not as pirates or smugglers, but as Englishmen, heretics.

Through all England, through all Spain the story of what had happened at San Juan de Ulua spread like wildfire. All those involved came to a decision: Queen Elizabeth, King Philip, John Hawkins, Francis Drake. And history opens out like a fan made of these four names.

This is how Queen Elizabeth took her revenge:

In Plymouth there was a Spanish ship carrying 500,000 ducats. It was the money King Philip was sending to the Duke of Alva in Flanders to pay his troops. Pursued by French pirates, the ship had sought refuge in Plymouth — a ship belonging to the King of Spain had put in at a port of his friend, the Queen of England. But suddenly the captain realized that he had stepped into a hornets' nest. There was not an Englishman, from the highest to the lowest, who was not determined to take this half-million ducats from Spain. To Philip this was consecrated money, because with it the Duke of Alva could pay his soldiers, who were killing Huguenots and Lutherans! Were the English people to tolerate this? Never. But how could they prevent it? This was the problem. Bishop Jewel dispelled the last scruples of the Queen's conscience — as though this were necessary, observes Froude — by pointing out that it was a laudable act to intercept funds that were designated for the slaughter of Protestants. Sir Arthur Champernowne, the Vice-Admiral, offered a solution: the Spanish boat was in his custody, and he had said to the captain: "Have no fear for your money and your ship while these guards are here; the Queen's honor is at stake." But even as he said this, he wrote to Lord Burleigh (Sir William Cecil, the Lord High Treasurer): "If Your Excellency approves, I can fall upon this ship with the help of some of my friends [incidentally, Sir Arthur's son was cruising in the Channel with three pirate ships] for the benefit of Her Majesty, though some blood will be shed in the venture. Not only will I do this, but I shall take upon myself the blame, so that this sizeable treasure may pass into the hands of the Queen. I cherish the hope that once the severe storm of her disapproval has passed — which the Queen must show at first to hide the facts — I will find the balm of her favor, as befits the risk I shall run for her sake. . . ."

But it was not necessary to resort to such measures. A simpler method was found, observes the distinguished author of *English Seamen in the 16th Century*. The idea was born in high places. It was suggested that the money be sent by land to London, where it would be safer. The Queen's troops took it into custody and, employing every precaution, deposited it in the Tower of London. At this point, the Queen's treasurer discovered that the 500,000 ducats in question were a loan Philip had received from the bankers of Genoa, and that until the money had been delivered in Flanders it could be considered not Philip's property, but the bankers'. It happened that the Genoese were in London, and the Queen said to them: "Isn't this a coincidence? This is exactly the sum that I need." And the 500,000 ducats were transferred from Philip to Elizabeth with the smoothness and simplicity with which a check is drawn.

This is how John Hawkins took his revenge:

The Queen had put him in command of several of her ships. He was a member of Parliament, well known as one of the rich men of Plymouth and as the hero of somewhat shady adventures. With these claims to fame, and the reputation of being a trader above everything else, he secured an audience with the Spanish Ambassador. He wanted to discuss a very intimate matter with him, he said: he had had enough of the Queen; she was niggardly, grasping, ungrateful — you know it as well as I do, Your Excellency; it's public knowledge — and she had never been willing to reward him for his services. There were in the fleet plenty of others who, like himself, would be glad to desert. What was going on in England was senseless, and it was all Elizabeth's fault. Hawkins grew more and more excited as he talked. If Spain was willing, Hawkins was prepared to help to overthrow her. The Ambassador — though it is hard to believe — gave credence to Hawkins, and passed the proposal on to King Philip. Philip was a fox: "If Hawkins is prepared to do this, let him come here and talk with me." But Hawkins was a slyer fox: "It is impossible for me to go, but I am sending my friend Fitzwilliam, who is my alter ego, and he will back up everything I have said; all I ask in return is that my men who are imprisoned in Seville be set free, and that I receive the necessary money to put things in motion." The King listened to Fitzwilliam, and everything was agreed upon. The Queen knew every step that was being taken from the letters Hawkins sent Sir William Cecil, the Lord Treasurer. The last one said: "My very dear Lord: I trust Your Honor will be well pleased to know that Fitzwilliam has returned from Spain where his proposals were favorably received not only by the King but by the Duke of Feria and the other members of the privy council. . . ." In this way the Queen learned of all the plots that were being spun against her. The conspiracy that was to bring Mary Stuart's head to the block now came to light. Every one of Hawkins's men returned to England with ten pounds sterling in his pocket, while John Hawkins received the £40,000 he had lost, according to his accounts, at San Juan de Ulua. This time it was Hawkins who laughed last.

And this is how Philip II took his revenge:

As there was not a shadow of doubt in his mind that his mission on earth was to crush the English, and as he was not an ordinary king but an instrument of God, he held his tongue and bided his time. England, that little heretic island, had become puffed up with pride because of her warships and her pirate ships. He would put an end to this. He would build the greatest armada of history, the Invincible Armada, which would strike unexpectedly in the darkness. Under the prow of its ships the shores of England would tremble and the bold English masts would be cut down like feeble reeds. From the high forecastle, the hand of the Inquisitor-King would deal implacable punishment.

And this is how Francis Drake took his revenge:

Twenty-six, handsome, daring, he belonged to a different school from these other three sly actors; his tactics were offense. He lacked the cunning of his cousin John Hawkins and the patience of Elizabeth. He was as strong-willed as Philip, but he outdid him in swiftness. All the world now recognizes that Drake possessed genius, vision, and daring. There is only one black mark against him: running away in the battle of San Juan de Ulua. Those who were saved with him praised this as a strategic withdrawal; the others reproached him for having deserted Hawkins. But these were academic discussions, which interested neither Drake nor Hawkins. Drake kept his men in training, serving a few months in the Queen's ships, but he was really preparing to complete his discovery of the Caribbean after the pirate manner. For two years, with one or two ships, attacking a galley here, a port there, he had familiarized himself with the salient points of the New World. One day the young ladies of Cartagena, watching from the roof-tops, witnessed the amusing type of warfare the Englishman was carrying on there against the Spanish ships. He was fighting — they said — not for honor, but for gain. That was the truth. But the outcome was that he burned two Spanish ships, seized a little gold, and then smilingly sailed away, with the Spanish doubloons jingling merrily in his pockets. On the coast of Darien he discovered a small, neat bay, so well hidden that it could harbor a whole little fleet without anyone's suspecting its presence. This was Puerto Escondido (Hidden Harbor). Beautiful hills, good hunting, better fishing. Not far away was Nombre de Dios. This was nothing but a squalid little village of miserable huts, on the pest-ridden coast. But over a bridle path across the Isthmus of Panama the convoys of mules arrived at Nombre de Dios, laden with all the silver of Potosí, as though it were sacks of potatoes or corn. When Drake returned to England he could say to his people: "Come on, lads, sign up; it gives me pleasure to inform you that I have discovered America." And so he had, another Columbus.

This time when Drake set out, his objective was the mule train. The trick consisted in knowing when the royal fleet was due, and on what day the mules would be crossing the mountains behind Nombre de Dios — then fall upon them! All this had to be worked out on the ground. The affair took several months, but the outcome was that Drake did waylay the mules and returned to England with the hold of his ships loaded with bars of silver and saddle-bags full of gold. The tales of this voyage went to form the legend that was to make the name of Francis

Drake immortal. It was told how he joined forces with the run-away Negroes who had revolted against the Spaniards, and how at the same time that he drew information from them and used them in his raids he taught them their prayers and instructed them in the "true" faith; between foray and foray, he seemed, as his father had been, an upright pastor. It is said that in the first assault on Nombre de Dios, he was in the very house where three hundred arrobas of the king's silver were deposited, and he came away with empty hands. This was not his fault. At the very start of the attack he got a bullet through the leg. He said nothing, so his men would not lose heart. But suddenly they saw him stumble and fall to the ground in a widening pool of blood. He urged them to leave him and press the attack, but his men knew that Drake was captain, pilot, guide, and pastor to them, and that without him they would be unable to chart their course at sea or find their way through the jungles of Darien. So they abandoned the attack, carried Drake to the ships, and withdrew to the little island of Bastimentos, where they made camp until Drake, who was also the ship's doctor, had cured his wound and was ready to resume his plans. One day a Spanish officer came to Bastimentos bearing a white flag. He wanted to know if it was true that Drake had led the attack. "Just as you have heard it," answered Drake, who received him, "I am Francis Drake, at your orders." The officer was filled with amazement and delight: he had seen Drake with his own eyes. And Drake, always the perfect gentleman, insisted that the visitor dine with him. Seated at the table, Drake plied his guest with the excellent wine that was part of the booty seized in the raids. Like two great lords, they shook hands. "Until we meet again, when I come back to Nombre de Dios." At Cartagena he seized a fine ship. As it was large, he put all his men aboard it. He called a carpenter whom he trusted completely, and said to him in secret: "Don't let anybody know about this, but tonight I want you to scuttle the Swan." The Swan was the ship in which he had spent the three best years of his life. His men loved it as one loves a faithful dagger. Drake reasoned: this, which was like a part of myself, no longer serves me; let it rest on the floor of the bay. When the ship began to sink, he was the first to lament the mishap: "God in Heaven, the *Swan* is sinking!" And then: "But what can we do? It is the will of God." And they all boarded the new ship. Then came his meeting with the Frenchman, Captain Têtu. They greeted each other with cannon shots that threatened to blow their vessels out of the sea, but when they discovered that they were both pirates, they embraced each other, joined forces, and on their last night together sat up until after midnight dividing the gold and silver which they weighed out on a Roman balance.

The best story of all, naturally, is that of the assault on the mule train. Drake had to wait over five months, keeping his men busy with minor depredations, forays into the Magdalena, and exploration of the coasts until the fleet should arrive. When the time was near he sent away his ships and made his way into the hills with most of his freebooters. The runaway Negroes helped him. On the summit of a hill there was a tree. "From the top," they told him, "you can see the Pacific Ocean." "Let me be the first to see it." Like a red-haired cat he climbed lightly up the branches and looked out over the sea. On that day in 1573 he felt himself another Balboa. He was the first Englishman to gaze upon these waters. "That shall be my sea," he mused; "I shall sail it, and fight the Spaniards for it." It was a vow. Then, they say, he went into the city of Panama. As a boy he had been page to the Duchess of Feria, and he spoke Spanish like a native; so now he acted as witness before a notary, and requested and received permission to leave the city as though he were from Medina del Campo or Valladolid. The night of the assault was thrilling. The mule-train traveled at night to avoid the heat of day. Hidden in the bushes along the path, the pirates barely breathed, and every now and then laid their ears to the ground to see if they could hear the tinkling of the little bells the mules wore on their collars. In order to recognize the members of their own band in the darkness, the men were wearing their shirts on the outside of their clothes. The mules arrived. There were over two hundred, and not one got away. The spoils were magnificent — silver from Potosí and the pearls, gold, and jewels of a rich Spaniard. It was like the story of Ali Baba. The account run up at San Juan de Ulua was being settled with interest.

Drake reached Plymouth one Sunday. The people were at church, but the news of his approach seemed to travel through the air. Drake's ships have been sighted! There come Francis and his forty thieves! When the minister raised his eyes from prayer the church was empty. In the twinkling of an eye, all Plymouth was at the harbor. People's eyes were wet with tears of happiness. The Sunday sun had never shone so bright on Plymouth; it was the sun of El Dorado. The emerald sea turned to pearls as it broke against the dark, shining hulls of the ships. The pirate's beard gleamed like a ruby, and his eyes flashed with the sparks struck from the flint of his victories.

"He reached London," wrote Fray Pedro Simón of the Order of Saint Francis, "after the most prosperous pillage and voyage, and he was received with the applause that usually accompanies wealth, for even the Queen gave excessive demonstrations and attentions hardly in keeping with her royal standing; but, after all, she was a woman, and some of this may have originated in the greed and desire to bury her hands up to the elbow in the rich booty brought back by the Protestant; this is evidenced by the fact that, urged on by these rich spoils, he immediately planned another voyage, with all the ships and men and supplies we shall see, paid for by what was plundered from our coasts."

Drake's career progressed in prodigious fashion. He set to sea again with the Queen's ships. On the flagship he carried musicians to entertain him, and plate of silver and gold. He had to travel in style because he represented England. Whither was he going? Nobody knew. Pirates follow their captain's orders, and ask no questions. But he was going — let no one overhear this — to make the trip around the world. To sail that sea he had gazed on when he climbed to the tree-top on the Isthmus of Panama. And he went around the world. He made raids in

Chile, in Peru, and in Mexico. He placed a bronze tablet in California. Near Quito he captured the ship *Nuestra Señora de la Concepción.* The foul-mouthed Spaniards dubbed him "Cacafuego" (Shitfire). "The value of the booty was never ascertained; the exact figures were known only to Drake and Queen Elizabeth." A certain Doughty, a mysterious gentleman who had great backing at the court, told the crew, between beakers of ale, that he bore letters from the Queen giving him equal command of the expedition with Drake. He tried to stir up trouble for the captain. Drake gave him a drumhead trial, found him guilty, and himself hanged him from the yardarm so that everyone would understand that only one person was in command: Francis Drake.

This voyage around the world was England's great exploit during this century. After having crossed all the seas, the ships returned to England laden with spoils. In the opinion of some, Drake was on a par with Vasco da Gama, Columbus, Vespucci, and Magellan: the first had only sailed around the Cape of Good Hope; the second had discovered the Bahamas, Santo Domingo, Cuba, and Darien; the third reached the coast of Brazil, and the fourth had sailed through the strait that bears his name. But Drake had sailed around the world. The Duke of Florence hung Drake's portrait among those of the great princes of the day. From the wood of Drake's ship, *The Golden Hind,* a chair was made that is preserved as a relic at Oxford University. The Queen presented him with a sword bearing this inscription: WHOSO STRIKETH AT THEE, DRAKE, STRIKETH ALSO AT US. Drake presented to the Queen a brooch of emeralds. And these emeralds of Muzo, which Drake had plundered in the Pacific, were the jewels the Queen wore on New Year's Day.

The Spanish Ambassador was pale with indignation. He denounced everything Drake had brought back as being loot from the ships of King Philip. The Queen replied: "The Ambassador is right. Let us see what Drake has brought so we may return to the King what is his. Let a magistrate draw up an inventory." And for this task she designated Edmund Tremayne of Syden-

ham, in whom she had implicit confidence. As to how he fulfilled his commission, we may judge from the letter he himself
wrote to Sir Francis Walsingham:

"To give you some understanding how I have proceeded with
Mr. Drake: I have at no time entered into the account to know
more of the value of the treasure than he made me acquainted with;
and to say truth I persuaded him to impart to me no more than
need be, for so I saw him commanded in Her Majesty's behalf that
he should reveal the certainty to no man living. I have only taken
notice of so much as he has revealed, and the same I have seen to
be weighed, registered and packed. And to observe Her Majesty's
commands for the ten thousand pounds, we agreed he should take
it out of the portion that was landed secretly, and to remouve the
same out of the place before my son and I should come to the
weighing and registering of what was left, and so it was done, and no
creature living by me made privy to it but himself. . . ."

A few days later, Drake was made a knight; with this, the
family entered the ranks of the nobility. Shortly afterwards he
married the daughter and heiress of Sir George Sydenham; in
her manor house, with her hooped skirt of brocade, her lovely
flower hands, her lace ruff and necklaces, Elizabeth Sydenham
looked like a queen. Sir Francis was elected to a seat in Parliament. Lady Elizabeth Douglas Fuller Eliott-Drake, one of the
last-flowering branches on the family tree of Sir Francis, has
published a handsome volume entitled *The Family and Heirs
of Sir Francis Drake*, in which all these memories are evoked. It
carries exquisite prints of the embossed golden goblets the
Queen bestowed upon Drake, and curious details such as this:

"The chests of coins and boxes of jewels which Tremayne made
note of were deposited first in a tower near Saltash, and later in that
of London; but the sum that Drake was advised to remove privately
was left in Radford in charge of his friend, Christopher Harris. It
has been suggested that in reality these ten thousand pounds were
by way of compensation for the losses he, Hawkins, and his mates
had suffered during the trading expedition of 1548, when their cargo
was treacherously seized by the governor of San Juan de Ulua. If this
was the case, as the Queen had, on this occasion, been one of the

adventurers, it is not unlikely that a considerable part of the money hidden in Radford passed quietly into her royal hands. . . ."

With all this prestige, Drake could now plan a large-scale venture into the Caribbean. Everybody wanted to share in it. The merchants of London subscribed seven ships. The other ports of England followed their example. The Queen contributed two of her own. Drake had thirty craft under his command; never had a freebooter enterprise assumed such proportions: 2,300 soldiers and sailors, all well armed. This was a life-or-death undertaking for the cause of England. The Queen's favorite poet, Sir Philip Sidney, that flower of knighthood, ran away from London to join Drake. Elizabeth, who was jealous of her poet and kept him at court like a favorite ornament, flew into a rage. Her messengers raced to Plymouth to bring back the youth. Drake returned him to them with great pleasure; he wanted no one cutting in on the glory of this adventure. The jealousy of the Queen and that of the pirate were in agreement in this instance.

The boats set out at leisurely speed. Drake's plan was not to leave one city of the Caribbean unscathed. He made a brief stop at Vigo, and another at the Cape Verde Islands, where he set fire to the city of Santiago; only the hospital was left standing. This was a piece of unnecessary brutality, for which Drake may not have been responsible; it is impossible to say whether the troops were moved to this violence because they found no gold or because they found too much wine. That there might be no repetition of such hot-headedness, Drake exacted an oath from his men, battalion by battalion. And the ships set their course toward the Caribbean. "The worst of it was that Drake was going to begin hostilities without war having been declared," writes Corbett in his admirable history of the period, and he adds: "But in this he only anticipated the enemy. For a long time it had been an open secret that King Philip was making his preparations to attack the independence of England. The only crime of the Queen's admiral was beating the Spaniards at their own game."

The Caribbean gave Drake a grim reception: yellow fever. Several hundred of his men died of the plague. The original plan to raze the entire coast had to be scaled down. But the first objective was carried out with complete success — an assault on the oldest city of the Caribbean, the city where Columbus's remains reposed, the first lamp lighted by Spain in the New World, Santo Domingo. In reality nobody had ever made such an attempt before, its defenses seeming inexpugnable. When word reached the city that Drake's fleet was approaching, the Spaniards sank two ships at the mouth of the harbor, practically sealing off the entrance. And those manning the cannon never took their eyes from this spot. Drake knew that it was impossible to take a city in the Caribbean by frontal attack; it was like trying to ward off cannon balls with a wooden shield. So by night he put his army ashore on a beach far from the city. Then when the ships drew up within range of the shore batteries, and the artillery was leveling off against them, Drake's infantry fell upon the city from the rear, and in the twinkling of an eye Santo Domingo was in his hands. The nuns took refuge in the hills, where they lived like frightened birds. Maids and matrons fled without even stopping to put on their shoes, while Drake's drums and fifes played a victory march as his troops poured into the city's plaza. The cannon he had taken in Santiago now helped him to spread terror among the Spaniards.

From the point of view of plunder, Santo Domingo was a disappointment, but the effect on the Spaniards' morale was shattering; few things ever affected King Philip as did this. However, the city was no longer the center of affairs it had been in the days of the Conquest. The great trading mart, the citadel, was now on the mainland: Cartagena. Santo Domingo had become the intellectual center of the Antilles. In 1538 Pope Paul III had raised the college founded by the Dominicans in 1510 to the category of a university, and it now enjoyed the same privileges as the University of Salamanca and Alcalá de Henares. This same rank was given to the institution founded years before by Hernando de Gorjón. These were the two first universities of the New World. One of the first bishops sent there was Alessandro Geraldini, the Italian humanist, who shares with Peter Martyr and Lucio Marineo Siculo the honor of having brought the Renaissance to the Spanish world. It was he who described the building of the cathedral in Sapphic Adonic verses, probably the first written in Latin in America. When Drake entered Santo Domingo the captains of the Spanish armies were all men of learning; they could carry on a conversation in Latin, but they did not know how to light the fuse of an arquebus. The names of the four captains were: Licentiate Fernández de Mercado, Licentiate Villafañé, Licentiate Aliago, Licentiate Acero. As though Drake were to be stopped by diplomas! The soldiers swarmed through the streets looking for booty. There was nothing. Fine clothing, and furniture like that to be found in the great houses of Spain, but not even a silver dinner service. For the heat of the tropics the hidalgos preferred china or glassware. Rubbish, grumbled the soldiers.

Ransom negotiations got under way. The sum Drake set was out of all reason. Each day that went by, he set fire to a block of the city, as though to lend persuasion to his words. His men found their task difficult; the houses were of masonry, and the fire made slow progress; they had to use cannon to help bring the walls down. By noon the heat was unbearable. Yet every twenty-four hours another block lay in ashes. The first day Drake had sent a Negro with his message. The sending of such an emissary was considered an insult by the white Spaniards, and one of the more insolent ran him through with a lance. The Negro managed to drag himself back to Drake, and died at his feet. Drake selected two Dominican friars from among the prisoners, and with a great ruffle of drums and blaring of trumpets he hanged them in sight of the Spaniards. Every day, he sent word, I shall hang two prisoners until you put to death the officer who lanced the Negro. What could they do? The Spaniards hanged their own officer.

The soldiers kept on searching. Sometimes they found jewel boxes, gold coins that had been thrown into the wells. The pillage of the churches was more remunerative; not a chalice, monstrance, candlestick, or censer was left. The holy vessels

were saved out and went to decorate the sideboards of gentle
men in London. "We burned all the wooden images, we broke
and destroyed whatever we found in the churches, and we took
much silver, money, and pearls that had been hidden in wells
and other places."

But Drake could barely squeeze out a ransom of 25,000 ducats.
The fact of the matter was that the island could not raise any
more. It took thirty-one days of struggle to amass this sum.
Thirty-one blocks of the city lay in cinders. And Drake left for
Cartagena de Indias.

The news of what had happened in Santo Domingo spread
like a prairie fire. Through the islands and on the mainland it
was told how the Dominican friars had been hanged, how the
soldiers had spat on the images of the Virgin, how the city had
been burned, and how not a bell had been left in the church
towers, nor a cannon in the fortress, nor a necklace or an emerald
in the family strong boxes. In New Granada fine armies of young
blades were mustered to go to the defense of Cartagena. Orders
were received from King Philip himself: they were to be on the
alert, for the Englishman was coming. Nobody in Cartagena
took the threat too seriously. Would the Englishman come?
Wouldn't he come? The priests sent out letters: For God's sake,
let them be ready, for the man was a scourge and he would not
spare the fortress of the New Kingdom. But how could he break
through the defenses of the city? The bay had two entrances:
the Boca Chica was closed off by a chain; the Boca Grande was
defended by forts and cannon. The señoritas remembered when
they had seen the pirate for the first time from the house tops,
and they said, he will come, he will come. And they waited with
curiosity, fear, excitement. There were rogations, processions.
From the pulpits, sermons were launched against the heretic.
And the soldiers laid bets: By God, By the Devil. . . .

And then the ships appeared!

> . . . *of funereal color*
> *Were pennons, banners, flags.*

The Indians had sown all the roads with poison-coated arrow-heads. By mule, by canoe, through gullies, on the highways, there was the terrified rush of nuns, children, women, and old men to take refuge in the hills and woods — please God they are not bitten by snakes! — and to hide whatever treasure they possessed.

The ways of the heretics were incomprehensible. The attack on Santo Domingo took place the first of January of 1585 — "for the glory of God and the honor of the Queen," said Mr. Mason. It was Ash Wednesday when they reached Cartagena, as though purposely to offend Our Lord. It was known to all that Drake never failed to eat meat on Friday. And when he sat down to the table he never failed to say prayers in English and to read the Bible, that Bible of Edward VI.

Poor Don Pedro Vique, who was in charge of the defense of Cartagena, did what he could: he threw up a stone trench a yard and a half high, mounted four cannon on the ground, and armed two galleys with rams and ten extra pieces of artillery. He placed three hundred musketeers, one hundred pikemen, and two hundred Indian archers at the most strategic points. But Drake, who was the Devil himself, was too much for Don Pedro. He repeated what he had done in Santo Domingo. When his ships reached Boca Grande he had already put his men ashore on the peninsula. The landing was made at ten o'clock on a night that was blacker than a pocket. The first knowledge the defenders received of this landing was fire from the English muskets. Don Pedro flew to defend the approaches by land, but his forces were as nothing against the powerful squadrons of Drake. Don Pedro describes the scene in his own words: "I set out with my sword drawn, shouting and calling on my men to follow, and when I was out of the trench and combating the enemy I turned my head to see if our soldiers were following me, and I saw that instead of obeying my orders they had turned their backs and were running away as fast as they could." The only voice to be heard among the soldiers was one shouting "Retire, gentlemen!" They all obeyed. In his letter to the King,

Don Pedro was still sputtering with indignation: "It is a shame, but I had the most pusillanimous vassals."

Not only had Drake captured the prize jewel of the Spanish crown, but now he had the strongest city on the mainland. He committed only one unforgivable error, according to an English historian: not having raised the British flag over the walls and fortresses of Tierra Firme for all time. But Drake was there to get the gold and carry it to his Queen — he knew her. He refused to discuss ransom terms with anyone but the governor and the bishop. When they arrived he received them courteously and affably. Drake asked for a million ducats' ransom. If it was not forthcoming, he would set fire to the city. The sum was unreasonable, they protested. Drake answered: "Observe that there has been no plundering, as there was in Santo Domingo, and this is the capital of Tierra Firme." And that was the truth. The Spaniards had had time to remove everything from the city except a skin or two of wine or oil, and some iron and soap. The city's wealth had been buried in the woods. The discussion over the ransom was long drawn out. There were days when Drake was on the point of losing his patience. Once, going through the governor's desk, he found a communication from the King referring to him as a corsair. This was intolerable. "One day," he said, "I shall meet the King face to face, I shall throw this lie into his teeth and take satisfaction with my own hands." The negotiations dragged on for a month. Drake had begun his block-burning system, and three naves of the cathedral had already been burned. At last he agreed to the figure of 110,000 ducats. For everything he received he issued a receipt, written in Latin, which the governor filed away in his archives.

There were already a thousand and one reasons for Spain and England to be at each other's throats. But there was one that was definitive, and this was Mary Stuart, who after twenty years of imprisonment finally lost her head, not because she had gone mad in the midst of so many Protestants, but because it was

155

severed from her shoulders by the executioner at Fotheringay Castle. A few minutes before the execution, the Dean of Peterborough exhorted Mary to change her faith, beginning his speech: "The hand of death rests upon your head, and the ax has been laid to the root of the tree — " "Prithee, Master Dean," Mary interrupted him, "do not torment me; I do not wish to hear you; I am firm in my Catholic faith." When the headman's ax carried out its brutal task, the last link had been severed between Protestant England and Catholic Spain. The shipyards of Spain were working day and night, turning out ships for the Invincible Armada with all possible speed. England should have been laying her defense plans, but the thought of authorizing the expenditure of a farthing kept the Queen awake all night. The only one who hit upon a solution was Sir Francis Drake: to slip into the port of Cádiz and burn King Philip's ships. Cádiz could not be a harder nut to crack than Cartagena had been, nor the Mediterranean rougher than the Caribbean. So he slipped into Cádiz, fired the ships, robbed the warehouses, and with a fair wind made off to sea again as though this were just part of the day's work. No great power ever suffered a worse surprise. The Spanish admiral fell ill and died of the shock. It took Philip a whole year to recover from the blow and refit his fleet. History says this was how Drake singed King Philip's whiskers, as he had vowed to do in Cartagena, and, at the same time, dealt Admiral Santa Cruz a knock-out blow. But, besides, on his way home, he captured a Portuguese ship, the *San Felipe*. It would be hard to say which was the more important for England's future — what happened at Cádiz, or the taking of this ship. The *San Felipe* was carrying a cargo of spices, silk, money, and Negroes from the Orient. Among the captain's papers Drake found the complete key to Portugal's dealings with the Far East. This gave rise to the formation of the East India Company — that is to say, of the British Empire. "One might well ask whether, if it had not been for Drake, the crown of India would ever have rested on the brow of Queen Victoria."

A year went by. The moment was approaching when the question of the dominion of the seas was to be decided. The

Invincible Armada was moving against England, commanded by the Duke of Medina-Sidonia, a gentleman who got seasick the minute he set foot aboard a ship, and who could not tell the difference between a shallop and a caravel. He tried in vain to avoid the responsibility thrust upon him, but to his arguments Philip replied: "These matters are not in the hands of man, but of God; the one who will lead our ships to victory over the Protestants will not be you, but God." England, on the other hand, made use of admirals who had received their training in the Antilles. The fleet was in command of Lord Howard, with Sir Francis Drake and John Hawkins as vice-admirals. But luck played no small part in England's victory. The Queen was reluctant to lay out the money to equip the fleet; the admirals encountered serious difficulties in supplying their troops. The greater part of the ships belonged to the merchants of Plymouth and of London. When the Spanish ships hove in sight, Lord Howard and Drake were having a game of bowls. When the look-out arrived with the startling news that the Spanish fleet had been sighted, Drake had the ball in his hand. All eyes turned toward him. He calmly remarked: "There is no hurry, gentlemen; there is plenty of time to defeat Spain; let us finish the game." The battle took place, with the defeat and dispersal of the Spanish fleet. The highest-ranking prisoner taken was Don Pedro Valdés. He was handed over to Drake, who treated him like a guest in his home. Don Pedro painted a huge portrait of himself which still adorns the walls of Sir Francis's manor house. In all the churches of England, services of thanksgiving were held for the victory over the Armada. For years banners and trophies commemorating the event hung from the vault of St. Paul's; the best were those captured by Drake's unerring hand.

If Drake's childhood lullaby was the sound of the waves that rocked the boats of Plymouth, the song of his youth and his manhood was that of the Caribbean winds. It was there that his untrammeled genuis found full scope for its audacity, there that he learned how to wipe out reverses with strokes of daring. Bandit, navigator, soldier, pirate, statesman — all these callings he learned on that indomitable sea. And with his eyes fixed on the Caribbean, he now set out on the voyage from which he was never to return.

A huge fleet had been assembled for this expedition: twenty-seven ships, twenty-five hundred men. The Queen had given the joint command to Francis Drake and John Hawkins. Since the days of San Juan de Ulua the two cousins had not set out together for their sea. "God made them, and the Devil brought them together," said the Spaniards. Drake, as always, was on the side of boldness; Hawkins, as always, or more than ever, counseled prudence. In Guadalupe, Hawkins began to slow down his speed, and they lost one ship there to the Spaniards. Another, which had become separated, arrived almost a wreck. Things were off to a bad start. The Spaniards put the crew of the captured vessel on the rack, and they confessed everything: the main body of the ships was with Drake, bound for Puerto Rico. And while Hawkins lagged, the defenses of Puerto Rico were being strengthened. Drake had taught the Spaniards to be on guard.

The first attempt of the English to assault the city was disastrous. A cannon ball hit Drake's own cabin, killing one of his best friends and wounding another. The worst of all was that Hawkins was dying — dying, as was his destiny, in the Caribbean. His last words were for the Queen, and they were full of sadness; he told her of the failure of the expedition, and he left her a legacy of two thousand pounds to make up for her losses in the enterprise. There was no time to be wasted on funeral ceremonies. Drake attempted a second assault; the Spaniards had blocked all the entrances, and the commander of the fortress was shrewd and divined Drake's thoughts. Wherever Drake attempted to advance, the Spaniards were ready for him. He lost many of his men. It was useless to persist. These were no longer the times of Don Pedro Vique. Drake had to make off, without a pound of booty, and leaving many dead behind him.

At Río Hacha he found nothing. The news of his arrival had spread, and wherever he went there were only deserted villages. Baskerville set fire to settlements for miles around. Río Hacha was left in ashes. At Ranchería they had a little better luck:

Drake got pearls enough there to pay for the outfitting of the fleet. But there was no ransom money. Santa Marta was deserted. He did not dare make an attempt on Cartagena. And the ships of the King of Spain — this time there were many of them — were encircling him from a distance. They were afraid to close in, but there they were. Nombre de Dios was but a shadow of its former self. They found nothing there, so they set fire to it. Baskerville started out overland with troops for an attack on Panama. They were caught in a storm, their powder got wet, the Spanish army came out to meet them, and the only way to save themselves was a swift rightabout-face.

This was the melancholy procedure of the last expedition. Drake knew he could not return to England with empty hands. His services in the raid on Cádiz and in defeating the attack of the Invincible Armada had never been properly rewarded. The Queen was frightened by his audacity, and there were many who, like her, looked askance at deeds of violence. Drake had been out of favor at the court for months on this account. The only thing that could redeem him would be to return in triumph, his ships bursting with gold. But he had taken no booty and his men were dying of dysentery. He himself had been attacked by it. But he feigned that all was well, saying to them: "We're going to Trujillo in Honduras, and you will see how we shall take more booty there than we ever dreamed of." Drake was still Drake. The young men greeted the suggestion with shouts of enthusiasm.

Drake shut himself up in his cabin; he could feel death hovering over him. And as with Hawkins, it carried him off, on January 28, 1595. The new recruits, the old hands, looked at one another in helpless terror. When the body had been placed in its weighted coffin and consigned to Drake's sea, the sound of the cannon firing a final salute echoed in the ears of the crew with a dismal and hollow sound. Their guiding light had sunk into the sea. The survivors were only shades, and it was a group of frightened shades that made its way back to England. Through the islands of the Caribbean, through Tierra Firme, the news rang like a triumphant peal. He was poisoned, he was poisoned!

Lope de Vega wrote a long poem celebrating the death of Drake. It was published with a sonnet of praise by Miguel de Cervantes and a letter of presentation by Don Francisco de Borja. The poem was entitled *La Dragontea*, and Lope explained that: "Each time the name Dragon is mentioned, and everything referring to it, it is to be understood that Francis Drake is meant." Two hundred, three hundred, almost four hundred years have passed, and the shade of this pirate still wanders uneasily about the Caribbean. In Venezuela, when children are naughty, they are told: "If you don't behave, the Englishman will come — Drake will come and eat you!" And terrified, the children quaver: "Mamma, I'll be good, I promise, but don't call the Englishman." But the children of Offenburg in Germany think differently. There stands a statue bearing this inscription: "*To Sir Francis Drake who brought the potato to Europe, A. D. 1586.*" Thus to the children of this "Aryan" land Sir Francis is a kind of Santa Claus, and perhaps in moments of enthusiasm they say to their mothers: "Mamma, when I am big I'm going to be like good old Drake who went to America to bring us potatoes."

In the schools along the Caribbean the children are taught that back in the sixteenth century there was a bandit by the name of Drake who amused himself by hanging monks and profaning the image of the Virgin; the children cross themselves in horror. And if they should chance to visit England (as happened to the author of this book) they will be shown a table in London "at which Queen Elizabeth was pleased to dine with Drake." This is interesting because it shows that history has two sides, and everything depends on which side of the fence you happen to be on.

Father Simón, in his history of Drake, found the following explanation of his success:

"If we consider these events from a Christian point of view, we may say that they were the same as when a father punishes the mischievousness of a child with a stick, and then throws the stick into the fire. And this stick was Francis Drake, through whom God in His infinite justice punished the transgressions of His Christians who were living thoughtlessly. And He then threw the stick into Hell. And they were improved by the punishment, though they lamented the slight loss of what the enemy had stolen from them at times, which was as though God had taken away their gold and silver from them to throw it on the dungheap of England; but this was so that the Catholics should put their trust in Him rather than in riches. All these considerations and the food for Christian thought contained in them may be found, better than we can put it, in Chapter VI of the Second Book of the Maccabees, which runs as follows . . ."

For his part, Drake looked upon himself as the instrument of God to punish those lands to which the Spaniards had carried the "poisonous infection of Popery." These are his words, taken from *The World Encompassed:*

"There is not a city like Lima, Panama, or Mexico, not a town or village, or a house in these provinces that is not corrupted with all the sins of Sodom. The pope and his anti-Christian bishops, employing their immoral methods, work with tooth and nail to hide in darkness the light of the Gospel. In the city of Lima, not two months before our arrival, there were certain people, to the number of twelve, who were seized, questioned and condemned for professing the faith. Six of these were tied to the stake and burned; the remainder are in prison, and will drink of the same cup in a few days. . . . Finally, we received news of a rich ship which was loaded with silver and gold, and on its way to Panama, and we followed it. . . ."

In the final sentence above, Drake is referring to the adventure in which he took among the booty the emerald brooch he presented to Queen Elizabeth.

IX

EL DORADO, THE BEGINNING AND THE END OF THE GOLDEN AGE

Elizabeth was two years and eight months old when her mother was executed. Neither shame nor resentment ate like a canker at her pride. . . . Nor did the scaffold matter seriously: it was an instrument of state to which the great families of the age paid tribute in turn. A Mantuan, describing England in the middle of the century, remarked that "many persons, members of whose families have been hanged and quartered, are accustomed to boast of it. Lately, a foreigner, having asked one English captain if anyone of his family had been hanged and quartered, was answered, 'Not that he knew of.' Another Englishman whispered to the foreigner, 'Don't be surprised, for he is not a gentleman.'"

J. E. NEALE

At the beginning of the century, when the conquistadors were plunging through forests and over mountains as though the Devil were at their heels, the spur that pricked them on was El Dorado. The tale of that Indian chief who had plunged into the gold-covered lake set Spaniards and Germans rushing through Ecuador, Colombia, and Venezuela, over savannas and wastelands, torrid valleys and frozen heights. They all finally came together at the presumed goal of their wanderings — the plains of Bogotá, where there were no gold mines, and the inhabitants were countryfolk who sowed their potatoes, fashioned vessels of clay, wove blankets of cotton, and dug salt from the bowels of a mountain. Such gold as they had, they had received from other peoples in exchange for their baskets of salt and their cotton blankets. El Dorado continued to be an elusive will-o'-the-wisp. The conquistadors turned their backs and set off in search of new adventures. Only one cherished the dream, Don Gonzalo Jiménez de Quesada.

Jiménez de Quesada was the first to reach the plains of Bogotá. He carried out the conquest, founded the city on August 6, 1538, in the name of the Emperor Charles V, and fashioned the New Kingdom of Granada, which was the name given to the lands later to be called Colombia. When this took place, Quesada was about the same age as the century, or a little older. He was eloquent, smart of appearance, and extravagant. He had his own ideas. He returned to Spain, traveled through Italy, wrote books of history and accounts of his trips. But his thoughts were elsewhere — fixed on El Dorado. He was made *adelantado*, marshal. He returned to America as governor of Cartagena. But the seacoast did not satisfy him; the high plains called to him, the uplands, that strange inland region where he found a mine of emeralds. And all the time he cherished his dreams.

He returned to Bogotá. Up the steep streets that climbed the hillside he went thoughtfully. His once jet beard was now gray with touches of white. More than sixty years had passed over his head. His legs moved clumsily. As happens with all riders, who look so fine on horseback, he was awkward afoot. Affable and diplomatic, with his calm voice he helped to smooth out the differences that arose between hidalgos and the judges of the Royal Tribunal. He no longer swaggered or boasted or threw money about in the taverns as when his forty years had rested lightly and gallantly on his shoulders like a Cordovan cape. In the armchair at his lonely house (for he had no family in these parts), he read and wrote sermons. But his dream was ever-present.

One day he made up his mind and requested permission to conquer El Dorado. He wished to leave it as an inheritance to his heir. Over there, behind those mountains that the dawn tinted with gold and the sunset enveloped in gold, there must be lands as rich as those of Peru and Mexico. More than half of America lay to the east of the Andes, spread out over prairies and forests like an endless sheet of emerald. What was in those jungles? What was carried in the waters of those thousand rivers that rushed down the mountainside into the Orinoco and the Amazon, where the mystery — perhaps the destiny — of the New World lay? That was surely the land of El Dorado. Because thirty years before, he had carried out the conquest of the New Kingdom of Granada, he was universally respected, and it was assumed that he had a basis for his belief. His request was granted. He was now seventy years old. What he was about to attempt was sheer madness. But — as happens so often with madmen — the gravity of his countenance and the dignified reserve of his attitude seemed a discreet curtain that modestly veiled his good sense! And so all the Sanchos of the New Kingdom eagerly followed this Don Quixote, with their horses, their donkeys, their swine, their chickens, their Indians, and their slaves.

It is touching to think of this crowd intoxicated with the dream of burying their arms up to the elbow in the golden sands of an old man's vision. It was not now as it had been in the days of the early explorations, when only soldiers undertook these tasks; now it was whole families, women with babes at their breasts, carrying their household goods and their songs with them, climbing the mountainside, eastward bound. It was a whole people on the march, a migration of the deluded. Along the mountain trails there moved the conglomerate mass of horses and people, the pigs grunting, the Indians staggering under their loads, the Negroes shivering with cold. As they came over the crest of the highest hills, there before the eyes of the hungry people opened up the limitless green plain of the east, crisscrossed by the glasslike threads of rivers flowing into the Orinoco. Eyes and minds were suspended in a joyful silence. This was a romantic people. And, for all his grave exterior, the leader smiled with the smile of a grandfather beside the cradle of an infant.

The end was disaster. Hunger, death, the murderous knife that would have buried itself in the back of the general himself; and so it went on until the last horse was devoured and only a handful of the vast throng that started out managed to make their way back to Santa Fe de Bogotá.

El Dorado was an invention of the Indians to rid themselves of the Spaniards; the shrewder of the chroniclers had so understood it, and to everyone in Santa Fe with average intelligence it was self-evident. Things are always so crystal-clear when seen in retrospect. Jiménez de Quesada was more than aged. His ulcerated skin was falling from his flesh. He could hardly stir from his chair. He had lost everything he had. Yet . . . he continued to dream of El Dorado. He was incurable; the older he grew the more stubbornly he clung to his illusions. He was approaching eighty, and he returned to the wars. He directed the last battles of his life from the litter in which he was borne by his men. When the hour came to settle his affairs and depart this life, he said: "I believe in the resurrection of the dead." And he left to his niece, to that exemplary María de Oruña, the daughter of Andrea Jiménez de Quesada, who was living in Spain, one single legacy: the dream of El Dorado. As for his books, he willed them to the library of a convent.

When María de Oruña received the news of the death of that astounding uncle who had died in the mountains of America, where the hills are made of salt and emeralds, she did not hesitate. "Antonio," she said to her husband, Captain Antonio de Berrio, "we must go and claim the inheritance of Uncle Gonzalo. Ask to be made governor of El Dorado." And straight to the court went Antonio de Berrio and María de Oruña. They were fashioned from the same clay and impregnated with the same spirit as Jiménez de Quesada: mad as hatters. Antonio had been a cavalryman in the war against the Moors of Granada, and he had put one of the Moorish kings to death; he had fought in Italy, in Flanders, and in Lombardy; he had been a captain in the infantry and the cavalry, warden of fortresses — in short, a soldier of the King. His Majesty named him General of El Dorado and Governor of Guiana. On his arrival in America he was enchanted by the beauties of the Orinoco. He pointed its waters out to his son: "They will be yours." On the island of Trinidad he founded the city of San José de Oruña. Then, on the banks of the Orinoco, Santo Thomé. The governor spent four years fashioning a little republic to his own liking. And all the time his ear was alert for the information he needed — the whereabouts of El Dorado.

Report had it that the city of Manoa, the capital of El Dorado, was on the shore of a lake called Parimé. In the background was a shining hill of gold. The city was said to be the largest of all that the Indians had built in America. The legend was turning into reality. Don Antonio sent these details to the court of Castile by Domingo de Vera. In Toledo, in the Mancha — Don Quixote's native heath — there was a stirring among the hidalgos, who wished to participate in the conquest of El Dorado, just as the trusting dwellers of Bogotá had followed Jiménez de Quesada. Domingo exhibited necklaces, discs, and earrings of gold as samples of what was to be found for the taking in Guiana. Old soldiers, squires, nobles, a son of the president of the Royal Council for the Indies — all applied for places in the ranks. Married men sold their property and business and embarked with their wives and children. Over two thousand persons sailed for the island of Trinidad and Guiana.

History repeated itself. They had come in search of the fabled city of Manoa; what they found was jungle and swamps, hunger and pestilence. Chigoes and worms ate them alive; at night voracious crickets tore away bits of their noses and ears, and the victims were too weak even to utter a cry. Berrio, too, was marked for assassination, but friars managed to stay the murderous hands. There were days in this tiny little colony when fourteen people were buried in a single day. To add to their woes, there was the menace of Indian war-clubs and axes. This was El Dorado.

Captain Berrio was the type of Spaniard who is a match for adversity. His stubbornness and his dream lent him strength. Jiménez de Quesada had assigned to him, as the mission of his life, the conquest of El Dorado. When Berrio married María de Oruña he married the chimera. But the strange thing is that in this Guiana of El Dorado — which was nothing but a green hell — Berrio encountered an Englishman possessed by the same madness. This was another son of Devon, the homeland of Hawkins and Drake; he was no adventurer, however, but one of the outstanding gentlemen of the court. He had been educated at

Oxford, and was extraordinarily endowed. His poems are to be found in all anthologies, his speeches are famous, his *History of the World* is one of the monuments of the Elizabethan Age. Moreover, he was handsome, gallant, and a fine soldier. With his large, deep-set eyes, his oval face with its pointed beard, broad forehead, the long, slender fingers of his courtier's hand, as he appears in the portrait in the National Gallery, he might have been one of the gentlemen painted by El Greco in his immortal *Funeral of the Count of Orgaz.* He was Sir Walter Ralegh. The Queen had taken Ralegh's heart and laid it on the balance of her affections. It is impossible to say which weighed heavier, Ralegh or the Earl of Essex; it is a delicate problem that involves the romantic legend of the Virgin Queen.

When he was seventeen, Ralegh joined an army of volunteers that went to France to fight on the side of the Huguenots against the Catholics. In this heated religious fray the boy risked his life every day for four years. He returned to London with the glory of a common soldier, but as he was well born, he went to the Middle Temple. This, in other ages, had been the proving ground for knights; now, it was where young men familiarized themselves with the mysteries of the law. But Ralegh did not study law; he read books on history, and those of Spain in the language of Castile. He came to know the New World through the extraordinary *Relations* of the chroniclers. Drake knew that Spain was the enemy because his mariner's sense told him so; Ralegh became aware of it through his reading. The soldier now allowed himself only five hours a day for sleep and rest; the remainder of his days and nights were spent poring over books until the call of war led him to the field of battle once more.

England did not fight Spain face to face; she helped the rebels in the Low Countries. Philip II did not fight England face to face; he gave aid to the Irish rebels. The reasons were religious, political, and economic; in each of the three fields the rivalry of the two kingdoms was manifest. Ralegh set forth to fight Spain in the Netherlands with the troops of the Prince of Orange. This experience was of brief duration. There was soon another enterprise that attracted him more, that of Sir Humphrey Gilbert, his half-brother. Sir Humphrey was the first to think of the conquest of America for England. He was not interested in smuggling, raiding, or pillaging: he desired to plant the Queen's standard in the lands of the New World. He was thinking, too, of finding the passage to the Orient, not through the Antilles but to the north. The Queen granted him a charter for six years. Sir Humphrey and Ralegh fitted out a fleet several times, but each time they were held back by adverse winds. All a man could do in those days was to kneel and pray to God for a favorable wind. Sir Humphrey was unfortunate to the end. Ralegh was to make another attempt later. But for the moment there was a more immediate opportunity to fight Spain and the Catholics: Ireland. Sir Humphrey Gilbert had fought in Ireland, too, and he left Ralegh certain useful lessons. When he had been governor of Munster there, after he had defeated the rebels, he had the prisoners marched to his tent between a double row of stakes on which the heads of their comrades were hung.

Philip had sent troops from Spain to assist the Irish rebels. Ralegh joined the Queen's forces under the command of the Earl of Ormonde. One day the earl took the mayor of Youghal prisoner, and hanged him from the roof-tree of his own house. The rebels were fighting under the Desmonds' standard. When James Desmond fell into Ralegh's hands, he was tried, found guilty, and quartered, his head and legs being set over the gate of the city of Cork. The countryside of Ireland was laid waste, the cities were reduced to ashes. Against the landscape the gibbet reared its ugly structure. In the fortress of Carrig-a-Flyle, fifty Irishmen and nineteen Spaniards under the command of an Italian — the Pope having added his mite — were forced to surrender; they were all hanged.

Ralegh's star was now in the ascendant. He was one of the heroes of the Irish rebellion; he had reduced fortresses and put Spaniards to the knife without cost to the Queen. He was the friend of the poet Edmund Spenser. Leicester introduced him at court. A good Protestant soldier, who could turn a neat sonnet, young, handsome — these were the best credentials a man could carry at the Renaissance court of Queen Elizabeth. Ra-

legh began to acquire titles and honors. Of the lands confiscated
from the Irish Catholics, twelve thousand acres were assigned
to him. The nobles were eaten up with jealousy. Leicester, who
had been his sponsor at court, now introduced another young
man who soon restored things to their proper balance. This was
Robert Devereux, Earl of Essex. The Queen was fifty-three;
Ralegh, thirty-five; Essex, twenty — and youth won the day. Ralegh, who was captain of the guard, could hear, behind closed
doors, the laughter and merriment of the young man and the
Queen, to the sound of music and other pastimes. Essex never
returned to his home until the twittering of the birds announced
the dawn.

But Ralegh's life was not circumscribed by the court. His
mind was on other things, such as the conquest of America. He
came to an understanding with Drake, and obtained from the
Queen authority to conquer such barbarous and remote lands of
the New World as did not belong to any other Christian prince.
He planned an assault on Panama. He spent £40,000 of his own
fortune on preparations for the first large-scale colonization of
North America, to be known as Virginia in honor of the Queen.
He was still the gallant cavalier. But from Virginia Sir Walter
introduced a filthy vice, which Elizabeth found detestable: tobacco. By one of life's little ironies, however, tobacco became
king, and if Queen Elizabeth were to return to her court today
she would find people talking of Virginia tobacco as though it
were a home product.

But Sir Walter Ralegh, the inventor of Virginia, one day committed the worst social crime of which he could have been
guilty. The historian who said that "to love any woman other
than the Queen at the court of Elizabeth was sacrilege and
blasphemy" voiced the consensus. Nobody dared to confess that
he had fallen in love with someone not the Queen; love affairs
must be carried on furtively; when Essex married, the storm
rocked the palace for weeks. But Ralegh's crime was unforgivable: he paid suit to one of the ladies-in-waiting, and they
were secretly married. There came a day when the affair could
no longer be covered up, and when it reached the Queen's

knowledge her orders were inflexible: to the Tower with Sir Walter and his lady! From prison Sir Walter wrote the Queen the tenderest love letters, romantic beyond belief, and so hypocritical that one could not conceive them outside the atmosphere of the court. Suddenly he had a luminous thought: El Dorado!

If the Queen was willing, if she would release him from the Tower, he would go to Guiana and bring her such wealth as Pizarro had never found in Peru. The Spaniards were already on the scent; Antonio Berrio was looking for it. In a Spanish ship captured by Captain George Popham extensive correspondence had been discovered on "The New Dorado." All the books that Ralegh had read in the Middle Temple now became a glittering castle raised and adorned by his imagination. To him it was a self-evident fact that the descendants of the Incas had taken refuge in the Guianas with all their treasures. There was a great city there — the largest in the New World — Manoa, where Atahuallpa's successors still reigned. England had failed to realize that it was the gold of America that had brought the insignificant kingdom of Castile out of its obscurity and set it up above all the others of Europe. This was because Englishmen had not read the accounts of the conquest; Ralegh refers to them all, and to prove his point he quotes that paragraph in which López de Gomara tells of the palace of Huaynacapac, the direct ancestor of the Inca of Manoa:

"All the service of his house, table, and kitchen was of gold and silver, or of silver and copper to make it stronger. In his chambers there were hollow statues of gold that seemed those of giants, and life-sized figures of all the animals, birds, trees, and plants of the land, and all the fish to be found in the waters and seas of his kingdom. He also had ropes, sacks, baskets, and knapsacks of gold and silver, and piles of gold bars stacked up like kindling wood. In a word, there was not a thing in his land of which he did not have a replica in gold. And they even say that the Incas had a garden on an island near Puna to which they went when they wanted to be near the sea, where the vegetables, the flowers, and the trees were of gold and silver. And the gold waiting to be smelted in Cuzco

was lost after the death of Huascar, for the Indians hid it so that
the Spaniards would not be able to take it and send it to Spain."

Ralegh was more credulous, or more ingenuous, or (why not
admit it?) madder than Jiménez de Quesada, his niece María,
and Captain Berrio put together. He not only believed López
de Gomara's flights of fancy, but he said: "No, that gold was
not lost; it is in Guiana, at Manoa. It was sought for by Orellana, Ordaz, and Lope de Aguirre the tyrant. Juan Martínez
reached the city of Manoa; he was there for seven months, and
in that time he was not able to see it all. On his deathbed he
confessed this to a priest in Santo Domingo, and, to save his
soul, he handed over to him a gourd full of gold nuggets he had
brought back with him."

The story had the desired effect. The doors of the Tower
swung open for Ralegh. The people of London were of the same
clay as those of Seville: everybody wanted a place in Ralegh's
expedition. And thus hordes of Englishmen flocked to the island
of Trinidad. In Guiana, Berrio had been warned of the invasion
and had prepared his defenses. But Ralegh knew more of warfare, and one morning he fell upon the Spaniards without warning, killed the guards, set fire to the city, and took Berrio prisoner. The latter, finding himself defeated and a captive, had no
choice but to tell Ralegh all he knew. Ralegh, like the courtier
and gentleman he was, treated him with all deference, and
seated him with himself at table. He swiftly began his prepara-
tion to go to El Dorado. Berrio, a simple and honest soul who
had been at this undertaking for over twelve years, told Ralegh
of the difficulties he would encounter going up the Orinoco. But
there was no turning back for Ralegh; to return to the Queen
with empty hands would mean the loss of his head. Out of what
he heard from Berrio and what he saw himself, he fashioned his
famous book — Discovery of the Empire of Guiana — which
was to unhinge the minds of many who came after him, and
which was quickly translated into Latin, French, and Dutch. Its
full title reads: "The Discovery of the large, rich and beautiful
empire of Guiana, with a relation of the great and golden city

of Manoa (which the Spaniards call El Dorado), written by Sir Walter Ralegh, Knight, Captain of her Majesties Guard."

Father José Gumilla, in his *El Orinoco ilustrado*, tells how he once tried to find out through how many mouths the Orinoco emptied into the Caribbean. After traveling for years, and making a thousand inquiries, unable to reach any conclusion, he questioned a pilot who had been living on one of the islands of the delta for fifteen years. "I tried to draw up a sketch on the basis of my observations and the pilot's additions. After we had listed thirty mouths by their names, he said that he did not know any more. For this reason, neither my plan nor that of any other map-maker is or can be exact in the listing of the mouths; some say there are forty; others, fifty-five; many, sixty. It is all guesswork. . . ." Thus the Orinoco, behind the shield of its islands and its mouths, was to preserve its mystery for centuries. For a distance out at sea, its currents flow without mingling with the other water. Ships are at the mercy of this enormous mass of waters, which at this point turns the Caribbean into a tempestuous, fresh-water sea. This was the river and this the sea on which in 1595 the gentleman from the court of London made his first contact with that land of wonder which he had known only through books.

Like all the knights of El Dorado, Ralegh dreamed too much to be a good conquistador. He tried to limit his account to precise observations, but it was as though there were something of himself in the forest, the river, in the New World, something that made him love the trees, the water, and the light that shimmered in the tropical heat. To be sure, his sketch of the river showed only sixteen mouths, but he found the inhabitants of the region (who had at first looked to Father Gumilla like devils) as attractive as they had seemed to Amerigo Vespucci. In his opinion the women had no reason to envy those of Europe on the score of beauty, and differed from them only in their cinnamon color. Of the wife of one of the caciques he wrote: "I have rarely see a better-favored woman. She was of good stature, with black eyes, fat of body, of an excellent countenance, her hair almost as long as herself. . . . I have seen a Lady in England so like her as but for the difference in color I would have sworn it might have been the same."

Because the inhabitants were so handsome, it was quite fitting to think of Queen Elizabeth as the great *cacica* of Guiana. The idea pleased Ralegh's fancy: "I made the Indians understand that I was the servant of a Queen who was the great *cacica* of the north, and a virgin, who had more caciques at her command than there were trees in their islands. . . ." Whereupon the Indians began to refer to Ralegh's queen as *Azrabeta Cassipuna Aquerewana*. Thus the knight of Devon added another ornament to the English royal crown — an Indian feather. But all he sent was the feather; the gold remained here. At the end of his book Ralegh implored the Queen to embark upon the conquest and extend her rule from Guiana to the limits of the lands of the Amazons, "so these women shall hereby hear the name of a virgin who is not only able to defend her own territories and those of her neighbors, but also to invade and conquer great empires." Ralegh set to work to win over the native chieftains, telling them that the English were enemies of those Spaniards who had tried to enslave the Indians and had treated them with such cruelty. But the English were more powerful, and Ralegh boastingly described how the Invincible Armada had been destroyed off the coasts of England.

There is not a sour note in all Ralegh's book. He found everything to his liking. From the moment he first came into contact with the Indians he began to eat their fare — iguana eggs and fermented corn liquor. "I never saw a more beautiful country, nor more lively prospects; hills so raised here and there over the valleys, the river winding into divers branches, the plains adjoining without bush or stubble, all fair green grass . . . deer crossing in every path, the birds toward the evening singing on every tree a thousand several tunes, herons of white, crimson and carnation perching on the rivers side, the air fresh with a gentle easterly wind, and every stone that we stopped to take up promised either gold or silver by his complexion."

Nor did he omit any of those fabulous details which might

arouse the interest of people as curious as the English: the arma-
dillo, whose tail he mistook for a horn; the huge lizards the
natives called *caimanes* (caymans); the houses built in the tree-
tops; the delicious pineapples; the Indian girls who could be
bought for three or four hatchets each. The Spaniards had done
a brisk business, buying girls twelve or thirteen years old for
three hatchets, and then selling them in Margarita for fifty or
a hundred pesos. Finally he spoke of the monsters: the tribe of
the Ewaipahoma, the headless warriors, whose eyes are in their
shoulders and their mouths in the middle of their breasts, and
who have a long mane of hair that grows backward between
their shoulders. When Shakespeare read these reports, he introduced this new human type into a passage of *Othello*:

> *Rough quarries, rocks and hills whose heads touch heaven,*
> *It was my hint to speak — such was the process;*
> *And of the Cannibals that each other eat,*
> *The Anthropophagi and men whose heads*
> *Do grow beneath their shoulders. . . .*

Ralegh realized that it was impossible, with the handful of
men under his command, to undertake a conquest that would
make England Spain's rival for empire. The Orinoco, he reasoned, was the route to Quito, Popayán, Lima, and the New
Kingdom of Granada — the whole map of the Spanish colonies
in South America. From the information he had gleaned, he
concluded that Lake Parimé, on whose shores stood the city of
Manoa, was the size of the Caspian Sea. It had been prophesied
to the Indians that the English would come and drive the Spaniards out of their lands and that the great Queen of the North
would rule them lovingly. It was imperative that a Mercantile
House be organized in London like that of the Spaniards in
Seville. With these ideas Ralegh embarked on his homeward
voyage. The *llaneros*, the plainsmen of Venezuela, sing a song
whose refrain runs:

> *Whoever goes to the Orinoco*
> *Either dies or comes back* loco.

Ralegh's first voyage to Guiana was in the nature of a survey, a preliminary draft for the future British empire he was dreaming of. To collect more complete information, one of his companions remained in Guiana. Ralegh set out for home and burned down Cumaná on his way back because it refused to supply him with provisions. At Río Hacha and Santa Marta he set fire to a number of houses until the inhabitants showed themselves liberally inclined. He arrived in London bringing with him the son of a chief, tobacco leaves, some feathers, samples of ore, and a bag of potatoes. (English historians include two schools of thought: one credits Drake with introducing the potato to Europe; the other, Ralegh.) The Queen must have been disappointed when she found that this man she had released from the Tower to discover El Dorado had brought her only an Indian, some tobacco leaves, some feathers, and some potatoes. But, as Ralegh now wore an aureole of prestige, he was allowed to live luxuriously in his own home, though he was barred from the court. He wrote his book about Guiana. His glory increased. The legend of El Dorado revived under his pen. New expeditions were outfitted.

Times changed, and Ralegh was restored to the Queen's favor. Spain was still the enemy, and he was the man to direct the war. An attack against Cádiz like that which Drake had executed was decided upon. The English ships were armed, and aboard them sailed those two rivals of long standing: Ralegh and Essex. Essex traveled in princely state. Ralegh's cabin was adorned with paintings and works of art. Once more the Spanish citadel was humbled by the English. Ralegh was the hero of the day. In London the star of Essex, that spoiled darling of fortune, began to decline. So wounded was his pride that one day he dared to raise his voice to the Queen, and laid his hand on the hilt of his sword as though to draw it against her. It was the end of the road for him. Ralegh, who owed everything to his own unshakable determination, to knowing how to ride out the storm, won everything that Essex lost. Essex, in desperation, finally showed himself in open rebellion, and it was Ralegh who was entrusted

with setting in motion the machinery that brought him to justice, to prison, and finally to the block for treason. On the eve
of his death, Essex humbly confessed himself to be the vilest of
sinners. The sentence pronounced on him has all the flavor of
the epoch: "They shall be conducted to the Tower of London,
and from thence through the city of London they shall be
drawn to Tyburn, and there they shall be hung, and living their
entrails shall be removed from their bodies and burned, and
their heads shall be cut off and their bodies divided into four
parts, and their heads and these parts shall be set up in such
places as the Queen shall assign." The Queen, in her own handwriting, signed the death sentence. The sole reservation she
made was that the special provisions fixed by the judge should
not be carried out. She "condemned her lover to her mother's
death." When the Earl of Lincoln saw her sign the sentence
he could not believe his own eyes; twenty times he had seen
the Queen and Essex embracing. . . . From the armory Ralegh saw the executioner carry out his mission with three strokes
of the ax.

These were twilight scenes. The Queen was old. Ralegh had
reached his zenith at the time when she, helping her faltering
steps with a cane, was moving toward the grave. Tears came to
her eyes whenever she recalled Essex. She would soon be traveling the same road. Ralegh, who was lame from a wound received in Cádiz, and whose hair was showing signs of gray,
would have enjoyed his power more if it had come earlier. He
took the waters at Bath, and enjoyed long conversations with
Shakespeare. In London he was to be seen among poets, writers,
and artists. When Elizabeth felt the hand of death upon her,
she sent a present to King James of Scotland who would succeed her on the throne, with these lines: "Lord, remember me
when Thou comest into Thy Kingdom" — the prayer of the
good thief to Jesus on the Cross. . . . And she died.

Ralegh's day of triumph was short-lived. When the new King
ascended the throne, it became evident that the courtiers had
poisoned his mind. Ralegh was now shorn of his privileges, and
another was named captain of the guard. The ministers spread

a snare, not too subtle, but sure of effect: they invented a tale to the effect that Ralegh was involved in a conspiracy to dethrone James in favor of the interests of Spain. He was imprisoned and brought before the judges, as Essex had been. Their purpose was not to try him, but to find him guilty. He saw that, as the last favorite of the dead Queen, he was to be made the scapegoat of the mob. With a dagger thrust he attempted suicide, but the blow failed of its purpose, and he was brought to trial. On the way to the court he was the target of the grossest insults, and the populace threw pipefuls of tobacco upon him. But at his trial he tore the prosecutor's charges to shreds and made him look ridiculous. He defended himself with courage, elegance, logic, and wit. Naturally, he was found guilty, but the same crowds that had insulted him on his way to trial now acclaimed him. The King saw which way the wind was blowing and commuted the sentence. From the window of his cell Ralegh saw the other prisoners executed; he had been told to prepare for the same fate. But, like the King, he could scent the change in the air; and he smiled, for he knew he would be spared.

He spent long years in prison. His wife, loyal and devoted as ever, accompanied him. A legend of gallantry and heroism had sprung up around Ralegh's name. In the Tower there was a terrace on which he used to walk; centuries have gone by, and it is still known as "Ralegh's Walk." The King's son visited the prisoner to learn from him things his father's ministers did not know. The prison cell was a study. Ralegh received and devoured old books, and wrote his monumental *History of the World*. A Faustian spirit, he carried on chemical experiments, working out a formula for a balm that the Queen herself used in her household, and discovering a method of converting salt water into fresh for use on long voyages. For his thoughts were still on Guiana; he was only awaiting a propitious moment. James's ministers were sinking into obscurity. The kingdom was badly governed. Cecil — that powerful former friend who had sent him to the Tower — had died when the wind changed. Ralegh wrote the memorable letter containing the phrase: "It is a beautiful fate to die for the King, not at the hands of the King."

177

And he saw to it that the magic words *El Dorado* reached the King's ears. James saw the gleam of gold in the offing. Ralegh managed to convey to the venal hands of Lady Villiers the £1500 she demanded for procuring his release. She was the mother of George Villiers, the King's favorite, James being a man who always needed to have a handsome youth around on whom to lavish his caresses. With £700 more, Ralegh could have left the Tower, without having to go to Guiana; another £1500 would have won him complete pardon for the rest of his life. But he was not able to raise so much money, nor did he want to give up the Guiana venture, being himself under the spell of El Dorado.

At last, in 1616, white-haired at sixty-four after long years of imprisonment, Ralegh saw the streets of London once more. They seemed like the faded decorations of some old theater. Faces had changed, and to most he was a stranger — a legend, indeed, rather than a real person, a knight of the Order of El Dorado rather than a Londoner, a figure that had stepped out of a tapestry. . . .

In London and in Plymouth, soldiers, sailors, gentlemen, old salts, friends of Ralegh's in other days, were preparing to follow the lead of this man whose footsteps had echoed in the life of England for over half a century. He was no longer the gallant captain of the guard who rode at the Queen's side in the handsomest suit of silver armor the streets of London had beheld in many years. But his broad forehead bore the imprint of fantastic experiences. Ralegh — chemist, scholar, poet, favorite, and victim — knew the secret of three magic words: Guiana, Orinoco, El Dorado. The Spanish ambassador grew uneasy; his source of information (who would believe it?) was King James himself, who was betraying his own people in order to curry favor with Philip III.

When the ships weighed anchor at Plymouth in March 1617, Ralegh gave his orders: a psalm would be sung every evening; blasphemy would be punished; no distinction would be made between soldiers and sailors; gambling, cowardice, and gluttony

were forbidden; precautions were to be taken against fire. It was
a brief disciplinary code made to fit those for whom it was designed.

As the fleet approached the Caribbean, there were signs of ill
omen — a hurricane, pestilence. The bodies of the stricken were
thrown overboard, among them some of Ralegh's most faithful
friends; he kept the somber record in his diary. At Trinidad they
went ashore, and a scouting party of the best soldiers was sent
out under the command of the man in whom Ralegh had the
greatest confidence, Keymis. They were to ascend the Orinoco
as far as the mines — five ships and two hundred and fifty men,
among them Ralegh's son.

The party reached Santo Thomé, but the Spaniards were
waiting for them with loaded cannon. (King James's information had not gone unheeded.) Nevertheless, the struggle was
unequal. Don Diego Palomeque, the governor, assembled all
the fifty-seven inhabitants and armed them. They had only two
cannon, which they set up on the river banks, and four stone
mortars, which they mounted in the city. The English, in two
strong columns, drowned the Spaniards' bravery in their own
blood. The governor died of knife wounds; so did Ralegh's son.
Keymis did not leave a stone standing, so infuriated was he by
the unexpected resistance, which had taken a heavy toll of his
men. The soldiers sacked the church and the council hall. The
city was put to the torch. Not even the convent of San Francisco escaped the flames. The priest, who was ill, was unable to
leave his bed; afterwards the Spaniards found him roasted in the
ashes. The invaders carried off even the bells to their ships; and
fifty quintals of tobacco.

But all this violence was fruitless. Keymis did not have men
enough to go on looking for the mines, and he knew that if he
discovered them it would be the Spaniards who would reap the
benefits. For twenty days, as he sailed along the banks of the
great river, the green flames of the trees that quivered in the tropical heat, the silence of the heavy-hanging night over the crystal
wheel of the Orinoco, the howling monkeys, and the red herons
that shot through the air like arrows of blood — all seemed to

repeat to the voyagers' imagination the fateful words: You shall not pass.

Keymis returned to Trinidad. He had to tell Ralegh of their failure, and also of the death of his son. At this news Ralegh bowed his head; his life no longer had any meaning. El Dorado had faded away like the twilight that loses itself in the ebony nights of the Orinoco. The Caribbean was now the sea that had swallowed up Drake, Hawkins — and his son! Guiana was but a jungle; the expedition, an abysmal failure. Numbly he turned to Keymis, his old friend: "You will tell the King of your defeat." These words fell on Keymis's ears like a blow of the headsman's ax upon his neck. Ralegh wrote no more in his diary; but in his letter to his wife the wavering of the pen is the trembling of his heart.

Keymis set down an account of what had happened, and handed it to Ralegh. To Ralegh it seemed meaningless, but he answered: "This is your affair; you can take it to court." Keymis, unnerved, retired to his cabin, loaded a pistol, and fired it against his heart. The shot missed its mark and glanced off a rib. Undaunted, he seized a knife — and his comrades found his body in a pool of blood. As Ralegh sailed his little fleet back to England, the ships seemed decked with funereal crape. The Spanish ambassador requested an audience with the King — a brief audience, for he had only one word to say. When the King received him, he spat out the word: Pirates. But the King promised to satisfy the Spaniards — Ralegh would lose his head to atone for the death of Palomeque and the burning of Santo Thomé. Much water had flowed over the dam since the brave days of Elizabeth, who was every inch a king!

Ralegh was sixty-five years old. Friends he had almost none. When he entered the Tower this time, he knew there would be no pardon for him. James was concerned over just one thing: to avoid another trial at which Sir Walter might once more elude punishment with his speeches. When Ralegh was asked if he had any request to make, he said: "One: that I be beheaded like a gentleman — not hanged or quartered." "This world," he wrote, "is but a great prison, from which a certain number are selected for death each day." He sought to give his loyal wife courage and solace, but she, poor woman — whose whole life had swung like a delicate pendulum between her son and her husband — felt her soul faint at the thought of facing what remained of the future, without them, alone.

Those farewell verses of his that are to be found in every anthology of English poetry were composed in prison:

> Even such is time, that takes in trust
> Our youth, our joys, our all we have,
> And pays us but with earth and dust; . . .
> But from this earth, this grave, this dust,
> My God shall raise me up, I trust!

At the foot of the scaffold, Ralegh pronounced his last speech. It is a gem of English oratory. In simple language he explained his activities in Guiana, denied the trumpery incidents of which he had been accused, and spoke face to face with eternity. His last words were: "I will speak but a word or two more, because I will not trouble Mr. Sheriff too long." These words were, first, to state that he had never rejoiced over the death of Essex, and, second, to ask all those who were listening to offer a prayer for him to God, whom he knew he had gravely offended because he had been full of vanity and had led a sinful life — "having been," he said, "a soldier, a captain, a sea captain, and a courtier, which are all places of wickedness and vice; that God, I say, would forgive me, cast away my sins from me, and receive me into everlasting life. So I take my leave of you all, making my peace with God."

He removed his cape and doublet. He called the headsman, who had been concealing the ax, and asked to see it. "Do you think it frightens me?" He took it in his hands, tried its edge, and turned smiling to the guard: "This is a powerful medicine, but a doctor that cures all ills." He forgave the headsman, and asked which was the best position in which to lay his head. Then he gave him the signal to proceed. '. . . The head was placed in a pouch of red leather, wrapped in a velvet cloth, and sent in a coach to Lady Ralegh.

Never, said the people, had they seen a man so serene and brave. The poets wrote elegies that were passed from hand to hand. And Sir Walter Ralegh returned to the tapestry out of which he had stepped to embark upon the conquest of El Dorado, with all his sins, violence, ambitions, misfortunes, greatness, books, and arms; and into the background were woven the islands of the river with sixteen mouths. Only the kiss of the executioner's ax was needed to give him an undisputed place in the romantic realm of legend.

BOOK II

THE SILVER AGE

THE SIXTEENTH CENTURY was a dynamic age; the Conquest, which was violent, was accomplished with sword, musket, and dog. The seventeenth was of a different texture. The pirate and the conquistador were followed by the personages of the colony. Steel armor was supplanted by the lace, velvet, and white gloves of the viceroys. The great figure in the colony was the *oidor* — the hearer, or judge; as his name indicates, he was all ears.

The problem now was not that of killing Indians, but of incorporating them. Through the underground channels of love the two races had come together and continued to do so. The mestizo appeared, bearing within him the remote voices of Virgin America and the rich voices of old Europe. The two bloods ran side by side in the same vein, pulsated in the same heart. The dreaming mestizo was lulled to sleep by the crooning lullaby of his Indian mother and the martial hymn of his father, the conquistador.

, The times no longer admitted of dramatic solutions to the problems life presented. It was necessary to rest and meditate. And gossip. Above the new settlements of clay-tiled roofs and thatched huts, a white tower rose into the air. At dawn the bells summoned the Christian to matins; at dusk the angelus sent him to his rest. Through the bull's-eye of the church, the playful fingers of the twilight reached in, caressing the niches of gold, the polychrome virgins, the cherubs with faces of Indian babies. Out of dreams and prayers these altarpieces had been born, in which the illusion of El Dorado was no longer a spur to battle, but was the imagery of a naïve yet complex mysticism in which miracles took place that satisfied the candor of the new converts, and in which there were reminiscences of Saint Teresa and Saint John of the Cross. The religious sense of America was not formed by racking the imagination in a monastery cell, but by sending the soul forth over the open roads, the wide rivers, the nights of silver in a sylvan world where the storm that turned brooks into torrents and tore mighty ceibas up by the roots alternated with tender dawns that palpitated in a drop of dew.

In the sixteenth century few women came out from Spain. And those that did were redoubtable, as daring as the rest of the crowd. By comparison with the courtly, refined viceroy Don Diego de Colón, his wife, María de Toledo, was the better man of the two. In Panama, Pedrárias Dávila's lady played as important a role as he did. And Pánfilo de Narváez's wife looked after his interests in Cuba with better sense and management than he ever showed. When Hernando de Soto set out on the conquest of Florida, he left his wife as governor of Cuba in his stead, and she displayed great skill, astuteness, and courage in her task. When Beatriz de la Cueva, the Unfortunate, lost her handsome husband, Don Pedro de Alvarado, her demonstrations of grief equaled those of Doña Joanna the Mad, but when it came to asserting her claims to the governorship of Guatemala she brought to bear a daring and determination that only the cataclysm that reduced the old city of Guatemala to rubble could defeat. It was earthquake, tidal wave, and death that conquered her; as long as her opponents were only men, she saw them bow like stalks of wheat before the impulse of her will. These were the governors' ladies. It is not necessary even to mention the women of the rank and file; the governors' ladies are colorless by comparison with them.

With the seventeenth century, women lost their daring, venturesome impetus. There followed a kind of twilight sleep, enlivened by domestic cares and absorption in local gossip fed by the books of the period — picaresque, scandalous chronicles, manuscript copies many of them, which were passed from hand to hand. The women of great spiritual impulse turned to the poetic metaphor. A flower of Lima, Saint Rose, perfumed the early years of the century. In Mexico it was Sor Juana Inés, in whose verses profane and sacred love jostle each other. The poems of Amarilis, veiled and coquettish behind her pseudonym, crossed the wide seas in reply to those Lope de Vega addressed to her. The sixteenth century was a period of disequilibrium and genius. The seventeenth moved on an even keel, and with well-turned phrases. The colony read. A year after *Don Quixote* was published, there were fifteen hundred copies of the book circulating in America. Don Quixote and Sancho became household figures. In Lima and in Mexico they appeared in masquerades, and everybody recognized and applauded them — all this less than three years after Cervantes had sent his immortal knight and squire into the world.

The empire of Spain in America was in the mountains, in the uplands of the Andes, removed from the temptations of the sea and the menace of the English. The conquistador, who was from the inland Castilian meseta, preferred this. Besides, there was the established tradition of the Indians. Charles V could not know America better than did Moctezuma, Atahuallpa, or Sacresaxigua; and these rulers knew very well why the mountain heights were the proper seats of government. There was only one battle front left: the Caribbean. But for England, too, the seventeenth century was no longer the age of Hawkins and Drake. The pirates themselves wanted to rest, to make their camps and colonies, to find themselves Indian women, and to throw in their lot with America. Instead of sailing around the world, as Drake had done, Morgan made his trip around the Caribbean; and instead of setting out on his adventures from Plymouth, he sailed from Jamaica. To know the world, one island suffices, and more.

X

THE SEVEN–COLORED ARCHIPELAGO

Anda, jaleo, jaleo,　　　(Come on, shake it up, shake it up,
Ya se acabó el alboroto　(The shouting is over
Y vamos al tiroteo,　　　(And the shooting's going to start,
Y vamos al tiroteo. . . .　(And the shooting's going to start. . . .)

SMUGGLERS' SONG

Tʜᴇ ᴍᴀɪɴʟᴀɴᴅ belonged to the Spaniards. Mexico, Peru, Central America, New Granada, Chile, and the Plate region were all viceroyalties or governorships. In the Caribbean, Spain's interest centered upon the large islands — Cuba and Hispaniola. For the refuge and solace of the pirate crews, there remained all the little islands scattered through the sea: the Lesser Antilles, which must be the peaks of a mountain chain that once extended from the Florida peninsula to the Guianas, and that in some remote geological age were submerged beneath the waters. Of these, some were volcanic, others pleasant plains, mesas of the sunken range. Seen on the map, they form a line of dots, like the "dots of suspense" used by writers when they want to suggest mystery, emotion, or irony; the reader's attention is caught and he smiles; an understanding is established between him and the author, a mixture of complicity and malice, as though the writer and the reader had winked at each other. Something of this atmosphere prevailed in the Lesser Antilles. They constituted a margin reserved for adventure, smuggling, clandestine activities, where outlaws formed associations that were more intimate and loyal than those between law-abiding citizens. There the Huguenots persecuted by the Catholics set up their camps, and the Catholics persecuted by the Puritans, the Puritans by the Arminians, the Jews by the Christians, the Caribs by the Spaniards, and the Spaniards by the law. Each island was the haven and refuge of men with blood-stained beards and knives ever unsheathed. The boldest was chosen captain. If they were of those who attended mass, they did so with all fervor; if of those who hated the Pope, they hated him from the bottom of their hearts. As enemies they were implacable, but when they loved, their devotion knew no limits. The warm, wayward winds, the open sea, and the islands themselves fostered a state of liberty that made a man smile, forget his cares, and take a sensual pleasure in living. On some of the islands there were herds of wild bulls, and of swine that had multiplied with the fruitfulness characteristic of the land. On the beaches the turtles, their heads swinging like pendulums, laid their eggs in the hot sand.

The islands bore the names of sweethearts, saints, hopes, adventures, that the sailors had bestowed upon them. To the discoverer it seemed as though by some magic touch a fitting name might make the islands lucky. In the chain baptized by Columbus he wrote his own story, which anyone who understands cabbalas can read. The list of the Caribbean islands is like a mystery story; in each name there is hidden a dream, a prayer, a misfortune, a joke: Barbuda, San Cristobal, Monserrat, Sombrero, La Tortuga, Marie-Galante, La Deseada, Granada, Bonaire, La Margarita, La Mona, Los Frailes, Gran Caimán, El Caimancito, Cayo de Roncador, Cayo de Quitasueño. . . . Even the groups of islands have charming names: the Windwards, the Leewards (which seem to move with winds), the Virgin Islands, recalling the legend of the Middle Ages.

And this is how the islands were settled:

We spoke first of the French pirates. Not once but many times they sacked Santa Marta and Cartagena. In Cartagena, on the eve of the day the sister of the governor and founder of the city was to be married, they fell upon the city so unexpectedly, while everybody was sound asleep, that the women had just time to flee in their nightgowns. The governor, sword in hand, defended the front entrance to his house while his sisters and nieces "climbed down from the back." The loot amounted to 200,000 pesos of gold, and it would have been still more if the Spaniards had not fooled them by melting down the copper candlesticks, and by putting on a great show of tears and grief as they turned the ingots over to them.

But these were tales of bygone days. Now the pirates wanted to found colonies. A detailed report on Guiana had been presented to Henri IV of France. Ralegh's book had stimulated the lively French imagination more than the soberer English mind. Never was a more harmful fable put into circulation. Besides, Samuel Champlain (whose name would later be associated with the conquest of Canada) was a curious traveler who had visited Santo Domingo, Cartagena, Mexico, and Havana, and who presented to the King an account illustrated with water colors. Champlain had no thought of war; his idea was to conquer lands that Spain had not occupied, to share with her the wonders of the New World. These ideas found support. An expedition whose objectives were the Amazon, the Orinoco, and the city of Manoa was organized. Daniel de la Touche de la Ravardière came with it; he gazed in wonder at what he saw and returned wild with enthusiasm. Henri IV appointed him Lieutenant-General of Guiana, and his companion, the naturalist Mocquet, "Curator of the Curiosities of the King."

As might have been expected, Henri IV died in 1610 at the hands of an assassin. But Marie de Médicis, who became regent, followed in the footsteps of his fantasies, and sent La Ravardière out again, accompanied by an uncle of Cardinal Richelieu, Alphonse du Plessis, and a high-ranking Knight of Malta, M. de Razilly. The expedition was a huge success; La Ravardière returned with six plumed Indians who were exhibited at the Louvre. Their dances were the first typical American sight ever beheld in Paris. The court crowded to see them. The paintings of Leonardo da Vinci that had been exhibited under the patronage of Francis I had caused far less stir than our Arawaks. Louis XIII, who was a child, hung the collar of Saint Louis about their necks. Moreover, La Ravardière's name was linked to one very definite accomplishment: the foundation of Cayenne. After him came the businessmen. In Rouen a company was formed, and an industrialist of Lyon was put in charge of colonizing Guiana. Finally there came Brétigny, who was appointed governor. He was the first resident official the natives saw; so great was his severity that he became known as "the Nero of Guiana." A native arrow that buried itself between his eyes dispatched him to the other world. Despite this unpleasant episode, Guiana maintained its prestige, and when Condé wearied of the intrigues of European politics he dreamed of coming out to Guiana — a plan he never realized — and setting up there his ideal republic, his Utopia. This was Cayenne in the seventeenth century, a dream of liberty.

Richelieu saw things more clearly. These islands were strategic bases. The man to conquer them was Pierre Belain d'Esnambuc. Esnambuc was the younger son of a noble family, and he had come out to the Caribbean to seek his fortune as a pirate. With Urban de Roissey he had roamed these waters. They had fallen upon boats loaded with hides, sugar, and tobacco. Their camp was on Saba, a perfect island for purposes of piracy. And Esnambuc, whose wings were growing, returned to France to seek the support of the crown. He presented himself before Richelieu, showed him tobacco leaf, and told him of the sea and the islands. The result of this was the organization of the *Association des Seigneurs des Isles de l'Amérique*. Richelieu was one of the stockholders; he put up £10,000. Others were the Quartermaster-General of the Navy, the president of the Exchequer, and the treasurer of the savings bank; nobody turned up his nose at these companies. Esnambuc was to go to these islands to colonize, and to fight, pursue, board, attack, overpower, sack, and with any kind of arm or instruments of war capture pirates or anyone else who attempted to interfere with the movement and freedom of trade of French ships or those of France's allies.

Saba became the lair of this fearsome brotherhood. Esnambuc shared the island with the English, who were plying the same trade. Said the Spaniards: "God raised them and the Devil brought them together." It would be well for the reader to bear the name of Esnambuc in mind, because a direct descendant of his became Empress of France: Joséphine, the Creole from Martinique, who turned Napoleon's head.

France was on the threshold of greatness. A few years later Louis XIV would gleam like a rising planet against two declining monarchies: that of Spain, which was setting in the dismal twilight of the Hapsburg dynasty, and that of England, where the crown was about to pass from the weak hands of James I to those of his son Charles, whose head would finally come to rest upon the block. So magnificent was the atmosphere in which Cardinal Richelieu moved and had his being that perhaps for this reason even the lair of the pirates in the Caribbean reflected a little of the splendor of the court. He sent out Philippe de Lonvillier de Poincy, steward of the order of Knights of Malta, as governor of Saba, Martinique, Guadalupe, and Marie-Galante. The smugglers watched him come ashore on the burning sands of Saba (where the heat was so great it cooked the turtles' eggs) with much pomp and ceremony, attired in the magnificent habit of his order, his cape floating about him, the white cross of Malta on his breast and the jaunty velvet cap over one ear. The gentleman formed his court. Three hundred slaves and a hundred servants were at his orders. He built a castle, surrounded by gardens, in the center of a walled enclosure. One day the comptroller of the *Association des Seigneurs des Isles de l'Amérique* came out to ask him for an accounting; like the gentleman he was, Lonvillier de Poincy received him with loaded cannon and threw him into jail. Now he laughed at the company and "worked for the general good." As was customary at court, he had his love affairs. Poetic satires were printed which merely spread what everyone already knew; the author went to jail. The pirates liked this governor. They looked upon him as their captain, he extended his rule to fourteen islands, and the French Antilles began to flourish. The knight was a devout Catholic, and churches were erected. The colony was inaugurated under the sign of the Cardinal with a mass which the pirates followed in silent devotion. One day, on Tortuga, Captain Daniel became so annoyed with a rascal who was not paying proper attention to the mass that he got up from his place and shot him dead. A number of Huguenots had entered the colony, and the knight decided it would be better for all concerned to keep the two sects separated. He suggested to Captain Lavasseur that he organize a settlement for them on Tortuga island. This was the traditional hide-out of buccaneers and pirates; Huguenots, Lutherans, and heretics were admitted. Lavasseur made himself captain and, following the example of his master, Poincy, as soon as he felt himself safely established he shook off his tutelage, and informed him that there he was in command. High on some jutting rocks, he built himself an inexpugnable stronghold that commanded the entrances to the island. It could be reached only by a rope ladder, which was lowered only for friends.

The Dutch made their entrance upon the scene in a different manner. They did not begin as pirates, like the English or French. In Holland, after a forty-year war, a liberal, middle-class republic had developed that was to challenge Spain for the dominion of the seas with the same cool, methodical calculation and the same determination by which it had wrested its very soil from the sea in a triumph of engineering. All the last part of Philip II's reign was a ceaseless struggle against these stubborn folk who refused to go on belonging to a foreign crown. Of all the struggles of this period perhaps there was none more determined than that of this handful of men pitted against the world's greatest empire. And in the end their flags flew upon the seven seas, and they developed one of the most powerful maritime forces the world has seen. As a matter of fact, Spain's absurd claims on Holland gave rise to nothing but a ruinous and foredoomed war. Between Spain and Holland, on land, lay France, always hostile; and by sea, England, always a menace. Toward the end of his reign, Philip II began to take a clearer view of the problem and to seek a peaceful solution. Philip III could have found a way out of the situation by gently loosening the bonds that linked him to the nettlesome little republic. But he was a weak king, under the sway of the Duke of Lerma; completely lacking in judgment, he failed to realize that the glories of Philip II were over. All he could see was that the Dutch Republic was a hotbed of heretics, and he was going to clean it out. One day, without warning, he seized all the Dutch ships in Spanish ports, and turned their crews over to the Inquisition. It was a severe blow to the Dutch. But Holland was going through one of those periods of upsurge when adversity becomes a stimulus to determined, aggressive action.

Necessity obliged the Dutch to draw on all the resources of their ingenuity. Holland had a mystic faith in herself. There was not a field of human activity into which the rising republic did not venture. Her bankers developed financial institutions that four centuries have not destroyed. To Spain's amazement, her sailors answered the challenge by making themselves masters of the seas. The Dutch theologians were the most active and wisest in the world of Protestantism. A Dutch navigator who had spent years in Spain and Portugal, Jan Hugo van Linchoten, assembled the most complete collections of maps, and took them back to his country to show its merchants the routes of the world. A geographer, Mercator, revolutionized his science, introducing a new system of map projection. Even the English, when they were unable to secure from their own rulers the support they needed, went to Holland and put themselves at the service of the new nation. It was under Dutch auspices that Hudson made his voyage to North America and discovered the river that bears his name. Dutch ships traveled to the Far East. Amsterdam became the center from which pepper, nutmeg, and cloves — spices worth their weight in gold — were distributed to the rest of Europe. The art of warfare of that day had its most notable exponent in Maurice of Nassau, son of the great William the Silent; he defeated the Spanish legions on the shifting sands, the moving dunes where the brave men of Castile were led to their death by the stupidity of leaders who substituted daring for sense.

Jacob Meemskerk, the navigator who explored the polar routes that did not become navigable to the world until four centuries later, was the pride of the Dutch navy. It was his destiny to match forces with the Spanish fleet. His twenty ships were ranged in battle order against the twenty-six commanded by Juan de Ávila. Meemskerk died in the battle, but his comrades avenged him by destroying Ávila's fleet. When his body was carried through the streets of Amsterdam, the whole nation turned out to render to the memory of this popular hero such homage as had never been shown before. Philip III had to bow to the naval victory of the Dutch and open peace negotiations — "with those men of butter," says a historian, "who milk their cows on the bed of the ocean, live amongst trees every one of which they had to plant, in a garden that they made out of a mud-flat."

The Dutch utilized the peace to lay out more ambitious plans. They had been working for thirty years on the idea of a company, and now the idea took shape. It was supported by the most convinced Protestants, the most active merchants, the most resolute soldiers. It was to be a business battle waged against the Spanish treasury. The plan was to bring from the East Indies tobacco, sugar, dyewoods, and hides, and to sell slaves, knives, mirrors, cloth, and flour in the West Indies. Great warehouses would be set up in Amsterdam, and the islands would be headquarters for free trade or smuggling, whichever the circumstances dictated. These were the plans not of kings but of the middle class. Thus the Dutch East India Company came into being, with a monopoly grant of twenty-four years.

The struggle was characterized by a variety of incidents, from the religious propaganda that converted Holland into the leading publishing center from which the Bible was distributed with the joyous enthusiasm of a budding fanaticism, to the rise of Piet Heyn from pirate to admiral of the republic. Erasmus had cut away the trunk of the medieval tree with his fine-toothed saw. Barneveldt, the statesman who unraveled Holland's political skein when it became tangled, was brought to the block because he was not so anti-Spanish nor so zealous a Protestant as the times demanded. Piet Heyn attacked the Spanish fleet off Matanzas in Cuba; his booty in silver and pearls amounted to twelve million florins (five million dollars).

These were the Dutch who soon began to make their appearance on the Caribbean horizon. They were to be found everywhere — on the coasts of Panama, Barbados, the Tortugas; in Guiana or Martinique, Providencia, Saba, St. Eustatius. . . . The French crown forbade the French to buy anything from the Dutch, but if they had obeyed they would have starved to death. Three-quarters of the merchant marine that sailed the seas was Dutch. Each year over a hundred ships called at the French islands of the Caribbean. As there were very high duties on tobacco and other products of the Antilles in France, the inhabitants of the islands found it easier and more profitable to sell to the Dutch and let them supply the world. Besides, the Dutch ships were cleaner; fewer passengers died of plague in the crossing.

In the West Indies the Dutch, French, and English got along well enough together. They were all brothers under the skin. On one occasion, a Dutchman, Guerin Spranger, was the governor of Guiana; the French fleet sailed into the harbor demanding the surrender of the place; Spranger calculated his strength, realized that it was useless to resist, and proposed that the French captain pay him 21,850 florins for his plantations. The money was paid, and the province was handed over without a shot's being fired; the whole transaction occupied a page in a ledger. When a Dutch boat reached a port held by the French, it was received by everyone, from the governor down, with open arms; smuggling was legitimate business.

After this fashion the Dutch installed themselves in Curaçao, Aruba, Bonaire, Saba, St. Eustatius, and Nevis, where they prepared cakes of salt and sent whole boatloads of them to Europe. The affairs of the Company prospered greatly. One of the finest sights of Amsterdam was the Company's buildings, of timber and brick, the upper stories crowded under the sharply sloping roofs down which the December snows slipped. Every day of the week the manager could climb up on a barrel before the door, and put this riddle to the merchants who crowded around: "A boat has come from Curaçao loaded with . . . ?" "Gold!" shouted one. "Rum!" "Sugar!" "Lumber!" "Silver!" "Pearls!" "Hides!" "Salt!" In Guiana the Company's headquarters was a fortress, with high-walled corrals where the Negroes were herded like animals waiting for the boat that would take them to the Caribbean. In Curaçao, amidst canals and drawbridges, houses were springing up like those of Amsterdam, Bruges, and the various cities of the Hanseatic League, with stone and timber fronts, and steep roofs down which rolled the water in the rainy season or the sunshine like oranges in December. In Curaçao the houses were painted Prussian blue, vermilion, chrome yellow, and parrot green, for it was not the same living among the fogs of the northern seas as under a sky of indigo blue. Here the factor could ask *his* riddle: "A boat has come from Amsterdam loaded with . . . ?" "Knives." "Looking-glasses." "Perfume." "Chintz." "Canvas." "Wine." "Oil." "Flour." "Whites." "Blacks." "Freemen." "Slaves." "Calvinists." "Huguenots." "Jews." Jews, for example, came by the boatload to Guiana, Negroes to Martinique, white and black to Curaçao. And the islands gradually turned into lands whose names have a double meaning. The day would come when at the mention of Curaçao some would think of the little island with its houses of stone and timber, its canals, and its bridges that go up and down, while to others it meant the liqueur that one drinks drop by drop to savor better this perfumed cream of the Antilles. Is "Havana" a city, or the bluish haze of a cigar? The French say: "Jamaica is an island." And British pride answers: "Jamaica rum," as though to overshadow the rum of Martinique. Thus the Caribbean has become a sea of smuggling, smoke, and alcohol.

As for the English, one must pick up the thread where Ralegh dropped it. The fact that he had his head cut off was merely an occupational hazard, which instead of destroying his prestige enhanced it. People went on talking about the Amazon and El Dorado. Now the outstanding Puritans of London had their eyes fixed on the other side of the Atlantic: Guiana, the West Indies, Bermuda, Massachusetts. As with the Calvinists of Holland, it is hard to say whether they put greater fervor into religion or into business. Many Englishmen had been following Drake's example in the Antilles. Lords of high degree had fleets of ships that brought them a splendid revenue by preying upon the ships of "Catholic" Spaniards. When England signed a peace treaty with Spain, the companies of corsairs moved to Holland and allied themselves with their Dutch brothers. The Spanish ambassador in London wasted his time spying on the Earl of Warwick and his friends, who were accused of engaging in pirate enterprises; the ships sailed from Ireland, Dartmouth, from ports far from London. In Venezuela the Spanish government forbade the planting of tobacco for ten years in the hope (which proved idle) of putting an end to the contraband trade the English and Dutch carried on from Trinidad.

There came a moment when relations between England and Spain grew strained again. Whereupon King James authorized the formation of the "Company of Gentlemen of the City of London to explore the Amazon." Captain Roger North set out with a fleet, accompanied by Thomas Warner. They had hardly got under way when the King was seized by scruples, and North on his return from the Amazon went to the Tower. Warner was luckier, because by the time he returned the storm had blown over. He formed another company, and came out to Saba, the northernmost of the Lesser Antilles. Like the French, he gave up the idea of establishing himself on the mainland, the graveyard of so many dead hopes, and set about getting a foothold on one of the islands. He came to an agreement with Esnambuc, the Frenchman, and they divided Saba between them. Warner was eventually appointed the King's lieutenant — the first appointment of a colonial authority in the West Indies by the English crown. One day while Warner was in London the Spaniards came to the island in warships. The English and the French scattered like frightened rats to other islands in the archipelago until the Spanish admiral had left, when they came back as big as life. Business was going well. Every year £12,000 sterling of tobacco was exported to England. It should be added that Sir Thomas Warner was admirably adapted for his post, since he was particularly close to the Indians, having fallen in love with a pretty Indian girl; and the fruit of their union was the half-breed Edward Warner, the first important descendant of an Englishman of distinction and a native.

But events of serious import were in the making. In England, the persecuted Puritans — faced first by James's failure to adopt a straightforward policy, and, following this, by the dictatorship of Charles I — were drawing together in a close brotherhood. A group of Puritans who had taken refuge in Holland came out to settle in North America in 1620. The leaders of Parliament, which had been dissolved by the King, gathered to draw up plans counseled by their indignation and fervor; if necessary, they would all emigrate to America. In the group there were the Earl of Warwick, Lord Holland, Sir Thomas Barrington, Lord Brooke, and John Pym, Cromwell's forerunner. Cromwell himself, though at the moment he had no special significance, was very close to the group and undoubtedly received his inspiration from them, and was destined to continue the work of these determined and unyielding gentlemen who at the moment composed the most vigorous party in England. The most active member of the group was Lord Robert Rich, Earl of Warwick; the most courtly, Lord Henry Rich, Earl of Holland. In their private conduct the members of this family were not typically Puritan. The wife of one of them had caused a great scandal in English society owing to her illicit love affair with the Duke of Devonshire. The Earl of Warwick, who had his own fleet of pirate ships, dealt in slaves too, and was the owner of the first shipment of Negroes sent to Virginia. The Earl of Holland's activities were less flamboyant: he received a commission for using his influence with the King and Queen. But such conduct was common among many of the great English families of the day.

The interest of the group now centered upon the islands of St. Andrew and Providence, lying off the coast of Panama on the route taken by the Spanish fleets bearing homeward the treasures of the mainland. Earlier, the Puritans had gone to Massachusetts and the Bermudas; the present venture was bolder, for they had invaded the inner ring of the Spanish possessions. How had they come to take such a step? It was due to a letter from a Mr. Bell, who was in charge of their business affairs in Bermuda. Things were not going well in Massachusetts, and Bermuda had no future because it lay off the trade routes; but Mr. Bell painted a glowing description of some islands that were not occupied by the Spaniards, safe from the Caribs, fertile, and pleasantly situated, by name St. Andrew, Providence, and

Fonseca. And where was Fonseca? It was a place in the Caribbean equidistant from Providence and Cuba. It was thus shown on many maps, and for over two hundred years it had been alluded to, but finally sailors grew weary of searching for it and came to the conclusion that it had been a figment of someone's imagination. With Mr. Bell's letter in his hands, however, the Earl of Warwick set about organizing the company. A smuggler and slave-runner, Elfrith, was sent out to make the first exploration; he found the islands as they had been described, and met there only a few Dutchmen. He laid the foundations of a settlement — New Westminster — and of a fort — Fort Warwick. In London, in a house in Holborn, Warwick called his friends together. It was agreed that the Earl of Holland should be named president of the company to secure a charter from the King. For this service he was to receive £200 in shares. But the acting head and manager of the company was to be Pym.

Things started very well. The first Pilgrims, those in Massachusetts, had actually sailed from Holland, where they had sought refuge, later crossing over to Southampton in order to embark in the *Mayflower*. This new group set out nine years later — in 1629 — from the Thames estuary in the *Seaflower*. The Earl of Warwick, who had been one of the patrons of the Amazon venture and, to a certain extent, the head of the Massachusetts enterprise, had never been so full of hope as over this present undertaking. The *Seaflower* carried only ninety Pilgrims, all men and boys; the women were to come later. The shareholders were wealthy persons from the east of England; the colonists were nearly all from Devon, Drake's home county. They were divided into three groups: farmers, workmen, and servants. The minister, as long as he stayed single, was to live in the governor's house to set an edifying example. They all swore an oath of hatred against Spain. But Pym, who took the long view, thought to himself: Today the enemy is Spain, tomorrow it will be Holland. And his advice to the settlers was: "Be friendly with the Dutch, but don't trust them too much." They were ordered to plant only half as much tobacco as corn. While they were waiting for their first harvest, Elfrith the pirate visited the neighboring islands to buy oranges. As was to be expected, as soon as he was left to his own devices, he found it much pleasanter to ply his trade than to go gathering oranges. It was considerably easier to be a Puritan in Massachusetts than in the Caribbean. Even Pym saw that an Englishman could not work in the torrid zone of Providence the way he could in the temperate zone, so he allowed Negroes to be brought in. The first friendship the Pilgrims of Providence struck up was with the pirates of Tortuga, an island that is now known as Hog Island, for to every man there must be a hundred pigs there. But in London, on the books of the Company, it was known as "Island of the Association." Naturally, this did not refer to the association between the men and the pigs, but to that of the Puritans and the pirates. Elfrith went out there to cut dyewood to ship back to England, but instead he sold it to the Dutch and the French. Smuggling begins at home. In Providence the minister lost his Christian vocation, and had to be sent back to London. The Pilgrims requested the Company to send them cards, dice, and gaming tables — and what they got was Bibles.

And so time went by, not unprofitably. The colonists began to toy with the idea of conquering Central America. They could begin with the coasts of Nicaragua, Honduras, and Darien. The Company's statutes were modified in London, and instructions were sent out. The English were to move cautiously, so as not to arouse the Spaniards' suspicions; Drake's name could be effectively invoked among the Indians, and they were to carry on evangelical labors. The explorations began, but they failed. The Dutch had already been there and had spoiled things for everyone; they had forcibly stripped the Indians of their gold necklaces and nose-rings, and had made bitter enemies of them. And the Puritans were taking no chances with Indians on the warpath.

The Pilgrims had been in the islands for almost six years, and the situation was not so favorable as at first. Spain had managed to get out of her entanglements in Europe and was beginning to take measures. A group of Spaniards sent out by the governor of Santo Domingo fell upon Tortuga, which the Company had strongly fortified, and not an Englishman was left there. Fortunately, many of them managed to escape, following the prudent example of the governor who, as soon as he sighted the ships, made off without any other explanation than "Each for himself. . . ."

The alarm spread from Providence and St. Andrew to London. The settlers prepared to fight. It was no easy matter to enter Providence, since the mouth of the bay is so narrow that only one ship can enter at a time, and the entrance can be closed off. Sentinels were on watch day and night. Everything was ready — fortifications, cannon, and muskets. And prayers. In London they were not thinking of religion but of war. On the day when Pym returned to his seat in Parliament, it was to ask: "Why should not England establish an empire in Central America like the one the Dutch are setting up in Brazil? Why cannot we wrest from the hands of Spain this second Brazil?" And when the governor of Cartagena sent his ships against Providence, the English received him with the roar of cannon. For seven days he tried in vain to find some way to enter through the reefs that form the natural defenses of the island. He sent an emissary to warn the English that if they did not leave the island he would be back with reinforcements and drive them out. The English dared him to try. The governor returned to Cartagena under cover of darkness. The rejoicing of the English was echoed in London.

The colony, which until then had been, at least theoretically, a haven for Puritans, now became a center of warfare and piracy. The King authorized reprisals against the Spaniards. Pym called a meeting of the shareholders to raise more capital; he was thinking of the reconquest of Tortuga, and with this in mind put the fleet in charge of an experienced smuggler who came out with recommendations attesting his gentlemanly rank and his military skill. In Providence military service was made obligatory. In St. Andrew, which up to this time had played a secondary role, a shipyard was set up, and small-tonnage merchant ships and raiders were built. The Spaniards called the islands dens of thieves and pirates; the answer of the English was a plan to sack

Santa Marta. And as they planned it, they attempted to carry it out. The expedition set out under the command of Mr. Rous; the ships boldly entered one of the perfect bays of the world, in whose depths they could see — reflected against the horseshoe of golden sands that encircles these blue waters — the houses gleaming as white as coconut meat. Rous landed and attacked as though he were Drake. But the Spaniards were stronger this time, and they took Rous and his soldiers prisoner. Rous was sent to a prison in Spain, from which he managed to escape by bribing the jailers with money sent him by Pym. Later he was elected to Parliament. A thumbnail sketch of Mr. Rous would read like this: From pirate ship to the Santa Marta prison; from the prison of Santa Marta to that of Cartagena; from that of Cartagena de Indias to that of San Lucar in Spain; from prison in San Lucar to Parliament in London.

Providence continued to be the dream Paradise, not only of the English but of the Puritans of Massachusetts as well. England was now the battlefield of two factions that hated each other heart and soul. The party opposed to the King, the Roundheads, who had organized the Providence Company, thought of leaving for the Caribbean, and asked permission to do so. The island was on the point of becoming the haven of the lords and gentlemen of the opposition. A brother of Lord Forbes had been proposed as governor. Pym planned to raise the capital investment to £100,000. Absurd though it may seem, this nest of pirates and drunkards, where there was a coal-black Negro for every white man, was regarded in London as a Paradise on earth. And this was not the only time.

And in New England, where the government had become an unbearable theocracy, the colonists were establishing friendly relations with those in the Caribbean. Ships from Providence reached Boston loaded with Indians, Negroes, and other native products. An ever-increasing number of Puritans began to make plans to leave New England for Providence, sold their property, and sent a representative to London to take the necessary steps. Pym gave their proposal a cordial hearing. According to him, Massachusetts was not the spot appointed by God as their haven.

And so the first group left Boston — thirty men, five women, and eight children. Was New England going to be depopulated to find a Paradise in Providence?

History grew more exciting. Newman and Jackman revived the tradition of the great pirates. An independent republic of buccaneers was planned in Central America, with a flag of its own. A democracy of bandits — it sounds like a fairy story. Butler, the new governor of Providence, successfully attacked Trujillo in Honduras. The Spaniards of Cartagena set out for Providence again, and again they returned with their tails between their legs. Butler celebrated their failure with a massacre of prisoners, carried out at the same time as the religious ceremonies ordered to celebrate the victory. When news of this reached Cartagena, Admiral Pimienta swore with rage and took an oath of vengeance: this affront would be washed out with blood, and he himself would drive the English from the islands of Providence and St. Andrew. It was said that Butler had a number of monks in prison, and this put fire into the Spaniards' hearts. The ships were prepared. Pimienta was a man of bravery, but of cool judgment. He planned the attack with the precision of an experienced strategist. His ships sailed straight to the spot from which the attack was to be launched. On the island the English were fully prepared; each man was at his post, and the cannon were ready with fuse waiting only to be lighted. The island had fourteen forts, manned by fifty-six large cannon and one hundred and forty-eight smaller ones. But Pimienta managed to break through and put his two thousand men ashore. There were howls, knife-thrusts, shots, oaths, blasphemies — and silence. The Spaniards had won a total victory. The friars emerged from their jail to chant a Te Deum. The English were put in prison, and the Englishwomen were put aboard a ship bound for London. Pimienta collected half a million ducats for the coffers of the King of Spain. The Pilgrims who were coming out from Boston heard the news en route, and promptly turned back. When they re-entered Boston everyone said that it was "a warning from Heaven."

In London, Pym saw his dream drown in a pool of blood.

The pirate Jackman raided Trujillo in Honduras, Jamaica, the coast of Cartagena, Guatemala, Darien. . . . These were little bonfires that did not affect the course of events. The Puritan Paradise had fallen into the hands of the Catholics of Spain. Providence, the home of the Pilgrims of the *Seaflower*, was lost. And by one of those curious quirks of history, it devolved upon the English poet of the century, John Milton himself, to tell the story of it. As secretary to Oliver Cromwell from 1649, it was Milton who wrote what amounted to a declaration of war against Spain: *Scriptum domini protectoris contra hispanos* (1655), a brief in defense of the Company of Providence in which the capture of Tortuga and Providence by the Spaniards and their attack on the ships of the Company are set forth. The great poet wrote the prosaic account of this other Paradise Lost, which Cromwell was to try to compensate for by the conquest of Jamaica.

It must not be imagined that on these rainbow-hued islands there lived only English, Dutch, French, Spaniards, Indians, Negroes, Jews, Huguenots, Catholics, and Puritans. On the contrary, those who gave them their real local color in the seventeenth century were the buccaneers and filibusters. Their history is the history of these men, who invented a style of fighting that was all their own. The other pirates, cast in the European mold, did the same things in the Caribbean that they did in the English Channel; theirs was still the French or the English school applied to the American medium. But not the buccaneer; he was not under the orders of any king in Europe. His king was his captain, and the captain was the member of the band who wielded the swiftest knife. Everything was share and share alike, as between brothers. When they were at home on their island, they organized themselves into Boy Scout parties and went into the hills to hunt pigs. They dried the meat in the sun and smoked it on platforms, over wood embers — *a la bucana*, as they said; treated in this way, the meat retains all its flavor, like the sausages of Spain or Thuringia, and may be kept for months. It is said that the Caribs did this with their enemies, cut up into quarters; it sounds exaggerated, but anything is possible.

"Let's go buccaneering." And at buccaneering they spent the days and weeks, sleeping in the hills, stretched out on the beach, in a joyful state of savagery. It was a rule that they never changed their clothes (when they wore any) nor washed away the stains of pig or human blood.

At other times they set out to sea without definite objective, just to see what might turn up; each carrying some dried pork or turtle meat, his pistol, and his knife. If they ran out of meat they went ashore on some island, preferably one held by the Spaniards, who were the common enemy. The first person they met was greeted with the question: "Where are the pigs?" — and if he did not take them to the pen, they sent him to hell with a knife thrust. And so on until they found the pigs, butchered them, dried their meat, and carried it to the ships in canoes. Then came the raids. The secret of their success was the lightninglike rapidity of the attack. Of the booty, nobody took anything for himself. It all went into a pool to be fairly divided by the captain when the trip was over. Each one received his share, and then got drunk. When they had drunk up everything, they put to sea again. Those who spent more time on the water than in the hills were called filibusters. In English a corsair was known as a *freebooter*, and this word, when sprinkled with a little West Indian rum, became transformed into *filibuster*.

The buccaneers and filibusters were pirates of the Old World who found life much pleasanter in the islands and resolved to make them their new home. Or they were servants the settlers had brought out from France, England, or Holland. Some of these servants were country boys lured away from Europe to serve without wages for three years; at the end of this time they received £5 or £10, and were allowed to leave. Others were young boys whom the pirates had stolen from villages and cities in Europe as the gypsies have been accused of doing. The servants were treated worse than slaves because the masters tried to get all they could out of them in three years. In order to save their lives, some would offer, in the second year of indenture, to stay on for three years more, with the hope that — following the same economic law — the master would be somewhat easier on them. The first opportunity he got, however, the servant would run off to sea or to the hills until he was lucky enough to find a camp of buccaneers who might admit him to their fraternity. To become a buccaneer was a step up in the social ladder. Life became a pleasant affair, almost the ideal existence. Raveneau de Lussan was an honest, upright person who became a buccaneer in order to pay off his debts. And lest one judge him too severely, it should be borne in mind that in Europe failure to pay one's debts was punished by having one's ears or nose cut off, not to mention a prison sentence. At any rate, Raveneau's was a fine gesture.

The buccaneer always had a close friend in the gang, his partner. This partner was his accomplice, comrade, and heir. Besides, all were brothers. When at sea they ate only two meals a day, and all gathered about the pile of meat and ate as much as they liked, regardless of whether he was captain or cabinboy. In dividing up the booty, the first share was for those who had been maimed in the attack. It was a form of social security. A man who lost his right arm received six slaves or six hundred pesos; the right leg was worth five hundred pesos; the left, 400; an eye was worth only a hundred pesos, and had the same rating as a finger. But these injuries were not taken too seriously. One of the great heroes was "Peg-leg," and the loss of an eye seemed to bring good luck.

When the filibusters returned to their camp, the tavernkeepers were waiting for them. The same thing happened in Amsterdam, says Esquemeling, with the sailors who returned from the East. The bandits were then gay, generous, and drunk — very drunk. Some of them bought kegs of rum or wine, and set them up at the door of their houses; everybody who went by had to have a drink with them. When fighting they were ferocious. They would tie their enemies naked to a tree, stick them full of balls made of palm thorns dipped in oil, and then set fire to them. If the prisoner died screaming, it was a sign that the Devil was carrying off his soul; if he died without a whimper, it was agreed that he was a brave man. Another procedure was to lash the prisoner until he bled, then put honey on the wounds to attract the mosquitoes. . . .

The best book on the buccaneers was written by Hendrik Barentzoon Smeeks, a Dutch physician who traveled on the ships of the Dutch East India Company and West India Company. His books were so entertaining that they were soon translated into all languages. His book on the buccaneers was written under the name of "John Esquemeling." The author says he will tell nothing that he has not seen or heard. He was taken out of the Indies, he says, as a servant, and resold to a kindly master who, after working him for a couple of years, said to him: "If you want to, you may go free, but you must promise to pay me what I paid for you when you make your fortune." Whereupon Esquemeling did the same as Raveneau, and joined the buccaneers to earn money. His master let him go as free as Adam — which, explains the author, means that he sent him off without a rag to cover his nakedness.

THE ISLAND OF
CROMWELL THE PROTECTOR,
AND OF
MORGAN THE PIRATE

With their mixture of courage and guile, of emotion and hard-headedness — a bit of Odysseus and a bit of Achilles seemed to be combined in every Greek — they were born to be seamen, that is, initially, pirates. Thucydides mentions this profession by name, and expressly adds "that no stigma attached to the business."

EMIL LUDWIG

WHILE the Puritans were carrying on their guerrilla warfare in the Caribbean, Spain was enlarging the scope of her Catholic activities over dominions on which the sun never set. Thousands of Franciscans, Dominicans, Jesuits carried their missions into jungle, mountains, valley, and upland until there was not a corner of the New World where a church did not raise its white belfry, where a sermon was not heard every Sunday, or the Indians were not taught the catechism. In the City of Mexico one of the largest and richest churches of the world went up; in Quito and Chuquisaca, high in the remote peaks of the Andes, the interior of the churches was covered with goldleaf, a sight to be found nowhere else in the world. Down the mighty Paraná, which runs through virgin jungles, at twilight — the hour of the Angelus — came great boats carrying Jesuits and Indians singing Latin hymns to the accompaniment of harps. Everywhere, from the far-flung territories of Mexico to the farthest limits of Chile and Argentina, carved altars were set up, images were painted, the rosary was recited, temples to the Virgin were dedicated. The blaze of Puritan fervor was but a quiet hearth fire, flaring up or dying down in Providence or St. Andrew, compared with this mystic Spanish bonfire, which lighted up half the world. The military conquest was over, and the Spaniards were making the transition from action to meditation, and America became a continent of souls, ripe for the hand of the religious reaper.

From Cádiz, fleets of twenty or thirty ships set out, so many bound for Hispaniola, so many for Santo Domingo, so many for Cartagena or Vera Cruz or Portobello. They came with their holds filled with skins of oil and wine, cloth for the shops, mercury for the mines; they returned with cargoes of silver. The flag under which they sailed was the banner of Christ, or more often that of the Sweet Name of Mary. When the sea was calm, in the afternoons the chanting of the friars could be heard from boat to boat. If it was Saint Ignatius's day and there was a group of Jesuits aboard, the rigging and masts were lighted up with paper lanterns from the evening before, and there were salvos of cannon and firecrackers. At dawn, mass was said on the bridge, and the gunwales were hung with white cloths. This was followed by processions, and hymns of ardent enthusiasm, for the Company founded by Saint Ignatius of Loyola was a militant order and its mysticism was bellicose. "Founder art thou, Ignatius, and general of the royal company, which Jesus has honored with His name. The legion of Loyola, faithful in heart, raises His standard on high. . . ." Following the feast of Saint Ignatius came that of Saint James — Santiago — patron saint of Spain. Its celebration gave the Dominicans, traveling in another ship, an excuse to vie with the Jesuits in splendor. Thus the crossing became a series of feasts, a kind of "Holy Week in Seville" on the high seas, a procession moving over the waters and through the sails, those white hands of the wind.

Among the friars there were some who were the worst in Spain, others who were good, though not overblessed with intelligence, and who had vegetated in their parishes or grown fat in the shadow of the convents. Some were holy, humble men, others were of an ingenuous, unquestioning faith; not a few were ambitious, having learned how to pull the wires of preferment in Spain, and now hoped to put their knowledge to good use in the green pastures of the New Continent. Gifted and learned artists and scholars there were, too, like the Bishop of Puerto Rico, Bernardo de Balbuena, who has gone down in literary history as one of the great Spanish poets of all time. On the governing board of the convent of La Merced, in Santo Domingo, there was a friar, a member of the executive committee, by name Gabriel Téllez, who, despite the sluggishness that weighs down the eyes at the hour of the siesta, made this shrewd observation: here "the climate develops men of keen intelligence, though inclined to be lazy." In the world of letters this friar is known by his pen name, Tirso de Molina. And alongside such subtle and finely endowed friars there were the bronze-voiced orators who rose in their pulpits to stir up factions, defy the civil authorities, terrify the Indians, and threaten the whites, making of the sermon a battle standard, and of the blessing, a blunderbuss. Others allowed themselves to be led from the narrow path by the temptations of the World, the Flesh, and the Devil, giving rise to scandals that bring a blush to the pages of the chronicles that record them, because a scandal involving a friar is doubly scandalous. Others were the purest of saints, like Saint Peter Claver, who was the balm of compassion for the Negroes in Cartagena.

Among the Dominicans who stopped in America on their way to spread the gospel in the Philippines was Brother Thomas Gage. Of an old family of English Catholics, he had been educated in the convent of the order in Spain. His brother was head of a college and a don at Oxford. But the closer Brother Thomas came into contact with the Spaniards, the more his British blood took the ascendancy and asserted itself. On reaching Mexico, he changed his plans and gave up the trip to the Philippines. He visited Guatemala, Nicaragua, Panama, Portobello, Cartagena, and Havana. Finally he returned to England, renounced his vows, declared that he considered himself fortunate because now he could see the Gospel in the light of liberty, and, with the passion that characterizes converts, lashed out at the Jesuits and Dominicans and thundered against the bishops and the Pope — the latter seeming to him the true Anti-Christ, who sold indulgences and authorized the idolatries of Gage's old companions, the Dominicans.

Now the ex-friar devoted himself to recalling all the abominations he had witnessed: the other friar with whom he got drunk in Cádiz, and their ensuing conversations; the scandal of Father Navarro in Guatemala who, as a consequence of a love affair with a lady of society, was cut by her husband and had his face scarred for life, etc. All this appeared in his book A *new survey of the West Indies*, which was a fiery appeal to England to snatch the conquest of the mainland from Spanish hands. The book had a great success, and was translated into several languages as the first document to give a reliable account of what was going on in those Spanish colonies barred to foreigners.

Cromwell did not need much urging to launch an attack against Spain. He was the intellectual heir of the group that founded the Company of Providence, and he belonged to the turbulent anti-Popish school of the coast of Devon that had carried on its pirate warfare under the cloak of Queen Elizabeth. Now Thomas Modyford, a planter who had set himself up in Barbados and accumulated a fortune, pleaded with him to send out an expedition against the Antilles, and the sometime Friar Gage, not content with having published his book, described his travels before Parliament, saying to the English: "The moment has come for England to make an assault in America against the Pope and against Spain." Cromwell planned the expedition; the orders were to attack Santo Domingo or Puerto Rico, and from there to strike at Cartagena or Havana. The admiral of the expedition was Sir William Penn, father of the colonizer of Pennsylvania; the general was Robert Venables. There were thirty-eight boats carrying twenty-five hundred hardened soldiers, the dregs of Cromwell's armies, the scum of London. The chaplain of the fleet was the ex-Dominican, Thomas Gage.

In an address to Parliament, Cromwell said: "Our great foreign enemy is Spain, our natural enemy because of her enmity against all that is godly. . . . The truth of the matter is that there can never be peace with a Popish state; sign anything you like, but rest assured that they will keep their promises only to the point at which the Pope says Amen." And to Admiral Penn he handed a statement of grievances which read:

"The King of Spain has carried out cruelties and inhuman abuses in America not only against the Indians and natives, but against all the people of other nations who inhabit those lands he has forcibly snatched from their legitimate owners in violation of the common law and the law of nations. He has put many men to death and imprisoned others, and up to the present has forbidden trade with us and with the others nations, to the point of committing hostile acts against us, in violation of the treaties existing between the two nations, alleging that these regions of the world belong to him because they were given him by the Pope. . . ."

When the expedition reached Barbados, the first island at which they stopped, and where Thomas Modyford had his plantations, many volunteers wished to join it. Making war on the Spaniards had an unfailing attraction in the Antilles. Modyford was more than pleased at the plan of the British government to change the flag of the New World. Venables offered the bound servants of the plantations their freedom if they joined him. In this way his army grew by leaps and bounds, and from every island came new recruits. The force of 2,500 men with which he set out from England had become 6,873 by the time he reached Santo Domingo in 1654. The Spanish governor, the Count of Peñalva, had only a few hundred soldiers with whom to meet the attack. If the directors of the expedition had used a little judgment, they could have annihilated the Spaniards. But good sense was the one thing Penn and Venables lacked. The admiral and the general were at cross-purposes. Penn smiled every time Venables made a blunder, and Venables made a blunder every time he gave an order or mapped a campaign. The army went ashore on a desert coast. To reach the Spanish forts, the soldiers had to advance for days and days through lands devoid of shade and water. Venables had not allowed them to carry brandy, which on such undertakings is medicine, stimulant, staff of life. One day he announced to his men that when they entered the city there was to be no looting; the indignation this produced was so great that hundreds of them threw their arms on the ground, declaring that they would not fight on those terms. And so this horde he led, but of which he was not the leader, was routed by the few Spaniards under the command of the Count of Peñalva. And if the Count had had a thousand soldiers to pursue them, not one man would have been left to tell the tale.

Now what could they do? Return to London defeated and lose their heads? No — there was still a way out: the conquest of Jamaica. In Jamaica the Spaniards had no troops at all. The English, French, and Dutch had taken other islands with a handful of buccaneers. Here all there was to do was cross an arm of the sea and plant the flag. And this they did. A tiny group of Spaniards took refuge in the hills, from which they made guerrilla sorties, but in reality all they did was to cover the escape of the women to other islands with their children and their belongings. And thus Jamaica passed, one might say for good, into the possession of the English. Nevertheless the defeat that Penn and Venables had suffered was staggering. When they presented themselves before Cromwell in the hope of offsetting their failure in Santo Domingo by their success in Jamaica, the Protector already had quarters ready for them in the Tower, where they spent several weeks paying for their ineptitude.

The new governor of Jamaica understood his job well. On August 14, 1656 he issued a decree ordering 1,701 Bibles distributed among the soldiers. On August 26, 1659 he ordered £20 sterling paid to John Hoy out of the treasury funds for fifteen dogs to hunt Negroes. Jamaica had become general headquarters for buccaneers and filibusters. They could be seen with their fierce faces, bright blue eyes, and bloody shirts, eating off gold and silver dishes. Some of their horses were shod with gold.

Back in the days of Columbus, with the object of bringing the light of the Gospel to the New World, the Spaniards freed convicts from prison and sent them out to teach the catechism. Now Cromwell, inflamed with religious zeal, did the same thing. He gave orders that convicts, vagabonds, and light women were to be rounded up throughout the British Isles — since they pre-

vented good people from living in peace and were no use in war
— and were to be transported to Barbados and Jamaica, where
the plantation owners could buy them and use them for five
years. The terms *vagabond* and *light woman* included Catholic
priests and boys and girls who professed that abominable religion. "We must," Cromwell said, "clear England of this pollu-
tion." Ireland was the ideal spot in which to carry out this plan,
for thus at the same time the death of the Protestants killed in
the latest Catholic uprising would be avenged. Cromwell's son
Henry went to Ireland as general of the troops, his father having
explained to him how to hunt down boys and girls and send
them to the Bristol jails, whence they would be sent out to the
West Indies. The son's letters reveal touching filial understanding:

"I shall not need to repeate any thinge abote the girles, not doubt-
inge but to answer your expectations to the full in that; and I think
it might bee of like advantage to your affaires there and ours here, if
you should thinke fitt to sende 1500 or 2000 younge boys of 12 or
14 yeares of age to the place aforementioned. We could well spare
them, and they would be of use to you; and who knows, but that it
may be a meanes to make them Englishmen, I meane rather, Chris-
tianes."

The English government really displayed great concern over
turning these stubborn rebels into Englishmen. A law was issued ordering them to trim their beards, to dress after the London fashion, and to drop such grotesque names as McCormick
and O'Hara for others that fall more pleasantly upon the English ear. The law suggested that to this end they take the names
of cities, such as Sutton, Chester, Trim, or Kinsale; or of colors,
like White, Black, or Brown; or of trades, such as Smith or
Carpenter; or of offices such as Cook or Butler. Refusal to comply with the law was punished by confiscation of property.

In four years, sixty-four hundred white slaves rounded up in
Ireland and Scotland were sent out to the West Indies. The
population of Jamaica seven years after its conquest was fifteen
thousand. In Barbados the plantation owners waited impa-
tiently for the arrival of the Bristol boat, and paid fifteen hun-

dred pounds of sugar a head for their purchases. Girls were in high demand, especially if they were attractive.

"It was a measure beneficial to Ireland [wrote an English historian], which was thus relieved of a population that might trouble the planters; it was a benefit to the people removed, who might thus be made English and Christians; and a great benefit to the West India sugar planters, who desired the men and boys for their bondmen, and the women and Irish girls in a country where they had only Maroon women and Negresses to solace them."

But Barbados and Jamaica were insatiable. The sugar plantations grew, and the demand for workers increased. Ireland and Scotland between them could not fill it. Children began to disappear all over England. As the ships glided down the quiet waters of the Thames, bound for the West Indies, the cries of despairing mothers could be heard from the banks calling down curses on the kidnapping sailors' heads, and pleading for their little ones. The complaints became so numerous that eventually they aroused the City Council of London. The practice of stealing children, says the report, is "a thinge so barbarous and inhumane that nature itself, much more Christians, cannot but abhorre." With grown-ups, other procedures were used. They were made drunk, and when they woke up they were on the high seas, destination Barbados. In the life of the average Englishman, Barbados loomed like a horrid specter. A new verb was coined: "to barbado." If a girl disappeared from home, it was because the slave traders had barbadoed her. Even politicians were barbadoed. Seventy gentlemen of the opposition were seized and taken to Plymouth by soldiers, and embarked there on the *John of London*, which carried them to the Bardados market. The system lasted for years. It was said that the Queen received a percentage from the business. After all, a political prisoner was no better than any other criminal, and in London a maid who stole £4 from her mistress's purse was sentenced to be sold into four years' bondage in the West Indies.

But experience on the plantations showed that the black slave was better than the white. To cut cane, grind it in the mills, and endure the tropical sun, the Negroes of Africa had proved more satisfactory than the Londoners. The disadvantage was that the Dutch handled the traffic in Negroes, so that British trade was the loser. And others were taking a hand in the game; a Genoese company had obtained authorization from Spain to sell 24,500 Negroes. England could not view all this with indifference. "The Company of Royal Adventurers to Africa" was organized. The Queen, the Duke of York, and Prince Rupert, as well as all the principal figures of London, held shares in it. Nothing could be more illuminating than to examine the long pages of its ledgers, with their columns of entries and disbursements: "1673, May 6: 204 negroes; sold for —— pounds of sugar; average price per head £17/11; 1675, February 5: 322 negroes; sold per head at £18/19 (117 women); July 26, 115 negroes; sold per head at £14 (arrived in poor shape, bad business)." Thus, from 1645 to 1667, while hundreds of whites emigrated from Barbados to Jamaica, the number of Negroes imported rose from 5,680 to 82,023. Naturally, the whites were treated with less consideration than the Negroes: if they slowed up at their work they were beaten; if they did their tasks well, it was assumed that they could do more, and their hours were increased. One day the cup ran over; the white slaves started a rebellion — or at least it was said that they were plotting to kill their masters; as punishment or warning eighteen of them were hanged.

Thus, in keeping with the spirit of the times, Barbados and Jamaica flourished. They had become the centers of great commercial intercourse. A document drawn up by the sugar planters and rum distillers stated that they employed twenty thousand Negroes on their plantations, that the crop was worth £200,000 annually, that they sent out two hundred and twenty-six ships a year, and that their exports topped those of all Spanish America. From Massachusetts came mules for the grinding mills, cloth, wood for barrels; the ships sailed back loaded with sugar, rum, Negroes from Africa, wine that had been brought in on Dutch ships, and salt from the neighboring islands. Jamaica's principal industry was piracy. Admiral Christopher Mings seized booty to the value of £300,000. In a single assault on Cumaná he took twenty-two chests full of silver coming from New Granada.

The Spaniards were pinning their hopes on the accession of Charles II to the English throne. At first the new king used very guarded language, but his statements claiming Jamaica and certain other islands as English possessions were as unequivocal as thou   had   been Cromwell speaking. A nephew of Cromwell'   mas Whetstone, put himself at the head of the Jam   tes, and the new governor of the island, Lord Windsor, declared that he would live in peace with the Spaniards of the Caribbean as long as they respected the freedom of trade. This was the most diplomatic and discreet way of declaring war. Shortly afterwards Admiral Mings made the first attack on Cuba. He fell upon Santiago in what seemed like a revival of Drake's days. The church, the hospital, the entire city indeed, were reduced to ashes. The church bells were taken to Jamaica. The cannon of the fortress were taken to the Tower of London, where they were placed on exhibition to the natural satisfaction of all beholders. The spoils were estimated at over half a million pounds. The raid on Santiago was followed by that on Campeche in Mexico, where the fortress was captured and fourteen ships passed into Mings's possession. A young man worth watching took part in both these raids: Henry Morgan.

Thus, while in London the Spanish ambassador was sometimes received and sometimes not, and there were times of war and periods of peace (so called), beyond the line — to use Drake's expression — there was no peace. In the Caribbean, violence, daring, and exchange of hostilities were the order of the day.

The most important thing that happened in the West Indies under Cromwell, something hardly mentioned in the accounts of the period, was the arrival of Henry Morgan. It is not known exactly when he first came out to the Caribbean. Nobody after Drake left such a strong impress on the lands lying about this sea. To the Spaniards he became "The Pirate" by antonomasia. In the history of Esquemeling's buccaneers, he is the central figure, and the account of how he hanged prisoners by their thumbs, stuck lighted matches under their fingernails and burned their faces with oil-soaked leaves, is like an etching of the period. But Morgan had been operating with the approval of the authorities of Jamaica; he was knighted at the court, became governor of Jamaica, and died rich in honors. If he had been born a century earlier he would have shared all Drake's risks and renown. When Esquemeling published his book, Morgan was indignant; he retained lawyers to sue the publishers for libel, and subsequent editions of the book in English came out with a prologue that was a paean of praise to Sir Henry rather than a mere apology.

When Admiral Mings returned to Jamaica after sacking Campeche, three daring captains, Morgan, Jackman, and Morris, decided to go on with their crew and raid the Spanish cities of the mainland. Altogether they had not many more than a hundred men, yet enough to assault Villa Hermosa in Tabasco. It would have been too risky to continue northward, to Vera Cruz. The south was not so well defended, less explored. This was the world of the ex-friar, Gage. And southward they headed. They crossed the gulf of Honduras, sacked Trujillo, and went on to Nicaragua, entering the country by way of the Mosquito Coast, where the Indians sided with the English. The plan was to fall upon Granada, that fine city on Lake Nicaragua, which lay closer to the Pacific than to the Atlantic. It meant a long trek overland, but the adventurers did it, and accomplished what they had set out to do. Granada, naturally, was not expecting this visit, especially as Spain was at peace with England. The looting was splendid, and the Indians and the English shared in it merrily. The Indians believed the day had come when the fair-haired followers of Morgan would replace the Spaniards as rulers of these lands. Granada was really a handsome city; the governor of Jamaica said it was as large as Portsmouth. It had seven churches, a handsome cathedral, and many schools and convents, all built of stone. In the cathedral alone Morgan took three hundred prisoners, nearly all priests and nuns. The truth of the matter is that all Granada had to defend itself with was the bronze of its bells. Morgan returned to Jamaica a conquering hero. His mailed fist had descended on the very spot Cromwell's ambitious eye had fixed upon, right between the kingdoms of Mexico and Peru. Morgan was not yet thirty. The pirates idolized him, the authorities respected him, his cousin loved him — and he married her. He was a hard drinker, he had money, and he could take his time; there would always be work for him in this sea, which was beginning to be his private preserve.

Following this adventure of Morgan and his merry lads, another captain of Jamaica, Mansfield, undertook one no less daring. His plan was to push still farther south, to Costa Rica, and thus finish covering the map of Central America. Among his six hundred men every accent could be heard: there were Englishmen, Flemings, Frenchmen, Genoese, Greeks, Levantines, Portuguese, Indians, and Negroes. It was the Foreign Legion of the Caribbean. Cutting through the forest, falling upon haciendas, they made their way. The Indians fled before them, as terrorized as the whites. The legionnaires reached Turrialba, but they were headed for the capital to sack Cartago. Mansfield had informed the governor that he was coming there to take a cup of chocolate and find out if the girls were as pretty as he had heard. The governor was Don Juan López de la Flor. No wonder the buccaneers nearly split their sides laughing at such a romantic name. To make it still funnier, the priest of Teotique was named Don Juan de Luna, and "Don Juan of the Moon" was the one who kept "Don Juan of the Flower" informed of the pirates' advance. There was still more to the joke: in Cartago they were expecting Our Lady of the Immaculate Conception to protect them. She was carried in procession through streets so thickly strewn with flowers that the steps of her barefoot faithful could not be heard. Into the air rose the flame of the tapers and the sound of prayers. How the buccaneers laughed! But this time it was the Spaniards who laughed last, because Mansfield, who was no Morgan, was afraid to set out on the almost impassable trails to Cartago, and because the governor, in spite of his name, was not the feeble reed he might have been thought. The people said the Virgin had worked a miracle: Mansfield had to put back to sea. He took by surprise the island of Providence, which twenty-five years before had been the refuge of the English. As soon as the Spaniards learned of this, they sent ships and drove the English out again.

Of all these adventures the one point that was clear was that the Caribbean was still a pirate sea. In Jamaica the buccaneers, bored with doing nothing, propagated the rumor that the Spaniards were getting ready to attack them. If the governor did not authorize Morgan to take the offensive, any day the English would have their houses burning around their ears. In the face of a danger of this sort, it was the English tradition to put defense and attack into the hands of their sea-dogs. Morgan drank and waited. The alarm grew. Everybody on the island said that the governor of Cuba was fitting out a fleet to send against Jamaica. All right; it was time for Morgan to start.

Morgan made his preparations. Everybody wanted to join him. With five hundred men in ten ships, he reached the Isle of Pines on his way to Havana. There he was joined by two hundred more, in two more ships. Some Englishmen who had escaped from prison gave him information about the defenses of Cuba. These were more powerful than had been believed. For a year the bishop had been after the authorities to finish the walls and fortifications of Havana. The bishop had been a soldier in his youth, and knew how to prepare for a fight. Morgan realized that if he tried a frontal attack on Havana he would be knocking out his teeth against a stone, so he drew off, hid his ships in Jardines de la Reina — a garden of bare rocks and sand dunes — and entered along the undefended coast to fall upon Santa María de Puerto Principe. Before the people knew what was happening, the invaders were in the streets. The defense was organized behind improvised breastworks and from housetops. Over a hundred of the inhabitants and the mayor were killed in the skirmish; Morgan's men made off with bulging knapsacks, driving before them a herd of a thousand fat steers that they slaughtered and prepared in Caribbean style; their ships were well stocked with "bucana" as they sailed away.

Their next port of call was Portobello, which had taken the place of Nombre de Dios on the coast of Panama. One of the greatest military engineers of the century, Juan Bautista Antonelli, had advised Philip II to found the new city looking out upon a bay where, with typical Spanish hyperbole, it was said that three hundred galleys and a thousand smaller craft could find accommodation. To be sure, iguanas and snakes circulated freely through the streets of Portobello, and snakes and scorpions had the impudence to go right into the houses. At night there were concerts that were deafening, for there is no bigger, noisier frog anywhere than those to be found here. When Champlain passed this spot he remarked that there was no worse or more worthless place in the world. The garrison had to be relieved every three months because of the fevers, and it was said that cows did not breed there or chickens lay eggs. Yet, what a fine sight Portobello was on the days the fleet arrived from Spain, and the luggage of the viceroys en route for Peru was put ashore, and merchants swarmed eagerly around to see what new things had been sent out from Castile, and the mule-trains arriving from Panama dropped their loads of silver ingots on the wharves, where they were piled up like cord wood. The cathedral, the market place, the hospital, the custom house, and the governor's residence were all of stone. With the fortress of San Felipe de Todo Fierro on one side, the castle of La Gloria, the fort of San Jeronimo, the walls defended the harbor like two stout arms. Seen from the sea, Portobello was an impressive sight; from the rear, its only defenses were snakes and frogs. The streets disappeared and were lost in the brush, swamps, and canebrakes, crossed only by a bridle path. Morgan knew all this, and knew just what he had to do. If he tried to enter through the mouth of the harbor his ships would be crushed in the embrace of the protecting arms of stone and lead. But if he took the road used by the frogs and the snakes, he could, like them, enter the market place without interference. The plan was a daring one, and the French who were with him backed out. He went on without them, left his ships at a remote spot along the coast known as Bogotá, and in a day's journey, most of which was made in canoes through the bayous, was at the outskirts of the city. An Englishman who had been a prisoner of the Spaniards acted as Morgan's guide. Of the three fortresses that had to be subdued, the first fell without a struggle, but the city was awakened, the bells sounded a tocsin, and while the raiders were sacking the church, the shops and homes, the governor fortified himself in one of the redoubts, and began to fire upon the English. To silence him, Morgan had only knives and pistols. Through the crack of gunfire could be heard the cry of "English dogs, pirate bandits, Protestant swine," and others that will not bear repeating. "Filthy Papists, Spanish braggarts, chicken-hearted monks," retorted the English, along with other epithets that must likewise be omitted. To attack the fortress the walls had to be scaled. Every time the English attempted this, the Spaniards repulsed them, hurling heavy rocks down from the battlements. Morgan found a solution that assured him victory: at the point of a pistol he made monks and nuns run up the scaling ladders. The governor was stabbed to death, and along with him the stoutest defenders of the fortress. The president of the tribunal of Panama paid the ransom; but, as Morgan's prowess was so amazing, he sent him a polite message asking him to show him the arms he had used for his triumph. Morgan sent him his pistol, with these words: "Keep it for a year, Your Excellency, and I'll come back for it." To which the governor replied: "I am returning it to you, for it is only right that you should know that you are not going to take Panama as you did Portobello; but as a consolation prize you may keep this emerald ring in token of my admiration of your audacity. . . ."

The pirates were on top of the world. They laid their plans for new expeditions. Cartagena eluded Morgan's clutches only by a miracle. When the ships were ready to set out on the raid, the flagship blew up and half the men seated at the table with Morgan were transported straight to the other world — "to hell," was the comment in Cartagena; "it was the Virgin of the Popa who performed the miracle." And there was not an inhabitant of Cartagena who did not visit that Virgin's shrine to light a candle of gratitude. Morgan then turned his glance on Maracaibo, in 1669 a less powerfully fortified stronghold. He marched into the streets with a ruffle of drums after the garrison capitulated. The inhabitants fled to the woods. Morgan subjected his prisoners to a variety of tortures, and in this way learned where the treasures of the city were hidden and dug them up. He spent a month in Maracaibo; it seemed as though he would never leave. Then he went on to Gibraltar, and cleaned that out. With his ships loaded with meat and gold and silver he prepared to return to Jamaica. Suddenly he found himself bottled up; the Spaniards had closed the entrance to the harbor with their ships. Whereupon Morgan employed a stratagem the English had used against the Invincible Armada: he prepared a fire ship, and the little craft, loaded with explosives, advanced against the Spanish fleet. Many tree trunks had been dressed up with caps and shirts to give the appearance of a strong force of soldiers prepared to attack. At the very moment the ship drew alongside the flagship, as though to board it, the fuse went off and the ship became a mass of flame moving through the Spanish fleet setting the ships afire. Morgan reached Jamaica with loot amounting to 250,000 pesos — all the gold and silver of the churches — Negroes, and wine. He sat down to drink and take his ease. The governor awarded him a great grant of land, and Morgan became an honest, respected planter. After the centuries that have passed, the visitor is still shown Morgan's Hill, Morgan's Valley, Morgan's River, where his plantation was.

A brave Spaniard ventured onto the shores of Jamaica, and nailed to a tree a challenge to Morgan. Was this to be endured? Morgan had only to go to the market place, walk through the taverns, and show himself. Port Royal was a city of drunkards and adventurers; everyone rose to follow him, even the French. The city council gave him letters beginning with the prescribed formulas: "To Admiral Henry Morgan, Esquire, Greetings!" Thirty-eight ships, a hundred and eighty cannon, 1,320 men. All Jamaica seemed to embark upon the waves. On to Panama! From the fortress of San Lorenzo at the entrance to the Chagres River, through which Morgan planned to make his way to Panama, his ships were sighted. This was fair war, no surprises. The governor was in the fortress with three hundred and fourteen Spaniards. Its stockade and walls seemed impregnable, and with the shout of "English dogs!" the Spaniards greeted and defied

Morgan's men. But ever since Maracaibo, Morgan seemed to have made a pact with fire; it was to be his arm. Again and again his troops were thrown back by these Spaniards, who were in no mood to yield. Finally Morgan managed to land his fire balls against the stockade and ruin the fortress. Even amidst the ashes the Spaniards defended themselves furiously. Only ten remained unwounded. Nearly all, from the governor down, died in the fray. Some threw themselves from the walls into the sea, preferring death to becoming Morgan's prisoners. The breaching of the entrance was hard, but the road to Panama lay open. It was the Spaniards, now, who leagued themselves with fire. Everywhere Morgan advanced through ashes. The Spaniards burned all the villages along the road. The Indians and whites fell back toward the Pacific, defying him: "We'll wait for you on the plain, English dogs!" Morgan followed the mule trail. These were days of hunger, but of hope, too. From the headlands Morgan pointed out to his men the western plains that merged into the sands where the Pacific spread its lacy foam. There the Spaniards were drawn up in battle formation, but the sight of the white houses of the city in the background lent the buccaneers an irresistible impetus. The inhabitants of Panama barricaded themselves in the side streets. Morgan's men leaped the barricades like agile hounds.

Panama was one of the largest cities of the New World. Travelers, often blessed with a heated imagination, compared it in wealth and beauty to Venice. At fair time, fifty thousand people gathered in its streets. The lamentation of the Negroes confined in the great warehouses of the Genoese company echoed through the air. In the homes of the rich merchants, with their ceilings of beautifully carved beams, dinner services of hand-hammered silver shimmered. All this magnificence was but a sheet of ashes the day after the assaults. Morgan entered between walls of flame. Who had set fire to his triumph? No one could say. For a whole month his greedy men dug about in the ruins. Considering the importance of Panama, one hundred and seventy-five heavily loaded mules and six hundred prisoners was not much of a prize for the homeward trip. Above all, the French considered themselves duped, and hatred was in their eyes as they glared at Morgan who, when it came time to divide the spoils, made them take off their shoes to be sure they had not hidden anything. This was the twilight of Morgan's career as a buccaneer.

Then began the career of Morgan the gentleman. He went to London. The attack on Panama had been made while England and Spain were at peace under the terms of the treaty called the Peace of America, drawn up to include the sea of the West Indies. Morgan and the governor of Jamaica, as his accomplice, were sentenced to prison. But this sentence was merely a formula for diplomatic purposes; the governor spent some time in the Tower, a mark of distinction, and was honored on his release. Morgan rose to heights of fame. He had correspondence with the King. He was made a knight. The King presented him with a snuffbox bearing the royal effigy surrounded with diamonds, and appointed him to be lieutenant-governor of Jamaica with Lord Vaughan. Jamaica now received flattering attentions from the English government. The person who drew up the instructions for its proper government was none other than the greatest English philosopher of the day, the man from whose treatises the spokesmen of the French Revolution took their ideas about the sovereignty of the people and civil and religious freedom and from whose maxims Jefferson drew the essence of the Constitution of the United States: John Locke. For the moment it was Henry Morgan who was entrusted with putting Locke's theories into practice. What an interesting experience it would be to reconstruct an imaginary conversation between these two men on the excellence of wisdom and the excellence of meat prepared *a la bucana*!

Sir Henry spent the last years of his life in Jamaica as a rich and upright citizen. Under the influence of his friendship with the King and the philosophy of Locke, when he was in office he pursued the pirates with relentless zeal. But there was a part of his past he never abandoned: his bottle of rum, always close at hand. He died the death of all rich men — because of infirmities, some say; others, because of the doctor's mistakes. But be that as it may he died in August, 1688, and each of the ships in the harbor fired a salvo of twenty-one shots. Among these ships was one that was most fittingly named for the occasion, the *Drake*. In the church, which was crowded with dignitaries and adventurers, the minister preached an inspiring sermon. Some years later an earthquake destroyed the church, and a tidal wave engulfed the cemetery and Morgan's tomb. But as a monument to Morgan's memory there stand the thick walls of the monastery of San José and the cathedral tower in old Panama, through whose cracks emerge the green branches of huge trees. The Spaniards, after the fire, moved the city to another site.

XII

THE COCKFIGHT

Here the men wear their arms as though they were taking part in a carnival.　　　　　JEAN DU CASSE

Depuis Drake et l'assaut des Anglais mécréants
Tes murs désemparés croulent en noir décombres
Et, comme un glorieux collier de perles sombres
Des boulets de Pointis montrent les trous béants.
　　　　　JOSÉ MARIA DE HEREDIA
　　　　　(A Cartagena)

(Since the assault of Drake and his English rogues
(Your neglected walls have crumbled in decay,
(And like a glorious necklace of black pearls
(Display the gaping rents torn by de Pointis.)

For more than fifty years unhappy Spain had had to fend off the attacks of all the European powers. Now, to her satisfaction, she was able to sit back and watch a number that had not been scheduled on the program. Until yesterday, in the buccaneer camp or on the bridge of the pirate ship all her enemies had been brothers-in-arms, and, comrades all, had attacked to the cry of "All against Spain!" Suddenly, the gang began to break up, and the Caribbean turned into an international cockpit. Each of the islands flew its own colors, though there were many that changed them according to the way the game was going. If the spur-gaffs did not always show, it was because the cockers were sharpening them for the fight. There in far-off Europe, in England, France, and Holland, the players were watching the fight from a distance, laying bets, egging on the combatants like professional gamblers. But from the amphitheater of its colonies on the mainland, Spain took in the show with the enjoyment of a spectator who has been admitted on a free ticket. Naturally, she ran the risk that these old ex-comrades might suddenly recall her, and make her pay the costs of the whole performance. At times they invited her to put a cock into the ring, and take a hand in the game. But she bided her time. It was natural that, on this occasion at least, she should be content to look on while the others shed their blood.

In general these wars were complicated affairs; in 1665, Holland and England were at war; in 1668, France and England. In 1667 England, Holland, and France signed a peace; in 1670, peace was signed between England and Spain. In 1672 Holland was at war with France and England; in 1673, France and Spain were at war. In 1673, Holland and England signed a treaty of peace; in 1678, France and Holland signed a peace. In 1689 England, Holland, and Spain were at war with France; 1679, peace; in 1702, England and Holland were at war with France and Spain, and so forth. . . .

These were sea wars, and the Caribbean was the sea. News reached the Caribbean slowly; when mails arrived announcing peace, the fleets had sailed out the night before to attack the enemy; and when they were informed of war, by some happy presentiment the adventurers already knew of it, and had followed their "hunch" without waiting for confirmation. The motto of the fighter in the Caribbean was: "Always be ready; better an hour early than a minute late." At times the kings went through the gestures of reproving this tendency to jump the gun, but the reprimand was always followed by a reward. We have seen that the road to knighthood involved a brief stop-over in the Tower of London.

At first, Huguenots, Puritans, Jews, Lutherans, Calvinists fought the Spaniards because they were Catholics. The thought of the gold and silver to be seized lent zeal to their efforts. This was no longer the Golden Age, however, but the Leather Age. Leather, sugar, Negroes, and tobacco were now as valuable as gold had once been, and it was just as profitable to seize a Dutch boat as a Spanish. And the French Catholics attacked the English Protestants; the English Protestants, the Dutch Jews; the Dutch Jews, the French Catholics. The Lutherans zealously assaulted the cowardly Papists; the Papists, the converted Jews;

the Jews, the besotted friars; the friars, the Protestant dogs. . . .
Each group put into his rallying cry the choicest adjectives in his
vocabulary.

The struggle, however, was not left wholly in the hands of
private enterprise. This was the situation in the beginning; then
the governments were but the wall that reflected the shadow pictures made by the pirates of the Caribbean. When the Devon
sea-dog raided Panama, the Queen meekly followed his lead. The
islands were the adventurers' personal property. When the first
companies were organized in France, the King bestowed his
blessing upon them and became a shareholder in them, but the
companies appointed the governors. After a few years, the companies were dissolved; there was no one to exercise a check on
the governor, and the State, which meanwhile had been developing as the new force in European politics, decided to inter-
vene. The islands became, so to speak, floating provinces of the
mother country. For France, the King appointed the governors;
official fleets made their appearance in the Caribbean, under the
command of crown officers, and openly flying the French flag.
Holland and England followed the same procedure. At times,
war was fought in the Greek manner — that is, no holds were
barred in deceiving the enemy. Thus Lord Willoughby, attacking the French in Saba, sailed in flying the French flag. But the
fundamental change was that the Caribbean was no longer run
as a stockholders' corporation, but now formed a part of what,
ironically enough, is known as the society of nations, whose
members smile only to bare their teeth, and shake hands only
to show their claws.

Wars were made and unmade in Europe for reasons compre-
hensible only to Europeans. They always had something to do
with politics, which was never clearly grasped in the Caribbean.
The inhabitants of this region considered an opportunity to fall
upon a Dutch ship enough excuse for war; and nobody could
understand why, because William of Orange had married a niece
of Charles II, there was to be an end to the war between Holland and England. The French, for example, made heroic efforts
to dislodge the English from islands they had occupied for years;

but then came the Peace of Breda, and all spoils had to be returned to the vanquished. Of the Peace of Ryswick one historian wrote: "Naval expeditions had been sent out, armies landed, battles fought, sieges laid, invasions repulsed; yet, when the war ended at last, neither nation retained a foot of the other's territory." It was incidents of this sort that created a lack of any sense of responsibility in the men who fought in the West Indies. They had to do only one thing: fight. How, why, on what side, ultimately became a matter of indifference. The Spaniards had been fighting the English for a hundred and fifty years. One fine day their captains told them: "We are now allies of England, and tomorrow we go out together, Spanish and English, to fight the French." Which was exactly what happened in Haiti. This, however, did not hinder them, as soon as the battle was over, from calling each other "Protestant dogs" and "Papist cowards."

Let us first consider the French. France had a more complete sense of the State than the others. Moreover, her king was an absolute, Catholic sovereign. From the time Cardinal Richelieu put his canonical finger in the statutes of the first company organized for America, he said very explicitly that only native-born Frenchmen, Catholic, Apostolic, Roman, would be admitted into the French Antilles. But the Church in France was flexible and mundane, different from the Church in Spain. King Henri IV's remark that "Paris is worth a mass" was fairly typical of the general attitude of the country. For this reason, there were Huguenot officials in the islands, and the French colony of Tortuga was Huguenot. The important thing was not the Church, as in the case of Spain, but the State. "L'état c'est moi," said Louis XIV, and in the wake of these four words moved a whole mighty, proud kingdom, with its army of officials, all this powerful machine directed by cardinals like Richelieu and Mazarin, or by ministers of the genius of Colbert. Thus, while the structure of bureaucracy was being set up in the French islands, in the English the plantation owners were getting an ever tighter grip on things. English sovereignty rested in the hands of His Majesty's subjects; wherever they carried the flag, they took with them a bit of this sovereignty. At the French court the King said: I am the State. In Jamaica, Barbados, and Nevis, the Englishman said: I am the Empire.

The King of France entrusted the government of the islands of Saba and Santa Cruz to the Order of the Knights of Malta. "Just as the knights," he wrote in a long and impressive document, "have made the island of Malta in the Mediterranean a bulwark against the infidel, so must you do in the islands of the Caribbean." The second governor was none other than a nephew of Saint Francis of Sales. M. de Sales went forth to war accompanied by Jesuit priests who, on the eve of battle, instead of allowing the soldiers to "waste their time" on military preparations, drilled them in spiritual exercises. Of course, a government cannot give itself over wholly to piety, and the first thing M. de Sales did was to draw and quarter a certain Boisson, an irascible fellow, a drunkard and trouble-maker, who insolently demanded the abolition of certain taxes and underscored his words with a pistol shot that almost killed the governor. The head, arms, and legs of the traitor were placed on view in various cities of the island, in keeping with the custom of the day. Then the governor started a war against the English, and went about it so enthusiastically that he was finally killed in combat.

The Catholic standard of France attracted the Irish. Many of them fled from Jamaica and Barbados to take the oath of allegiance to France. They formed a regiment of their own, under the command of one M. Coullet, a strange personage whose life reads like a novel. He was born in the palace of the King of France. His father was the commander of the regiment of Navarre, his mother the governess of the children of Louis XIV's brother. When Coullet was of an age to choose between the brilliance of the court and that of the Caribbean sun, he preferred the latter, being an adventurer at heart. When he reached the Caribbean he set about recruiting the Irish under the banner of the Pope. When the French invaded the English islands they burned down the property of the English but respected that of the Irish. The Protestant churches were turned over to Catholic priests. The Irish could now follow the dictates of their conscience in religious matters, and were profoundly grateful to M. Coullet. Then he transferred his activities to the islands where the Caribs and the Negroes had revolted against the English. The Negroes greeted him with shouts of: "Here comes *compadre* Coullet. My compá Culé, my compá Culé!" And the Caribs hailed him in the same fashion. He was popular with everyone. When he talked to the Caribs, he appeared before them naked, his body painted red. One and all, they looked like devils. In tribute to his victories the Caribs brought "compá Culé" the leg of an Englishman, smoked in buccaneer style.

The battalions of Negroes fought under their own officers, who shortly before had attempted to provoke an uprising against the English. To some of them the French gave generals' uniforms, complete with cocked hats and swords, and promised that after victory was won they should have white women as their spoils. Never did the drums beat out a more stirring battle call.

In Mexico, and in Quito high up in the heart of the mountains, the bell that called to the Angelus swung in a golden circle like the halo that surrounds the saints' heads. No turmoil came to disturb the quiet hour of prayer. But below, the islands seethed with fire, brandy, and the volley of guns. There the change from action to meditation did not take place after the manner of the gentle mutations in the lives of the mystics. The filibusters sought their peace of soul after they had dispatched their enemies to the other world.

"One day [relates the Dominican priest Jean-Baptiste Labat] I was preparing to return to my parish, when our father superior detained me to officiate at a high mass the filibusters had ordered said the next day, at which they were going to receive communion in fulfillment of a vow they had made during a fight in which they captured two English ships. We spent all Friday morning hearing their confessions. Then a mass in honor of the Virgin was celebrated with great solemnity; I officiated at it and blessed three huge loaves of bread presented to me by the captain, who was accompanied by his officers, to the music of fifes and drums. A corvette and the two prize ships, which were anchored in front of the church, fired a salvo as mass was begun, when the Host was elevated, when the blessing

pronounced, and for the Te Deum sung after the mass. All the filibusters brought their offerings: a candle apiece and thirty sous or
a silver crown in money. Those who received communion took it
with the greatest devotion and humility. When I visited the corvette
I wanted to buy a box of butter and one of candles. I asked the
boatswain how much they were and he answered: 'Pick out what
you want, Father, and then we'll fix up our accounts.' I made my
choice, and when I went to pay him he told me they had taken so
much booty that he was not going to charge me for those trifles;
and he gave me besides fifty bottles of beer and cider, saying it was
the least they could do in return for my coming to hold mass for
them, and that he hoped I would commend him to God in my
prayers."

Father Labat goes on to say that the idea prevalent in Europe
that the filibusters are not devout is unfounded, for they always
put aside a part of their booty for the Church, and when in their
raids they find things appropriate for church use, they always
bring these back to their own parish.

Father Labat, whose book was to become one of the classics
of this world of the Antilles, found the life of the filibusters so
well suited to his tastes that he built a watch-tower near his
church and set up a cannon on it. His marksmanship was so good
that in many a hard-fought battle the filibusters called on him
for help. Before Father Labat another Dominican, Father du
Tertre, wrote his *Histoire générale des Antilles habitées par les
Français*. In this book, which described man in a state of nature,
du Tertre, according to one historian, anticipated Rousseau by
a hundred years.

Father du Tertre says that the Antilles were once a hell for
Indian women and a paradise for Indian men; but that now
they are a hell for Frenchmen and a paradise for Frenchwomen.
This was somewhat exaggerated; the truth is that men and
women shared alike the dangers and fears of daily life. And in
the background hovered that difficult problem of balancing the
human materials that were assembling there. To keep a proper
equilibrium between the sexes, it was often necessary to mix a

diversity of colors. In the wars, the women were never outdone by the men in enthusiasm and courage. This has always been the case, and if the reins of government were handed over to the women, contrary to what many people think, there would be more wars than there are now. A typical figure of these times is Magdalena of Valence, the daughter of William the Silent, who served one of her father's cannon with greater courage and efficiency than any other gunner.

At the beginning, keeping order in the islands was a serious problem. The governor of Martinique, Jean Charles de Baas, Marquis of Castelmore, as a security measure issued a decree regulating the activities of "Protestants, Jews, inn-keepers, female vagrants, and other undesirable elements." Apparently the governor had no trouble lumping these different groups together and reducing them to one common denominator. It should be added that the Marquis was the perfect gentleman, and that his brother, M. d'Artagnan-Montesquiou, was the living model of one of Dumas's three musketeers. But when d'Ogeron was appointed governor, the policy changed. He formulated the principle of the desirables among the undesirables. The islands could not be properly governed as long as the men were footloose, and he appealed to his superiors in France for shipments of girls. One hundred and fifty arrived on the next boat. Historians are divided as regards the social standing of these aids of law and order. Obviously, they were not out of the top drawer. But they seem to have worked out satisfactorily and to have quickly acquired "many of the virtues of frontier life: they became veritable Amazons who could shoot, ride, and hunt as well as their husbands."

The handling of the color problem presented great difficulty. The government viewed with alarm the increase of mulattoes. Restless, touchy, tricky, impressionable, they were an obstacle to peace and order. Ordinances were issued forbidding white men to cohabit with Negresses. If a Negro child showed evidence of having white blood, its paternity was investigated, the offender was fined two thousand pounds of sugar, and the Negress and the little mulatto became the property of the hospitals.

Since to the friars in charge of these institutions, this was manna from heaven, they developed into highly skillful detectives in such matters. One of them made a name for himself as an expert by reason of his success in these investigations. But one day he suffered a set-back at which the judges nearly killed themselves laughing. It was a case in which a certain French gentleman was accused of being the father of a little pickaninny. The expert appeared before the religious court in charge of such cases, and when the Negress came in with the child in her arms, without waiting to be questioned she walked over to the expert, and, pointing to him, said to the little mulatto: "Look, there's your daddy!"

In his book Father Labat has a long treatise on the way to discover whether a baby is a mulatto. It is not easy, since during the first month the color is vague, but he works out a method based on the tint of the half-moon at the fingernail base and of certain unmentionable parts. Father Gumilla, in *El Orinoco Ilustrado*, says the sign is to be found in a different place. But this was really a matter for anthropologists. The real problem was the moral one. Father Labat was, for instance, confronted with the case of a white girl who was going to bear the child of a Negro. When the girl's father learned of it, he lost his head, as might have been expected. The only advice Labat could give him was to sell the Negro at once for transport to another island and send the girl into the back country so that no one would know about the child when it was born. Fortunately, a Pole turned up who offered to marry the girl and make himself responsible for the child. Labat ends his story: "And we married them with all possible speed, before the Pole should change his mind."

For more than half a century, with only short breathers, France and England had been at war with each other. But occasionally they joined forces against a common enemy, Holland. It is interesting to see how this tiny nation that had emerged from the mud now defied England, France, and Portugal as boldly as she had challenged Spain a century before. Her colonies were to be found in the Far East, in Brazil, North America,

Guiana, and the West Indies, and for the first time in history a breastwork of masts protected a battle-line that circled the earth. The Brazilians managed to drive the Dutch out of Recife. The survivors went to Martinique and Guadaloupe, where the French gave them a cordial welcome. They made up a group of industrious planters, and brought the first cuttings of sugar cane to these islands. Although they were Jews, it is said that the Catholic authorities even went so far as to change the calendar so these new brothers could observe their Sabbath.

In North America the English proceeded against the Dutch as efficiently as did the Brazilians. The Dutch, having bought the island of Manhattan from the Indians for 60 florins (the equivalent of $24), had built a pretty city of brick and timbered houses, with sloping roofs and windmills — a replica in the New World of a typical port of Holland — to which they gave the name of New Amsterdam. Charles II of England planned to seize the city by surprise. The idea was to attack without warning, capture it, and, once the prize was in his hands, declare war. In secret he bought from Lord Stirling his claim to Long Island for £3,500, transferred the title to his brother James, at that time Duke of York, and with the same secrecy ordered the fleet to attack. The Dutch in New Amsterdam must have had some suspicion of what was in the air, for they ordered the ships about to sail for Curaçao to remain in port, and prepared to defend the city. But the suspicion seemed so groundless, and the assurance they received from Holland was so convincing, that the ships were presently allowed to sail, and New Amsterdam was left unprotected.

At that moment — it was August 27, 1664 — the English fleet appeared. The commander demanded the city's unconditional surrender. Peter Stuyvesant, the governor, hurriedly threw up barricades along Wall Street, and the Dutch flag flew defiantly from the fort. But this was merely a gesture, a sop to pride. They were no match for the British, and the burghers realized that there was nothing to do but surrender. King Charles II handed the colony over to his brother, the Duke of York (later James II), and the name "New Amsterdam" was erased from the maps and replaced by "New York." At the Peace of Breda, Holland had to bow to the inevitable and hand her old colony over to the British; in return, she received Surinam — that is, Dutch Guiana. Thus England paid with some patches of jungle along the banks of an unexplored river, five degrees above the Equator, for the site of New York City and its surrounding territory.

In Guiana the Dutch displayed their characteristic tenacity. On the flooded shores they undertook against the sea and the elements the same kind of struggle that had wrested Holland from the ocean. Future generations would find there another New Amsterdam — but it would be just a group of wooden houses and a Botanical Garden. This seems to have been Holland's destiny: to begin with an empire and wind up with gardens. It is not a bad idea. However, the Dutch now made Guiana the center of their slave trade, and introduced sugar cane, coffee, and tobacco. The planters, with their wide straw hats, white shirts, and heavy leather boots, sipped their coffee, drank quantities of beer, and smoked their own tobacco in handsome meerschaum pipes.

The set-back the Dutch had received in Brazil and North America was not decisive. The sea was still theirs, and France and England joined forces to wipe them off the map. The Dutch had an account to settle with England, to pay back the treacherous attack that had robbed them of New Amsterdam. In 1672 they attacked the English fleet in the Channel and won the victory of Texel, "the most painful military humiliation the English had known since the day William of Normandy disembarked in Sussex." The English fleet was burned at Chatham, and the Thames was blockaded. England had to sue for peace. There remained the problem of France, and the place to attack France was in the Caribbean. But here the Dutch were not so fortunate. In Guiana they advanced as far as Cayenne, but the French drove them back. Curaçao was on the verge of falling into French hands; fever checked the soldiers advancing on the island. But saddest of all was what happened at Martinique. De Ruyter, the admiral who had helped defeat the English in the Channel, was unable to subdue the capital of this island of

Negroes and sugar. He had to withdraw in humiliation, pursued in defeat by fever and dysentery. The corpses of hundreds of his men strewed the waters, to be devoured by sharks. And finally, off the tiny island of Tobago, the whole Dutch fleet came under the fire of the French, and this time it was the Dutch who were destroyed. Fortunately, the Dutch were saved from slipping completely downhill by the circumstance of the marriage in 1677 of William of Orange to his cousin Mary, daughter of the Duke of York and niece of Charles II. Thus peace with England seemed assured, and France could not continue to challenge the Dutch by herself. At the same time, the victorious French fleet was wrecked on some reefs, and the broken spars floating on the waves were mute testimony to the unpredictable turns of the wheel of fortune in the Caribbean.

The next war found the English, Dutch, and Spaniards allied against the French. France was approaching the logical goal of these conflicts: Spain was the real enemy. In the first acts of the drama, fortune swung like a pendulum. The English fleet, four thousand men and forty-seven ships attacked Martinique unsuccessfully. Then the English and Spanish together won a victory on the island of Santo Domingo. But the French began to see the light. There were Cartagena, Portobello, Vera Cruz, the Spanish colonies. The old enemy, the real one, was that spectator who had been sitting back for years, rubbing his hands and watching the cockfight from the benches. L'Olonnais, a ferocious fellow who was described in Esquemeling's book as opening a prisoner's breast with his sword to tear out the victim's heart and eat it raw, had set the example with his sack of Maracaibo. A Dutchman and a Frenchman — "all brothers against Spain" —, Van Horn and Grammont, had raided San Juan de Ulua. And, finally, Louis XIV had what seemed a Heaven-sent communication.

In the Bastille there was a Huguenot who was expiating the crime of having, while living in Holland, made mock of the Catholic Church. In an attempt to secure his freedom, he wrote a report to one of the French King's ministers, outlining a plan of attack on Cartagena that would line the royal pockets with silver. The plan fascinated the Baron de Pointis, second-in-command of the fleet, and the baron persuaded the King. There was only one danger: peace might break out between Spain and France — God forbid! Plans were speeded up. Pointis persuaded some wealthy Frenchmen to invest money in the scheme. Although nobody knew what fortress was to be attacked, the mirage of galleons loaded with silver captivated them once more. Du Casse, the leader of the filibusters in the Antilles, was instructed to hold himself and his worthies of knife and pistol in readiness.

Since the days of Drake, Cartagena had multiplied its fortifications, despite the fact that Spain's problem was far more complicated than that of either England or France, whose possessions consisted of tiny islands on which one or two fortresses were sufficient defense. Spain had to fortify her territories on two oceans from the Straits of Magellan to the coasts of Mexico. It had been great foresight, or great good luck, to build the principal cities far inland, among the mountains, out of reach of the pirates. But there were the ports, and each port had to be a citadel. In the reign of Philip II, Antonelli was entrusted with working out a plan of continental defense, and the first step was building fortresses on the Straits of Magellan. Then he laid out that vast system of fortifications which stood for centuries as part of the stone girdle that was Virgin America's belt of chastity, to which belonged the walls and fortresses of Portobello in Panama, on the island of Puerto Rico, Morro Ridge in Havana, San Juan de Ulua in Mexico, and Cartagena in New Granada. And in these plans Cartagena stood out as the major redoubt on the mainland.

On to Cartagena, ordered Baron de Pointis. Du Casse, leader of the buccaneers, tried to dissuade him from the hazardous undertaking. Why not try Portobello, Vera Cruz, or Havana? But the secretive and stubborn Baron, with the Huguenot's plan in his pocket, had not come out to discuss plans. He was a soldier carrying out the King's orders, and that was all there was to it. Du Casse limited himself to assembling his men, and signed an agreement with Pointis as to his share of the spoils. The buccaneers always looked with suspicion at these important figures arriving from France.

In Cartagena it was hard to recruit volunteers; nobody believed in the possibility of an assault. When Pointis was sighted approaching with twenty-six ships, carrying over five thousand men and five hundred and thirty-eight cannon, the defenders of the city, struck with surprise and bewilderment, made frantic last-minute efforts. Don Sancho Jimeno was cut off in the fortress of Bocachica, and the governor failed to send him the reinforcements he needed. He had no choice but to surrender. He yielded to the urging of his own officers, but he had, it is said, put up such a gallant resistance that the Frenchman returned his sword to him in tribute to his courage. Don Sancho surrendered the fortress with tears of shame and rage. Behind it lay the city, enveloped in its walls, without men to defend it or a head to govern it. Pointis brought his cannon ashore one by one, set them up, and began methodically bombarding the walls where he believed they could be breached. He strung a pontoon bridge opposite the tower of Santo Domingo, and from it hurled bombs into the city. Twenty-two hundred men fell like a punishment from heaven upon the churches and important buildings. The cathedral had a hole torn in it; the parish church of the Blessed Trinity was perforated, and a bomb exploded in the chapel of the hospital while the Blessed Sacrament was exposed. Through the streets ran women, brave youths, cowardly youths, old people, falling over one another, all mad with fear. The officials of the Inquisition, who had been guarding their headquarters, realized that the hour for flight had come. They hastily tied up chests, boxes, and bundles of papers from their secret files, and quickly judged such cases as were pending, lest the French should enter before the heretics had received their just punishment. Up the mountain trails, buffeted by drenching rainstorms, fled the city's population, "many being drowned on the way, others buried in the mud, and many more dying of hunger." Finally the breach that Pointis had been working at was opened. The French swarmed in and the Spaniards capitulated. The terms were that all articles of value be turned over to them; the conqueror allowed the defeated to keep their clothes and their furniture. "Finally arrangements were made to hand over the city, and the governor departed with the regular troops and volunteers, with guns loaded and lighted fuses, standards flying and four artillery cannon." All this took place in 1697, on the 3d of May, the month of the Virgin. Pointis ordered a Te Deum sung in the cathedral in thanksgiving for the victory God had bestowed upon French arms.

The officials of the Inquisition were stupefied to see the buccaneers — such devout Catholics, and now in the service of His Most Christian Majesty, Louis XIV — kill a friar of the order of Saint Francis because he begged them not to despoil the Virgin of her gold crown, smash the statues of Our Lady of the Rosary and those of the saints "because they were enraged at the slight amount of gold used to ornament them." And they dressed up a statue of Saint Michael in grotesque fashion, stood it in one of the windows of the Tribunal of the Inquisition, and used it as a target, afterwards throwing the remains on the dung-heap. "They took from the Tribunal rooms the garments and caps worn by the penitents, and dressed themselves in them, some taking the part of the offenders and others the part of the ministers of the Holy Office, making a mock of the proceedings of an auto-da-fe, such as the reading aloud of the sentences, all with great scoffing and mockery."

Typical of the looting is this brief inventory of what was taken from the official of the Inquisition, Don Pedro Calderón: in money, in a box, 32,894 pesos; and "six chocolate cups, a salt cellar, two bowls, a chocolate pot with several various pieces inside, a chamber, a washbasin, a ewer, two candlesticks, a pot with a spout, six medium-sized plates and two smaller ones, two small platters, two large ones, two serving dishes — all of silver; a necklace of thirty-three links, and another of thirty-six beads, both of gold; a string of ninety-eight pearls, two necklaces of baroque pearls, and a bracelet; a collar of gold with a cross of emeralds and eleven links; a gold rosary; a gold brooch with twelve pearls and an emerald in the middle; a pair of gold and emerald earrings with emerald pendants, two gold rings each set with seven diamonds, a pair of earrings of burnished gold. . . ."

When the French finally withdrew from Cartagena, suffering more from attacks of dysentery than from anything else, they were confronted with the problem of dividing up the loot. The buccaneers set up a devil of a fuss; they felt that Pointis's men were cheating them. All they received was 40,000 crowns, and there were those who said the booty had amounted to 100,000,-000 pesos. Pointis admitted to 8,000,000 crowns, and in his report he wrote that a considerable amount had been lost because the inhabitants of Cartagena managed to get out a train of one hundred and twenty mules loaded with gold. Whatever the truth was, the exasperated buccaneers returned to Cartagena to finish fleecing it. Although this was in violation of the agreement made with the authorities, the fact is that, by torturing a number of people and sacking convents and dwellings, they brought their share up to a million crowns. Baron de Pointis was shocked by this conduct, and in a report he submitted on his expedition he belittled the help received from the pirates, saying that they were cowards, that they created difficulties in the attack, that they gave no evidence of daring, but only of gluttony. Yet they must have been a help, these old pirates who knew their way about the Caribbean blindfolded. And when Du Casse presented himself at the court of Louis XIV, the King acknowledged his claim to a larger share for his buccaneers, made him a knight of the Order of St. Louis, and promoted him to the rank of admiral.

Strange indeed, and typical of the shifts of fortune in political spheres, is the end of this pirate captain's career. With the death in 1700 of the moronic King of Spain known to history as Charles the Bewitched, the Hapsburg dynasty came to an inglorious end and, in the person of Philip V (the Duke of Anjou), was replaced by the Bourbons. A complete reconciliation took place between the courts of Madrid and Paris. French philosophers and statesmen became King Philip's advisers, and Louis XIV, as a mark of special deference to this grandson who was the new King of Spain, offered him the services of Admiral Du Casse.

Philip showered honors and posts of responsibility upon the admiral. It was now Du Casse who convoyed the fleets bearing gold and silver from Mexico and Peru. Nobody was better qualified to carry out this task. And, as final mark of honor, King Philip conferred upon the former pirate the Order of the Golden Fleece, worn by the grandees of his court.

XIII

EDINBURGH AND COPENHAGEN
SET THEIR COURSE SOUTH

*This door of the seas — El Darien — and the key of the universe,
with anything of a sort of reasonable management, will of course
enable its proprietors to give laws to both oceans, and to become
arbitrators of the commercial world, without being liable to the fatigues, expenses, and dangers, or contracting the guilt and blood of
Alexander and Caesar.*

WILLIAM PATERSON

ON THE shores of the Baltic Ocean and the North Sea lie several kingdoms which, to our eyes, lack the precise, clear-cut
contours of France or England. In their remoteness they have
something of the quality of a legend, a fairy tale. Norway's history is like the pictures seen in a magic lantern; its midnight
sun illuminates a landscape that hardly seems real. The palace
dramas of Stockholm seem new shoots from the old trunk of
Nordic legends. Denmark is to us a tale of the Castle of Elsinore. Edinburgh, Dundee, Aberdeen, Inverness, seem scraps of
ballads rather than names of cities. Europe, as we know it, ends
at the north in London, on the borders of France; we must make
an effort to extend it to include Holland. From there on the
Nordic world lies in the charmed realm of imagination, of
dreams.

But it is not just an arbitrary fancy on our part that converts
the North into the dreaming forehead of Europe's countenance.
The long winters in which these nations of fishermen gather
about the hearth fires, the long summers when they lie in their
forests under a sun that never sets, fire the imagination of the
old man spinning tales for his grandchildren, of the poet who
leads his hero along the path of the sagas. Grieg's music showed
us a world inhabited by trolls and fairies. Andersen's tales gave

wings to the imagination of all the children of the world. Stevenson immortalized the Caribbean in his *Treasure Island*, whose appeal to old and young is eternal.

The dreams of these northern realms lead always from the mountains toward the sea. The sea is in the very marrow of their bones. It is visible from every mountain peak. Denmark is a jigsaw puzzle of islands; Norway, a series of valleys through which the fingers of the sea reach to the very foot of the flanking mountains. High above, against the clouds, crowning the rocks, stand armies of pines whose green lances pierce the sky. Every village is a port; the cradle that rocks the little ones is a boat. The Vikings were the first riders to mount wooden horses; galloping over the plains of the sea they reached the Black Forest by way of the Rhine, and along the Arctic trails they came as far as the outposts of America.

All this happened long ago. . . . But tales were beginning to reach these lands about other seas, eastern seas, seas of America. These were being conquered by nations of shepherds and peasants like the Spaniards, or by newly fledged republics like Holland. The former had come home with nuggets of gold; the others, with ships loaded with cloves, sugar, rum, and pepper. The Scots saw no reason why they should take a back seat for the English — or why London, and not Edinburgh, should claim dominion of the seas. Copenhagen felt the same way. When Denmark, Norway, and Sweden were united under one king, Copenhagen was the key to the Baltic, and Denmark, with the help of the other Scandinavian countries, held the princes of northern Germany in check. King Hans, who laid the foundations of the Danish fleet, had the satisfaction of defeating the Hanseatic League. Christian II, last of the kings of the three nations, founded a Scandinavian Company of the Indies, and was preparing a great expedition to make conquests in America and explore the routes to the East. The division of the Scandinavian peninsula into Norway and Sweden brought these plans to a halt. Denmark reefed its sails. Its king, a humanist and a friend of Erasmus, brought scholars to the court, introduced the printing press into Denmark, encouraged the university, and converted Copenhagen into a most hospitable center for those who love to gather about the warm glow of the lamp of wisdom. But the adventurous urge was at work again. A renaissance was taking place in Denmark, and the dream of the Caribbean entered into it. Hans Nansen, an Icelander who had spent his youth wandering about Danzig, Amsterdam, Gluckstádt, Hamburg, and Copenhagen, and Erik Neilsen Schmidt, who knew the Caribbean so well that two of his ships had been seized there by English pirates, reached Copenhagen one day with a cargo of tobacco and rum from the West Indies. This was all that was needed. The same enthusiasm prevailed at the court as in the port. Shortly afterwards, from the battlements of Elsinore could be seen the sails of a ship setting out for the remote island of St. Thomas. The King had selected it to plant the Danish flag there.

On maps, the island of St. Thomas has the shape of a handsaw. The sea, lapping its rocks, forms a thousand coves that are impossible to guard, a pirates' paradise. The Danish Company of the West Indies was organized with a twofold purpose: it was to operate in Africa and in America. There it would hunt Negroes, and here it would sell them as slaves, settle the island, do business with the pirates, and carry on smuggling. The King, the Queen, and Prince George were the first to invest in the company.

St. Thomas was practically deserted. When the Danes arrived they found only three Indians, and to keep one of them from running away the governor cut off his leg. This first governor was George Iversen, the son of a baker. Sixty-one convicts, released from prison, were the first settlers. Then French, Dutch, Germans, Jews, and English began to trickle in — refugees, all of them. The unhappy governors were at their wits' end to know how to keep order among settlers whose antecedents were not doubtful, but all too clear, who spoke every language and had served under every flag. To make things worse, when sugar cane began to be cultivated and ground, St. Thomas became famous for its rum, known as "Mata Diablos." Instead of killing devils (as its name suggests), this rum filled the body of its drinkers with them.

In Copenhagen the King did everything he could to protect his enterprise. Every state employee was obliged to invest ten per cent of his earnings in company shares. But the problem was human rather than economic. The first years of the company were harassed by great conflicts on a tiny stage. Iversen had to defend the island against French attacks. He became ill, and homesick for Denmark, and asked the King to relieve him. He was succeeded by Nicolas Smit; but Adolf Smit, the latter's brother, who was in league with the pirates, rebelled against him and seized the government. To bring order the King again sent out Iversen, who by this time had recovered from his homesickness. But Iversen never reached St. Thomas; he was bringing out another load of convicts who mutinied on the way and tossed him into the sea. Next the King sent out a converted Jew, Gabriel Milan, who spoke four languages and had strange ideas of how a colony should be governed. He threw the Smit brothers into jail. He taught the Negroes to obey; for trifling infractions he impaled them alive or chopped them down a foot in height. The complaints reached Copenhagen. A new governor was sent out who laid siege to Milan and imprisoned him. After the governor came a judge, Mr. Mikkelsen, who cleared up the situation by sending Milan and the Smits to Denmark in chains.

At Denmark's back and somewhat in its shadow, a state was emerging that was to cause substantial changes in the world. At the moment, Prussia was barely edging its way into the society of nations. Frederick William of Brandenburg — the "Great Elector" whose son was to be the first King of Prussia — could not consider undertaking a maritime enterprise on his own. He tried first to interest Denmark, then Austria, and finally Spain, in an East India Company by which the Hohenzollerns might better their fortunes. He achieved nothing. But one day, a sly and shrewd Dutch promoter who had been unable to make any headway in his own country approached the Elector. Benjamin Raule was known to have made a fortune as a ship-chandler, and lost it; what he wanted now, like many other malcontents, was to do as much harm as he could to the Dutch company, and he laid before the lord of Brandenburg a vast plan to catch slaves, make pirate raids, trade with the West Indies, and have a share in the conquests. Frederick William listened enchanted to his siren song, and appointed him director of the proposed fleet. Thus Raule rose to power, and not long afterwards the two first Prussian expeditions set out for the Antilles and the coasts of Guinea. "When in August of 1680 the fleet of six warships and a fireship — the *Brenner* — sailed for America from the port of Copenhagen, the curious spectators who watched it depart never dreamed that they were looking at the embryo of what was to become the German Imperial Fleet which was to play a dominant role in the Baltic for two centuries."

The newly launched fleet made a few unimportant hauls, which only whetted its appetite. Evidently, until Prussia possessed a port of her own in the West Indies, it was a waste of time to think of new enterprises. Benjamin Raule's plan was to establish a slaving station in Guinea, and make arrangements with the Danes to use the privileges of St. Thomas. In this way, by utilizing the support of Prussia's powerful neighbor Denmark, Raule could satisfy his personal ambition, which was to harm the Dutch company by cutting in on their slave trade. "It is common knowledge," Raule explained to the Elector, "that the slave trade is the source of the Spaniards' revenue from the Indies, and whoever supplies them with slaves will have a share in this wealth." It was not hard to convince Frederick William that there was a great future in slave-running. The Brandenburg-Danish Company was organized under the Dutchman's seductive spell. There were to be two boards of directors, one in Copenhagen, the other in Emden. The general manager was to live in Copenhagen. The Prussians would be given land in St. Thomas for their plantations and warehouses, on which they were to pay Denmark a tax. The island would be under Danish sovereignty. Calvinists and Lutherans would have freedom of worship; Catholics and Jews would be tolerated as long as they made no trouble.

In the Antilles the sugar cane of His Highness of Hohenzollem flourished and his slaves toiled under the hot sun. A new Elector of Brandenburg, dazzled by the glory of Louis XIV, was pulling wires to have himself crowned King of Prussia. But things were not going well between Prussians and Danes on St. Thomas. The last thing the Prussians were thinking of was paying the taxes that had been agreed upon. It enraged them that the Danes insisted on using their own scales to weigh their output of tobacco and sugar. The Prussian factors hit upon a method of evading what they considered tyranny: to conquer Crab Island and transfer to it their slaves and warehouses. But when they reached the island, they found the Danish flag hoisted there.

The Danes, in turn, were growing irritated. The governor forbade the colonists to buy anything from the Germans. When the day came for the Germans to pay what they owed, they refused to do so. The governor upbraided them, invoking their signed agreements, their loyalty to their king, their honor. He was wasting his breath. Then the governor sent for a smith, went to the Germans' warehouses, pried open the doors, and took possession of the sugar and tobacco, a list of which was carefully entered in the ledger, and all weighed on Danish scales. The echoes of the conflict were heard in Copenhagen and in Berlin. The Prussian factor wrote Frederick that the Danes were drunken, bloodthirsty beasts. New agreements were drawn up in Denmark extending the Germans' term of payment. In St. Thomas the Danish governor again had to enter the Prussian warehouses by force. The year 1701 rolled around. Frederick was king. In the city of Königsberg, the Elector of Brandenburg converted the Hohenzollerns into a royal dynasty. The partnership with the Danes was liquidated. The final accounting showed that the King of Prussia was in the Danes' debt to the tune of 1,028,729 pieces-of-eight. This was what the Prussian attempt to get a foothold in the Antilles had cost.

The Danes breathed a sigh of relief. They had other troubles. At times, fearing Spanish attacks, the settlers fled the islands. But they returned. In times of war St. Thomas was an international refuge, principally — and ironically enough — for the

Dutch. A census of the population revealed that there were one hundred and forty-eight whites, of whom sixty-six were Dutch, thirty-one English, seventeen Danes and Norwegians, seventeen French, four Irish, four Flemish, three German, three Swedish, one Scotch, one Brazilian, one Portuguese, and the rest — the great majority — blacks. At the beginning, power for the cane grinders was supplied by windmills. Then mules were used. The Negroes tended the grinders, feeding the cane into the revolving cylinders. Sometimes a slave would carelessly let his arm slip in too far, the juice would drip out mixed with blood, and another Negro would rush over swiftly with an ax. There was always an ax handy so that the mill would not drag the body in after the arm and spoil a lot of good syrup.

The day on which the entries in the ledgers were made in money instead of pounds of sugar represented a great step forward in bookkeeping. West Indian products were carried in Danish ships to Copenhagen, Elsinore, Christiania, Trondhjem, Lübeck, Danzig, Stettin, Königsberg, St. Petersburg, Stockholm, Gothenborg. . . . The company lasted for eighty-four years. Then the islands passed under the King's control, and remained in Danish possession until the United States bought them in 1916 to strengthen its Caribbean defenses.

In Edinburgh, the Scots forgathered in taverns to discuss their problems, and they saw red whenever the conversation turned on London. It was enough to make the calmest man's blood boil to see how London was trying to grab all the markets. The world was big enough for everyone, in those years at the end of the seventeenth century, and the people of Edinburgh and Dundee were just as good as those of London. And in the city itself, there were many who resented the special privileges enjoyed by the East India Company. A Scottish company to interest more people in these overseas enterprises would be the solution. This matter was being discussed in Scotland as Parliament was about to convene. A law would have to be passed authorizing the undertaking, and a majority of votes would have to be lined up. To make sure of these votes the members must be wined, dined, and perhaps other, more substantial perquisites might be useful. It has been possible to reconstruct exactly what took place, because, being Scotch, the promoters of this venture kept an exact account in their journals of how much each of these attentions had cost in pounds, shillings, and pence. One of the moving spirits in the enterprise was James Balfour. This is a name worth remembering; the Scotch came into the Caribbean, and there Balfour picked up pirate yarns of buried treasures and dream islands. It was a favorite topic of conversation in his home. And as one of his descendants was Robert Louis Stevenson, it is easy to see how *Treasure Island* came to be written, as well as other tales by this incomparable story-teller.

So at times in William Ross's tavern, or at The Ship, McClurg's Saloon, the Widow Graham's, or Patrick Steel's tavern, the friends of progress forgathered, a little in the manner of conspirators, to plan the organization of the "Company of Scotland trading to Africa and the Indies." The Scottish Parliament convened in Edinburgh. Affairs on the Continent had made it impossible for King William III to come to the opening, as was customary, but the Marquis of Tweeddale, acting for him, declared in his brief address that he would view with favor the formation of such a company. Only half a dozen words, but they were sufficient to open the door to the burgeoning plans of the citizens of Edinburgh.

The projects of James Balfour and his friends had been a little hazy. All they knew was that, setting out to sea, one discovered lands of great wealth. Exactly where these lay, and how to reach them, were questions they had not thought through. But in London there was another Scotsman who told them what they needed to know — William Paterson.

The life of William Paterson held an irresistible attraction for the citizens of Edinburgh. When he was seventeen years old, fleeing religious persecution, Paterson had gone from Bristol to Amsterdam, where — like the good Scot he was — he made himself at home in the taverns, and where he heard about the Antilles, and whence he set out in search of adventure. He went to Jamaica and other islands. He learned about — he may have practised — the pirate's calling. At any rate he made the acquaintance of two famous buccaneers: William Dampier and Lionel Wafer. These two gentlemen, one a naturalist, the other a surgeon, by a series of circumstances that could happen only in those days had taken part in some of the most famous buccaneering exploits, had crossed the Isthmus of Panama, sailed the Pacific, and explored the coast of Africa. The result of these adventures was a famous book whose manuscript Dampier carried in a bamboo tube to save it from shipwreck and protect it against damp.

William Paterson's views differed radically from those of these two Bohemians. He returned to Europe carrying in his mind the plan of a great company trading with the Indies. One of the first persons he went to see was the Elector of Brandenburg, who at the moment was not in a position to take advantage of his services, as he shortly afterwards did of Raule's. Paterson himself postponed these plans to carry into effect another, which was to make him famous: the founding of the Bank of England. He went to London, interested the King and the rich men of the City in his project, and thus in 1694 this great institution came into being. It was engendered in the mind of a Scotsman whose school of business had been the gatherings of Caribbean buccaneers. Paterson was made director of the Bank of England, but he was not a man to sit behind a desk waiting for customers to come to him. He left the bank and began to lay the plans for his West Indian scheme. And while he was turning it over he learned of the project of his fellow Scots, and he wrote them at once.

Paterson put things bluntly. It was a waste of time to think about the Far East; the future was in Darien, on the isthmus where Dampier and Wafer had won their spurs. The isthmus was the real nexus of the world, because through it the routes of East and West must pass. Whoever makes himself master of Panama can dictate his terms to the world. His words were so convincing that it seemed that the adventurer who had founded the Bank of England would now convince the gentlemen of Edinburgh and London that their manifest destiny was Panama.

As a result of Paterson's letters the Scottish company was

transformed into the Darien Company. Just as England had founded New England in the north, Scotland would found New Scotland in the isthmus. The scheme was fantastic, for no one had less claim to these lands than Scotland. Spain had had her flag planted there since the days of Columbus. It was the point of departure for the conquest of the Pacific, and through it had passed all the great figures of the Spanish conquest. But these were trifles light as air to the mind of a buccaneer. His plan was accepted, but the destination of the expedition was kept secret. The prospectus referred only to the company of "Africa and the Indies." The colonists themselves, when they went aboard, did not know where the ships were found for. Paterson became the leading man in the company. James Balfour was filled with surprise and indignation to learn that Paterson was to receive a huge sum as reimbursement for the expenses incurred in acquiring his knowledge of Darien, while *his* claim for the pounds, shillings, and pence he had spent buying votes in the Scots Parliament was ignored. But Paterson could not be bothered with such trifles, and he renounced the money. The plan was far more important than a sum of shillings, and he left for London to promote his undertaking there. The City was his element.

But as soon as the East India Company got wind of what was afoot, it reacted without mercy toward the Scots. The rich shareholders had no intention of letting these upstarts threaten their monopoly; they moved court and Parliament, brought the matter to the King's attention, and stirred up a veritable hornets' nest. They demanded an investigation of the passage of the bill in the Scottish Parliament. The King sided with the East India Company, and removed the Marquis of Tweeddale from his post for the disservice he had done with his speech authorizing the formation of the company. And this was not the end of the affair. It was said that the Scots had bought the Duke of Leeds for five thousand guineas. Could such things be? The East India Company painted a doleful picture of the future of England if the Scots were not tied short: peddling their wares and everywhere cutting the ground from under the feet of honorable English merchants, making themselves masters of the City of London itself. . . . The House of Lords approved a resolution estopping the English from buying shares in the Scottish Company, and the sailors and ship-builders from working for them in any way. The East India Company received further powers to combat the fledgling enemy. And the House of Commons, not to be outdone, demanded the severest sanctions against twenty-three persons, from Lord Belhaven down, for having sworn to uphold the statutes of the Company. To save the Company's books and their own skin, the Scots had to flee London precipitately.

Scotland's national pride was wounded. In the cafés of Edinburgh and Dundee, conversation was punctuated with angry pounding of tables. Rich and poor, women and men, dukes and countesses, shoemakers and tailors, everybody in Scotland was now behind the company. When the shares were put on sale, people stormed the offices to subscribe their patriotic contribution, until far into the night. The Duchess of Hamilton was the first to subscribe with three thousand pounds. Then Countess Margaret, a thousand for herself, and a thousand in her son's name. The Very Worthy City of Edinburgh invested three thousand pounds, and the tiny village of Queensferry, a hundred. On the Company's books were to be found the names of "rich man, poor man, beggar man, thief, doctor, lawyer, merchant chief."

And to complete the capital needed, since London was hostile, there was the Continent. So to the Continent went Paterson and John Erskine. They would also have to buy there the ships England refused to sell them. The name of John Erskine is associated with the first Scottish colonies in America, when a group of dissenters went to settle Stuart in South Carolina. Now Erskine was the most active promoter of the new company. Patriotism burned in him like a flame. His name, like those of all the members of his family, appears repeatedly on the books. But he was not content with the passive role of financing the project; he wanted a more active part. He and Paterson worked like beavers on the Continent. In Lübeck they received the cannon that had been manufactured for them in Sweden by the

Czar of Russia's armorers. In Amsterdam they bought ships. In Hamburg they planned to open an office to sell shares in the company.

When news of this reached London, the haughty gentlemen of the City flew into a rage. The King's minister addressed a long letter in Latin to the council of Lübeck and the senates of Bremen and Hamburg, advising them that the Scots were acting contrary to the wishes of the king. Hamburg was the scene of the bitterest battle. When it was learned that Paterson and Erskine were planning to open an office there, with the authorization of the senate, and put a sign on the door reading: "This is the office of the Scotch Company," the English minister wrote the senate as follows:

"We the Under-Subscribers, Ministers of His Majesty the King of Great Britain, have, upon the arrival of Commissioners from an Indian Company in Scotland, represented at two several times to Your Magnificences and Lordships, from the King our Master, that His Majesty, understanding that the said Commissioners endeavoured to open to themselves a Commerce and Trade in these parts by making some Convention or Treaty with the City, had commanded us most expressly to notify to Your Magnificences and Lordships, that if you enter into such Conventions with private men, his subjects, who have neither Credential Letters, nor are any otherwise authoriz'd by Authority, that His Majesty would regard such proceedings as an affront to his Royal Authority, and that he would not fail to resent it."

The office of Paterson and Erskine was not opened in Hamburg.

Suddenly a rumor began to spread through London to the effect that what Paterson and his supporters were planning was to found a settlement in Darien. The secret had leaked out and reached the King's ears. What and where was Darien? People began to recall Drake's reports, the book of the ex-friar Thomas Gage, the exploits of Morgan. . . . And a book had just appeared with fresh news, that of William Dampier, the buccaneer. But in London Dampier played the role not of buccaneer, but of naturalist. The book was dedicated to the president of the Royal Society, and in scientific circles its contents aroused curiosity and admiration. Dampier and Wafer were in London, and they were called to Whitehall to converse with some of the great figures of England; among those present were Sir Philip Meadows, a friend of Milton's, and the philosopher John Locke. Times had indeed changed. A few years before, Dampier and Wafer, seated around a blazing campfire on an island off the coast of Darien, had been discussing with all the pirates of the Caribbean, convoked in an assembly, the best way to make a surprise attack on Panama. And now, in the most fashionable section of London, these two buccaneers were saying to the cream of society and science the very same thing Paterson had said: that Darien was the key to America. And the English were thinking the very thing the pirates had been thinking, but more determinedly: that the Scottish company must be knocked on the head.

It should be observed in passing that the success of the two old buccaneers was without parallel. Their influence was felt even in the highest literary circles. Through them Daniel Defoe learned about a mutinous sailor aboard a ship on which Dampier and Wafer [1] were sailing the southern seas, who refused to obey his captain and was marooned on the island of Juan Fernández, near Chile, where he lived alone until he was rescued by other English sailors. This was the origin of *Robinson Crusoe*, the scene of which was laid on an island in the Caribbean near the mouth of the Orinoco. Not only the English, but the Scots, too, wanted to talk with the buccaneers. By roundabout paths, after dark, Wafer visited a certain house in the outskirts of Edinburgh. There he was respectfully questioned by the worthy members of the Company who wanted to do what Paterson had done years before: get direct information from a buccaneer. The secret of success in the Caribbean was to lie in keeping on friendly terms with the buccaneers.

[1] There is also a story that Defoe met the sailor in question, Alexander Selkirk.

Excitement was mounting in Scotland. A petition was sent to the King protesting against the campaign of which the Company had been the victim in Hamburg. Haste was made to get a second expedition under weigh, and if the King did not like it, he could lump it. The enterprise had come under national auspices. Paterson's star was setting; a friend of his had embezzled company funds, and though Paterson had been the chief victim his prestige had been destroyed. His name was removed from the list of directors, and if he wanted to go to Darien he would have to go like any ordinary settler. The ships were being loaded at the docks. Their destination was still secret, but a joyful presentiment quickened the hearts of these poor credulous searchers for the rainbow. "On the 26th of July of the year 1698, the whole city of Edinburgh poured down upon Leith to see the Colony depart amidst the tears and prayers and praises of relations and friends, and of their fellow countrymen. Many seamen and soldiers whose services had been refused because more had offered themselves than were needed, were found hid in the ships, and when ordered ashore, they clung to the ropes and timbers, imploring to go without reward with their companions. Twelve hundred men sailed in five stout ships." Of all this there remains an impassioned lyric testimony, the poem *Caledonia Triumphans*.

Paterson sailed with his wife. As the days went by, his services became more and more valuable. It had been his idea; he knew where they were going. Among the sealed orders that were opened at the several ports of call, there was one which provided that Paterson was to be made a director. The dream of the old promoter was taking shape. Once more his eyes beheld the sea of his youth, the sea where he had buccaneered and that had rocked the cradle of his imagination, where the idea of the Bank of England had been born, and which now inspired — so he believed — something far more important.

At last the islands of America hove into sight. There were the Virgin Islands, then the Popa headland, which guarded the bay of Cartagena. Then Dorada island, and the coast of Darien! The colony was to be called New Scotland; its capital, New

Edinburgh. The flag was one of the prettiest America was to know for centuries, and in it, for the first time, appeared the three colors — yellow, blue and red — that Francisco Miranda was to use a hundred years later to call the free men of America to proclaim their independence.

The first reports sent back to Scotland were overflowing with early optimism. A constitution was drawn up, government was conducted soberly and prudently. All was done as befitted a republic, a kingdom. The Indian Diego, a cacique of the region, was showered with attentions. He was invited to a dinner, plied with liquor until he was drunk, and given a scroll investing him with the title of "Commissioner of the Colony." He was the ally the Scotch were looking for against the Spaniards. The union between the colonists and the Indian acquired on paper the tone of a treaty drawn up by agents acting for European powers: "Treaty of friendship, union, and perpetual confederation, agreed and entered into between the RIGHT HONORABLE THE COUNCIL OF CALEDONIA and the EXCELLENT DIEGO TUCUAPANTOS ESTRADA, Chief and Supreme Leader of the Indians inhabitants of the lands and possessions in and about the rivers of Darien and San Matolomé. . . ."

The arrival of the Scots caused general alarm. Messages flashed among the Spaniards from Cartagena to Panama to join forces against the interlopers. From London came letters to all the governors in the West Indies and New England to give them no support. These letters, signed by the royal secretary, Vernon, were in the same implacable tone as the message to the senate of Hamburg. The settlers of Jamaica petitioned to have these inopportune competitors removed. The governor of that island addressed a note of apology to the Spanish governor of Cartagena informing him that although the Scots recognize the King of England as their sovereign, they are not English, and the English do not intend to become involved in their schemes. At the same time he issued a proclamation that was like a declaration of war: the Scots can die of hunger, for Jamaica will not sell them one pound of flour. Hardships followed, a little famine, and fevers that decimated the population. Paterson's wife died; Paterson took sick; Panama was organizing an army to drive out the intruders.

The Scots were stubborn. They had not lost faith. They prepared to defend themselves, and they succeeded. The army from Panama, instead of attacking, decided to besiege the settlement, and camped in the neighboring mountains. But only birds, Indians, and snakes can live in the mountains of Darien. In addition to the hunger and fever that were beginning to thin their ranks, there came a hurricane that destroyed the Spanish camp. The army decided to withdraw to Panama. There was only one engagement — to be exact, a skirmish — at Tubuganti, but it was celebrated from New Edinburgh to Old Edinburgh as a military triumph. This was perhaps the only pleasant episode in the whole venture. On this occasion, fate was propitious, but when one of the Scottish ships set out for Barbados in hope of finding succor, it was wrecked near Cartagena. The captain and crew fell into the hands of the Spaniards, who sent them as prisoners to the dungeons of Cádiz in Spain.

To try to continue was to attempt the impossible. The morale of the colony had been destroyed; most of the settlers were drunk all the time. It was therefore decided to abandon the colony. Paterson, a sick man, could not oppose the decision. The survivors were crowded aboard three ships. One shipload reached Jamaica; at sword's point they had to force the governor to let them come ashore, to such lengths did he carry his cruelty. The Scots eventually came to form part of the population of Jamaica, and were one of the best groups in the colony. In New York the other ships received a less hostile welcome; there was a large Scottish colony there, and they helped these victims of an unkind fate to return to their own country.

While these misadventures were taking place, a second expedition was being fitted out in Scotland, where news traveled slowly. Resentment against London was growing. There were rumors that all was not well, but the ships set out without waiting for more news. They carried such supplies as, in the opinion of a Scot who had never left his own shores, were needed by a settlement in the Caribbean: beer, hardtack, gunpowder, knives, razors, needles, twenty-nine barrels of pipes for tobacco, four boxes of hats, fourteen reams of paper. . . . Among the crew were a gunner, an expert smelter of metals, a minter of coins, and a Jew born in Curaçao who claimed to know Spanish, Portuguese, Italian, French, Dutch, English, and the languages spoken by the Indians on the coast of Darien.

When the bad news began to come in, the excitement in Edinburgh was tremendous. Some said that the delay in sending out reinforcements was the fault of James Balfour, and the crowds stoned his house. With this example before them, the directors of the Company made haste to send out a ship so there should be no further complaints. But it was plain that if King William III continued to oppose the project the Company would not be able to fight England, Spain, the fever, hunger, and drunkards. The Scots drew up a petition to the King asking him to withdraw his opposition to the Company and to convene Parliament. The King stonily replied that Parliament would be convened only when the needs of the kingdom made it necessary. The Company insisted: *Because* the interests of the kingdom make it necessary, we humbly beseech its convocation. A representative was chosen to deliver the petition in person to William. When at last he consented to receive the delegate, his answer was that he was the judge of when Parliament should be summoned, and that the gentlemen could have spared himself the trouble of traveling to London with this paper. Darien was driving a deep wedge between England and Scotland.

One day in London, Lord Peterborough walked into Parliament with a little book published in Edinburgh setting forth the reason for the failure of the Scottish colony: London's opposition. The Lords' indignation knew no limits. The book was declared lying, scandalous, and treasonable, an insult to the honor of the King and Parliament, designed to create jealousy and animosity between England and Scotland. It was ordered burned by the Lord High Executioner "at twelve noon, in the courtyard of the palace, in the presence of the city bailiffs." And a search was to be instituted for the author or editor, who was to be imprisoned.

Indignation ran equally high in Edinburgh. The King yielded to the point of offering to intercede with the Spanish government to free the prisoners taken in Cartagena, granting the Scots in the West Indies equal rights with the English, and announcing that the Scots Parliament would be convened on May 14. It was decided in the cafés of Edinburgh that until the King approved the Darien project he would receive no support from Parliament. But on this point he was as stubborn as the Scots. His representative had unequivocal orders against the Company. The session was inaugurated. Not a word did the King's representative say on the subject of Darien. The Scots passed a motion to give this matter priority over any other consideration because it was a matter of vital national interest. Then another motion was presented declaring that the settlement of Darien was legitimate and sound. This occupied the sessions of the two first days. On the third, the representative of the crown announced that he had a cold, was hoarse, and could not speak, and that because there were urgent matters that he needed to talk over with the King the sessions would be suspended for the time being while he returned to London. Thus this famous meeting of Parliament was limited to three sessions. The representative did not return.

It was at this time — late, as usual — that word of "the victory of Tubaganti" reached Edinburgh. On Thursday morning the news was received, and that same afternoon the group that met at Steel's tavern ordered celebrations. Lights were displayed in the windows of all loyal Scotsmen, and the name of the Company in large letters. Salvos boomed out. All Edinburgh got drunk. Certain windows remained dark. "Those are the houses of those who are not behind the Company! Stone them!" A druggist and a printer had been put in jail because of the Darien pamphlets. The populace assaulted the jail, broke down the doors, and freed the druggist and the printer. At dawn the next day the patriots were still singing, though a bit hoarse. It had been the celebration of independence day.

Law and order had ceased to exist in Edinburgh. The authorities tried to restore it after the drunkards decided to call it a day. Troops patrolled the streets and guarded the city gates. An edict was issued forbidding illumination and fireworks. The four leaders of the mob that stormed the jail were ordered exiled from Scotland. Their ringleader, a butcher, was to receive two hundred lashes. When the sentence was to be carried out, a crowd gathered and followed the butcher and his cronies. They showered them with flowers. Bagpipes skirled. The executioner brought the whip down so lightly on his victim's back that it looked as though he were tickling him. The crowd shouted: "You hurt him and we'll kill you!" It was one of the gayest spectacles ever seen in Scotland. Once more all Edinburgh got drunk. Once more the streets echoed with songs.

But in Darien there were no songs, flowers, or skirling of bagpipes. Drunkards there were, not because they were happy, but out of loyalty to a national tradition. The King's harsh orders continued in effect. When the colonists' ships went by Monserrat, they were not allowed to stop to take on fresh water. Then came war, and this time the Spaniards had organized a real army. The governor of Cartagena himself was in command of a fleet of three large ships and eleven smaller ones. The Scots had only six. The settlement was besieged and every road cut. If they held out they would have only rats and snakes to eat. A herald approached with a message from the governor telling them that with the ships in Rancho Viejo and the troops in the Matanzas River he could wipe them out, but that instead he called upon them to yield to save their lives. The besieged settlers answered that, through lack of an interpreter, they could not grasp what the governor had said in his letter, but they understood that the forces he had assembled on land and sea were a threat to them. However, this did not intimidate them because they were men of honor, and because they believed they had a right to be there they trusted in God, who would protect them.

Two, three, eleven days went by; the governor tightened the siege without firing a shot. On the twelfth day a launch drew alongside his boat carrying this message: "Most Illustrious Sir — When we replied to the letter you sent us a short time ago, we said that for lack of a competent interpreter we could not fully understand its meaning; later we came to understand it better; we find that you bade us leave this neighborhood. Considering the grave detriment that may follow if the friendship which today prevails between the King of Great Britain and the Catholic King should be broken on our account, we have thought it well to send these lines to inquire what conditions you offer us. We await your reply, and meanwhile are, Most Illustrious Sir, very devotedly . . ."

What had become of the Jew who spoke seven languages? Had fever made an end of him? The war had turned into a language problem, which was finally worked out by the governor's writing to the besieged in Latin and talking to them in French. He was really anxious to avoid bloodshed, and he allowed them to depart in their ships with flags flying, drums beating, and each soldier fully supplied with ammunition. And this was the end of the Darien settlement. The ships drifted aimlessly about the Caribbean. One of them came to grief on the reefs of Cuba. Two others, anchored at Charleston in Carolina were shattered to matchwood by a hurricane. Very few of the settlers returned to Scotland. Among these was a Presbyterian parson who published a little book recounting the misfortunes they had undergone; at the end he prayed that the day might come when they could avenge themselves on the Spaniards "whom we left alive because of our lack of ammunition." Thanks to the generosity of the Spaniards, he said, we were able to take ship, but we reached Jamaica crowded together like pigs in a sty.

Another minister was saved, Archibald Stobo, one of those who went ashore at Charleston. He played a more important role in history, for a great-great-grandson of his was destined to cut the Gordian knot of Darien: Theodore Roosevelt.

These conflicts between Scotland and England over the question of Darien kept on for years. It was the most serious problem King William III bequeathed to Queen Anne in 1702. In London a Scottish boat was seized in the Thames on suspicion that it might be setting out for the Indies. In retaliation the Scots seized as pirates the crew of an English ship that fell into their hands. The crew were tried and two were put to death, to the great delight of the spectators. The Scots Parliament ordered three books dealing with the Darien venture burned by the hangman as offensive to the national honor. The Parliament in Edinburgh became so touchy on the subject of Darien that the English prime minister wrote one day: "I have occupied, in my struggles with it, the most difficult and troublesome position held by anybody in the past century." For some years the union of the two kingdoms — which went into effect in 1707 — almost foundered over the Darien venture. The memory of William III, who had stood in the way of the greatest undertaking of his reign, was forever execrated in Scotland. When almost a century later someone in Edinburgh suggested raising a statue to him in commemoration of the English Revolution of 1688, an anonymous writer addressed a letter to a newspaper saying: "I think this is a fine idea, and on one face of the pedestal there should be a bas-relief in memory of the Scotch colony of Darien." Nothing more was said about the monument.

As for Paterson, his somewhat prophetic words have come down through time, like an echo of his venturesome dreams. In his judgment, the opening of a canal or some other means of communication across the isthmus represented the solution to a universal problem. If the English and the Scots, he said, become involved in internal quarrels, some other power will profit by the idea. Darien, to him, was a wondrous spot, as was the Bay of Uraba, where a fleet of a thousand ships could find anchorage. If the English do not want to concede the privilege to Scotland, let them organize a company in which London shall hold two-thirds of the shares. . . . Paterson was an incurable optimist.

"Darien [he wrote] lies between the golden regions of Mexico and Peru; it is within six weeks' sail of Europe, India and China; it is the heart of the West Indies, close to the rising colonies of North America. The expense and danger of navigation to Japan, the Spice Islands, and all the Eastern world, will be lessened one-half; the consumption of European commodities and manufactures will soon be doubled. Trade will increase trade; money will beget money; and the trading world will need no more to want work for hands, but hands for work. . . . Darien possesses great tracts of country as yet unclaimed by any Europeans. . . . Their crystal rivers sparkle over sands of gold. . . . The bottom of the sea is strewn with pearls. . . . There a New Edinburgh shall arise; the Alexandria of old, which was seated in a barren Isthmus, and grew suddenly into prodigious wealth and power by the mere commerce of Arabia and Indie, shall soon yield in fame to the NEW EMPORIUM OF THE WORLD."

BOOK III

THE AGE OF ENLIGHTENMENT

TO THE MEMORY OF HERNANDO DE LA CALLE

THE EIGHTEENTH CENTURY was the century of revolution. It is fascinating to see, as one studies it, how the first sparks appear, then isolated flames, until it becomes one gigantic bonfire. In Europe, when the French bourgeoisie launched upon the French Revolution, the traditional order of power was completely upset. The Church lost its political strength, the monarchy either toppled from the throne or yielded to the pressure, first gentle, then violent, of the philosophers, the economists, and the orators of the Third Estate, who were charting a new course for the world. The tug-of-war was begun by the middle class which, by its enterprise, intelligence, and daring, had developed industry and broadened the horizons of commerce. These were the *nouveaux riches* who were demanding their share in affairs with the uproar, justice, and insolence that has always characterized them. First they invaded the halls of government, they got the

267

nobles out of difficulties, they dressed like lords. Then they took over the machinery of government. The philosophers, looking on with satisfaction as the former masters tumbled from their seats, celebrated the downfall with volumes of sarcasm. The poor kings applauded the advance of liberalism and — before they realized what was happening — found themselves engulfed in a tide of revolution. Voltaire was not a philosopher; he worked out no profound system of thought; he was a sardonic journalist with an entertaining, encyclopedic pen, who scratched about on the dunghill of daily life with the gleeful maliciousness typical of the period.

In America, too, the eighteenth century was the real century of revolution. It was then that the three great and decisive uprisings of this hemisphere took place: that of the English colonies, in the North; that of the people, in South America; that of the Negroes, in Haiti. The War of Independence was delayed in the South until the nineteenth century, but the first cry, and the full-grown revolutionary spirit, appeared with Mompox and Antequera in Paraguay, with Tupac Amaru in Peru, with Galán in New Granada in the second half of the eighteenth century, and in the masses of *comuneros* that spread from Venezuela to Paraguay over the range of the Andes, from the expanse of the mesas to the lowest valley of the slopes, all moved by a single spirit. In the Caribbean the most stirring struggle of all was that of the Negroes, whom neither England, nor Spain, nor Napoleon's pride could crush.

The eighteenth century in America had its "encyclopedia," too. And, thanks to an oversight on the part of the Bourbon kings, the most dangerous books circulated there. Even in the pulpits the bishops mingled phrases from Rousseau with orthodox doctrines without realizing what they were doing. French and Spanish savants came to America. We had a walking, living, active encyclopedia. Societies of "Friends of the Country" were organized, and Masonic lodges, which were one and the same thing. The Jesuits were expelled, and in every institution of learning left vacant by them new studies were introduced; instead of metaphysics, mathematics and natural sciences were taught. A cult of science developed where all concern had hitherto been with theological problems. Libraries were opened, newspapers were founded, circles were formed to discuss questions of the day. This was followed by the War of Independence.

The movement of the eighteenth century in America shows a few outstanding names, but in general it was an anonymous activity, sometimes subterranean. Here, contrary to what happened in France, it was not the newly rich who initiated it — it was the people, the community, the unknown citizen. A woman of the masses was the first to arouse the peasants against the edicts of the viceroy, a Negro who had been a servant in a hotel or some gentleman's coachman, a lady who held a gathering of intellectuals in her home. In the uprising of the *comuneros*, five or ten names come to mind, but the revolution stemmed not from them, but from the masses, the hundreds, the thousands, the hundreds of thousands of humble folk seeking their little beam of light through the darkness of the world.

The eighteenth century began in the Caribbean with the rediscovery by the French of the Mississippi. It ended with a failure of Napoleon's: the war with Haiti.

XIV

CRADLE SONG OF THE MISSISSIPPI

*O Louisiana, lost colony, land that our fathers discovered and con-
quered, distant are the days when the flag of France floated over
your cities and your rivers. . . .*

EUGÈNE GUÉNIN

THE MISSISSIPPI appeared on the map of America a hundred
and fifty years late. The Amazon, the Plate, the Orinoco, the
Magdalena already had their place in history and legend; their
waters had reflected the shadows of heroes forever linked to
them: Orellana, Aguirre, Irala, Quesada. They were rivers old
in the world's geography when the Mississippi was still to be
discovered. Hernando de Soto had become a blurred memory in
the history of America; a hundred and thirty years after his
body was submerged in the waters that carried him to eternity,
in Canada they were talking of the Mississippi as of a new world
awaiting discovery. The Comte de Frontenac, who was governing there in the name of the King of France, sent out Father
Marquette to see whether the river was a fable or really existed.
Early in 1673 the missionary, with a handful of men, proceeded
westward from Quebec along the Great Lakes, made his way
southwest and south, and discovered the river on May 17, 1673.
He sailed down it in a canoe, dipping his hands again and again
in its waters to feel the caress of the current, and with joy and
fear returned to Quebec to give the news of his discovery. For
a whole day the bells of the cathedral rang out. The settlers
gathered about the altar to give thanks to God. The governor,
"who though removed from the court had not forgotten its tactics," proposed that the river be given the name of Colbert, in
tribute to Louis XIV's minister.

A man with imagination, Robert Cavelier de La Salle, asked
permission to undertake the conquest. He had no doubt that this

stream flowed into the Gulf of Mexico, and (Canadian ideas of geography being fantastic in the extreme) he maintained that, to the north, the river communicated with China. La Salle already saw the Mississippi teeming with ships laden with silk, cloves, and pepper sailing into the Gulf of Mexico and proceeding to French ports. As Frontenac listened to him, he felt that plans of such magnitude were too much for a governor of Canada, and that it would be better for La Salle to go to France and discuss the matter with the King.

La Salle was a great success at the court. King Louis XIV sent him back to Canada with full authorization to undertake the expedition. He was accompanied by an Italian gentleman, Tonti, son of the man who devised the "Tontine" plan of life insurance by groups — a money-saving scheme that had captured the imagination of many. With Father Marquette, La Salle and Tonti traveled across the lakes and began to descend the river. Their party was made up of twenty-three Frenchmen, eighteen Indians, ten Indian women, and three children. They reached the point where, back in the sixteenth century, Hernando de Soto had given up the discovery. Eventually they came to the Gulf of Mexico itself. La Salle took possession of the river. A notary drew up a legal record of the act; the priest sang a Te Deum; La Salle set up a post bearing the following inscription: "In the reign of Louis the Great, King of France and Navarre, April 9, 1682." The soldiers shouted "Long live the king!" — two dozen hoarse voices attempting to fill the vault of the sky and reach to the plains of the sea, when indeed no one standing on the opposite shore would have been able to see or hear them. The Indians looked on silently; they understood nothing of what was going on. At the foot of a cross a lead plaque was buried bearing an inscription that began: "Ludovicus Magnus regnat, Robertus Cavelier, cum Domino de Tonty. . . ." In the notary's record the river is referred to as the "Colbert."

Back in France, Louis XIV honored the fortunate discoverer; the nobles listened to his tales in amazement; and a second expedition was fitted out. From now on, the history of North

America was to center on this great river, though La Salle would not live to see it. On the trip back he attempted to enter through the Gulf of Mexico, but he was unable to find the river's mouth. The party spent an anxious interval exploring the coast. The captain of the fleet grew impatient, and went off without its leader. La Salle pushed into the plains of Texas, a tiny group following him. Unable to find his way back to the river, La Salle fell victim to an assassin's dagger. It was the destiny of the three discoverers who revealed the secret of the Mississippi to the world — de Soto, Father Marquette, La Salle — to die obscure deaths just as they had the prize within their hands.

The discovery had been made. Now came the struggle to see who should carry out the conquest. An outlet through the Mississippi was the natural development of the French colonial empire in America. Unless France hurried, however, England would steal a march on her, for it was said that the English were already assembling Huguenots to found a settlement at the mouth of the river. The French in Canada regarded this matter as their personal affair: the initiative had been theirs, and the colony was to be theirs. Charles Le Moyne was an old Frenchman who had been born in Dieppe and had come out to America where he founded one of those families whose pride rests partly on their size. His fourteen sons indeed gave M. Le Moyne a claim on the consideration of his neighbors. But, besides, he had brought up his flock to serve the King of France. When they grew up they were to be found in many high administrative posts, thus honoring the memory of their progenitor. Of these sons, two had won their spurs in skirmishes with the English around the Hudson's Bay country: Pierre, Sieur d'-Iberville, and Jean-Baptiste, Sieur de Bienville. The King put the conquest of the mouth of the Mississippi into their hands. An old buccaneer, Laurens de Graff, who had been with Du Casse and had helped raid Cartagena, steered the ships through the Gulf of Mexico. This time they found the river's mouth.

The brothers divided the work of the undertaking. Iberville took charge of communications; he came and went between

France and America, carrying news and bringing supplies. Bienville explored the coasts. He was twenty-six years old, he was clever and agreeable, he could talk to the Indians in their native tongues, and he smoked the peace pipe with them, painting his face white like theirs. News of the progress trickled back to Canada, and all sorts of rumors were set afoot. It was said that in these new lands there were huge rocks of emerald, and a special machine was devised to break them up. France was skeptical about the riches of the colony because the Canadians had the reputation of going off half-cocked. But the great engineer Vauban believed in them; he conceived of the French colonial empire as a huge arch resting on three points: Santo Domingo, the capital of Louisiana, and Canada. The great dream of Iberville's life was to destroy Boston and New York, and drive the English out of there. Yellow fever carried him off before he was able to accomplish these laudable projects.

The Sieur de Bienville founded New Orleans, probably in 1718 — that international window adorned with beautiful French grille work, from which mulattoes and quadroons, smugglers and pirates, looked out upon the turbulent life of the Caribbean. It was to become famous throughout the world for its cooking, its Mardi Gras, duels, quadroon balls, gaming houses, and establishments for ladies of easy virtue. New Orleans was destined to be North America's key to the Caribbean. That was evident. But building a house in New Orleans was a real problem. In the flood season the river overflowed the streets. The subsoil was like porridge. Levees had to be thrown up along the river banks, and the houses built on piles. Living in this city dedicated to the Duc d'Orléans was like living on an island floating on a mudflat.

The Sieur de Bienville modeled his mud pie lovingly. Skeptics looked on doubtfully; rivals, suspiciously. Du Casse in Santo Domingo refused to take New Orleans seriously. The Spaniards of Pensacola — that colony situated between the Mississippi and the peninsula of Florida — were not hospitably inclined toward their new neighbor. To the north the fierce Natchez Indians were on the alert; they might decide to help the French, or they might massacre them. In New England the English were priming their muskets. And on whom was Bienville counting for support? A motley, undisciplined group that was already splitting up into factions. The priest wrote reports attacking Bienville. Bienville replied that it would be better if, instead of having a shop and selling like an Arabian Jew, M. le Curé devoted his time to administering the sacraments. Four hundred Huguenots in the English colony applied for permission to move into the French settlement on condition that they be allowed freedom of worship. The King replied that he had not driven the Huguenots out of France to tolerate them in his American colonies.

Thus New Orleans emerged as a symbol of what these colonies of the southern United States had been and were to be. There was not an inch of territory around the Caribbean that had not been the scene of a struggle. In 1565 a shipload of French Huguenots settled on the Carolina coast. The Spaniards fell upon them and hanged the few survivors from trees, with a placard affixed that read: "Not because they were Frenchmen but because they were heretics." Whereupon Condé, in France, sent over another company of colonists, who fell upon the Spaniards, hanged the few they took alive, and left the sign: "Not because they were Catholics but because they were murderers." The international courtesies had been observed. The Spaniards of Pensacola set out against the French of New Orleans, but their ships foundered in sight of port. The French politely rescued them, gave them clothing and arms, and sent them away. Bienville used a different procedure with the English: when they made their appearance he fooled them into thinking he had a great army, and the English, knowing that discretion is the better part of valor, withdrew.

But the most serious problem was the internal situation. Bienville was standing on a shaky mud pedestal in the midst of a settlement that was getting out of hand. The settlers fell in love with Indian women, and then no one could induce them to come back from the woods. An appeal for women was made to

France; twenty-three were sent out. Their arrival caused a sensation, but the joy was short-lived; the selection had been carelessly made. One high official remarked: "M. Clarembault, who sent them, must have been more concerned with their looks than with their virtue. All the settlers are fine, upstanding men, and not too particular about the past of these girls they marry." In France this criticism was filed away for future reference.

Thirty years had elapsed since the day La Salle planted the arms of Louis XIV at the mouth of the Mississippi, and so far no one could see what financial profit there had been. Louis XIV's extravagance had brought French finances to the verge of ruin, and he showed no inclination to continue spending money on these lands when it could be used for greater display in Versailles. So he made up his mind to hand over this empire La Salle and Bienville had won him to Antoine de Crozat, a businessman reputed to be the richest man in France. Crozat saw the possibility of great enterprises in these lands that were several times the size of France: furs, gold, emeralds, slave-trade, and — best of all — smuggling. Bienville was supplanted by the governor sent out by Crozat, who was none other than M. de La Mothe Cadillac.

Cadillac, like a number of other figures in this narrative beginning with Hernando de Soto, has achieved immortality because centuries later his name was given to a make of automobile. He was, above all, a man of clear judgment whose every word carried a nugget of wisdom. Within a short time after his arrival, like all Frenchmen he was writing *Mémoires*. His style was terse and pithy: "This colony is a monster without head or tail. . . . A lie has a better chance of getting a hearing than the truth. The mines of Arkansas are a myth. The beauty and fertility of this land, a phantasmagoria. The writers have said that this land was like the Isles of the Blessed; I never saw anything worse. The Mississippi is not a navigable river. Six months of the year it is a raging torrent; the other six it is dry, without water enough to float a canoe. . . ."

The priest of the colony, too, wrote his *Mémoires*: The settlers from Canada were all fugitives from the law, nobody obeyed the precepts of his religion, and though a few observed the Sabbath and the feasts of the Church, the majority spent their time in gambling dens and saloons. Almost all were drunkards, blasphemers, and gamblers who made a mock of religion and its ministers, and preferred to live with Indian women rather than take the vows of matrimony. According to the priest, there were only two ways of straightening out this state of affairs: either bring in established families from France or Canada, or let the Frenchmen marry the Indian women. And he ventured to add a third suggestion, which was that France send out young unmarried women — "but more carefully selected than the last, more settled and better fitted to become the wives of men of position and official standing."

The inevitable feud sprang up between Cadillac and Bienville, and the people took sides, as happens in any village anywhere. Bienville's explanation of their disagreement was that Cadillac was angry because he had not wanted to marry Cadillac's daughter.

All this took place in an insignificant little city, where there were but a few hundred white men, considerably more Negroes, and thousands of cows, pigs, and chickens. The smuggling enterprise had not worked out. Crozat had hoped to introduce his merchandise into Mexico, and one of the settlers, disguised as a peddler, set out to size up the market. He crossed prairies and mountains, stopping to talk with farmers, entertaining the guests at the inns with the account of his adventures. When he reached the capital, the viceroy had him thrown into jail. But the Frenchman was smart: on the way he had left a pledge of love with a Spanish officer's daughter. The viceroy released him from jail, invited him to dine with him at the palace, and gave him a good horse so that he could hurry back to marry the Spaniard's daughter. . . . That was no way to lay the foundations of business. Crozat had to admit his failure. He confessed that this empire was too heavy a load for him, and he was giving up the undertaking.

Louisiana returned to the crown just as France was going through one of it severest crises. In 1713 His Magnificence Louis XIV had died, leaving the public treasury stripped. The national debt amounted to 1,600,000,000 francs. In Paris the people were dying of hunger and cold. The Duc de Saint-Simon proposed that the nation declare itself in bankruptcy and convoke the Estates General. In the council presided over by the Duc d'Orléans, this plan produced the effect of a bombshell. Something must be done. And at this juncture, not long after the Sun King's death, there appeared on the scene a fantastic Scotsman, John Law, whose name will be forever associated with one of the most fabulous schemes of speculation in the world, and with the history of the Mississippi.

Like William Paterson, John Law was a great promoter. He was born in Edinburgh where his father, a jeweler, initiated him into the world of business. The boy was restless and a gambler. He went to London, secured entry into society circles where people gambled and talked politics. He fought a duel, left his adversary on the field, and fled to the Continent. He visited Holland, France, and Italy, and he seemed to have been born under a lucky star. In Paris, in the salon of the actress who was the toast of the day, La Duclos, he played for breath-taking stakes. Politicians, artists, and scientists were his friends. He came to the gambling houses with heavy bags of gold, which multiplied under the magic spell of his luck. People began to grow suspicious. The police expelled him from France, and he went to Germany and Italy. He laid schemes of financial reforms before the governments of these countries, and was expelled from them, too. But by this time he had become one of the richest men in Europe; his fortune was estimated at £2,600,-000. Would he not seem the proper person to straighten out the tangle of French finances, employing the same audacity he had used at the gaming table?

The Duc d'Orléans dropped the suggestion to his ministers. He was one of the many Law had dazzled with his financial schemes. Law's idea was to found a state bank, with branches in all the leading French cities, to issue paper money, collect taxes, and put an end to usury — a bank that should be authorized to carry on commercial operations, associating with itself the most influential men in France as stockholders. In 1716 the plan was put into operation as a private enterprise. With the backing of the nobility and the bourgeoisie, the Banque de France began to flood the country with paper money, and presently a mantle of well-being and prosperity covered the memory of Louis XIV, whose popularity had begun to wane in the hunger-ridden land.

The bank was only the first step in the Scotsman's plans. It was followed at once by the organization of the "Great Mississippi Scheme" which was to undertake the colonization of this incomparable valley paved with gold and emeralds. In the remotest corner of France, pictures were displayed showing the arrival of the French at the Mississippi, and below each an inscription that read: "Note the coins of gold, silver, copper, lead, mercury. As these metals are very common and the Indians have no idea of their value, they trade pieces of gold and silver for knickknacks such as knives, brooches, mirrors, or little bottles of brandy." In the Bois de Boulogne and at the theaters, Indians were exhibited, and all Paris flocked to see them, from the Duc d'Orléans and the nobles of the court down. The shares of the bank and of the Mississippi Scheme skyrocketed. Bienville was appointed governor of Louisiana, and began to assemble a fleet to take out settlers, tools, and food. Never had the French ports been the scene of such feverish activity. The masses were revivified by the vision of wealth, and Law was considered a genius — the Ace, as he was affectionately termed, who was performing the miracle of restoring France to life. The streets leading to the bank and the company offices were jammed with people. Decrees were issued to encourage the settlement of Louisiana; vagrants and beggars were to be sent there, offenders against justice, girls who had been incarcerated in La Salpetrière. Gangs known as "Mississippi Highwaymen" were organized to go into the provinces and "persuade" prospective colonists; they received ten francs for every quarry they brought in. Five thousand were rounded up in Paris. At times the victims made trouble. One hundred and fifty girls who had been taken by main force to La

Rochelle to be put aboard ship turned on the soldiers and —
scratching, biting, and kicking — managed to break loose. Fortunately the soldiers were able to load their guns, and six of the
girls were killed and twelve wounded. Order was re-established,
and the girls went aboard. When these methods threatened to
reflect on the good name of the company, a cordial invitation
was extended to the Swiss and the Germans. Peasants and harassed citizens of those countries were entranced by the prospectus, the posters, and the coat-of-arms of the company: a golden
horn of plenty, symbolizing the Mississippi, adorned with fleur-
de-lis, upheld by two savages, and pouring forth over a field of
silver and emerald. Whole families left their native land to choke
the highways of France. Hunger, pestilence, and fever decimated their numbers, but some of them finally reached those
swampy shores where Bienville was struggling (like the hero he
was) to shelter and distribute these waves of immigrants which
the genius of the Scotsman was pouring out upon the virgin territories of America.

And legends began to form. Every immigrant had a past. Who
could he be? A murderer, an impoverished nobleman, the hero
of some amorous adventure? A good yarn often enhanced the
prestige of a family. The haughtier and better-looking were
probably the illegitimate offspring of royalty. New Orleans came
to be full of people whose origin was a mystery. Among a group
of Germans there was a woman of singular beauty who married
the Chevalier d'Aubant. Nothing was known of her past, but
the nails of time, scratching and scratching at her secret, eventually brought out that she had been the wife of the Czarevitch
Alexis Petrovich, a son of Peter the Great. The Czarevitch was
a beast, and the princess had one day feigned death to escape
his brutality. And there she was in New Orleans, the wife of the
Chevalier d'Aubant. Anyone who had any doubts could get a
picture of the princess and compare them. . . .

John Law managed to get out of Paris alive by the grace of
God and the help of the Duc d'Orléans. The bank and the company had crashed on May 29, 1720, and the sound of its fall had

filled the streets of Paris with weeping and wailing and gnashing of teeth. At the height of its dizzy rise, the company had declared two-hundred-percent dividends. Voltaire said that the paper money issued represented eighty times the nation's wealth. People sang in the streets:

> Lundi, j'achetai des actions,
> Mardi, je gagnai des millons,
> Mercredi, j'ornais mon ménage,
> Jeudi, je pris mon équipage,
> Vendredi, je m'en fus au bal,
> Et samedi à l'hôpital.[1]

Those who were on the other side of the ocean, in New Orleans, had to get on as best they could. Bienville, at war with the Natchez and the Spaniards, had acquitted himself well. He had taken Pensacola. But he also was fighting gossip and slander, which flourished like the green bay-tree in New Orleans, as well as such adversities as the hurricane that destroyed the church, the hospital, thirty houses, and three of the ships anchored in the harbor. He issued the Black Laws, which began: "*Article 1*. All Jews are to be expelled." He issued an ordinance imposing severe penalties on opening other people's mail, because it had become intolerable that the very last person to learn the contents of a letter was the person to whom it was addressed. And after forty-four years in Louisiana, struggling to make it into a French colony, he received a letter from the court ordering him to present himself in France to answer charges of improper conduct in office.

Languidly, like a slow-motion picture, the colony dragged on. Groups of nuns arrived to found convents, hospitals. Negro slaves, for the cotton plantations. Girls, who married soldiers. Each new family that was formed received a grant of land, a cow,

---

[1] Monday, I bought some shares,
Tuesday, I was a millionaire,
Wednesday, I furbished up my house,
Thursday, I got into my carriage,
Friday, I went to a ball,
And Saturday, to the poorhouse.

a calf, a rooster, five hens, an ax, and a gun. Money was completely unstable. Bills were printed on paper and cardboard. France found all this very tiresome. It bored the ministers to have to listen to news of the colony. King Louis XV wanted no more of it, and, besides, he was a poor devil. The colony was in danger, and France did not know what to do. Aid was asked from Spain. In pleading tones one of the ministers begged the ambassador in Madrid to intercede with the Spanish king to have the governor of Havana send help to New Orleans. This was the beginning of the end. Louis XV, with the help of his minister, hit upon a brilliant idea: to present Spain with this worthless colony.

XV

THE WOULD-BE GENTLEMEN, THE ENCYCLOPEDIA, AND THE COCKED HATS

The Pyrenees have ceased to exist!
Louis XIV

THE LAST Spanish monarch — though the title might seem a misnomer — of the haughty Hapsburg dynasty was Charles II; historians are divided as to whether he should be known as The Impotent or The Bewitched. Until he died (without issue) in 1700, he dragged out his ailing years dominated by his wives and confessors. At the opening of the eighteenth century the throne of Spain was the stake in the game of intrigue played with every card in the deck by the courts of France and of Austria. France won; Philip of Anjou, grandson of Louis XIV, became Philip V of Spain; and the War of the Spanish Succession was on in Europe.

It was a stroke of fortune for Spain that things fell out this way. Over the Pyrenees trooped the brilliant throng that had flourished in the France of Louis XIV. The sober black garb that had become traditional among the Spanish nobility since the days of Philip II, the somber sable velvet that chilled the blood and silenced the tongue, was now exchanged for coats of pink and blue brocaded silk with ruffles of lace at throat and sleeve, gold-buttoned satin vests, and, crowning it all, three-cornered hats to set off the curled periwigs. Even the bishops and archbishops now lived like princes of the Renaissance; the day of emaciated friars, *memento mori*, was over. And during the same period these transformations spread to the farthest reaches of America. In New Orleans, Caracas, Mexico, Santa Fe de Bogotá, and Lima new viceroys made their appearance, as did the Archbishop Caballero, learned geographers, and — who

would have believed it? — even Frenchmen. They burst upon
the colonists with a riot of colors, an assortment of new books,
clothes, and sciences that were the amazement of the Creoles,
the delight of the mulattoes, the horror of devout old women.

This was not alone the result of the ascent of the Bourbons to
the Spanish throne. It was that Spain was shaking off its leth-
argy and awakening. It was the tone of the century. All Europe
was undergoing a complete overhauling. In England the philosophers had thrown open doors that would lead to a political transformation. In Denmark the court was an academy. In
Russia musicians, poets, and writers were giving new splendor to
the palace of the Czars. In Prussia a court was developing that
would in time be the amazement of Europe. But if there was
one nation that could greet these happenings with the youthful
enthusiasm accorded a revolution, that was the Spain of the
eighteenth century. It was a century that did not, perhaps, pro-
duce works of great depth; for the times were not suited to solitary meditations, but rather to considering the whole world as
a spectacle where the mind no longer sought the answer to eternal doubts, but launched itself on the breathless race of progress.

The first clash came with the Inquisition and the Jesuits.
These had been the two arms of the Hapsburgs, and therefore
the two strongholds the Bourbon ministers had to reduce. In
Spain there were nine thousand convents and seventy thousand
friars. If not a third, at least a fourth of the population of Spain
were friars, nuns, clergymen, lay members of religious orders,
hermits, or persons who had taken a vow of chastity. In every
house the seat at the head of the table was occupied by some
member of the Holy Office. The government had put into the
hands of the Inquisition many civil functions: the enforcement
of the laws against usury, smuggling, circulating alloyed coins,
and exporting horses. Someone had even suggested a plan by
which the church of Toledo should take charge of the army;
that of Seville, of the navy; and that of Malaga, of the galleys
and prison camps of Africa. The Church had wielded this om-
nipotent power in the heart of Madrid and in the most remote
corner of America.

The reaction was initiated by a new school of philosophical and political thought — that of the regalists, whose purpose was to restore the prestige of the State, to enable it to talk with the Papal See as power to power. When the Bourbons ascended the throne, Pope Clement XI, under the pressure of the Emperor, almost at bayonet's point, continued to favor the Austrian claimant. Philip V handed the Nuncio his passports, closed the embassy, and calmly sat back. Rome yielded. France acted as the Pope's intermediary in restoring relations. Peace was made on Spain's terms, and Spain's representative at this time was an alert, truculent man of great learning who exerted a vast influence in Spain at the time this new policy was adopted: Rafael Melchor de Macanaz.

Macanaz sought to bring about the revival of Spain through the development of agriculture, commerce, science, and industry. He wanted to send students of painting and sculpture to Rome; to create "Patriotic Societies" to study the economy of the different regions and to bring in experts from other, more advanced countries so that Spain might profit by their experience; and to found an academy of arts and sciences. The Jesuits and the Inquisition opposed Macanaz with every means at their disposal, for they realized the threat his plans represented to them. Macanaz advocated the closing of all convents founded after the reform of Cardinal Cisneros — that is, those established under Hapsburg auspices. The convents, he said, deprived agriculture and industry of workers, and were the cause of Spain's stagnation. As for the Jesuits, Macanaz held them to be the unrelenting enemies of episcopal authority and of the State; if the State were to seize their archives one day by surprise, it would find ample proof of their ambition, duplicity, and pernicious tenets.

The chief magistrate of the Court of the Inquisition was Francisco Judice. Judice had coveted the archbishopric of Toledo, and Macanaz had frustrated this ambition. The prelate never forgave him, and when he learned that Macanaz was drawing up the plans for a concordat with the Holy See, he set into motion the machinery of the Inquisition, and forbade the reading of French books containing ideas of the kind that Macanaz was promulgating. Philip V became indignant; he ordered the Inquisition's edict torn from the church doors and forbade Judice to set foot in Spain again.

Macanaz's ideas had firmer roots in the people's soul than in the King's mind. Philip was popular because the side he had taken symbolized their hopes. Their eyes were open, and even if the King were to retrogress, an awareness had developed in the intellectual classes and in the rising middle class. In the last analysis, all this was merely the spirit of the age. The people's resentment against the Jesuits often took violent forms. When the convent of the Company was being built in Zamora, army protection was necessary because as fast as a wall went up the people tore it down. When the Jesuits went to take possession of a property that had been willed them in Toro, the people stoned them away. In Vitoria the town council, the Franciscans, the Dominicans, the whole population, opposed them when they attempted to found a school there. It did not matter that the Jesuits were the King's confessors. The day was to come when another king, with the backing of Rome, would proscribe them from all Spain's possessions.

To be sure, Philip V was not a man remembered for his strength of character. When in 1714 he married a second time, his new queen, Elizabeth Farnese, sided with Judice's supporters. Macanaz, who saw the storm coming, asked permission to visit a spa in France, and there he took the waters for ten years, thus keeping out of jail. Though Philip lived on until 1746, most of his remaining years were melancholy to the point of madness; he would, for instance, get up at two in the morning to go fishing, he took a dislike to all forms of personal cleanliness, and he tried to ride the horses in the beautiful palace tapestries. But even though Elizabeth Farnese held the reins in Spain, and Macanaz was taking the waters in France, the reformers' teachings had not fallen on barren ground. The Basques founded the Guipuzcoana Company, and the first society of "Friends of the Country" was organized. Out of these beginnings came the Enlightenment, the Illuminism movements, the Masonic lodges that brought the Spaniards into contact with men of Philadelphia, England, France. In a word, it brought about the Basque renascence.

The plan of the Guipuzcoana Company was ambitious: to put the new mercantile, political, and philosophical ideas into play from the Pyrenees to the American colonies. Macanaz's ideas were to be shipped across the Atlantic. The progress of Holland, England, and Denmark had been founded on similar ventures. The Basques hoped to carry these same ideas into effect on a different basis. Their flag was not the pirates' skull and crossbones. Nor were their ventures a mere commercial undertaking, or circumscribed by religious fanaticism. Along with its merchandise, the Guipuzcoana Company took to the American ports the volumes of the *Encyclopedia.* By coincidence — or perhaps as a counterbalance to fanaticism — it set up its headquarters in the same city and the same street where the soldiers of the Company of Jesus had their barracks and their birthplace. Thus the two great Basque enterprises stood face to face. The Company's shares were put on the market, and the outstanding members of the bourgeoisie of those provinces showed their confidence in it by becoming stockholders. King Philip bought two hundred shares for 100,000 pesos. He was following to the letter the advice Macanaz had given him years before: that, in order to dispel the idea that trade was unbecoming a gentleman, the King should be the leading figure among the businessmen. The Guipuzcoana Company was to have a monopoly of trade with Venezuela, was to extend the cultivation of chocolate, and to drive out the Dutch smugglers.

In July of 1730 the Company's boats set out from the port of Pasajes on the Basque coast. When they reached Puerto Cabello in Venezuela, the first reaction was one of distrust. The Dutch and Spanish smugglers bribed people to make difficulties for the new company. The planters refused to sell their cacao beans. But the Basques are famous for their tenacity and stubbornness, and, like a wedge, they drove their way in, and there was no power that could stop them. They finally persuaded the moneyed people of Caracas to invest in the Company; with shares producing a twenty-five-percent return, this was not too difficult. From the huge Company warehouses in Puerto Cabello, whose great stone doorways and wide wooden balconies recalled the architecture of the Basque manor house, far into the plains, dotted with herds of the Company's cattle, and on the plantations where the production of chocolate was being doubled, spread a wave of new-found prosperity. Basque settlers arrived in the country. The port of Puerto Cabello, which had hitherto been either a site of combat or a nest of smugglers, was almost unrecognizable; its new harbor was thronged with mule-trains clattering over cobblestone streets and hummed with the oaths and laughter of busy stevedores. And above all this din the employees of the Company, punctual, hard-working, and pleasant, were ordering everything with the most painstaking exactitude.

To Spain, too, there came a sense of well-being. Money was plentiful. The feasts of the Basques' patron saint, Ignatius, were now sponsored by the Guipuzcoana Company, which had stolen its saint from the Company of Jesus. The Count of Peñaflorida, president of the Guipuzcoana, built the finest palace ever seen in that region of Spain, and there he assembled musicians, writers, and friends of progress. One day the village of Vergara was preparing a great celebration. Vergara and Beasain were rival villages; for years they had been carrying on a dispute as to which was the cradle of a certain saint. After due consideration, the Pope had decided in favor of Vergara. In honor of this, Vergara had masses and fireworks, dances and rosaries. But the final touch was supplied by the Count of Peñaflorida. In his house on this occasion the rich mingled with the villagers, and, as the Count was an amateur of the arts, he and his friends, the gentlemen of Guipuzcoa and Biscay, put on a comic opera the Count had translated from the French and for which he had arranged the music. After the performance, the villagers danced their traditional folk dances, the guests gorged themselves in true Basque fashion, and the celebration wound up with everybody singing. All the guests congratulated the Count on the play, on his palace, and on the splendid banquet. Why not found a society such as Macanaz and the Asturian, Pedro Rodríguez de Campomanes, had outlined in their *Address on the Development of Arts and Crafts?* And arrange for meetings of people who would be interested in discussing the new ideas that were coming forth in other countries such as France, England, and North America? The Count's palace, with its fine library, its physics laboratory, its music room, would seem the ideal place for a forum of this sort.

The plan was enthusiastically received. There were to be seven meetings a year, and a different topic would be discussed each time. "The days of this symbolic week would each be devoted to the cultivation of a different branch of the encyclopedic tree: one day to physics, another to history, the third to music, and so on, until the hebdomadal span had been filled with multiple erudite activities. The seventh will be devoted to fulfilling religious obligations." In the initiations the ritual of the lodges was to be followed, and at the official inauguration it would be observed to the letter.

With the Vergara society serving as a model, other similar societies were immediately formed in Valencia, Seville, and Saragossa. Father Isla might make all the jokes he liked about "the would-be gentlemen of Azcoitia." The Company's ships entered Spanish ports loaded with chocolate and sailed back to America carrying books by Montaigne, Voltaire, and Rousseau. And soon there were societies like those of the "would-be gentlemen of Azcoitia" in Caracas, Bogotá, Quito, Lima, Buenos Aires, Havana. . . . The consequences were far reaching. New courses of study were introduced, scientific missions were organized, the metallurgical industry was developed in Bilbao. There was something symbolic about the tongues of flame rising from the blast furnaces. . . .

When in 1759 Philip's second son, Charles III, came to the throne, Spain was a cauldron seething with new ideas. The monarch placed himself at the head of this rebirth, determined to change the tenor of Spanish life. Macanaz's initial efforts to uphold the rights of the State were continued by the minister Manuel de Roda, and carried to completion by José Moñino, later Count of Floridablanca, who won from the Pope the bull for the expulsion of the Jesuits. In the field of literature, the Benedictine monk, Father Feijoo, year after year brought out the volumes of his *Teatro Crítico*, in which he threshed out for Spain everything that was being done in the world in the fields of science and philosophy. Jovellanos, statesman and writer, furthered the work of reform. The royal academies of language and history were founded, and the dictionary was published. Scampish, amusing Diego de Torres, author of almanacs, swept through the University of Salamanca like a whirlwind, setting the old professors by the ears, teaching mathematics, and planning the creation of an academy of mathematics to array the physicists against the metaphysicians.

One day, at the instigation of the superior of the Jesuits the book by Dr. Mesenghi on Christian doctrine was brought to the attention of the Inquisition. With slight variations from its first edition, this book had been circulating in the Catholic world and was considered a source of orthodox, approved doctrine. According to the Jesuits, it contained more than a thousand errors. A council of cardinals, by a vote of six to five, declared the work anathema. When the result of the findings was sent to Charles III, he instantly returned it to the Inquisitor-General, forbidding its publication. The Inquisitor, out of either shrewdness or stupidity, had already distributed the document among churches and convents, and had no way of recalling it. Humbled and frightened, he so advised the King. Charles ordered the Inquisitor exiled twelve leagues from the capital, to the monastery of the Benedictine friars of Our Lady of Sopetrán. From there he wrote the monarch, on his knees, imploring pardon. The King revoked the ban "because of my tendency to forgive a person who confesses his error and implores my clemency." The Inquisition sent him a letter of thanks. Charles replied: "The Inquisitor-General has asked forgiveness and I have granted it. I accept the thanks of the court, and I shall always accord it my protection; but it should not forget this indication of my displeasure at any hint of disobedience."

Matters reached a climax with the expulsion of the Jesuits early in April 1767. The Spanish crown took its place alongside other nations in their stand against the order. Don José Moñino had obtained the bull from the Pope, and had sent secret orders throughout the kingdom and the colonies that on the same day and at the same hour all the Jesuits' residences were to be taken over and the Jesuits removed. This had been the advice of Macanaz. In Madrid as in Guatemala, in Toledo, Caracas, Lima, and Santa Fe de Bogotá, in the jungles of Paraguay and the savannas of the Orinoco, on muleback, in canoes, or in sampans, with knapsack over shoulder the members of the order set out on the road to exile. In Cartagena, Vera Cruz, and Havana, as in Cádiz, ships were waiting to take them to other countries. They had learned of these secret orders in time to make ready — to hide the rich chalices, to secrete a gold doubloon in each cake of chocolate; but their influence was not great enough to induce the people to rebel at their exile. On the contrary, the next day, the friars of the other orders who could not bear them beamed with satisfaction, and the sermons preached from the pulpits had an undercurrent of "Praise be to God!" The government proceeded to occupy the Jesuit schools and to introduce into them the teaching of mathematics and natural sciences, all in accordance with the formulas of the illuminists, the encyclopedists, the mentors of "enlightened despotism." The libraries of the Jesuits, supplied with new books, served as nuclei for the public libraries that were coming into existence.

The court of Spain began to receive the visits of savants from all over Europe. As Louis XIV had said, the Pyrenees no longer existed. In Madrid and Seville, Cervi taught medicine; Virgili, in Cádiz, surgery; Quer, botany in the Botanical Garden of Madrid; Bowles, mineralogy. Ward drew up a plan to combat vagrancy; Godin directed the school of midshipmen; Casiri revealed to the world the priceless Arabic manuscripts preserved in the monastery of San Lorenzo. Under the patronage of the French Academy of Sciences, La Condamine, accompanied by

a group of French scientists, went out to Ecuador to measure
a degree of longitude on the Equator. Humboldt made his marvelous journeys through America which were to reveal to Europe the natural wealth and the human values of the New
World. Both La Condamine and Humboldt were accompanied
by Spanish scientists: Ruiz, Pavón, Mutis, Jorge Juan, Antonio
Ulloa. America had become the university of the world. It
seemed as though the Hapsburgs had locked all the doors in order
to hold fast to the secrets of this hemisphere, which was destined
to become the home of the free men of the world. With the
eighteenth century had come that era of discovery whose consequences were as great for America as for Europe.

The Caribbean was the first place where the old ideas, the
vested interests, came into conflict with American ambitions,
the theories of illuminism, enlightened despotism, and the desire for independence. And Caracas was the first place where
the spark was touched off. There was a profound contradiction
in the Spanish theories. The more that "enlightenment" spread
through America, the stronger became the feeling against "'despotism." It might almost be said that the influence of the new
theories was stronger on this side of the Atlantic than in Europe
itself. The Creoles were ambitious, they had been thwarted by
the Spaniards, and their enthusiasm for science — which had
been, if possible, more neglected here than in Spain itself —
became a veritable furor. Little magazines began to appear in
Madrid, containing a condensed version of the best that was being published in the journals of various countries on politics,
science, and history. In format, technique, and choice of articles,
El Espíritu de los Mejores Diarios of Madrid was a counterpart
of our present-day *Reader's Digest*. The greater part of the selec-
tions in this Madrid review were from English rather than
French periodicals. Moreover, the spirit of Philadelphia, where
the Declaration of Independence was soon to be proclaimed, was
manifest in its pages. From the time of Macanaz and the Count
of Peñaflorida the Spaniards had been playing with fire. Magazines like the one in Madrid soon began to appear in Mexico,

Guatemala, Bogotá, Quito, Lima, Buenos Aires, and Havana. Something important was going to come from all this: the independence of Spanish America.

The Creoles in America were beginning to feel their oats, and the conflict with Spain was approaching the boiling point. The populace, too, was in a revolutionary mood. In the back lands of Venezuela this took the form of an insurrection against the Guipuzcoana Company. Juan Francisco León, acting judge, had been notified that he was to be supplanted in his post by the Basque Echeverría, and he advanced on Caracas with a mass of barefooted followers shouting: "We don't want justice at the hands of Basques! We want Islanders or Creoles — but no Basques!" (León had been born in the Canary Islands.) The governor was unable to check the rioters. They marched through the streets with flags flying, trumpets blowing, and drums rolling. The town council was called into session, and agreed to notify Spain that it had accepted the demands of León's followers. The town crier stood at the street corner demanding in a thundering voice: "In whose name is Juan Francisco de León acting?" "In the name of the whole province!" roared back the people. The better to conduct his government, León set himself up in the bishop's house, which resembled a barracks. In order to govern, he had to pull wires, make numerous commitments, dissemble, run many risks. To send secretly his own report of what had happened to Spain, he was obliged to go to La Guayra disguised as a friar. But as soon as the people returned to their fields, and the regular officials got over their fright, and reinforcements arrived from Spain, reprisals began. León had to flee to the mountains. He was tracked down, captured, and sent to Spain a prisoner. His house was razed and the ruins were sown with salt. But the people had learned to revolt.

Intellectuals of America went to Spain to take their place beside the natives in literary, scientific, and philosophical undertakings. Olavide, a Peruvian, was hailed by Jovellanos as his master; he was appointed intendant of Seville; he translated Voltaire, and he was one of those restless spirits who kept the

Holy Office, intent on extinguishing every spark that sprang up, on pins and needles. And when the forces of reaction were directed against him, he was brilliantly defended by another American, José Mejía of Quito. Zea, of New Granada, was named director of the Botanical Garden of Madrid. Jacobo Villarrutia, of Santo Domingo, was the editor of the *Correo de Madrid*; later he went to Mexico, where he founded the country's first newspaper. It would be impossible to list them all. America was very much to the front. In Barcelona a company was organized to trade with Puerto Rico, Cumaná, and Margarita. Havana was growing; it had a university and a printing establishment. Martin Aróstegui, a merchant of Guipuzcoa who had settled in Cuba, founded the Royal Trading Company of Havana, in which the King was a shareholder. Consulates, or merchants' universities, were set up to encourage commerce; in the Caribbean they began to operate in Caracas, Havana, Cartagena, and Vera Cruz.

How far all this was to go, no one could say. Humboldt and the other foreign scientists who visited America and had eyes to see and ears to hear, received the impression that we were on the eve of a profound change. French influence was a two-edged sword. On the one hand, France sought to bring order into ideas, to reduce to a clear system things that elsewhere assumed a cloudy, confused aspect. Moreover, it exalted the idea of liberty. In Spain, order could now make progress thanks to a rising, well-to-do middle class that was beginning to take over the posts and prerogatives that had formerly belonged to the nobility and the clergy. In America, the direct consequence of this new philosophy was the struggle for freedom.

XVI

THE TALE OF THE ENGLISH ADMIRAL AND DON BLAS, THE LAME, THE HALT, AND THE BLIND

Most monuments that are erected subsequent to the events they commemorate only perpetuate time-hallowed errors; one should even distrust medals struck at the time of the event. We have seen how the English, taken in by a false report, engraved on the exergue of a medal: TO ADMIRAL VERNON, CONQUEROR OF CARTA-GENA; the medal had hardly been struck off when it was learned that Admiral Vernon had raised the siege. If a nation abounding in philosophers has thus ventured to deceive posterity, what can we expect of peoples and temples abandoned to the crassest ignorance?

VOLTAIRE

LONDON was going through one of those moments when demagoguery in Parliament and mobs in the streets foreshadowed great events. In other words William Pitt — the elder Pitt, later made Earl of Chatham — was beginning his career. He was just thirty years old, in the flower of his years, and now for the first time he had an opportunity to take part in a great debate. He revealed his gifts as an orator, and his admirers went so far as to compare him to Demosthenes. When King George II opened Parliament in 1739 he asked the members to employ moderation; with less animosity and heat — he remarked — we shall not waste time in unnecessary sessions. But the King was unpopular. The newspapers published caricatures poking fun at his character. The opposition responded to the royal suggestion by bringing up the two topics most likely to excite discussion and arouse the masses: the reduction of the army and declaring war on Spain. These were Pitt's two theses. From all parts of the kingdom came petitions favoring this policy — from London, Bristol, Liverpool, Lancaster, Aberdeen, Edinburgh, Dundee, and even from Kingston in Jamaica and Georgia in North America. At eight o'clock on the morning of the final oratorical joust, over a hundred seats in the house were already occupied, and the gallery was crowded.

Pitt's target of sarcasm and attack was Robert Walpole, the Prime Minister. The latter had been trying to come to an amicable arrangement with Spain; the King did not want war. But the people were up in arms because not a day went by that the Spanish coast guards did not seize English vessels engaged in smuggling, and the growth of Spain under the Bourbons was looked upon as a threat to British supremacy. In the international world an alliance of France, Austria, and Spain against England was shaping up. The doughty spirit of Elizabethan mariners was coming to life again. To hell with the Spaniards! Spain was trying to keep the sole right to commerce with America for herself; she had permitted only the English South Sea Company to carry on slave trade with the Antilles, and this only once a year. Every time that Walpole tried to arrive at some friendly solution, the ambassador in London would uncompromisingly answer that the Spanish government would continue to seize all English ships in Spanish waters of America. It was a known fact that if a few Spanish coins were found on a ship this was enough for it to be adjudged a smugglers' craft. Moreover, in this, the Spaniards were quite right. This was the situation when the memorable session of Parliament dealing with the matter of Captain Jenkins's ear took place. The war that followed in consequence has gone down in history as "The War of Jenkins's Ear."

Robert Jenkins, a smuggler with headquarters in Jamaica, carried on his business as God or the Devil counseled. His ship was the *Rebecca*. The Spanish boat was the *Isabel*. On a day in 1731, the *Isabel* overtook the *Rebecca*, and Jenkins was taken prisoner. The Spanish skipper cut off one of Jenkins's ears and handed it to him, saying: "Here's your ear; take it to the King of England and tell him there's to be no smuggling here." For seven years Jenkins had carried his ear about in a bottle waiting to show it to the King and demand vengeance. Now in 1739 he managed at last not only to procure an interview with the King, but even to exhibit the ear in Parliament. The sight of that dried, shriveled appendage aroused the people to a fury. Walpole had lost. War was declared. The bells of all the churches in London were set pealing.

Most enthusiastic of all was the Prince of Wales. When Pitt finished his address, the Prince descended from the gallery, crossed the chamber, put his arms around Pitt and kissed him. Heralds went out to announce that the country was at war. They were followed by a huge crowd, among which went the Prince of Wales. As they passed the Rose Tavern the Prince called out for everybody to halt; then he was served a glass of wine in which he drank to the health of the people and to victory. The writers were infected with the spirit of the time: Samuel Johnson published a lyric effusion, and Pope followed him with precise verses.

Spain replied to this outburst in London with scornful pride and fitting sarcasm. Jenkins's ear became the laughing stock of Madrid; it was said that the ear he had shown was not his own but someone else's, that his had really been lost in some smugglers' fracas. The King of Spain charged that the English not only cut off Spaniards' ears and noses, but that at dagger's point they made their owners eat them. On the Basque coast a considerable number of Spanish sailors fitted themselves out as privateers, and in a short time sailed into San Sebastián with eighteen captured English vessels. It was said that in a year the Spaniards captured £234,000 of English shipping.

If Pitt was the most eloquent member of Parliament, no one had raised his voice louder than a brave sailor who had spent years in idleness and was eager for the smell of powder and the clash of steel. This was Sir Edward Vernon. He was a member of an old and distinguished family that had always moved in high places. His father had been Secretary of State under William III, his brother the English representative at the court of Denmark. Edward himself had had a brilliant career. Having entered the Navy at fifteen and a half, he had taken part in the battles of Malaga and Barcelona, where he had learned to fight Spaniards. Then he went out to the Caribbean, where he had the pleasure of seeing a fight with Spanish ships near the port of Cartagena. Afterwards he spent five quieter years in the waters of the Baltic. As a result of all this experience he spoke with authority, and what he promised was: "With six warships, Portobello is mine."

No war was ever so popular in England. Vernon was put in command of the fleet to be sent to the Caribbean. Another was to go to the Pacific. The Spanish empire in America would be caught in the pincers of the British Navy. The Pacific fleet, under the command of Commodore Anson, made a very good showing. It sailed around Cape Horn, stopped at Juan Fernández Island, attacked and set fire to the port of Paita in Peru, and in the neighborhood of Panama captured *Our Lady of Covadonga*, which yielded a booty of £313,000. But the chief interest of the war centered in the Caribbean. Vernon's orders were that he was to make war on "the Spanish dogs" — he was to destroy all the Spanish settlements in the West Indies and not let one enemy vessel go unscathed, no matter what means he had to employ.

And with six ships, as Vernon had promised in Parliament, Portobello was taken. To be sure, Portobello was but a shadow of its former self. The fortress was in poor repair, almost unarmed. But there floated over it the legend of its stormy past, and, the fortress guarding the harbor had at least a name that was like a coat of mail: San Felipe Sotomayor de Todo Fierro. The news of the victory, which seemed the fulfillment of a prophecy, aroused wild rejoicing in England. Vernon received a vote of applause in both Houses. Medals were struck on which his bust appeared with six ships in the background. The houses were lighted up, and from towns and cities messages of congratulation poured in to the King. The oldest taverns of England and Scotland changed their traditional names for others like Portobello, Vernon's Head.

The next move was discussed. Would it be better to attack Cartagena, or Havana? Cartagena was like a magnet to Vernon, but an attack on it would require a large fleet and a complete army. For the first time in the history of the English colonies in

America they were asked for aid. In Rhode Island, Connecticut, Massachusetts, Maryland, Pennsylvania, Virginia, and North Carolina companies of militiamen were formed. Thirty-six hundred North American soldiers were to go with Vernon, their ranks including youths, workmen, and rogues; and they had received a solemn promise of plunder. Five companies were recruited in New York. Military training was given at Annapolis. The King had promised their freedom to all in prison who were willing to join the expedition. Creditors were not a little disgruntled to see so many scamps get out of paying their debts. The mayor of Anne Arundel (Maryland) shared this sound opinion, and let his tongue run away with him. For saying "Damn King George and all his soldiers!" he was thrown into one of the vacated debtors' cells for lack of respect for the monarch.

Vernon was not too pleased with his American allies. He found them inexperienced, and he suspected that many of them were Papists, of Irish origin. Only in case of dire necessity did he entrust them with any important operation. Nevertheless, they proved brave and loyal. Among them was Lawrence Washington, George's half-brother. Vernon did not suspect that he was to find in this American a man capable not only of standing by him in defeat, but of honoring him in a manner far beyond what might have been expected.

In Jamaica, two thousand Negro machete fighters joined the troops.

Never had a more imposing fleet entered Caribbean waters: thirty thousand fighting men — fifteen thousand of them sailors — in more than one hundred and twenty ships. Vernon was admiral; Wentworth, the general of the landing forces. Vernon was acquainted with Cartagena; he had already made a trial bombardment, hurling three hundred bombs into the city. He knew that the entrance to the bay was defended by the stoutest fortresses of the Caribbean. He knew that its walls were the pride of Spain in the New World. Yet this was the same Cartagena that Pointis had assaulted, and now, within its walls, there were only four thousand soldiers to defend it, counting whites, Indians, and Negroes. Vernon had seven men to each defender. The problem lay in the stones.

The viceroy was in Cartagena, a most unusual circumstance. His presence, which was a stimulus to the Spaniards, added zest to the English attack. The commander of the stronghold was Don Blas de Lezo who, like the good Basque he was, was tenacious and very touchy in matters of honor. But a more mutilated soldier could not have been found in any army of the world. In 1704, at the battle of Gibraltar, Vernon and Don Blas had fought on opposite sides, but while Vernon was one of the victors and received a reward of two hundred guineas, Don Blas was not only among the defeated, but lost his left leg. In Toulon he lost his left eye; in Barcelona, his right arm. In each battle he left a piece of himself in exchange for a little glory. Louis XIV made him a lieutenant, and Philip V gave him a special reward. He was a brave man. In Barcelona, to bring a convoy to the help of the beleaguered city, he set fire to several of his ships, and came in under the protection of a double curtain of flame. The English knew all this, and Vernon knew he was dangerous on the offensive. Right after the capture of Portobello, Vernon wrote Don Blas a letter that was a perfect challenge. Don Blas answered him: "If I had been in Portobello you would not have assaulted the fortresses of my master the King with impunity, because I could have supplied the valor the defenders of Portobello lacked, and checked their cowardice. . . ."

Vernon spared no pains in the slightest detail of what was to be the great achievement of his life. It was not to be endangered by any laxity of discipline, any infraction of rules. His troops were a heterogeneous assembly. To be sure, this was the largest land and sea force ever gathered in these waters, but there were many drunkards in its ranks. And the Caribbean was sown to rum. The islands were better known by the brands on their bottles than by their flags. Rum, the admiral informed his men, "conspires against the health of sailors, ruins their morale, and makes them the slaves of brutal passions." It was not that Vernon was a teetotaler; it was that he believed in moderation. He ordered that liquor be issued twice a day on the ships, and forbade its being mixed with anything but water. A half-pint of water to a pint of rum was his formula. He did not realize that he was inventing a new drink, and that through it, by way of the tavern, he would achieve immortality. This mixture became the famous "grog," so named because his men called him "Old Grog" from the heavy grogram coat he wore in foul weather. The day was to come when, among drinkers, Vernon's name would be as closely associated with grog as Jamaica is with rum, or curaçao with the island that gave it its name.

In 1740 the siege got under way. It was a long and bitter struggle; if the inhabitants of Cartagena were forced to eat things that hardly bear mentioning, the English were battering their heads against the stone walls in vain. The admiral and the general were not getting on well. It seemed to Vernon that Wentworth dawdled; Wentworth felt that Vernon was giving him insufficient support. Days went by in the effort to take the fortress of Bocachica. As long as the Spaniards were there, Vernon could not maneuver his fleet into position. Every afternoon he sent Wentworth a letter urging him to make speed. Finally the fortress fell. Now Vernon's opportunity had come. In his enthusiasm he sent word to England: "The wonderful success of this evening and night is so astonishing that one cannot but cry out with the Psalmist: 'It is the Lord's doing and seems marvelous in our eyes.' " And — so sure was he that Cartagena itself was now about to fall — he issued orders to the effect that he would accept only unconditional surrender and no quarter granted. There are no words to describe London's enthusiasm. Total victory was hailed and once more medals were struck off celebrating the fall of Portobello and Cartagena. They were of more than two hundred and fifty different kinds — silver, copper, nickel, bronze, tin, and lead; and all had memorable inscriptions: "British glory revived by Admiral Vernon," "True British heroes took Cartagena," "Spanish pride humbled by Admiral Vernon," and the like. On some, Vernon appeared with six ships symbolic of the taking of Portobello. On others, Don Blas de Lezo, kneeling and holding out his sword to the Admiral. One bore the images of Vernon, Wentworth, and General Ogle (who had contributed nearly ninety ships to the expedition), and at the bottom two lion cubs, because on the day the news was received a lioness in the Zoo had given birth to two cubs which were named Vernon and Ogle.

But while medals were being struck off in England, Englishmen were dying like flies in Cartagena. The city neither fell nor surrendered. Don Blas, the one-legged, stood firm, and the viceroy remained at his post. As long as the fortress of San Felipe de Barajas or that of San Lorenzo held out, it was impossible to enter. Once again Wentworth failed to advance. The white men could not endure the heat; the Negroes could not endure the bullets. A Spanish prisoner whom they forced to act as guide led them to the steepest escarpment. This time the Americans were used — to run up the scaling ladders, Lawrence Washington leading them; but the ladders were too short, and the soldiers were mowed down. Besides, yellow fever was wreaking havoc among them. Wentworth refused to call on the ships' doctors, so as not to be under obligations to the admiral. Serving as surgeon in the expedition was a man who was later to win fame as a novelist — Tobias Smollett, who afterward wrote moving descriptions of the sick, of the wounded crying in vain for help. The army generals held their own councils; the officers of the fleet, theirs. Every afternoon there was an exchange of letters between Wentworth and Vernon. Seven thousand soldiers died in the attack on San Felipe. Finally, Vernon — or the general staff — made the bitter decision to raise the siege, withdraw in defeat. Don Blas, the lame, the halt, and the blind, watched the besiegers disappear down the bay. It seemed a miracle. Te Deums in the cathedral!

Vernon now planned to attack Cuba. But, how, with what forces? The campaign against Cartagena was said to have cost England twenty thousand men. Jenkins's ear, Pitt's speeches, the toast at the Rose Tavern were but a memory. . . . But Vernon and others who shared his views decided that what they had been unable to accomplish with cannon they would do with paper. And the war of the pamphlets began. But these pamphlets were not directed against Spain — it was Vernon against Wentworth and Wentworth against Vernon. The Spaniards collected "Vernon medals" for their amusement. Vernon said that, aside from two regiments of English veterans, all the others in the general's forces had been raw recruits — inexperienced young gentlemen and "scum of the cities who after having been used for some dirty job in England were rewarded with places in the army." His opinion of the Americans was no better: tailors, shoemakers, scoundrels. The replies from the other side were in the same tone. Vernon summed up his position in these words: "The responsibility for these misfortunes rests with General Wentworth; although I have little experience in land fighting, I believe, nevertheless, that if the sole command had been placed in my hands, Your Majesty's forces would have taken possession of Cartagena and Santiago. . . ."

Despite this defeat, the name of Vernon is linked to a monument far more important than all the taverns of Scotland and England that sought to honor him. And this is due to an American. Lawrence Washington remained so loyal to Vernon that when, on his return home, he built his house overlooking the Potomac, he named the place "Mount Vernon" — a place that in time was to become an American shrine. The admiral, who had had so little faith in the Colonials, at least believed in the Washingtons, and it may have been he who opened the way for George Washington to serve with the British troops, thus contributing his mite to the loss of the English colonies. . . .

XVII

THE PACT BETWEEN THE ENLIGHT-
ENED COUSIN AND THE
PLAYBOY COUSIN

*And so it came to pass that within the space of about half a century
after the settlement of Louisiana, France was reduced to the position of no longer possessing an inch of land in North America, where
she had once owned the largest part.*

GAYARRÉ

CHARLES III, the advocate of progress, who selected his ministers from among the most distinguished scholars and economic
and intellectual reformers, had a playboy cousin who was the
King of France, Louis XV. The narration that follows belongs
to the days when King Louis had put aside his legitimate wife to
give himself over, body and soul, to the wife of a "bourgeois
gentleman," M. d'Etiolés. This lady left her husband, and to
compensate her for the loss the King gave her the title of Marquise de Pompadour. When La Pompadour was nine years old,
a fortune teller had predicted that she would become the mistress of Louis XV. The odds seemed very long, for — aside from
the fact that her mother's antecedents were not at all clear —
her father had been condemned to the gallows. To reach Versailles from such humble origins seems quite a feat, but as La
Pompadour was the best rider and dancer in the environs of
Paris, she made the leap and landed on her pretty feet.

Louis XV was the most bored man in a century when the
French court exuded boredom, and every noble was afflicted
with ennui. The Abbé Galiani observed that Louis XV followed
the lowest of all trades, that of king, quite against his own
wishes, and the brothers Goncourt later called this the most
perfect portrait ever made of the King. At any rate, little by little
Louis XV turned over the government to his mistress. If any of

his ministers attempted to criticize, however lightly, anything
La Pompadour did, the King haughtily cut him short, saying:
"Whatever Madame orders is to be done, and that is all there
is to it." And Madame proceeded to build charming chateaux,
had a new program planned each day for the King, carried her
theater — a marvel of stagecraft — from one palace to the other,
and herself put on spicy, amusing little comedies. Life was a
whirl of gaiety, of which she was the center around which all the
court revolved, from the King down. It was she who brought together the authors of the *Encyclopedia* and encouraged them in
their work. It was she who seated at the royal table writers and
artists, beginning with Voltaire. She planned the wars, corresponded with the generals, sent daily notes to the minister of
war, brought in the Duc de Choiseul as chief minister, and
even lavished her affections on him, since nothing was too much
trouble for Madame de Pompadour. With perfect justification
she could have applied to herself the remark of Louis XIV:
L'état c'est moi. But unfortunately, Madame was not the statesman Louis XIV was. In her hands the empire disintegrated, the
monarchy became discredited, and the inheritance of the First
Republic was a State eviscerated by the cancer of the court.
While the sorry king dallied with her — and with other ladies she
herself picked out for him — that proud France which had once
stepped so high in the world was humbly imploring the help of
Spain to save itself from the final crash. And the sensible cousin
came to the aid of the frivolous cousin.

Louis XV was barely able to keep his nose above the mire that
was his own life. Charles III was at the height of his reign. It
was then that Charles conceived the strange idea of signing a
family pact, linking the destinies of the two branches of the
Bourbons. The pact was aimed at England, toward whose royal
house Charles professed cordial dislike. Spain could hardly have
picked a worse moment from any point of view. It gave England the excuse she needed to resume her campaign of attacks in
the Caribbean. The "Family Pact" was supposed to be secret,
but France lost no time in exploiting it, and London learned

about it before Spain would have wished. "I am not surprised at France's lack of secrecy concerning this pact with me," Charles wrote in a personal letter; "for in the first place, you know that keeping a secret always gives the French indigestion, and they have to spit it out; and, in the second place, they seemed to think that it suited their interests to make it known. . . ."

Pitt, who had been obliged to resign for having advised the attack on Spain, was now in his glory. An inquiry by the English ambassador in Madrid received from Charles III an answer that was like a slap in the face. England got its fleet ready. This time they would not make the mistake of attacking Cartagena, whose fortifications were now considered invulnerable, but would proceed against Havana. The governor of Cuba did everything he could to strengthen fortresses and walls, but when in 1762 Sir George Pocock appeared with his fleet, the hope of holding out grew very slight. Women, children, and old men took headlong flight to the interior of the island. Inside the citadel there were only about five thousand men, and Pocock had twelve thousand foot soldiers he had brought from England, three thousand supplied by New York and Jamaica, four thousand Negroes, and fifteen thousand sailors. The ratio was practically the same as at the siege of Cartagena, but there were two differences: here Admiral Pocock and General Albemarle were in accord, and the defenses of Havana were not like those of the mainland. The siege dragged out for sixty-seven days. The bravery of the defenders of the fortress of El Morro was heroic, but the English finally broke through, and this time their intention was to stay on the island. By the generous terms of surrender, twenty-eight ships set out for Spain, carrying the nine hundred soldiers and officers who had survived the defeat and who wished to return to their mother country. The booty was estimated at £736,000, which was divided up among the victors. The officers came off a little better than the soldiers: Pocock and Albemarle each put £120,000 into their pockets. Elliot, the next in rank, got £24,500. The generals each received £6,800; brigadiers, £1,900. The soldier's share amounted to £3/4/9, and the sailor's to £4/1/8.

And British rule began in Havana. At first the people offered resistance. In these words of its president the city council refused to take the oath of obedience to the English King: "My lord: We are Spanish and we cannot be English; do what you like with our property, sacrifice our lives rather than demand that we swear allegiance to a prince who to us is a foreigner." The ladies signed a petition addressed to the Madrid court stating that the surrender of the city was an act of cowardice on the part of the governor. The bishop refused to hand over to Albemarle a list of the priests with a statement of their livings, or to assign him a church in which the Protestants might hold their services. Albemarle set about smoothing out the difficulties with firmness, and sometimes with tact. He respected the attitude of the town council. He tried to bring the bishop to reason by threatening him with banishment. The bishop replied: "In spiritual matters I obey only the Pope, and in temporal, only my King; but here is my miserable body for you to do with as you like, heretics!" Restraining the impulse he must have felt to have him hanged, Albemarle sent a squad of soldiers for him the next morning; they lifted him out of his chair without letting him finish his breakfast and shipped him off to Florida. Every church had to pay a ransom on its bells; otherwise they were melted down for cannon. And finally Albemarle found two Spaniards, Peñalver and Oquendo, who were willing to help him.

At the same time, Cuba suddenly came to know "all the sweets of free trade." In the ten months of the English occupation, which ended July 6, 1763, almost a thousand ships entered the port of Havana; before this, the rate had been six a year. The shops were full of merchandise never before seen. It was a delight to visit the shops, where there was so much movement that it seemed like a constant festival, and where the money flowed like water; a pleasure to stroll down to the wharf and watch the crowds of sweating Negroes unloading ships. Agriculture took on new life with the settlers who arrived every day from England. The trading company founded by the Basques was the first to suffer the inroads of the invaders. Above the wreck of its defunct monopoly, free trade now flourished and business grew by leaps and bounds. This was a lesson the Cubans were never to forget.

Everything would have gone as merrily as a wedding bell for the English in Cuba if it had not been for the merchants and planters of Jamaica and Barbados. They had been fighting since the times of Cromwell to maintain a monopoly of the market, and now it made them green with jealousy to watch this competitor rising on the British colonial horizon. They directed all their efforts to seeing that England should return the island of Cuba to Spain when the war was over. The King himself gave the Spaniards his word that this would be done. And though Pitt, when the matter was discussed in Parliament, raised the roof with his protests, his eloquence could not outweigh the influence of the Jamaican lobby. England returned Cuba to Spain, and received Florida in return.

The Cuban occupation, then, was only an episode. The effects of the pact were much more strongly felt in the North because it was France who paid the piper when the war was over. England received Canada and the Mississippi Valley — the empire that had been in the making for a century. The only thing France kept out was the city of New Orleans; this was not for herself, but was to go to Spain to compensate her for the losses she had suffered. "Louis XV, who had stripped France with his execrable politics and had shamed her with his dissolute pleasures, now graciously offered Spain Louisiana as indemnity." It was the more amazing as Spain had not exercised the slightest pressure. Charles III's ambassador in Paris did not venture to accept the gift without first receiving his king's approbation. In New Orleans there were angry protests from the settlers. This city founded on the lands discovered by La Salle, and created by Bienville and even by the Paris grisettes and the ne'er-do-wells rounded up in Law's day, was French to the backbone. The residents of the city were happy; they were ideally situated to carry on their contraband activities with both English and Spanish. They would not be handed over to the Spaniards! In every parish a delegate was appointed to an assembly whose purpose was to declare loyalty to the King of France. Lafrénière, the orator of the day, harangued the people and fanned their patriotism to white heat. They paraded the streets, carrying the white flag of the worthless King, shouting: "Long live our beloved monarch!" A delegate was sent to Paris to inform the King that New Orleans would never be another's, but would always be the Creole daughter of the King of Versailles.

When the commissioner reached Paris, he went straight to the house of Bienville, now a graybeard of eighty-six. On hearing the story, Bienville threw his cape around his shoulders, and, shaking more with anger than with age, went to see the minister Choiseul. The minister heard him, but paid no attention to him. To him, as to Louis XV, Louisiana was a troublesome burden, and he smiled with pleasure at the thought that now the problem had been dumped in the Spaniards' lap.

When in 1766 the Spanish governor arrived to take over the colony, some of the people were still hurrahing for the King of France. The governor overflowed with Charles III's spirit of enlightenment; he wanted progress, science, learning. But the only thing that interested the dwellers of New Orleans was smuggling, quadroon girls, and houses of amusement. The contrast was interesting, because the governor was none other than Don Antonio Ulloa, that Spaniard who had been most closely associated with the great men of France, the person whom Voltaire had called a true scientist, who had accompanied La Condamine, Godin, and Bougher on the expedition to Ecuador. He was the author, with Jorge Juan, of a masterly work on America that, translated into French, had won him the respect of all and the esteem of scientists. New Orleans had never before had a person of this caliber as its governor. It was most unusual that he should have accepted this post after having founded the Museum of Natural History in Madrid, and having traveled through France, Denmark, Sweden, and the Netherlands on a mission for the King collecting information that might be useful in the reorganization of Spanish commerce and industry. But Charles III was keenly interested in the progress of America, and it was his policy to send men of high attainments to the colonies.

As a politician, Antonio Ulloa was not too gifted. He had come out with only eighty soldiers, assuming that this would be more than enough, since there were the French soldiers who would lend their services because he intended to pay them. They demanded the pay, but refused to serve. The Germans who had come out in Law's venture, and who formed a colony of their own, egged on the French to insubordination. The ladies raised a great to-do because Ulloa's wife, a Peruvian lady of title, did not call in a Creole wet-nurse for her child. The gossips whispered that Ulloa had forbidden the whipping of Negroes because his wife was so delicately nurtured that she could not stand their screams of pain! The Acadians, who had been driven out of the English colonies and had taken refuge with the French, were bristling with suspicion. And so the muddy waters of malicious gossip and sullen resentment kept rising around the distinguished governor and his wife until one day a riot broke out.

Four hundred Germans and Acadians, led by one Villère, marched through the streets shouting "Down with the Spaniards!", waving white flags, and cheering Louis *le bien aimé*. Feeling rose so high that finally the Spanish flag was hauled down, and Ulloa and his wife were put aboard a ship to save their lives. A petition was circulated demanding that he be removed from office — a petition addressed, naturally, not to Charles III, but to the "Bien Aimé." That was a night of celebration in New Orleans, with drinking, singing, and carousing. There was a wedding, and after the merry party had danced until dawn, and drunk until they could hold no more, they decided it would be fun to go down to the pier and serenade the Ulloas. The governor's lady — so delicately nurtured! — would be deafened by their songs. One of the revelers, in a final taunt of impudence, cut the cables of the ship, and it went tacking down the river, swept along by the current, until it was lost in the distance. By a miracle, Don Antonio and his wife reached Havana, whence they proceeded to Madrid to report to Charles III on the failure of a mission.

The truth was that New Orleans weighed very little with either the playboy cousin of Paris or the hard-working cousin who ruled in Madrid. The Creoles led a life of sensual ease, gossiping about the latest feud between Jesuits and Capuchins, drinking and gambling in the cabarets (which were supposed to close at nine o'clock) until the dawn, just as in the gayest quarters of Paris. They all had plenty of time to exchange ideas, make plans, concoct stories, and contrive schemes, seasoning life with café philosophy. In 1768, as soon as Ulloa had disappeared from the stage, the schemes went into operation. Why not an independent republic of New Orleans, governed by an assembly elected by the people? Pamphlets were published. There was much speech-making. The city that had defied France and Spain was dizzy with its triumphs. It had defeated Spain because Spain was represented by eighty soldiers, and it had flouted the orders of the King of France because Louis XV did not give a snap of his fingers for Louisiana. When the new governor of Spain, O'Reilly, of Irish extraction, appeared in the harbor with a fleet of twenty-four ships, well-manned with soldiers, the pamphlets about a constitution and independence were hurriedly tossed into the garbage, the white flags disappeared along with the memory of the "Bien Aimé," and the streets echoed to the cry of "Long live our King, Charles III!" There was a French accent to the shouts, but conviction as well.

In the square opposite the river, the French troops formed to present arms to the new governor. To salvos of cannon and rifle, with ruffle of drums and flying flags, General O'Reilly entered. Lafrénière, the orator of the rebellion, was the first to address him: "We are here, Sir, to assure Your Excellency of the colony's submission to the orders of Their Catholic and Christian Majesties, and to show you our respect for the virtues and military talents which have raised you to the high office with which you have been invested. . . ."

The new governor was in no mood for pleasantries. He had been asked to show clemency, but he immediately began an investigation into the recent disturbances. The new colony was going to be taught a lesson with a salutary example. A bonfire was built in the square, and the Negro executioner consigned to the flames the leaflets listing the colonists' grievances. The six judged responsible for the revolt against Ulloa were sentenced to death; but, being a man of noble sentiments, the governor decided that to have them hanged by a Negro would offend the colony, and therefore — since no white man was available who was experienced at that work — the six were to be shot. Among these the leading figure was Lafrénière, who pronounced a last speech, exhorting his companions to show no weakness; he refused to have his eyes bandaged, and asked a friend to send the bandage instead to his wife to give his son when he should be grown. Marquis, an old marine captain, followed his example; he refused to have his eyes bandaged, tore his shirt open, and shouted to the soldiers: "Shoot, sheep!"

It was all very French. The executed men became the first patriots. But the storm blew over quickly. O'Reilly soon imposed order, the colony flourished, the Spanish population increased, and so a new human layer was added to this city where every nation had contributed a different group of colonists, every continent had added another color, every language its accent, to form one of those rich olla-podridas which are the glory of the world's cuisine.

In twenty years the population of New Orleans had tripled. The governor created the municipal council, balanced the budget, and levied a tax of forty pesos yearly on the billiard halls, taverns, cafés, and inns in which New Orleans abounded. Every barrel of brandy brought in paid an excise tax of one peso, and this constituted one of the richest sources of income. A library was established, with books in Spanish, French, and Latin, though readers were few. Schools were opened. The court of the Holy Brotherhood was set up to punish those who robbed or murdered outside the city limits: those who denied God or the Virgin had their tongues torn out; those who spoke ill of the King were flagellated.

Meanwhile the Louisiana Territory had grown in importance. New Orleans, now more of a city, had become the strategic center for a new enterprise. The English colonies to the north had embarked on their War of Independence. Oliver Pollock, a rich, enterprising Irishman, who in the days of Governor O'Reilly had helped the Spaniards out with shipments of flour, had greatly increased his capital by trade with the colony. When the North American Revolution broke out, Pollock acted as confidential agent for the Continental Army, buying on his personal credit 300,000 pesos' worth of arms and ammunition. Bernardo Gálvez, the governor, openly assisted him. The Spaniards viewed with satisfaction this revolt against England, their lifelong enemy. Gálvez supplied Pollock with the money he needed, and, not to be outdone, the Council for the Indies wrote to the governor to bid him, if Pollock found it impossible to meet his obligations on time, not to press him, but to put his notes in the safe among the cash on hand.

Spain and France were determined to help the North American rebels. Count Aranda, the Spanish ambassador in Paris, was the first to advise his government as to the conduct to be pursued: to send money, arms, and ammunitions through private parties whose ships were safe from search, and also unattached officers who should offer their services to the Continental Army, pretending that they needed work. In Pensacola and Jamaica, France and Spain had spies planted. In Santo Domingo, a half-million Tournois pounds was placed at the disposal of the revolutionists, and another half-million was sent them in arms shipped from French ports. Beaumarchais, the author of *The Barber of Seville* and *The Marriage of Figaro*, organized a kind of War Service, with a large fleet carrying abundant supplies for Washington's troops. In France, Benjamin Franklin was a center of attraction, and Count Aranda was one of the first persons to talk with him. Although Franklin knew little French and Spanish, and Aranda knew no English, the latter grasped what it was that America needed, and the former, Spain's attitude of good will. This North American emissary secretly entered Spain, and elaborate precautions were taken so that he could accomplish his mission without being received at court. But the facts came out, and the purpose was so manifest that Spain wound up declaring war on the English king. And the better to help the colonists, it was decided to make New Orleans the center of operations.

Bernardo Gálvez, the governor, was only twenty-one, but he was intelligent, enterprising, and bold. He detested the English cordially, and he had the complete support of Spain. The Gálvez family was closely linked to American affairs. Bernardo's father was governor of Guatemala, and his uncle was Minister for the Indies. As soon as war was declared, young Gálvez seized all the English ships within his jurisdiction. In a short campaign he captured Baton Rouge and then turned back and laid siege to Pensacola, which was forced to capitulate. This was his greatest achievement. All western Florida was now under Spanish control. Everything Charles III had been obliged to cede to the English in return for Cuba was reconquered by this bold stripling.

And while Bernardo was executing his campaign, his father, Don Matías, was carrying on that of Central America so successfully that he was rewarded with the office of viceroy of Mexico. He drove the English out of the fortress of San Fernando de Omoa, attacked and defeated them in their Campeachy-wood logging camps in Honduras, and harried them wherever he could find them.

This time the residents of New Orleans loved not only their governor, who had covered himself with glory, but the governor's lady as well. She was lovely, intelligent, and kind, and — that no detail of perfection might be lacking — she had been born in New Orleans! After the death of his father, Don Matías, Bernardo succeeded him as viceroy of Mexico. He was now the great gentleman, and he built himself a beautiful palace in Chapultepec for himself and his Louisiana lady.

Louis XV died, his name ever since being associated with a style of furniture and with the Pompadour. Louis XVI succeeded him. The French Revolution followed. France invented a number of extraordinary things: a machine to cut off heads, the *Marseillaise*, and the flag of the republic. Then came General Napoleon Bonaparte, the First Consul.

Charles III died, and in Spain the Bourbons passed from the noonday light to darkness. Charles IV was the poorest sort of excuse for a king. His queen, Maria Luisa, was food for common gossip, and she and her favorite, Godoy, were the subject of the rabble's indecent songs. King Charles spied on his son Ferdinand; Ferdinand betrayed his father; the people swept Charles out like a piece of trash, and crowned Ferdinand king. The court was on a level with the father and the son. On the other side of the Pyrenees, the real French eagle, Napoleon, was destroying and creating kingdoms and republics with the ease of one who had come into the world with this mission.

And Napoleon decided that he would take the affairs of Louisiana in hand. The Negroes of Santo Domingo had revolted and he intended to bring them to heel and restore the French empire in America. New Orleans must return to France and become his base of supplies for the Caribbean. Napoleon knew that the degenerate court of Charles IV had the same idea of New Orleans that France had held: it was too much of a problem to bother one's head with. So by the terms of the Treaty of San Ildefonso, Charles IV handed Louisiana over to the First Consul in exchange for an Italian kingdom invented by Napoleon — Etruria, which was given to the Duke of Parma. One day the colonial prefect, Laussat, arrived to take possession of the colony in Napoleon's name. In his proclamation he said:

"The separation of Louisiana from France was one of the most shameful blots on the annals of the monarchy which in the hands of a weak and corrupt king signed a peace without honor after fighting an ignominious war. . . . No sooner had France, after a prodigious series of triumphs in the last revolution, recovered its liberty and its glory, than it turned its eyes toward Louisiana. To restore this natural order of things a man was needed to whom nothing that is country, greatness, magnanimity, or justice can be indifferent, who to the most exceptional martial gifts joins that of achieving from his victories the happiest results, and who, by reason of the endowments of his character, produces in his enemies terror, in his allies confidence. From now on, that man will preside over the destinies of France and Louisiana, and guarantee its happiness."

A few days later "that man" sold Louisiana to the United States for $3,000,000. And M. le Préfet, who with great solemnity had hauled down the flag of Spain and raised that of France, now — with equal solemnity — hauled down that of France and raised that of the United States.

XVIII

THE FRENCH REVOLUTION AND THE
NEGROES OF HAITI

The snake has eyes of glass;
The snake comes and winds around a tree;
With its eyes of glass, around a tree;
With its eyes of glass.
The snake moves without feet;
The snake hides in the grass;
Moving, it hides in the grass;
Moving without feet.
    Mayombe — bombe — mayombé!
    Mayombe — bombe — mayombé!
You hit it with the ax and it dies:
Go on, hit it.
Not with your foot, it will bite you;
Not with your foot, it will get away.
    Sensemayá, the snake,
    Sensemayá.
    Sensemayá, with its eyes.
    Sensemayá.
    Sensemayá, with its tongue,
    Sensemayá.
    Sensemayá, with its tail,
    Sensemayá.

                    NICOLÁS GUILLÉN

IN ALL the West Indies no colony had achieved the importance of Haiti, or Saint-Dominique, as it was more frequently called. Nowhere in the other islands were there such prosperous colonists, such flourishing business enterprises, finer plantations. In Jamaica the English had made a fortune, it is true, but not to the point where the island had become a decisive factor in the destiny of the British Empire. Cuba one day slipped out of Spain's fingers, and she hardly noticed its loss. But Haiti was the source that gave life to Marseille, Bordeaux, Nantes. Fifteen hundred ships a year called at its ports, many more than at Marseille. Twenty-four thousand seamen were employed on the seven hundred and fifty ships engaged exclusively in trade with Haiti. In Bordeaux there were sixteen factories refining sugar from the island; the sugar was imported, brandy was exported, and a hundred small industries had sprung up in connection with the distilleries. The merchants of Nantes had £50,000,000 invested in the island. The cacao of Haiti supplied France with all its chocolate, and in addition to the cacao, the island exported seventy-three million pounds of coffee and six million pounds of cotton. All this was produced by slave labor. The Negroes had cleared the forests and planted the coffee. They unloaded the boats, cared for the master's house, and hauled the cane to the mill. The Negro was a form of wealth, another domestic animal. The ships brought in Negroes and brandy. The rich people counted their wealth in so many mules, so many cows, so many Negroes. Nantes, Bordeaux, Marseille invested their capital in textile mills, factories, and Negroes. Out of this came that rich middle class which was to bring about the Revolution.

The settlers were happy, proud of their industry, of their busy port, of the beauty of Haiti, with its coffee groves that looked like a sea of foam when they were in flower, and became a shower of purple when the berries appeared. Everything bespoke solid wealth, prosperity. The rivers were crossed by bridges of stout Roman arches, and water was carried to the sugar mills in stone aqueducts. The colonists spoke of all this not only with the natural satisfaction money brings, but with pride in the humanitarian work they had accomplished, bringing the Africans out of the benighted darkness of their native land into the pleasant paradise of Haiti. There were half a million Negroes in Haiti to thirty thousand whites. For every white man who stood over them, lash in hand, there were sixteen Negroes at his service.

Port-au-Prince was a city of fine buildings. There were rich mulattoes who lived in European fashion. Theaters flourished; three stock companies entertained whites and mulattoes with performances of *Le Légataire universel, Cartouche, L'École des pères,* all the latest Paris productions. Producers grew rich in Cap François, too, which was known as the Paris of the Antilles. It was a Paris with a few slight drawbacks. When it rained, nobody could go out of the house for two days. The streets became rivers of mud. The system of sewage-disposal followed the old formula: "Watch out for the water below!" But what a sight it was to see the hairdresser visit his clients "in a suit of silk, his hat under his arm, a sword at his belt and a cane in his hand, followed by four Negroes. One of them combed the client's hair, another arranged it, a third curled it, and the fourth put on the finishing touches. The hairdresser supervised the operation, and at the slightest mistake he whacked the Negro, who went on with his work without saying a word, even though he had to pick himself up off the floor. When the task was completed the hairdresser departed with the same dignity and elegance with which he had arrived. . . ." In Cap there was a branch of the Philadelphia lodge where the rich Masons foregathered to discuss the *Encyclopedia* and progress. The city had twenty thousand inhabitants, of which ten thousand were slaves. Some of the mulatto women were ravishingly beautiful. There were gambling houses and houses of even pleasanter amusement; of the seven thousand mulatto women, five thousand were engaged in making life more agreeable for the gentlemen. The ladies of high degree were jealous of their brown rivals, and for good reason — and the white men of the rich mulattoes.

The Negroes of this "Paris of the Antilles" were publicly whipped in the streets, salt and lemon juice being put on the wounds to prevent gangrene from setting in. To punish a cook who let a cake in the oven burn, the mistress would go out to the kitchen and say: "Throw that nigger into the stove!" As the cook perished in the flames, the lady would return to her social obligations in the drawing-room, polite and unruffled. In the country the slightest disobedience was punished by burial alive; the culprit's head was left exposed, molasses was poured over it, and the ants finished the job. Of course, nobody liked doing such things. A Negro cost money, and losing one was like having a house burn down. But it was the only thing to do if the others were to be kept in line. When the ladies went to the slave-market where the slave-traders displayed their wares, they felt each slave all over with great care. Then, to undo any impression of familiarity this examination might have left, they would spit upon them.

Bringing in the Negroes from Africa was a problem. They would riot in the round-up pens and on the ships. The only way to handle them was to shackle them to long bunks, like counters, and take them on deck, chained together, once a day. To gain space they were sometimes packed in so close together that they could lie down only on their sides, fitting together like spoons. The stupid beasts had a strange propensity toward suicide. Sometimes when they were brought on deck to dance for the captain's entertainment, the more agile would throw themselves over the rail into the sea.

The Negro Mackandal planned a revolt once. He was a marvelous orator; it was said that he talked with the Devil. In the hills, the voodoo drum beat and the Negro women danced lascivious dances by the light of the campfires. They adored the Negro Mackandal. All the women fell in love with him as though he had given them some love potion. He had only one arm, and when he gesticulated he looked like a mutilated shade from hell. In a language the Devil himself might have used, he said the most hair-raising things. "Let us make an end to all the whites," he proposed one night at a voodoo gathering. "On the same day we will poison all the wells on the plantations, then we will set fire to the house, and chop the white men and women to pieces, and there will be no more whippings, no more masters or slaves." The plan leaked out and Mackandal was burned alive. But, like an aura, there floated in the air the poem in "savage Alexandrines" that Mackandal had declaimed at the voodoo gathering, the first hymn to liberty, a fierce hymn that ended by telling how God was thirsting for vengeance against the whites who had made the Negroes suffer and weep so, and would heed the Negroes' cry for their freedom:

Bon Dieu, qui fait soleil,
Qui clairé nous en haut,
Qui soulevé la mer,
Qui fait l'orage gronder . . .
Jetez portraits Dieu blanc
Qui soif d'leau dans yeux nous
Coutez la liberté qui nan cœur à nous tous.[1]

This is the Creole version of the *Marseillaise* composed by the Negro Mackandal forty years before the French stormed the Bastille.

Louis XIV had drawn up a code of laws for the protection of the Negroes. It was promulgated first in the islands, then in Louisiana. In this, France was imitating the laws issued by Spain in favor of the Indians. "In order to maintain the discipline of the Roman Catholic Apostolic Church and to regulate all matters concerning the state and position of the slaves in our islands." The code contained no fewer than sixty articles. It began by saying that the Jews, being enemies of the Christian faith, should leave the islands within the space of three months, under penalty of having their persons and goods confiscated; that the slaves were to be baptized; that the children born of concubinage were to be free; that the slaves were not to work on feast days, that they were to receive so many pounds of cassava each week, two suits of clothes a year. . . . The slave who should attack his master or mistress was to suffer the death penalty; if he stole a sheep, a goat, or a hen he was to be whipped and branded on the back with a fleur-de-lis; if he ran away, his ears were to be cut off and he was to be branded with the fleur-de-lis, and at the third offense, he was to be put to death. . . .

With all its limitations, the code was a guarantee for the slaves; in places it showed a glimmer of kindness, and it was a

[1] God who has made the sun
Which lights us from on high
Who raises up the sea
And makes the storm roar
Throw down the pictures of the White God
Who thirsts for our tears
Hear the sound of liberty in all our hearts.

law. Even if it was not carried out, it was a hope. "When the master thinks the slave deserves it, he may put him in chains and have him beaten with whips and ropes, but not give him torment nor mutilate his members under penalty of losing his slaves and receiving exemplary punishment." Le Jeune, a planter of Plaisance, refused to abide by these laws. A number of slaves had died on his coffee plantation, and he decided they had been poisoned. In trying to get to the bottom of the matter, he killed four Negroes and put two women to the torment. He pulled their arms and legs out of their sockets, burned their feet, and put spiked iron collars on them. The gentleman had carried matters to such an extreme that the Negroes appealed to the law. It caused a scandal; Le Jeune had put himself outside the law. He alleged in his defense that the poison that killed his slaves was in a box the women had hidden. When the box was opened it was empty. But had the provisions of the law been carried out against Le Jeune, it would have meant a victory for the Negroes, and so it became a test case. The planters of Haiti saw things clearly, and they closed ranks to defend Le Jeune. There were lodge meetings, reports, pamphlets, and speeches. Le Jeune was absolved.

It was always the same. In 1760 the Intendant Jean-Étienne Bernard de Cluny had come out to the island. He was in the full vigor of his early thirties, with a fine background of administrative experience in France, steeped in the *Encyclopedia*, and he had ideas on self-government; he opposed the aristocracy, which tried to assume control of the army, and he planned a complete reform in the island. This time it was the bureaucracy that blocked him, and he had to return to France. He became one of the greatest economists of France, Turgot's successor under Louis XVI.

The world was in a troubled state. The bourgeoisie, emboldened by its new wealth, had done a lot of talking; the nobility was visibly sinking deeper and deeper in degradation, and the idea of revolution was taking shape. The whites of Haiti wanted a voice in the States-General, the same as the people of Mar-

seille, Dieppe, or Nantes. They were a part of the French nation,
and one of the richest and most productive. It was an innova-
tion for the colonies to send delegates to the meeting of the
States-General, but not for nothing was the world on the eve of
a revolution. The colonists were supported by the commercial
cities of France, which lived on the colonies and were, in a
sense, the leaders of the new trend in politics. The colonists
wanted self-government in the island, as Cluny had said, and to
shake off the yoke of a bureaucracy imposed by the King. The
ambition of the French in France was this same thing: the natural desire of those who had the money to wield the power.
Legally or otherwise, the colonists of Haiti formed their assembly and elected representatives to the States-General. In Paris
they met at the home of the Marquis de Massiac, the owner of
a sugar refinery and a dealer in indigo. Haiti wanted to have its
own assembly, to vote its own taxes, and to preserve the power
and prestige of the white planters without interference from the
crown.

In the States-General the question of seating the delegates
from Haiti arose. The colonists claimed the right to twenty-four
seats. Like Mirabeau, Brissot, who belonged to the Association
of Friends of the Negroes, protested indignantly. "These gentlemen," he said, "count the Negroes of the island and elevate
them to the rank of men for the sake of securing this representation, but they want to represent them only to degrade them and
give them a subhuman status." Mirabeau was more graphic:
"Either the slaves are men or they are not; if the plantation
owners consider them men, let them free them and turn them
into voters eligible to hold a seat in this assembly; otherwise,
why do not we, in computing the number of deputies to which
the French nation is entitled, take the census of our mules and
horses?"

For the colonists to ask admission to the States-General was
to put the Negro question on the docket. In England a school
favoring the liberation of the slaves had been growing up. This
new attitude on the part of a nation that, until a short time before, had been demanding a monopoly of the slave trade, had

interesting origins. Adam Smith and Arthur Young, "the fore-runners of the new era, condemned the system of slavery as the most expensive in the world." The English had just discovered that it had been a blessing to lose their North American colonies, because everything could be produced more cheaply in India. Pitt informed his colleagues that half the slaves sold by the English in the West Indies were bought by the French of Haiti, and now the prosperity of that island was prejudicial to the interests of the Empire. Why not import sugar from the Orient? The experiment was undertaken and proved highly successful. Free laborers in India at a penny a day were much more profitable than expensive slaves in the Antilles. And thus the Abolitionist Society, which printed such humanitarian tracts, came into being. The generous spirits of France were captivated by their beautiful phraseology. And the Association of Friends of the Negroes was born in France, supported by men like Mirabeau, Brissot, Condorcet, Pétion. . . .

The poor Negroes of Haiti were unaware of what their new-found defenders were thinking and doing, but the rich Negroes, the emancipated, and the mulattoes, not only took advantage of this state of affairs, but sought representation in the States-General. Many of them had been educated in France, where their color had not been much of an obstacle, and they were in perpetual conflict with the rich whites of the island. The whites hated them for two reasons: because they were closer to the Negroes — the parents of many of them were still slaves — and because they knew that any mulatto rising would have the support of the Negroes. Besides, as they were less extravagant in their spending than the whites, many of them were money-lenders, and the whites had to undergo the humiliation of borrowing from them. Ordinances were passed forbidding the mulattoes to carry swords, to purchase land in certain parts of the island, and to be addressed as Monsieur and Madame. But the mulattoes flourished. Now they were the counter-revolutionists. They raised the standard of the monarchy against the bourgeois revolution of the plantation owners. The governor sought support among the mulattoes against the whites who resisted him, and thus the two supporting columns of the monarchy were the government employees and the mulattoes. The mulattoes finally won a place in the National Assembly at Paris, and in one of those moments of democratic intoxication when no one weighed his words, a former land-owner rose and declared: "I not only believe that the rights of the mulattoes should be recognized, but that the Negroes should be given their freedom." The mulattoes, for their part, behaved very intelligently. They accompanied their petition with a subscription for the expenses of the Assembly to the tune of 1,200,000 pesos. In Haiti the whites took reprisals; the man who had upheld the rights of the mulattoes was hanged.

But the mulattoes were now very powerful. Ogé, one of them, who was a friend of some of the most important figures in the National Assembly, made up his mind to carry the revolution to Haiti. He undertook a campaign and was defeated. He was tried, and no device of cruelty was omitted in the execution of his sentence. His arms, legs, and ribs were crushed by hammer blows, and he was then tied to a wheel, where he lay, face upward, until God should take pity on him and let him die. After death, his head was cut off and hung as a trophy on the road that led to his town, Dondon. Paris was horrified when it heard the news. Robespierre declared before the Assembly that if, to uphold the doctrines of liberty the Revolution had proclaimed, it were necessary for France to lose her colonies where such a system of slavery prevailed, it was worth the price.

The Negroes were overhearing everything the whites said. They were observing the efforts of the mulattoes. Back in the hills the Negroes were beating their drums and singing: "Better to die than to go on being slaves."

Nobody had thought of it, nobody would have thought it possible. Christophe, a servant in a Cap François hotel, laughed as he set the table and listened to the enraged whites. The Negro Toussaint, coachman of M. Bayon de Libertat, laughed, too. And even Dessalines, who was less than any of them — the slave of a Negro — laughed. They did nothing, they just listened. And they also listened to the beating of the voodoo drums. More

stealthily than a snake moves, the slaves carrying the summons
for the voodoo gathering moved from group to group.

Never had the voodoo rites caused such trembling, sweating,
laughing, and terror as they did that night of decision for the
Negroes. As the charmed serpent spread its coils, the mass of
Negroes who had come from every direction gathered about the
magic altar to take their oath. The whites thought a marriage
festivity was going on, and never realized that the drums were
sounding their death knell. As they danced, the Negro women
seemed more flexible than the serpent itself. The blazing torches
turned to blood the leaves of the trees and the rivulets of
sweat that rolled down the dancers' hips. The faithful drank
the hot blood of the sacrificial pig, which left a salty taste on
their lips. Boukman, Baisson, and Jean-François shouted the
war cries:

> *Eh! Eh! Bomba, hen! Hen!*
> *Canga cafio te*
> *Canga moune dele*
> *Canga doki la*
> *Canga li . . .*

Better to die than be slaves! It was the night of the 14th of
August, 1791.

Dawn was beginning to color the morning. The palms, the
banana trees, the brows of the hills were still silhouettes against
the rosy sky when the flames began to crackle in the sugar mills,
in the cane fields, in the masters' houses. The screeching of the
Negroes was like the shrilling of a thousand fifes. From every
house, every cane field, and every grove burst a Negro with a
torch. As far as the hills Cap François was a sea of flame that
spread and spread amidst the screams of terror of the whites and
mulattoes, and the shouts of rejoicing of the Negroes. The smoke
could be seen miles and miles away. With their gleaming machetes the Negroes were cutting down white men. The blood of
the sacrificial pig had been multiplied, and was spattering the
whole surface of Haiti. As the Negroes went leaping like devils
through the flames, it seemed as though they were wearing red

gloves and stockings. For three weeks it was impossible to tell day from night.

Reprisals followed. The cruelty of the Negroes had hardly equaled that of their masters, but the latter settled their account with a heavy hand. The whole length of the road leading to Cap François was lined with Negroes hanging from the trees. They had killed two thousand whites. The whites hanged ten thousand Negroes. A hundred and eighty plantations had become one hundred and eighty mounds of ashes. Two million dollars' worth of property had gone up in smoke. The celebration had lasted two months. And this was just the overture.

M. Bayon de Libertat's coachman Toussaint had been born in Africa some time in the 1740's. His father was a chieftain, the prince of Guiaou-Guinou, whom slavers had captured and brought to Haiti. Toussaint was quiet, resolute, intelligent. Though sickly as a boy, he grew stronger as he approached manhood. Becoming the best rider in his part of the island, he was known as "the Centaur of the Plains" — the same name that was later given to Bolívar. His master became very fond of him. He was baptized, he learned to read, and another Negro who acted as his teacher instructed him in a knowledge of herbs. He had become a coachman, a post of importance for a slave. He went still further, performing the duties of butler. He had read Herodotus' *History of the Wars*, Caesar's *Commentaries*, and that classic of the art of war, *Mes Rêveries* by Marshal Maurice de Saxe. But the book that most influenced him was that of the Abbé Raynal, *Philosophical and Political History of the European Establishments and Commerce in the Two Indies*. There he found the words that foretold the uprising. The Abbé wrote that the slaves were treated worse than dogs, but he saw the lightning that precedes the storm. "All that is needed is a brave leader. Who will he be? There is no doubt that he will appear; he will come and raise the sacred standard of liberty." As the coachman meditated on these words he fell silent and read them again. What if he . . .

The Negro Toussaint had not been at the voodoo gathering.
He was a good Catholic; he wanted no murders or arson. He
wanted the freedom of the Negroes — nothing more. There was
no fire on M. Bayon de Libertat's plantation. Toussaint ordered
the slaves to be quiet, and they obeyed him. There was something about the butler that commanded respect. But Toussaint,
looking on in silence, saw everything. He saw the tide of vengeance, the whites drowning his people in blood; he saw the fury of
the Negroes crowning the hills with flames. And he saw that it
was impossible to remain neutral. He took his mistress to safety
from the plantation and helped the family to escape to the
United States; then he joined the army of the rebellion. At first
the leaders looked askance at him because he had not been with
them in those first days when they had been like tigers thirsting
for vengeance. But there was a magnetic power about Toussaint.
His ability to read gave him prestige; his knowledge of herbs,
which — in their eyes — made him akin to a witch-doctor, the
dignity of his bearing, and the shape his ideas were taking. He
entered as a doctor; in a short time he was the leader of the
rebels. In the end he had become a thorn in Napoleon's flesh,
and was looked upon as one of the greatest men of his age.
Lamartine wrote a poem of which Toussaint was the hero. Au-
guste Comte praised him lavishly in his *Calendrier positiviste*.
Chateaubriand, in his *Mémoires d'outre-tombe*, accused Bonaparte of the crime of having assassinated Toussaint.

The reports of the Negro rebellion of 1791 filled France with
terror. Whites and mulattoes joined forces against the common
enemy. There were meetings of patriots, gatherings of statesmen, at which the whites, with a handsome gesture, said in
substance to the mulattoes: "We are brothers; let us overlook
our mutual shortcomings, forget offenses, and work together for
the peace of France and the good of all." The National Assembly proclaimed the equality of whites, mulattoes, and free Negroes. In Haiti the whites gave a sumptuous banquet to the
mulattoes, which the mulattoes returned in kind. The mayor of
the Cap said: "The dissensions which have existed heretofore

now belong to the past. We recognize no differences of color here; there will be only free citizens and slaves. As for the slaves, it is obvious that we are not going to bring them from Africa, at a great capital investment, to make them free French citizens in Haiti."

Toussaint had formed his army. He had six thousand men, determined to conquer or die. Negroes armed with cudgels, machetes, and axes seemed to spring from the hills, and the generals had decked themselves out in ribbons and decorations, everything shiny that fell into their hands. The more modest titles were not for them — they were all admirals, generalissimos, or at least brigadier generals; one called himself the viceroy of all the conquered territory. All were opposed to the revolution of the bourgeoisie. Suddenly they heard the shocking news: Louis XVI had been beheaded. It was almost unbelievable. A king beheaded! Toussaint said: "We must have a king. Let us go to Santo Domingo, place ourselves under the suzerainty of Charles IV, King of Spain, and make war against the republicans of Haiti." And the black torrent poured out of Haiti into Santo Domingo with savage shrieks of delight. The Spaniards, who were at war with France, offered freedom to all slaves entering Spanish territory, and confirmed the leaders in their titles of generals and admirals. Toussaint was ascending the ladder of success, and his name acted like a talisman. He was tireless, he seemed never to dismount from his horse; wherever there was danger he was there, and it was he who cleared the road for freedom. He no longer signed himself merely Toussaint, but with the name of battle he had invented: Toussaint L'Ouverture. "Brothers and friends, I am Toussaint L'Ouverture. Perhaps you have already heard my name; I have come to avenge you. It is my wish that freedom and equality reign in Haiti. I have come to win them. Come and join us, brothers, and we will all fight for the same cause." Toussaint carried out a lightning campaign. His army grew in every town he passed through. The Negroes had found their liberator. The discipline of his troops was as perfect as that of European armies, if not better. In this

war Spain had no leader who could be compared to Toussaint.
And he was as good a diplomat as he was a soldier. At the conclusion of the campaign the Marquis of Hermona received Toussaint with every honor and presented him with a sword in the
name of King Charles.

The whites lost lands, villages, and cities, and finally fled to
the United States. Their one salvation was to ally themselves
with the English, and the governor sent representatives to Jamaica to ask for help. Just as Toussaint and his followers had
gone over to Spain, the planters turned to England: "The citizens of Haiti, having no legitimate ruler to whom they can turn
to free them from the tyranny of which they are victims, invoke
the protection of His Britannic Majesty, swearing fealty to him,
and imploring him to preserve this colony and treat us as good
and faithful subjects until peace comes and the allied powers
decide the fate of the country." William Pitt in England saw a
new opportunity. Parliament stated that the war it was declaring
was not to protect the rich, but for reasons of security. Jamaica
began to send troops to Haiti.

In France the Revolution was progressing. One day there appeared before the National Assembly three delegates from Haiti:
Bellay, a former slave who had bought his freedom; Mills, a mulatto; and Dufay, a white man. They had come to take their seats
among the French representatives. One deputy arose and declared in impassioned accents: "The aristocracy of birth and religion came to an end in 1789; there remained the aristocracy of
color. Today we are taking the last step toward equality; a Negro
and a mulatto of Haiti are taking their place among us." The
speaker received a tremendous ovation. Another spoke: "The
Assembly has anxiously awaited this moment; I move that the
entrance of these new delegates be sealed by a fraternal embrace
from the president." Wild applause. The delegates came forward to the rostrum and the president embraced them and
kissed them on both cheeks. More applause. The next day the
Negro delegate spoke; it was to ask that slavery be abolished.
When he had finished his speech, Lavasseur rose and said these
few words: "When the Constitution of France was drawn up,

the French people did not remember the unhappy Negroes. Posterity will reproach us for this. Let us make good this oversight, proclaiming the freedom of the Negroes. Citizen President: let us not shame the Convention by arguing this step we are about to take." The Convention got to its feet. The Negro and the mulatto were led in triumph to the presidential rostrum, and once more received the French kiss.

Thus in 1793 was slavery declared abolished. A former Negro slave had made the heart of France in the city of Paris beat faster at a moment when France was at the climax of its political enthusiasm.

Toussaint was now able to ride under the banner of the French Republic. The Spanish governor saw his self-invited ally slip away from him, and Laveaux, the French representative who had come out to undertake what seemed a hopeless fight against the English, saw his recent adversary come back to join him in their common campaign. Toussaint was named brigadier general. He was going to fight against England, against Spain, against the whites in defense of the republic and liberty. But it must not be forgotten that Haiti was a land of Negroes. Many times Toussaint did not even have to fight; once, with a letter he stopped a battle, and three thousand Negroes came over to his side. Laveaux was taken prisoner by the mulattoes; his one hope was that Toussaint would arrive and liberate him. Toussaint organized an attack against Cap François and set him free. Any lack of respect for the governor — he stated in a proclamation to the city — would be a lack of respect for France. Toussaint's entry into Cap François was a day of glory. Laveaux assembled the townspeople, the army was drawn up in formation in the square, and Toussaint was publicly named the governor's aide. "I shall take no step," said Laveaux, "without asking his advice. Here is the man, the black Spartacus, whose coming the Abbé Raynal foretold, destined to avenge the oppression of his race."

The honeymoon between the French representatives and M. Bayon de Libertat's sometime coachman had begun. Toussaint's two sons were sent to France to be educated. Toussaint hovered the government beneath the wings of his victories, and the colony began to revive after the terrible devastation of the war. Plans to stimulate agriculture were begun. Schools were opened. France gave Haiti seven seats in its Assembly. And Toussaint managed the elections so skillfully that the commissioners sent out from France were elected to these seats. They departed from the island, and he was left alone. Alone he was about to defeat the English.

For a hundred years the defeat inflicted on England by Toussaint was kept a secret. "For years," writes the historian C. L. R. James, "Pitt and Dundas continued to pour men and money into the West Indies against what they were pleased to call bandits; but the negro country men, who until a short time before had been slaves, with the help of the climate and the loyal mulattoes, dealt Great Britain the greatest defeat her expeditionary forces had suffered from the days of Queen Elizabeth to the war of 1914."

The English, with the help of the white planters, had taken the towns of Jérémie, Port-au-Prince, Arcahaie, Saint-Marc, and Môle Saint-Nicolas. Wherever they established themselves, they restored their former privileges to the whites. Whitelocke had flooded the island with a proclamation exhorting the settlers to transfer their allegiance to Great Britain. In the name of the King he offered every facility to all burdened with debts. The Spanish governor of Santo Domingo, in turn, offered all this and Heaven, too, to those who accepted Charles IV as their king.

But the Negroes now turned on the English as they had turned on their owners, and would turn tomorrow on the Spaniards. They heeded only the words of Toussaint and Dessalines. And what black hands could not achieve, yellow fever did. England sacrificed some eighty thousand men in the struggle. During the year 1796 alone the expenses of the English forces in Haiti amounted to £2,600,000. One by one they had to give up all the positions they had taken. Finally the day came when Toussaint entered Port-au-Prince in triumph. There were church

bells ringing, triumphal arches, flags, carriages, white girls strew-
ing his path with flowers, dances, fireworks, banquets. Toussaint
allowed the English to withdraw to Môle Saint-Nicolas, where
the formal capitulation was to be signed. There General Mait-
land received him with his troops on dress parade and presented
him, in the King's name, with the silver service that had been
used at the banquet. Then His Britannic Majesty's troops were
reviewed by M. Bayon de Libertat's sometime coachman. Toussaint negotiated the treaty with the English as though he were
the ranking authority on the island. When the English general
came to keep his appointment, the Negro let him cool his heels
in the anteroom for some minutes. Lack of courtesy? Nothing
of the sort. When he appeared, he explained why he had kept
him waiting. He had been answering a letter, and he showed
him both the letter and his answer. The letter suggested that he
hold the Englishman prisoner, and in his answer he explained
that under no circumstances would he commit such an act of
treachery. The English, too, tried to beguile him. They offered
to make him king of the island, under British protection. The
Negro refused with equal firmness.

In France the reactionaries of the Convention were regroup-
ing their forces. Vaublanc had made a violent speech demanding
that measures be taken to check the aggressions of the Negroes
against the whites. In answer Toussaint wrote a letter to the
Directory which is one of the most remarkable documents in
favor of democracy that have been produced in America. With
serene bravery, with dauntless determination, this man who did
not know how to write, but could read, who dictated his letters
to five secretaries and then, before signing them, went over them
letter by letter, composed a series of documents that many men
of learning might envy. "France," he said, "will not be false to
her principles . . . will not permit the destruction of that which
most honors her, the degradation of the finest of her achievements, the revocation of the Decree of the 16th Pluviose, which
is an honor to humanity. But if this were to be done, and slavery
restored in Haiti, I must tell you that such an attempt would

be doomed to failure. We are prepared to oppose any threat to our liberty; and to defend it, we are ready to defy death. This, citizens of the Directory, is the attitude of the people of Haiti; these are the resolutions that Haiti transmits to you through me."

The whites had chosen Hédouville, one of France's most able generals, who had distinguished himself in the pacification of La Vendée, to go to Haiti and, first by cunning and diplomacy and then by force, to bring the Negro Toussaint under control. But Toussaint happened to be better at the game of diplomacy than Hédouville. He found all sorts of excuses not to meet him for an interview, and allowed him to govern meanwhile, which was the same as allowing him time to make mistakes. The pacificator of La Vendée knew nothing about Haiti; when he tried to supplant one of the Negro generals with a Frenchman the storm broke. Toussaint ordered the former servant of the hotel of Cap François and the Negro Dessalines, to attack, and Hédouville's only salvation was to take ship for France with such of his men as managed to escape. Toussaint entered Cap François in triumph, and his speech the following day was the complete affirmation of his authority. "Hédouville has said that I was the foe of liberty, that I want to go over to the English, and that I want to make myself independent. Who do you think loves liberty more, Toussaint L'Ouverture, the slave of Bréda, or General Hédouville, the one-time Marquis and Chevalier of the Order of St. Louis? If I had wanted to join forces with the English, why did I drive them out of the country? Remember that in Haiti there is only one Toussaint L'Ouverture, and all the world trembles when it hears his name. . . ."

The war now was going to be against the mulattoes. The last thing General Hédouville did in a final attempt to destroy what he could of Toussaint's power was to leave a letter for General Rigaud, a mulatto rival of Toussaint's, handing the power over to him and urging him to unite the mulattoes against Toussaint. The war that ensued went to unbelievable lengths in its violence. Dessalines was a black tiger who spared no one. The hatred of the mulattoes for the Negroes seemed greater than that of the whites for them. Only Toussaint was capable of forgiving. When he entered Cap François, following his usual custom he ordered the mulattoes to gather in the church. He loved to talk from the pulpit. The mulattoes obeyed the order in fear and trembling. Their lives were at the mercy of this ugly, powerful man, who seemed still more terrifying in his colored frock-coat. with his enormous sword, epaulets, ribbons, and gold buttons. They could hardly believe what they heard him say. He spoke of mercy and pardon. He wished to take no further advantage of his triumph. The mulattoes had been punished enough, and just as he was willing to forgive them, all the people should. Those who wished to leave to join their families would receive safe conduct; those who wished to remain would be treated like brothers and could count on his protection. When Toussaint stepped down from the pulpit, his hearers wept, acclaimed him wildly, called down blessings upon him.

Only the mulatto Rigaud refused to yield. One day when surrounded, he attempted suicide, but he finally managed to escape to France. Many of those associated with him fled to Cuba. Hatred became an obsession with them. Nor did the other Negroes show Toussaint's magnanimity. Dessalines lopped off heads with the greatest enthusiasm. "I told them to prune the tree," Toussaint said, "not to pull it up by the roots."

In a short time Toussaint was at war with the Spaniards. In Santo Domingo, the Spaniards kept up their slave trade. Toussaint decided to advise them to put an end to it. For this purpose he employed another French representative who had come out to Haiti, and to whom Toussaint dictated his message word by word. But when the commissioner transmitted it to Don Joaquín García, Governor of Santo Domingo, he let him know that he had written it under pressure from Toussaint, and that he could answer with some polite excuse that would satisfy the Negro and close the incident. Don Joaquín did just this, and sent the two generals who had brought him the message and their escorts back with a very cordial letter that said nothing.

But Toussaint divined what had happened; he arrested the French representative, deprived him of his powers, and said to his Negroes: "Now it's the Spaniards' turn."

Toussaint engaged in the war and won it without much difficulty, for the Spaniards had no army with which to oppose his troops, and the capitulation was effected with the greatest courtesy. Each side received due honor; the flag of Spain was hauled down with a salvo of twenty-one rounds, and that of France raised with twenty-two. Don Joaquín asked Toussaint to swear by the Blessed Trinity that he would govern the land he had conquered justly and faithfully. With all politeness the Negro answered: "I cannot comply with your request, but I swear from the bottom of my heart, before God who is my witness, that the past will be wiped out, and that the only purpose of all my decisions and acts will be to keep the Spaniards who now will live under the French flag happy and contented."

During the years 1801 and 1802, Toussaint was the ruler of the island from one end to the other. The French representative had discreetly left for home, as had his predecessors. Toussaint began to reorganize the administration in the Spanish colony, as he had done in Haiti. He drew up a new plan for the treasury, he lowered the tariffs, encouraged trade, stimulated agriculture, built roads and schools. Everything was carried out with military order and precision, in a manner that was at once European and revolutionary. He returned to Haiti from Santo Domingo. He was more active in peace than in war. The island had to shake off the effects of ten years of war. He had his own nephew shot for disputing his authority and encouraging an attempt at sedition. At last he took the decisive step: he selected a group to draw up a constitution. Things had reached a point where the country needed its own laws. Without having proclaimed his independence from France, Toussaint had been governing, dealing with foreign governments, making war, signing peace, and levying taxes, without giving a thought to the mother country except as a symbol. The commission to draw up the constitution was composed of whites and mulattoes, for he knew that among the former slaves, who did not even know how to read or write, there was none qualified for the task. Moreover, he never failed to utilize, as far as possible, the ability and training of the whites in the interests of better administration. He had invited his former owner to return, and all who were willing to serve under the flag of the Negroes, which in his hands stood for freedom. Not a few had accepted his invitation. In his palace he was in the habit of giving receptions and of holding smaller, more intimate gatherings, over which he presided, ceremoniously, politely, displaying at the same time an impenetrable reserve and a great solicitude to listen to all and show himself friendly and courteous. When he went out in the street, he was preceded by two trumpeters bearing silver shields, and a guard of fifteen hundred horsemen in handsome uniforms, while he wore a blue frock coat with red cuffs trimmed with gold braid, fringed gold epaulets, scarlet waistcoat, silk hat trimmed with red ostrich feathers, the tricolored sash of the Republic, and a long sword.

XIX

NAPOLEON, THE CREOLE EMPRESS, AND THE NEGRO EMPERORS

Napoleon, through a blur of contemptuous hatred, saw in Toussaint a black caricature of himself, whose very success, in some mysterious manner, seemed to cast a shadow over his own achievements. Such a mental picture made a violent assault on Napoleon's pride.

PERCY WAXMAN

AT THIS point Napoleon enters the picture. The connections of this son of far-off Corsica with the West Indies could hardly have been more intimate. After a lapse of three centuries the Mediterranean and the Caribbean were linked together once more, and this embrace took place in the First Consul's nuptial couch. At the very time the former coachman of M. Bayon de Libertat was making his stirring addresses from the pulpits in Haiti, defeating the English, French, and Spanish, and attiring himself in red and blue frock coats and plumed hats, a lovely Creole of Martinique, in whose veins ran the blood of two families prominent in the island from the days of the buccaneers, had formed a salon in Paris frequented by prominent figures of the day. Her name was Joséphine de Beauharnais. She was a widow. Her husband had paid his tribute to the guillotine. She had two children, and her tropical beauty was at its peak of perfection.

The day came when her son presented himself in the offices of one General Bonaparte, who, after a certain brilliant campaign, had been named commander of the army. He had come to ask for the sword of his father, the Vicomte de Beauharnais, who had been beheaded a few days before the fall of Robespierre. Napoleon graciously granted his request, for the emotion of this boy of fourteen had touched him. The next day the grateful mother called on the general to express her gratitude. And

337

this was how Napoleon Bonaparte of Corsica and Joséphine de Beauharnais of Martinique met. Napoleon was twenty-six at the time, Joséphine, thirty-two. A year later Napoleon married her. No other woman would ever hold the same place in the heart of the future Emperor of the French as Joséphine. She was his great love, his overwhelming passion.

Heroes are like bits of flotsam that the tides of the nations lift out of the void, raise to the clouds, and then engulf once more with dizzying rapidity. But never had there been such breakers, nor had heroes been raised to such heights, as in those days. The Negro Toussaint, the Creole Joséphine, and the Little Corporal of Corsica are three perfect examples of the period. It would be hard to say whose was the greatest prowess. The Negro's rise was unbelievable. The Corsican's astounded the universe. But Joséphine's took the breath away.

At sixteen Joséphine was a beauty who had come into flower under the stimulating caress of the Caribbean sun. The slaves who had brought her up, whispering tales of magic into her ears, had spoiled her; those nurses do spoil their charges, and Joséphine was affectionate, lovable, generous. She had the tropical languor of the planters' daughters, she bore a hammock in her soul, and she made her début in life with the simplicity of a child of nature, one who had grown up on milk that came warm and foaming from the cow, on baked plantain, yucca, and coconut. In Paris she had an aunt who had once been in Martinique, an ambitious, worldly woman, who took it into her head to launch Joséphine or her sister in Paris society. And this miracle was to become feasible because of that magnetic attraction possessed by the Venuses of the Caribbean which Amerigo Vespucci's roving eye had detected centuries before. A slave who could tell fortunes had read Joséphine's palm and told her: "You will be a queen." This was something fortune-tellers always told girls, but this one seems to have possessed a special gift. To another girl she had said: "You will almost be a queen." And to a third: "You, veiled, will be more than a queen." The winds of life scattered the three girls through the world. And, as the old woman had foretold, one — Madame de Maintenon — was almost a queen. The second was stolen by pirates and taken to Constantinople, where she entered the Sultan's seraglio and became more powerful than any queen. In Joséphine's case, the fortune-teller made a slight mistake in the title: she was to be not a queen, but an empress.

When Joséphine reached Paris her aunt took her in hand, polished her, taught her airs and graces, and married her to the Vicomte de Beauharnais; and her remarkable career began. It is hardly believable that one day the Pope, Pius VII, should have come to Paris to crown Napoleon emperor. When he reached Paris, the Pope was informed that he would also be a witness to Joséphine's coronation. The Pope and the Creole had a long heart-to-heart talk. Delicately Joséphine opened her heart to His Holiness. Her conscience was troubling her, for her marriage had never received the blessing of the Church. Although France had bestowed upon her the title of Empress, she realized that, in the sight of God, she was merely Napoleon's concubine. His Holiness arranged everything, and this time it was Napoleon who was surprised: in a quiet ceremony in the Tuileries, Cardinal Fesch united Napoleon and Joséphine in the bonds of holy matrimony. This was followed by a magnificent celebration, the greatest Paris had known in many a year. All France was there. A guard of honor of ten thousand horsemen. Uniforms, medals, gold, diamonds, and the carriage with the four imperial eagles bearing the crown, which the Pope set upon the brow of the Corsican adventurer. And Joséphine, beautiful as a goddess, with just a tinge of Antillean cinnamon in her complexion. Napoleon's sisters were pale with envy, rage, and jealousy — and they had to carry her train! To make them obey, Napoleon had had to use sterner measures than in ordering a battle. And in spite of everything, they almost made the Empress fall. The vixens let Joséphine bear the full weight of her robe. Only a Creole brought up like Joséphine, in the arms of Nature, could have managed that enormous train of velvet strewn with embossed golden bees and bordered in ermine. But Joséphine, though she was forty-one, looked twenty-five. Never had she seemed more beautiful. The hands of the Emperor were two caresses of love as he set the diamond diadem upon her lovely head. At the height of his glory Napoleon seemed to be repeating in the coronation gesture that ardor which lives in his letters like the incense of his devotion to Joséphine: "My happiness consists in being near you. . . . Your letters are the joy of my weary days. . . . I send you a thousand kisses as warm as my heart, as pure as you. . . ." Joséphine had not always followed the example of Caesar's wife, but the most appealing thing about the whole coronation ceremony was that it seemed a rebirth of love.

Let us leave Joséphine in Notre Dame and return to the Negroes in Haiti. Napoleon did not care for Negroes. As slaves, they had their place; one could even like them, as one likes dogs, as Joséphine had liked them in her childhood. But the only thing to do with a rebellious Negro was to cut off his head. Napoleon relieved General Dumas (father of the author of *The Three Musketeers*) of his command merely because his mother had been a Negress of Haiti. His first impulse when he became First Consul was to bring Toussaint's followers to heel. But aside from the fact that hostilities with Great Britain made it impossible for him to deal with Haiti, those returning from the island advised him to proceed with caution. He decided to send out representatives with a new proclamation ending with the words: "The sacred principles of liberty and equality for the Negroes will not be modified in any way." This proclamation was followed by a decree confirming Toussaint L'Ouverture as commander-in-chief of the Haitian army, and ordering this motto inscribed on the flags of the island: "Brave Negroes, always remember that only the French people have recognized your freedom and your equality of rights."

Toussaint received the delegates, but he was not pleased with the procedure the First Consul had followed. Napoleon should have addressed himself to him personally. For this reason he did not follow his suggestion as to inscribing the suggested motto on the flag. Napoleon did not want Toussaint to make war on the Spaniards, but Toussaint did so because he wished to establish complete control over the whole island. And, finally, Toussaint,

who had had the new constitution for the island drawn up,
handed a copy to Napoleon's representative, saying: "I would
ask you to return to France and place this constitution, with this
personal letter from me, in the hands of the First Consul." One
of the clauses of the constitution stated that Toussaint was to
send it to the French government for approval, but added that
owing to the suspension of laws and the urgent need for a system of government, he had been asked, by the unanimous vote
of the inhabitants of the island, to put it into practice. At the
same time it stated that Toussaint was to be the governor of the
island for life, and was to leave the name of his successor in a
sealed envelope to be opened only on the day of his death. The
representative called attention to the fact that the constitution
made no provision for the French authorities. "France," answered Toussaint, "will send her representatives to talk with me."
". . . As it has been approved, she will have to send you ministers
or ambassadors, like the Americans, Spaniards, or English."

In his letter to Napoleon, Toussaint said: "Citizen Consul: I
have the satisfaction of announcing to you . . . the constitution which augurs the happiness of the inhabitants of this island
. . . today under a single government. . . . The general assembly has asked me to put it in force provisionally, as the most
efficacious manner of setting the colony on the path of progress;
I have yielded to its desires. The constitution has been received
by all the citizens with the greatest manifestations of delight. Receive my greetings and my deepest respects. . . ."

When the commissioner reached France, Napoleon flew into
a rage. He would tear the epaulets from the shoulders of every
Negro. The commissioner explained to him that Toussaint was
very powerful and it would be the part of wisdom to proceed
cautiously. Napoleon had the commissioner deported to the island of Elba and began making preparations for war. Joséphine
helped him with a correspondence he carried on for some time
with Toussaint about a plantation belonging to her family. She
put it in Toussaint's charge; Toussaint sent her the accounts regularly, and asked her to send his sons back to him. Joséphine
lavished attention on the children, but did not return them; they

341

were hostages whom Napoleon could use to advantage when the time came. As soon as the war with Great Britain was intermitted by the Peace of Amiens in 1802, Napoleon announced an expedition against Haiti. The slaves had flouted France's authority, and national honor demanded vengeance.

To conceal the scale of the planned expedition, preparations were made in the ports of France, Spain, and Holland. It was to be larger than the one Napoleon himself had led against Egypt. It was something to see the greatest man in France assembling the forces of his allies, fitting out ships, and loading munitions for the purpose of getting rid of this Negro. "The best troops of France, the soldiers of Jourdan, Moreau, Hoche, Bonaparte, victors in Germany, in Italy, in Egypt were proceeding by forced marches to Atlantic and Mediterranean ports. France had never before seen such an array of naval power. Spain and Holland, as allies, were sending their quota." In two years France sent forty thousand men to Haiti.

The expedition was under the command of General Le Clerc. He was not only one of France's great generals; he was also Napoleon's brother-in-law. Pauline Bonaparte saw the invasion as a means of acquiring a kingdom for herself. Napoleon Bonaparte in France, Pauline Bonaparte in America: a nice fraternal division of the world. Her ship, on which Jérôme Bonaparte, the youngest brother, was also a passenger, was loaded with tapestries, furniture, paintings, musicians, artists, jesters . . . and Toussaint's sons. Napoleon had sent for them, had given a banquet in his palace in their honor, had presented them with fine uniforms, and had said to them: "France will give your father protection, glory, honors; you will carry him my message of friendship." At the same time he was giving General Le Clerc secret instructions for his campaign so that everything should be carried out according to plan. The action would comprise three phases. During the first, Toussaint was to be promised everything, all the Negro officers were to be confirmed in their rank, nobody was to be harmed, and measures would be taken only against those who revolted. During the second period, the rebels were to be hunted down and killed, and though the officers and

Toussaint himself were to continue in their posts, everything possible was to be done to discredit them. During the third period, Toussaint, Dessalines, and the others were to be sent to France if they offered resistance, there to be tried by a court martial and executed within twenty-four hours. If, on the contrary, they assisted in the work of pacification, they were to be sent to France without being deprived of their rank. These instructions, in Napoleon's own handwriting, are preserved in the archives of Paris.

Toussaint had seen what was coming in time, and had managed to buy thirty thousand rifles. His secret agents had warned him of the expedition, but they had failed to learn its proportions. When, from a hill-top, he saw the fleet arriving, he shouted, panic-stricken: "All France is coming against us!" This was but a momentary reaction, however. At once he leaped on his horse and began to organize the resistance. Not a ship was to enter the harbor. Better fire and death than slavery. Messengers flew as on wings to every part of the island. Le Clerc had planned simultaneous landings at different points, and his objective was Cap François. Pauline prepared her prettiest toilettes. A messenger was sent ahead to advise Christophe, the local governor, to organize a solemn reception. The former hotel servant received Le Clerc's delegate in his palace, a mansion befitting a lord, and regaled him at his table, which was set with a service of gold. The delegate was astonished at the display of luxury. "I have no authority to receive General Le Clerc," Christophe informed him. "I shall have to consult first with Governor Toussaint."

Le Clerc could hardly believe his ears when he heard his delegate's message. He sent him back to notify Christophe that he would brook no delays, and instructed him to distribute copies of Napoleon's proclamation among the people. The mayor, who got hold of a copy, had it read by the town crier. Opinion in the city was divided. But Christophe knew his duty. With that exquisite politeness characteristic of those who at some time in their lives have been lackeys, he was all amiability to Le Clerc's

343

delegate. He asked for forty-eight hours, by which time, at most, Toussaint's instructions would have arrived. Meanwhile he disposed his troops and gave them specific orders. All the inhabitants of the city were to be evacuated from the city to the hills. Every soldier was to have his torch ready. When Pauline Bonaparte and her General-husband entered the city, a curtain of flame was already spreading up the hills, and the city was a mass of ashes.

Hostilities began at once. Le Clerc and his troops threw a noose around Toussaint which was methodically drawn tighter and tighter. The Negroes fought like heroes or wild animals in the hills, but there came a moment when Toussaint seemed lost. Whereupon the Negroes feigned a heavy attack at one spot, Le Clerc's troops hurried to reinforce the position, and Toussaint and his men managed to break through the weakened line and make a perfect retreat.

There were long days, months, of tedious fighting during which Napoleon's troops suffered more than they had ever suffered on the other side of the Atlantic. At one time Le Clerc managed to establish contact with Toussaint by correspondence. He sent him his own sons bearing messages of friendship and a personal letter from Napoleon to the Negro, a long letter full of expressions of respect and consideration. Toussaint read it, and politely and quietly answered, sending Napoleon's general to the Devil. If France's intentions were those expressed in this letter, why had he entered as an invader and killed so many Haitians?

And to make this unending struggle worse, there was yellow fever. Le Clerc wrote Napoleon asking for new armies. Crushing the cockroach (as Napoleon phrased it) had not turned out such an easy job. The island was running blood. Might not diplomacy bring better results? Le Clerc began separate negotiations with Toussaint's generals, making them the most solemn and unlimited promises in the name of peace and their country, where all should be brothers sharing in the common glory of France. And he succeeded. The generals went over to him. There came a moment when Toussaint could no longer count on his general

344

staff, and he had no choice but to accept this dangerous peace. There followed a series of letters, emissaries, proposals, with Le Clerc always seemingly frank and conciliatory. Toussaint finally agreed to an interview with Le Clerc to bring the war to an end. All along the road, the crowds gathered to pay him tumultuous, affectionate tribute. He was the undisputed hero of his people. To the accompaniment of banquets, speeches, Te Deums, processions, parades, and church bells, peace was heralded in. Toussaint accepted it, but announced his complete withdrawal from public affairs. He wanted to go home, to enjoy its peace after so many years of conflict; he loved his wife, he adored his children. He took leave of his troops. Tears streamed down the savage faces of the soldiers, and those rude hands, in whose grasp the machetes had seemed brands of lightning, shook with emotion. Toussaint took the road to the hills, to his home. It was as though he were going to resume his dialogues with the herbs he understood so well.

When all seemed peace and quiet, they carefully laid the snare. General Brunet invited Toussaint to come and talk with him. Everything had been going along like a honeymoon, so Toussaint could hardly refuse. The two began to talk in the friendliest fashion; then Brunet asked to be excused for a moment and stepped into the adjoining office — and soldiers burst in through the doors demanding Toussaint's immediate surrender. By the same frigate that carried Toussaint to France, Le Clerc wrote asking for reinforcements. But the illustrious brother-in-law was not to live to see the outcome of all this plotting. Not long afterwards yellow fever carried him off. Pauline, who seemed to have lost her head, returned to France with dashing General Humbert as her lover. Justly indignant, Napoleon exiled Humbert to England, whence he fled to the United States, to make assurance doubly sure. Jérôme Bonaparte, too, threw in his lot with the democratic masses of the United States.

Toussaint was confined in the strongest prison in all Europe, the castle of Joux, which a knight had built in the time of the

Crusades to shut his unfaithful wife in. Thanks to the solicitous care of his jailers, he died there in 1803, in less than a year, this man whom England, Spain, France, and Napoleon together had been unable to conquer. Perhaps he was not a man, but a whole people. And indeed he continued his battle from the other world, for his spirit roamed the hills of his native land, just as when, on nights when his visions held him sleepless, the hoofs of his galloping horse had beaten out a song of freedom for the Negroes. The result of France's efforts in Haiti was mountains of corpses. Le Clerc was followed by Rochambeau, who capitulated. The final casting-up of accounts showed sixty thousand French soldiers killed. It was Napoleon's most costly campaign to date. And all for nothing. The Haitian casualties amounted to one hundred and fifty thousand.

Dessalines had himself crowned emperor with the title of Jacques I. When Francisco Miranda, father of the South American revolutions, stopped at the island, the emperor gave him an unbeatable formula for getting rid of the Spaniards: cut off their heads and burn down their houses. Jacques had made himself emperor because he considered himself with as much right to the title as Napoleon. He did not create a nobility because he alone was noble. On every hill-top he built a fortress. Assassinated, he was succeeded by Christophe, who had himself crowned king with the title of Henri I. The jewelers of the Cap made Henri's crown, scepter, and mace, which are three masterpieces of the goldsmith's craft. He built a church just for his coronation; after the coronation it was torn down. He created a nobility of princes of the blood, dukes, counts, and barons. The pattern of the European monarchies seemed to suit the African taste exactly. Henri-Christophe had twelve palaces built for himself; that of Sans Souci was as impressive as the finest French châteaux.

The inevitable dissensions arose and the island split up into a republic headed by Pétion and Henri-Christophe's kingdom. Pétion had been able to acquire an education, and his government was liberal and magnanimous. Personally he was modest, and he worshipped liberty. He offered Simón Bolívar his support when the latter, defeated, had taken refuge in the West Indies and needed it most. With Pétion's Negroes and a handful of whites, the Liberator invaded Venezuela; it was a decisive moment in his struggle, and he wanted to repay Pétion in some way. The only thing the latter would accept, the only thing he asked for, was the liberation of the slaves in Venezuela. Bolívar gave him his promise and fulfilled it.

To return to Henri-Christophe. The problem confronting Haiti was Napoleon's second campaign against the island. To those who had achieved their independence after such a desperate struggle, it was a question of life or death. The king put everybody to work, even old men, women, and children, day and night, in the forests and in the towns, setting up brick kilns, quarrying stone from the mountainsides, bringing in logs, and carrying cannon up the steep slopes to build a fortress. This fortress — The Citadel — was big enough to hold a large part of his people and was planned to withstand a siege of months or years, so strategically located on the heights and with walls so thick that it could be neither destroyed nor captured. The Citadel came to be considered the eighth wonder of the world. Yet, compared with the human factors that went into its construction, the gigantic structure is but a trifling testimony to the sacred fire that animated those impassioned lovers of liberty. There is no exaggeration in calling it the world's eighth wonder. Perhaps one could go further and call it the first wonder of liberty. On the summit of La Ferrière for centuries the Citadel would be visible, like a prolongation of the mountain, its walls rising sheer above the abyss, two hundred meters long, one hundred and fifty meters thick, and eighty-seven meters high.

Christophe's idea was to make the Citadel a fortress and a refuge. He had stored in it food, medicines, and arms enough to enable fifteen thousand men to withstand a year's siege behind its walls. Fourteen million pounds of coffee, eight million of cotton, and the same amount of chick-peas, rice, corn, and salt were stocked in the cellars, and the supply was replenished every three months. Elaborate cisterns had been built to catch

347

water, and pipes had been laid to carry it through the inner walls, which were four meters wide at their base. It was defended by three hundred cannon. Forty thousand rifles, swords, machetes, bullets, and tons of powder were there in expectation of Napoleon's attack.

"When the French army disembarks," Christophe's instructions ran, "every city, village, house, factory or any other building on the plain will be burned to the ground to deprive the invaders of all protection against the climate; all the population will withdraw to the hills; the bridges will be chopped down and destroyed; all the levees on the rivers and lakes will be destroyed, too, so that their waters can flood the roads; all highways are to be blocked; the cattle and horses are to be herded into the most remote and inaccessible places; every cart, coach, buggy, and everything that in any way might be useful to the enemy is to be destroyed or rendered useless — so that when the enemy lands he will find nothing but ashes and ruins, a land where devastation marks the spot on which cities, towns, and houses once stood. . . ."

But the Haitians had overrated Napoleon's intentions. He had learned a great deal from these distant wars, and he knew that no European army could resist both the Negro and yellow fever. Some years before, when he had dreamed of rebuilding France's empire in the New World and secured the return of Louisiana from Spain, he thought of making Louisiana a base from which to supply Haiti with food, cattle, and lumber and thus make the island the flower of the French colonies. At this time, like the show-off and lover of bombast he always was, he said: "France cannot resign herself to an inert existence, to that settled calm with which Germany and Italy content themselves. The English have scorned my offers of peace. So be it; I shall turn Haiti into one vast camp, and I shall have my own army ready there to carry the war to England's own colonies." These words might have been written in water. Napoleon gave up Haiti, and sold Louisiana. When he called a council of his ministers to discuss the sale, he summed up his ideas in one phrase: "Fifty million francs and not one cent less." One minister, bolder than the others, voiced his objections to the plan, and pointed out the possibilities of New Orleans for the future. "Lying as it does across from Panama, which will be the key of trade in the future, if France keeps Louisiana it can play a decisive role in the destiny of the New World." But Napoleon was determined to sell. "Fifty million and not a penny less. And by strengthening the United States with this territory," he went on, "what a headache we shall give England! And, anyway, I need fifty million for war."

In the background, the Negroes of Haiti, who, like rum, carry a wicked power within them, laughed with teeth as white as coconut meat.

Napoleon's troops never crossed the Atlantic again. Henri-Christophe died in 1820, five years after the white emperor had suffered final defeat at Waterloo and was languishing in St. Helena, philosophically waiting for death. Under these circumstances the black king could calmly depart for Hell, and so he did. On a mountain-top of Haiti his clenched stone fist, the Citadel, stands defying time, a symbol of the Negroes' impassioned fight for freedom.

BOOK IV

THE AGE OF LIBERTY

TO THE MEMORY OF TOMÁS RUEDA VARGAS

WHEN the nineteenth century made its entry, the stage was
set for it. The people had begun to shake off their chains, and
knew how war was waged. The Creoles were familiar with the
philosophies proclaimed in Europe by the sons of the Revolution. The doctrine of the rights of man had taught the individ-
ual that he possessed an inalienable sovereignty. The Social
Contract had outlined in concrete fashion the formula for con-
stituting a republic. The whites had their federation of states in
North America; the Negroes of Haiti, their kingdom. The bourgeoisie had set up its republic in France. Over the waters of the
Caribbean began to move the gallant, heroic figures of Miranda
and Bolívar. In Mexico Father Hidalgo sounded a peal that
shook the very stones of the old cathedral. Spanish America
seethed with an emotion that knew no frontiers. The armies
were on the march in all Mexico and Central America, from
Venezuela to Chile and from Argentina to Peru, all moving to
the magic watchword: Liberty. It was a word understood by all
— Indians, Creoles, and Negroes, poor and rich alike.

And the people lost their heads, and it seemed that their
hearts would burst their breasts. The intoxication of victory, the
rejoicing that expressed itself in the lyrical outpourings of ro-
manticism, made it impossible to bring lasting order in these
republics which for three centuries had been repressed and humiliated. America was still, and would so continue another hundred years, a lush jungle, a plain on which wheels had not yet
left their track, where the riders rode as though on wings, and
where there was a wild delight in heroic feats. These were by-
products of liberty.

Europe viewed this sight with curiosity, sometimes with horror. The Old World assumed too much the role of overlord,
tutor, guardian. At first, Bolívar and Miranda attracted the admiration of people as they traveled about the capitals of Europe.
Later, because of the astounding spectacle of our civil wars, the
expression "the savage lands of Spanish America" became a by-

word. Then came the determination to bring the New World within the circumference of some intelligible category, such as Latinism for example. To make a Latin America. Or a Spanish America. Ideas. Words, words, words. But all the excesses, ferocity, wars, heroic exploits, adventures, novels, and poems of the nineteenth century left a deep, undying residue in the spirit of those untamed cubs of America: their love of liberty.

In the background lies a dark, troubled history, as is the case with all true stories. Everything was to be found in the people who wrote them. If we were to remove the blots from the history of America, there would be nothing left: the black in our past is the coal from which the flames sprang. In the nineteenth century there was more barbarity in America, if such a thing is possible, than even in the sixteenth, the century of the conquest. At times the horses galloped through pools of blood. Bolívar's war to the death was one of total ferocity, and Morillo's reconquest was even more ferocious. We achieved our liberty through violence. In the same way we are today seeking justice with passion. History has so ordered our circumstances that life, for us, has a dramatic quality. Possibly the episodes of the nineteenth century will not be repeated, but they must be seen as they were, to feel the emotion peculiar to our history, which is that of constantly skirting the edge of an abyss.

A century that began in the Caribbean with Bolívar, and that came to a close in that same sea with José Martí, will remain an inextinguishable light in the history of mankind.

XX

THE TWILIGHT OF THE PIRATES

*"Tell your commander I found the principal of this gang so old an
offender, and so very bad a man, that I have saved him the trouble
of taking him to the United States. I hung him myself."*

JEAN LAFITTE

ENEMIES of mankind, *hostis humani generis*, is Captain Johnson's verdict on them in his history of the pirates. With their
black skull and crossbones flying from the mainmast, their sinister ships scudded along, raising a foam of blood before their
prows. Their legend was the legend of the Caribbean. At the
mere mention of their name, the Spaniards shivered in Havana,
the English in Kingston, the French in Martinique, the Dutch
in Curaçao, the sailors on the sea, the rich on land, and even, in
the shadow of the hills, women, friars, and children. In the days
of Queen Elizabeth a man could begin as a pirate and end up a
royal admiral. But there came a moment early in the eighteenth
century when the English found themselves the victims of their
own Frankenstein monster. The Empire was losing more ships
and money at the hands of the pirates than to the French and
Spaniards together. So the King finally issued his famous decree
ordering the pirates wiped out, with a clause providing that the
royal pardon would be granted to those who sincerely repented
their ways before September 5, 1718. There was to be a century
of struggle with the pirates before they were finally wiped out.

Captain Teach, "Blackbeard," who had spread terror throughout the Antilles, presented himself humbly before the governor
of North Carolina, and the governor extended the royal pardon
to him. The pirate, now a reformed character, married a sixteen-
year-old girl. The governor was witness to the ceremony, and,
touched to the heart, wished Teach "Health and a new life!"
Blackbeard went aboard his ship, and in a short time was sowing

panic throughout the countryside. From villages, from church steeples, from the decks of river boats, people watched fearfully, expecting at any moment to see the whiskers of this bold Scotsman, which spread greater terror through the community than the tail of any comet ever seen in the heavens. The pirate wore his beard very long, and braided with ribbons. Behind his ear he carried lighted fuses, to give him a more diabolical appearance and to have tinder always on hand for his pistols. At times the Devil shipped with him. Ninety would come aboard in port; later, when the roll was called, there would be ninety-one; and a few days later there would be only ninety. Old Cloven Hoof had come aboard and left, no one knew when or how. People drew a deep breath on the day when Blackbeard was taken; his head was cut off and hung as a trophy from the mainmast of his ship. It is said that at night his beard can still be seen flying through the hills like a comet.

The island of Providence in the Bahamas was the pirates' general headquarters. For some reason the majority of them were Scotsmen. They plied their trade around Cuba, Mexico, Martinique, and Cartagena. Their prey might be Spanish, French, or English — it was all one to them. In the years following the decree of the King of England, the English were the worst sufferers. The King spared no efforts in pursuing the pirates, and English ships patrolled the Caribbean. The pirates scoffed at them, and carried their depredations as far as the coasts of Africa. At times law scored some small triumphs. In Charleston, in New York, in Jamaica, pirate trials were held, at which the prescribed penalties were imposed. On one occasion, at White Point near Charleston, people had the satisfaction of seeing twenty-four pirates strung up from the trees. They had been comrades of Captain Bonnet, all from Aberdeen, Bristol, Dublin, Glasgow. The poor fellows had done all that was in their power to provide Stevenson with good models for his *Treasure Island*.

But it must be said, in fairness, that all nations were represented among the pirates. There were not a few from Jamaica, and some from New York. And there was the Spaniard, Don Pedro Gibert, from Catalonia, whom the ladies found irresistible with his sparkling black eyes, his teeth like two rows of pearls, his hair like a crow's wing, and his broad, bold forehead. One day he sailed out of Havana. From the Morro fortress his topgallant sail could be seen billowing over the green savanna of the sea. The first ship that crossed his path was the *Mexican* out of Salem, Massachusetts. Gibert stripped it of everything aboard, from the barrels full of money to the two gold chronometers, and then made for Africa. There he struck up a friendship with a Negro king, buried his loot in the sand, and bought ivory, tortoise shell, palm oil, and slaves. But the British men-of-war were on his trail, and caught him. He was taken to Boston to stand trial. The pirates were twelve: Gibert, Francisco Ruiz, Bernardo de Soto, Antonio Ferrer. . . . The defense counsel did everything he could to save Bernardo de Soto and the poor colored cook. On one occasion Bernardo de Soto had bravely saved twenty Americans. "The Sultan of Turkey," said the attorney for the defense, "can tie as many women as he likes into sacks and throw them into the Bosphorus without furnishing food for an hour's conversation in Constantinople. But that is not the case here; human life has a value for us; stop and think. . . ." Meanwhile Bernardo de Soto's wife had arrived, traveling all the way from Barcelona in an effort to save her husband's life. She threw herself on her knees before President Jackson, and he was so touched by her devotion that he granted her husband a pardon. The colored cook, too, was spared. "We shall die like brave Spaniards," were Gibert's last words. Father Varella, who had accompanied the condemned men to the gallows, said as the noose was adjusted about their necks: "Spaniards, ascend to heaven!"

The pirates of Havana attacked every American boat they encountered because the Americans were interfering with their slave-running. As the crews of the pirate ships were made up of French, Portuguese, Spaniards, and Scotsmen, they flew any flag that happened to suit their fancy, if they preferred it to the Jolly Roger.

Of a person born in the heart of noble England, within the precincts of Westminster, it is fair to assume that he is a gentleman. There are those who believe that pirates are born, not made, the same as a gentleman. Edward Low was born a pirate. At school he did nothing but bully his comrades. While still a stripling, he went to sea, following the pirate's trade in Honduras and the Leeward Islands until he was finally hanged in Martinique. The famous North American pirate Charles Gibbs showed his inclinations at a very age, too. He was born in Rhode Island, of good family; his parents, unable to control him by either rod or counsel, finally died of a broken heart. The boy had run away from home and shipped aboard a man-of-war. He was in the battle of Chesapeake Bay, but he did not like taking orders. He opened a feed store in Boston, hard by Tin Top, the tavern that was the gathering place for all the loose women and drunkards of the city. He was on friendly terms with all of them, lent them money, lost everything he had, and to repair his fortunes organized raids that took him all the way from Florida to Buenos Aires, where he married. It was said of him that he had killed some four hundred people. He returned to Havana and New York, and — as he had $30,000 in his pocket — he seemed a gentleman. When war broke out between Brazil and Argentina in 1826, Gibbs offered his services to Argentina and reported to Admiral Brown in Buenos Aires. He served as a member of the crew aboard the 25 de Mayo. He reports that the admiral said to him: "I want no cowards in the navy," and that he answered: "You don't need to worry about me." He served through the campaign with distinction. Later he learned that France and Algiers were at war, and he went to offer his services to the Dey. When he reached the desert and looked out over the sands, he observed: "This is no place for me," and came away. "It amused me to see the ruins of Carthage and recall the war they had fought with the Romans." He finally reached his proper place: New Orleans. There he found full scope for his talents. But he was finally caught, and this sentence was pronounced on him in New York: "To be hanged by the neck until dead, and his corpse turned over to the College of Physicians and Surgeons."

357

The elite of the pirate profession was to be found in New Orleans. It was the rendezvous of smugglers, the Versailles of the kings of the black flag. When Jean Lafitte strolled about the Place d'Armes in the Vieux Carré, his bold eyes, his handsome mustache, his wavy chestnut hair drew the glances of quadroons and whites like a magnet. He was a great gentleman, a familiar figure at the opera, at balls, and around the gaming-table. It was impossible to see him without thinking: "So this is Jean Lafitte!"

New Orleans was the natural center for smugglers. It was impossible for the English, French, and Spanish colonies or the young republic of the United States to take measures against these bold, shrewd traders in forbidden goods, who could slip easily through the channels and bayous of the Mississippi. Every island was a mystery camp. The camps were like the floating gardens of some enchanted tale that drew settlers and merchants from many miles around to bid for the goods Jean Lafitte had stolen from Spanish ships and auctioned off. As England had seized the islands of Guadaloupe and Martinique and had banned the importation of slaves, the planters of the South had to go to the pirate chief's island to replenish their stocks — to Barataria. It is curious to consider to what use the name of Sancho Panza's fantastic governorship was being put! Lafitte sold his slaves by weight, a dollar a pound.

Goods of the finest quality were to be seen in New Orleans. To be sure, the ladies' elegant brocade dresses were occasionally a wee bit spattered with blood: it is impossible to loot a ship without having a little blood splash about. But the drawing-rooms of no other city displayed so many mirrors, crystal chandeliers, and handsome furniture. Far finer than the balls given by the white ladies were those of the quadroons. Travelers from Europe made the trip just to attend these; the beauty of those daughters of handsome mulattoes and white gentlemen was such as to satisfy the most exacting standards of the other side of the Atlantic. The white ladies were so jealous of the quadroons that the governor finally had to issue a decree forbidding the latter to wear certain articles of luxury so that they would not outshine the leaders of fashion at the opera. But these efforts were of no avail; the attractiveness of these women aroused the most romantic passions, and New Orleans became the Mecca of duellists. Not a night went by that, in the near-by woods, one could not hear the pistol shots of some affair of honor, or see the flash of swords; and it was always over some quadroon. The cemetery was full of headstones whose sole epitaph read: "Fallen in an affair of honor."

It is interesting to note how New Orleans was becoming polished and refined, and acquiring a marked character all its own. It had a haughty pride and the most cultivated manners, which had their origin in the exaggerated sense of honor characteristic of professional gamblers and the gallant gestures acquired at dances where silks, mirrors, and good liquor abounded. And all this, a by-product of the somewhat irregular life of many of its inhabitants, was reinforced by the authentic distinction of the great gentlemen living on plantations where a refined, polished aristocracy was coming into being, the most cultivated and ceremonious of the country. The Place d'Armes of New Orleans looked like a corner of Europe. The Creoles found the manners of the other North Americans insufferable — the "Kaintucks," as they dubbed them. New Orleans was becoming a historic shrine; it was one of the places that pointed out to the traveler: this is where Pierre Lafitte was imprisoned; General Jackson slept here; this is the house that was prepared for Napoleon — just as the historic spots in Salamanca, Rouen, or Canterbury were displayed in the other hemisphere.

But, of them all, the most important spot was the old blacksmith shop where Lafitte started his business. It was here that the planters came and said: "I need twenty blacks." The next day Jean Lafitte would sail up one of the arms of the Mississippi with the planter, and in Barataria the buyer could pick out what he wanted. Lafitte's customers were treated as guests, dined on dishes of silver, served the best of French wines, and given fragrant cigars. The smugglers of Barataria recognized him as their captain. Protected by his prestige, his bravery, his knowledge and shrewdness, they all felt safe. And Lafitte's fleet was never idle, whether it was harrying the ships of the United States or of the English.

Lafitte never allowed himself to be called a pirate. "I am a corsair," he would haughtily insist, "and my flag is that of Cartagena." The Spanish colonies had risen against the King. Bolívar was waging ruthless war. In New Granada, Cartagena had been one of the first centers to proclaim its independence. Lafitte said that he had letters patent from the republic of Cartagena to attack Spanish shipping. On the island of Barataria the only flag flown was that of Cartagena.

The day came when Barataria was the terror of the seas. It was impossible to reach the port of Vera Cruz in safety. The big Mississippi boats were in a state of constant alarm. One captain, who had been boarded in the Gulf, made his way back to New Orleans and complained loudly in the square, in the church vestibule, on the corner, in the street, in the governor's house: Pirates, Pirates! And the echo answered: Lafitte, Lafitte! The streets leading to the square were thronged with people. The denizens of Barataria heard the uproar, but went on calmly selling oysters, shrimps, and crabs at their stalls. There was high indignation — and then, suddenly, craven silence. Arrogant and smiling, Pierre and Jean Lafitte made their way through the crowd, and all, high and low, responded to their defiant challenge. New Orleans respected bravery and daring.

One day, however, the governor decided that things had gone far enough. He had tried to clear New Orleans of smugglers. He had asked the legislature for help repeatedly, and it had paid no attention to his plea. He was not going to be humiliated in his own front yard any longer, and he prepared a legal trap. He invited the leading citizens to call at his office on confidential business, and there had them give testimony to be used at a trial *in absentia* of Jean Lafitte. A poster signed by the governor appeared on street corners: $500 reward to anyone handing over Jean Lafitte on charges of carrying on illegal traffic, refusal to appear before the authorities, violations of the law. . . . Two days later, on the same corners where the governor's placard had been posted, appeared one signed by Jean Lafitte. It was an exact copy of the first, with two slight changes: $500 reward to anyone handing over the person of the governor — and the signature was "Jean Lafitte." Once more New Orleans gaped in admiration at Jean Lafitte's audacity.

But on one occasion the governor happened to hold the trumps. Pierre Lafitte was in prison! Jean roared with anger. There were two lawyers in New Orleans, the best in Louisiana and among the most distinguished in the whole country: Livingston and Grymes. Edward Livingston had been mayor of New York City and Attorney General under Jefferson. Grymes was the prosecuting attorney of New Orleans; he resigned his office to undertake the defense of Pierre Lafitte with Livingston. There were no heights the power of the Lafittes could not scale. But the governor had staked his prestige on bringing Pierre Lafitte to justice. The lawyers were unable to get him out of jail. But, all the same, they received their fee of $40,000 agreed on with Jean Lafitte for his defense. When they went to Barataria to collect the money Lafitte entertained them in royal fashion. Grymes, who spent a week there, declared that he had never been the guest of such a perfect gentleman.

During the War of 1812 a small detachment of the English fleet put in at Barataria. The captain wanted to talk with Jean Lafitte. He brought with him letters from the crown offering Lafitte a large sum of money and a high post in the English navy if he would join England against the United States. Lafitte's brother was in the clutches of the governor, his links with the young republic were very feeble, and the only flag he had proclaimed was that of Cartagena. He showed the captain every courtesy and deference and, after reading the letters carefully, asked for time to consider the offer: he had to talk it over with his comrades, and as soon as they reached a decision he would let the captain know. Lafitte accompanied the officer back to his ship, thanking him warmly for this proof of esteem England had given him.

But the time that Lafitte had requested was used for sending all the letters from England to the governor and to a friend who was a member of the Louisiana legislature, adding a note of his own to say that as a good American he was prepared to come to the defense of New Orleans with all his men. All he wanted in return was an appointment to the army, and to have the ban against him and his followers lifted. The offer was a tempting one, for New Orleans' defenses left much to be desired, and what better soldiers could be found than an army of bandits? Nevertheless, the governor not only did not answer Lafitte, but organized an expedition against Barataria. In a surprise attack the government forces landed on the island and seized the warehouses where the merchandise confiscated amounted to over a half-million dollars. Many of Lafitte's comrades were taken prisoner and clapped into jail. Lafitte escaped by a miracle.

In spite of the loss of the island and his property, Lafitte was still unbeaten. He had arms and he had men. It was known that the English were preparing to attack New Orleans, and General Jackson arrived in the city to organize the defenses and meet the attack. On the council for the defense of the city there were several friends of Lafitte. In New Orleans they still point out a tavern where (they will tell you) Jackson and Lafitte met for an interview. Pierre Lafitte escaped from jail. All the pirates of Barataria, with Lafitte at their head, entered General Jackson's army. Once again Lafitte had become a popular hero. General Jackson's report of his action in the battle was most flattering. Lafitte's best friend, Dominique You, who had come out to America with Le Clerc's troops at the time of Napoleon's expedition against Haiti, was one of the heroes of the Battle of New Orleans. At the great ball held to celebrate the victory among the guests were the smugglers of Barataria in handsomely colored frock coats. But Jean Lafitte was the lion of the evening. The next day the girls wrote in their "dear diaries": "Last night I met Jean Lafitte"; and the matrons, "Jean Lafitte said to me" or "Jean Lafitte told me that once. . . ."

New Orleans returned to its normal life: opera, quadroon balls, duels, jokes, Creole cuisine, French wines, crystal chande-

liers, brocade gowns. In a great brick-flagged courtyard in Du-
maine Street, the quadroon Sanité Dédé acted the role of the
Queen of Voodoo. New Orleans had only one rival in voodoo:
Haiti. The city was the leading center of witchcraft; there one
could buy hairs, spider legs, cat's claws, and frogs' entrails to
ward off evil spirits, cast a love spell, put an end to one's enemies. A great effort was being made to prevent the further importation of Negroes from the Congo, who were responsible for
these superstitions; but to all the Negroes, regardless of their
origin, voodoo was a sacred thing. To deprive them of these rites
would have been like taking the Bible away from Drake. And
they gathered in hordes in the brick courtyard where Sanité
Dédé talked with the enchanted serpent; the animal's darting
tongue, like a quick-moving straw, answered all the questions.
The Negroes worked themselves into a frenzy, shouting, singing,
weeping, and laughing. Then they held a dance in the square.
Not far from this savage festivity — some three or four blocks
away — the gaming houses and houses of pleasure catered to
their fashionable clientele.

The heroes of Barataria found their humdrum existence bor-
ing. Lafitte dreamed of founding a new empire, a second pirate
republic. He went to Galveston and began to lay the foundations for his venture on the island of Campeachy. First he
bought eight ships, to which he soon added others. His enterprise began to flourish anew. Lafitte operated under the Mexican flag, or the Venezuelan, or that of Bolívar. A hurricane came
and swept away all the houses of Campeachy. Lafitte built them
up again. He was invincible as long as he was in his tempestuous
element. But the nineteenth century was too far advanced to
tolerate the continued existence of pirates. A military expedition
was organized to wipe out the new republic. The officer in command of the mission held an interview with Lafitte, who realized that his day was over. "Give me two months," he said, "and
you won't have any cause for complaint." "Agreed," answered
the officer; "I'll wait." Lafitte set to work returning his men to
everyday life. He settled them one by one wherever they preferred to be. And finally the island, with its stout brick houses,

its big warehouses, its unquestionable importance, was left deserted. The two months were up. Lafitte then set fire to everything, even blew up the buildings so that not a brick was left standing. In 1826, at the age of forty-six, he sailed off in one of his ships, and his figure was swallowed up by legend.

Dominique You had other ideas. He had stayed on in New Orleans, a peaceable citizen, well known, honored, and popular. In the Caribbean the history of Napoleon still floated in the air, as though caught in the palms' shaggy fronds. Dominique You had been, first and foremost, a soldier in the Grande Armée, and to him, as to every pirate, Napoleon was the great captain. Now Napoleon was a prisoner on St. Helena, and untold numbers dreamed of rescuing him from the English, setting him free, bringing him to the West Indies, to New Orleans, a locale befitting his genius. (People in the know reported that he had once hoped to come to America.) The mayor of New Orelans, who was a millionaire, said: "I will take care of the expenses." A magnificent house was prepared for him, and a ship was secretly dispatched to carry out the plan. The pirates' last dream was to rescue Napoleon and bring him to New Orleans. And this was Dominique You's last dream, too.

Later, old crones would tell their grandchildren, in low mysterious voices, that Napoleon had indeed been rescued. The body entombed at the Invalides in Paris was that of another man; the real Napoleon was in New Orleans. . . . And in a sense this was true — not because his bones ever came to rest in any New Orleans cemetery, where the coffins had to be weighted with stones to keep them from floating in the muddy marshes on which the city was built, but because the captain of the French eagles made his last eyrie in the hearts of the Barataria pirates, in the soul of the last corsair.

Before we take leave of New Orleans, one more romantic episode is worth recounting. A rich merchant of Nantes had made a fortune carrying silks, velvets, and wines to Santo Domingo. For years and years his lucky ship had sailed regularly through the English blockade without ever being boarded. The captain, whose name was Audubon, took his pleasure on the island, where he had a plantation. He also had a wife in Nantes and a chest full of pieces-of-eight. On one of his return trips to France he took a child with him. Where had he got hold of it? In Santo Domingo? In New Orleans? Having no children of his own, he adopted the boy. It was not considered too odd that there should be a mystery in the life of a sea captain doing a flourishing business between Nantes and the West Indies. But one day some inquisitive soul began to speculate: the boy was the same age as Louis XVI's son would have been by this time; the captain was from La Vendée, always a royalist stronghold; so . . . ? When the boy grew up he assumed a mysterious air with regard to his origin. In many a self-respecting city of America there is some family that claims descent from the "lost" Dauphin of France. And it was so with this boy. When he came out to America, everyone who heard him play the flute, the violin, or the clarinet, or watched him dance the gavotte, the pavane, the minuet, or saw him sitting pensively under the trees reading La Fontaine, felt sure that he was the Dauphin.

Captain Audubon had really brought the boy up with unusual care. He wanted him to study, to become a naval officer. But the boy preferred to hunt butterflies in the woods, collect nests, and paint birds. He was singularly gifted at drawing, and the captain took him to the great Jacques Louis David's studio in the hope that the painter of those elegant portraits, those heroic medallions, would initiate the boy in the secrets of his art. But the lad preferred drawing birds to making copies in charcoal of plaster profiles. Then, for some unknown reason the captain sent him to the United States, where he quickly lost the small fortune Captain Audubon had given him. These were the days when the frontier was moving westward, and the Mississippi was the highway of North America. Thus, following the Mississippi, the boy came to New Orleans. There he spent his days, months, and years along the bayous, through the countryside, around Natchez and on the island where Lafitte had set up his pirate republic, painting birds. Not one escaped the snare of Audubon's brushes, until one day he was able to present an album of the birds of America that was the most complete and beautiful that had ever been seen.

New Orleans was a center for artists, where they led a bohemian existence, many of them living on houseboats on the bayous. And here Jean Jacques La Forêt Audubon, when he found himself hard up, would paint a portrait of the shoemaker's wife to pay for a pair of shoes, or of the daughter of some rich merchant to get the money to send his wife a present. In this fashion he managed to exist until the world finally recognized him for the extraordinary artist he was; indeed, his paintings of birds have been sought eagerly ever since by connoisseurs. His success strengthened the belief of people in the romantic legend of his origin — a fantasy not inappropriate to one whose head, in a manner of speaking, was full of birds' nests. But the only thing actually known about him was that the infancy of this man who painted beautiful pictures had been spent on the boat of the Nantes captain — which was enough to place this episode of New Orleans life under the aegis of France.

XXI

GUERRILLA LEADERS AND
FILIBUSTERS IN CENTRAL AMERICA

I would exchange my life for the white halo
Of imbecile or saint; for the necklace
Painted on the fat Capet;
Or for the rigid shower that fell
Upon the nape of Charles of England.

LEON DE GREIFF

T HE French Revolution, the independence of America, the triumph of the middle class over the nobility, the emancipation of the slaves, the rise of free thought above the rubble of the Inquisition, all lend the nineteenth century a boldness without precedent. To the younger generation who had been held fast in the web of dogmatic precepts, it was as though the world were actually opening out before their eyes. In Mexico, Iturbide had himself crowned emperor; his ambition was to incorporate all of Central America into Mexico. In the South, the president of Paraguay declared war on Brazil, Argentina, and Uruguay. In Argentina, Rosas, supported by his wily gauchos, defied France. Colombia approved the most liberal constitution that had ever been written; Victor Hugo, hailing it as the greatest victory of the times, was stirred to a new faith in the destinies of man. The dictator of Bolivia set the minister of Great Britain on a donkey and had him paraded through the streets. The colonies, transformed into republics, planned ambitious systems. As the century moved onward, United States political leaders came to believe that it was the "manifest destiny" of their country to be master of the Caribbean, in an irresistible extension of the zone of influence of dollar diplomacy. In 1848 the discovery of gold in California, by one stroke of fortune, converted the wildest dreams into pale images of what reality had tossed into the lap of North Americans. A steady stream of covered-wagon trains galloped over the Western plains, and in Panama and Nicaragua every effort was made to improvise the quickest route to the gold fields of California.

Central America had been a field for religious struggles from the first moment of its independence. Certain ecclesiastic dignitaries were with the republic, others against it. From the archbishop to the lowliest Franciscan lay brother, they descended to the market place, and made use of every arm they could lay their hands on: paving stones, bottles, excommunication, bullets. The priest Delgado — one of the fathers of the independence and a leading figure in the conspiracies against the Spanish governor, who drew up the articles of the declaration of independence, and whose impassioned oratory was to be heard in every revolutionary committee meeting, gathering, and assembly — flung down the gage to the Archbishop of Guatemala, leader of the reactionaries. The archbishop threw the full weight of his authority into the right dish of the scale, but, for all the effect it produced, his staff and miter might have been of straw and cork. Central America had no intention of continuing as a colony. The republic constituted San Salvador a diocese, so as to limit the archbishop's jurisdiction, and appointed Father Delgado bishop. At first the friars refused to swear allegiance to the constitution; the government showed the mailed fist, and they ended by yielding meekly, promising to support the standard of independence and the constitution of the republic.

But in a little while discord was being fomented from the pulpits. The women divided into factions, following the lead of the various preachers. The Bishop of Salvador and the Archbishop of Guatemala each had his own advocate in Rome, and presently Pope Leo XII fulminated this sentence against Father Delgado: "You have done so many and such horrible things that the words of Scripture can justly be applied to you (and we say it with tears): You have entered the flock like a thief and a ravening wolf . . . to kill and destroy. . . . If, within the period set for the correction of your crime, you have not satisfied the Church . . . although it grieves us and (to use the

words of Chrysostom) we weep and lament, and our bowels
faint, as though we were cutting off our own limbs . . . we shall
have no choice . . . but to pronounce the sentence of excommunication against you."

In Quetzaltenango the adherents of the clerical party attacked
a doctor, Cirilo Flores, vice-president of the State of Guatemala.
He sought asylum in the church; but the women fell upon him,
tore out his hair, and beat him with sticks, and he climbed into
the pulpit. The priest then brought out the Host and pleaded
with the crowd to respect the sanctity of the church. But the
older women and some of the more hot-headed youths followed
the doctor into the pulpit, where they tore out his whiskers and
more of his hair. Finally they dragged him from the church and
beat him to death.

In Honduras, Congress declared that the decision of the Holy
See would not be considered valid in the country until approved
by the government. In Salvador, where the clerical party had
burned Dr. Herrera's library and all the friars had come out in
favor of the empire, the Congress ordered the convents closed.
Iturbide's troops thereupon invaded Central America.

These conflicts were only natural. Spain, whose power had
been absolute during the colonial epoch, had not prepared the
Creoles for self-government. In the United States, where the
North Americans had, for all practical purposes, been governing themselves since before the Revolutionary War, nothing
serious happened. But in Spanish America everything had to be
improvised, done by the trial-and-error method, and all this
when the masses were excited by the wars of Independence, and
the reaction had its Trojan horses, its fifth columns, where they
could cause the most trouble. There were high and noble ambitions, admirable plans put forth by wise, civic-minded men,
but they found no support in the unruly, illiterate masses, who
gave them no peace to settle internal problems and who were
under the subversive influence of foreign powers that took every
possible advantage of the troubled waters.

In the Congress of Guatemala a bill was passed authorizing
the opening of a canal between the Atlantic and Pacific. In 1822

Dr. Valle proposed a Pan-American Union. These were tributes to the religion of progress, to the brotherhood of the American nations, which were paralyzed by war. President Morazán expelled the Archbishop of Guatemala and the fire-eating priests who were making it impossible for him to govern. Lands held in mortmain were ordered sold. War broke out. Morazán was killed in the fray. Two capitals were set up in Honduras: that of the Liberals in León, that of the Conservatives in Granada.

In 1822 slavery was abolished in Central America. The following year the British Parliament, not yet able to take so radical a step, approved a plan providing for gradual abolition; whereupon the plantation owners of Jamaica addressed the following petition to King George IV: "If this island is to be the scene of a dreadful experiment, we beg that we may not be involved in the awful consequences. If slavery be an offense to God, so are anarchy, desolation, and blood. Let your Royal Parliament become the lawful owner of our property by purchase, and we will retire from the island and leave it as a free field for modern philanthropy to work upon." The United States would within one generation be approaching its bloodiest war because of the "irrepressible conflict" between the slaveholders of the South, whose whole system was based on a slave economy, and the liberal, humanitarian businessmen and farmers of the North, in whose factories and fields hardly a Negro was to be found, and who could therefore, without prejudice to their own interests, champion the cause of freedom.

In New Orleans there lived an impetuous young journalist, a graduate in law and medicine, who believed that slavery was the natural destiny of the Negro and the legitimate enterprise of the white man. William Walker also believed that it was the "manifest destiny" of the United States to swallow up the lands of the Caribbean. Moreover, he had the soul of an adventurer and history would remember him as the last of the filibusters. When his wife died of yellow fever, Walker, to forget his sorrow, hurried from New Orleans to San Francisco, where, instead of yellow fever, he encountered the gold fever. After a period of working on a San Francisco newspaper, he joined two expeditions whose purpose was to invade the Mexican territories of Sonora and Lower California and then to request their admission to the United States, using the system that brought Texas into the Union. These attempts failed; Walker was tried as a filibuster, but was acquitted. His fame as a leader began to grow.

Walker quickly envisaged another field for his activities: Central America. It would be easy to take advantage of the unrest that dominated those little republics, to get a foothold there. There was keen interest in his project among North Americans, because important shipping interests were being developed in Panama and Nicaragua as a result of the migrations from the East to California. Commodore Cornelius Vanderbilt had secured a contract from President Chamorro to set up a passenger service on Lake Nicaragua. The ships from New York came to the port of San Juan del Norte, where Vanderbilt's boats were waiting to take the gold-seekers up the river and through Lake Nicaragua. On the shore of the lake there were buses to carry them to the Pacific port. It was a splendid business, and the region offered unlimited opportunities. People in California and New Orleans were of the opinion that it would be far better if this cross-country region were under the American flag rather than in the hands of its own stupid inhabitants. Walker offered to establish a colony in Nicaragua. With fifty-six settlers he arrived in León, where he took an active part in politics and war and became head of the army. Before the Central Americans knew what was happening, the filibuster Walker, who was now only thirty-one, had made himself dictator of Nicaragua. Costa Rica, Guatemala, and El Salvador opposed him, but he had control of Honduras.

At first Walker was satisfied with being the head of the army, and carried on the government with a puppet president, Don Patricio. Don Patricio sent Father Vigil as Minister to Washington, where he was received by President Franklin Pierce. But soon Walker deposed Don Patricio and had himself elected president of Honduras. Eight days after taking the oath of office, he was visited by the Minister of the United States, who told him: "I have instructions from the President of the United States to advise Your Excellency that my country has decided to enter upon relations with this State." In his memoirs Walker mentions the high opinion he formed of this American diplomat, who had seen the situation of the country clearly and had been empowered to act without the interference and delays that Father Vigil had encountered in Washington, where the representatives of other countries had deliberately created hostility against him.

Walker had assembled in Nicaragua a large number of North Americans, whom he had gradually been bringing in, especially from California, where his writings had aroused keen enthusiasm; and soon all the high offices in the country were held by bearers of Anglo-Saxon names. Walker was empowered to declare and make war. One Sunday he hanged Salazar, a man who had opposed him, in the public square in the midst of general rejoicing, taking advantage of the fact that, since it was market day, more people could enjoy the edifying sight.

Walker's principles of government were the faithful expression of his character: English was to be made an official language on the same footing as Spanish. All lands were to be under white ownership. "All acts and decrees of the Constitutional Federal Assembly are hereby declared null and void." But the cardinal issue was that of slavery. "The mad rhapsodies of Rousseau," he wrote, "the sharp, keen sarcasm of Voltaire, infected the readers of that time with a kind of hydrophobia — a mortal aversion to the word 'slavery.' Hamilton and Washington, though struggling against the French notions, were still under the influence of the Genevese ravings about equality and fraternity. Mr. Jefferson not only yielded to the French fashions of thought and feeling, but actually cherished them as if they were the fruits of reason and philosophy." NO — Walker was far smarter than those misguided men. He knew what slavery signified in the modern world, in the world of progress: "The conservatism of slavery is deeper than this," he wrote. "It goes to the vital relations of capital toward labor, and by the firm footing it gives the former it enables the intellect of society to push boldly forward in the pursuit of new forms of civilization."

Flushed with his success, Walker made the fatal mistake of confiscating Commodore Vanderbilt's holdings. The Commodore swore he would make an end to the filibuster. He joined forces with the English of Belize and backed the revolutionists of Costa Rica. War followed, and Walker found himself surrounded and cut off in Granada. He planned to set fire to the city, but instead he gave himself up and was brought back to the United States. In New Orleans and even in New York he was treated like a hero. Everybody showered attentions on him, and he had no difficulty preparing a second invasion of Nicaragua. But this time his successes were more ephemeral. He had to leave the country again and return to New Orleans, where he stood trial. This, however, only enhanced his prestige. He was hailed as the last filibuster. And he made a third try. This time he was defeated by the English in Belize, who handed him over to the authorities of Honduras, who executed him in 1860.

Walker's friends went about the United States making impassioned speeches of protest. There were columns in the papers extolling his memory. Henningsen, who had been his companion on these campaigns, published a letter in a New York paper, the *Day Book*, which ended: "Far from thinking that the enterprising spirit which moved William Walker has been buried in the tomb, I can prophesy with all assurance that another daring leader will spring from every drop of his blood. Ever since the news of Walker's death, as a result of English intervention, has become known, I have been flooded with letters from stouthearted men, willing and anxious to fly to the scene of the tragedy, and from others prepared to lend us financial support. I shall answer them all, telling them to wait, and that, when the day comes, the cause will not lack a leader."

XXII

MIRANDA, LIBERTY'S KNIGHT ERRANT

He is a Quixote, except that he is not mad.
NAPOLEON

IT WAS the month of January of 1787. In the coach of Prince Gregory Potemkin — the Empress Catherine's one-eyed favorite — the Venezuelan, Francisco de Miranda, was traveling toward the Crimea. The horses were galloping over the ice-bound surface of the Dnieper. The Prince turned to the Venezuelan to say: "I imagine this must be a new experience for you, Count. You probably cross the rivers of your country in a different fashion."

On the passport the Minister of Austria had issued to Miranda in Constantinople, he was referred to as a count. The Venezuelan had no documents from the Spanish government, which regarded him as an enemy. Shortly before, the Spanish ambassador in London had received instructions from the Count of Floridablanca to treat Miranda as a smuggler. Whichever he was, count or smuggler, there was something about this traveler that attracted Prince Potemkin. He was a fascinating companion, with his tales of his military exploits and his voyages, of the strange life of the unknown continent of America, of monk-ridden Spain where the Inquisition exercised a medieval dictatorship lighted up by its autos-da-fe. Miranda looked in amazement at the vast herds of sheep, cows, and horses on the snowy steppes, the bands of Tatars and Don Cossacks who came to pay servile homage to the Prince. They stopped at a monastery of dervishes. Never before had Miranda known cold and snow like this. The peasants warmed their insides with frequent libations of tea and vodka. One day, in a city where they halted, they went to a concert. Miranda was struck by the perfect discipline and timing of the musicians. How did they manage it? "That's the

374

way we make music here," he was informed, "with a cudgel." Prince Potemkin told him the history of the Crimean War; it was the history of his life.

Miranda was thirty-seven years old. He may even have been a count. He belonged to the family of the Dukes of Miranda who, through their connections with the Caraccioli, descended from the same line as Saint Thomas Aquinas. In view of his blue blood, on his arrival in Spain at the age of twenty-two, he was made captain in the Princess's Regiment. The description of his coat-of-arms runs: "A shield with field of gules displaying five unadorned maidens' torsos." His destiny, as foretold by his heraldic device, was to be war and adventures among unadorned maidens.

But the thing the Prince found most entertaining was the vagabond life this adventurer had led. He had not gone to Spain to display his fine figure in the Princess's Guard. He had come to get acquainted with the world and to fight. After conducting himself gallantly in an African campaign, he was sent to the American theater, to the Caribbean. He came to Cuba, and from Cuba was ordered to Louisiana where the governor, Bernardo Gálvez, was setting out from New Orleans to make war on the English. Miranda accompanied him, and was one of those who entered Pensacola to haul down the British flag and run up the Spanish. Miranda's star was in its ascendency. In Cuba the governor took a liking to him, appointed him lieutenant-colonel, and sent him on a special mission to Jamaica. As might have been expected, he aroused envy and rivalry. He was accused of being a smuggler, and one of those interminable Spanish trials was instituted against him. While the charges were being piled up in the sluggish chambers of justice, Miranda put the sea between him and his accusers. He went to the United States. With this began that chain of travels whose links had stretched ever farther until here he was on the steppes of the Crimea.

The impulse behind all the activities of Count Francisco de Miranda was his love of liberty. Chance had brought him to the court of Catherine of Russia, herself an ambitious, amazing adventuress who, setting out from her cradle in a tiny, rude German court, had, by luck and chance, come to be this wanton, liberal ruler who enlivened the court of the Czars of Russia, surrounding herself with artists, writers, and dashing officers, and establishing that enlightened despotism inspired by her passionate devotion to Voltaire's writings.

After leaving the service of Spain, Miranda had witnessed the birth of the republic in the United States. His diary, which he kept without interruption, is filled with vivid pen-pictures describing the rise of this new Anglo-Saxon nation where the simple delight of the masses in their new-found State was used and directed by the ambition of its great leaders. One day when Miranda was in New Bern, North Carolina, the people were informed with a ruffle of drums that hostilities with England had come to an end. Four cannon were fired, "and about one o'clock there was a barbecue — that is, pig roasted in a pit — and a barrel of rum. Everybody, bigwigs, country people, the dregs and offscourings of the town were shaking hands and drinking out of the same glass. It would be impossible to conceive of a more purely democratic assembly, and it bears out all that the Greek historians and poets tell us of similar gatherings among the free peoples of Greece. Toward the end, some were drunk, there were a number of fights, one man was wounded, and when night came everyone went off to his bed, and with this, and the burning of a few empty barrels as fireworks, the celebration came to an end."

Miranda went to Philadelphia. He arrived there as Washington passed through the city on his way to Annapolis to present his resignation as commander-in-chief of the army to Congress. The streets were lined with men, women, and children cheering the hero "as though the Saviour had entered Jerusalem." During the days Washington spent in Philadelphia, Miranda sat at the same table with him. Washington, fifty-one years old and at the peak of his glory, afforded the untried young Venezuelan, who was only twenty-three, the inspiring sight of a man who had led a nation to freedom.

The peals of the Liberty Bell of Philadelphia had roused a deep echo in the heart of Miranda. He was transformed into the knight errant of liberty. In Boston he outlined the first plans for the independence of Spanish America, and talked them over with North American generals. From America he proceeded to London, hoping to find support there. Then, as he wandered about Europe, he studied the political life of the various countries, planning the system of government that would be best for the Spanish colonies when he swept into them with the war that should set them free. His was an ardent, questing youth, and, like his coat-of-arms, it was emblazoned with amorous adventures. In every city there was some woman who caught his admiration and for a brief pause held it, as did the cathedrals and the museums: moments devoted to passing pleasures. But his true love was his love of liberty. He belonged to an army of liberators that existed only in his imagination, and he was impatient for the hour of combat to strike. In the pursuit of his dream he had arrived in Russia.

Turning to Count Miranda, Prince Potemkin observed: "My dear Count, it would not look well for you to leave Russia without paying your respects to the Empress." So Miranda started for Kiev, where the court was. He left Kherson in a swift *kibitka* toward the heart of Russia, and toward the heart of Catherine. Forest, frozen rivers, villages whirled past him, until finally, from a height fifteen versts away, he could see the city with its gilded, onion-shaped church domes.

The Empress received the Venezuelan graciously and listened to his tales. It filled her with pride to see how superior she was to the reactionary Spanish monarchs. The somber despotism of the Inquisition made the favor accorded French letters at her court stand out by contrast. The jealous courtiers fawned upon Miranda because of the interest Catherine showed in his adventures. He was a living representation of two hemispheres, and always, in the background, was the new, unfamiliar world. Catherine affectionately pressed him not to leave because the weather was bad and the trip might be dangerous. She invited him to stay on in Russia as an officer of the army. She introduced him to the King of Poland. She saw that he was invited to all court gatherings. He was a guest at her table. Catherine was mature, experienced, intelligent, cultivated, licentious, and bold. Miranda was thirty-one at the time; Catherine, fifty-eight — old enough to be his mother. But the real object of his youthful ardor was the glory of becoming the liberator of America, and he departed from Russia. Catherine's letter and money smoothed his path in Sweden, Norway, Denmark, Prussia. He traveled under assumed names, since the Spanish ambassadors were pursuing him wherever he went; but in every country the Empress's protection spread its wings over him. He talked with kings, and explained to them what they should do for their countries' progress. He was on close terms with the different Masonic lodges. He kept himself in touch with what was taking place in America. The *comuneros* had made their bid for independence. . . .

In England Miranda sought an audience with the Prime Minister, William Pitt the Younger. Pitt received him at his country estate, and with him discussed the problem of Spanish American independence. Miranda explained his military and political plans. An independent empire was to be declared that should extend from the Straits of Magellan to Parallel 45 in North America, with the Mississippi as boundary between the United States and the new nation. Havana would still be the key to the Gulf of Mexico, and a canal would be dug through Panama to facilitate trade with China. A descendant of the Incas would be made emperor, and there would be a parliamentary system modeled after that of England, with a House of Commons elected by the people, and an upper house of native chieftains.

Pitt did nothing, and Miranda's plans got mislaid. Meanwhile, the French Revolution broke out on the other side of the Channel. Louis XVI was taken prisoner. Prussia declared war on France. The bourgeoisie was prepared to defend its triumphs to the death. It was an ideal situation for Miranda who might perhaps — since England seemed not to be going to take action in his behalf — be able to fish out of the troubled waters the aid he was seeking for the independence of America. Crossing the Channel, he was made a general in the French army and, under Dumouriez, served in the campaign of the North against the Prussians, witnessing their defeat at Valmy in August 1792. He laid siege to Antwerp, captured it, and, during Dumouriez's absence, acted as commander-in-chief of the French armies. One day he decided to confide to him his campaign for the Antilles, which was to begin with the reconquest of Santo Domingo; from this as a springboard, he would launch a drive on the other Spanish colonies and break once and for all "the chains forged by Cortés and Pizarro." Miranda was now a political celebrity, but he was already skirting the abyss of misfortune. In that swing of the pendulum which from now on was to keep him steadily oscillating between triumph and defeat, he was often to find that just as he thought himself on the verge of complete triumph, he would find himself in prison instead. Dumouriez, who finally turned traitor to the Republic, had planned his new campaign in the North badly. At the battle of Neerwinden, Miranda was forced to retire; he was arrested and tried before a revolutionary tribunal in Paris.

Miranda's trial aroused great excitement among the people, the intellectuals, and the poets. Haughty, unshaken, self-possessed, the Venezuelan confounded his accusers and made a memorable speech such as was highly esteemed in the Paris of the Revolution. The court absolved him, the people acclaimed and embraced him, and he was borne in triumph to his home. A few days later the Girondists fell and the "Mountain" came into power. Robespierre — the man of the hour — was no friend of Miranda's, and the Committee of Public Safety sentenced him to prison once more. He would have been shot, as were a number of his comrades, if Robespierre's death had not opened the prison doors for him.

Miranda's stay in France covered the tempestuous years from the stupid reign of Louis XVI through the chaotic triumph of the Revolution, the struggles of the Directory, and the warmongering of the First Consul. At one time he even dreamed, in view of his achievements, of becoming one of the consuls of

France. He visited the most fashionable salons, he corresponded with Mme. de Staël. Napoleon called him a Quixote without the madness of Cervantes's hero. The Directory ordered him imprisoned. He fled to England, disguised in a white wig and green glasses, and using the name of M. Mirandov. There he visited Pitt again at his country estate, and resumed his activities on behalf of the independence of America. Behind him, in Paris, he had left the memory of his love-affair with the wanton Delphine, Marquise de Custine, whose caresses had intoxicated Chateaubriand, Fouché, Alexander de Beauharnais. . . . One day France would engrave Miranda's name on the Arc de Triomphe in Paris.

It was the winter of 1805 in New York, the season when Santa Claus prepares for his annual trip down the chimney, and the children dream of the "sleighful of toys and eight tiny reindeer." Don Francisco Miranda and a Mr. Ogden had fitted out a mystery ship, the *Leander*, that would have made a pirate's mouth water. It carried over five hundred rifles, shotguns, and carbines, nineteen cannon, machetes, six thousand, five hundred rounds of ammunition, ten thousand flints, five tons of lead — only Mr. Ogden and Don Francisco knew all its contents. But the stevedores who carried the heavy cases aboard had their suspicions, and in the waterfront taverns there was much speculation. Where was the *Leander* bound for?

The snows of January were melting. The February days were getting longer. Spring would soon set the buds burgeoning. The sun was warming men's hearts and arms. Mr. Ogden and his associates went about quietly, inviting all who looked as though they might have a taste for adventure to sign on the *Leander*. The men who go down to the sea gave their fancy free rein; some said they were wanted to act as "the President's guard"; others said they were going to look for gold; most or all of them wondered whether it might be a filibuster raid. Which of them, from childhood, had not dreamed of becoming a filibuster? In 1806, New York was a city of nearly eighty thousand people, and its port seethed with ambition.

When the Leander weighed anchor and set sail, the two hundred Americans who had signed on still had no idea of their destination. The mystery was soon to be cleared up, for General Miranda, who could usually be seen on deck, seemed to be in command, and began to give a hint of his plans. The cases of guns were opened and the men put to polishing them. The ship's carpenters built racks for the lances. Those who had had military experience were appointed sergeants to train the others in the tactics of warfare. They were organized into companies. Miranda had invented a name: Colombia. He had devised a flag, the flag of Colombia — red, blue, yellow — which was flown from the main mast. For the first time the winds of America, the warm breeze of the Caribbean caressed this sacred symbol that fluttered like a flame, like a heart in the center of the blue firmament above the restless sea of the Americas. It was saluted by two hundred soldiers — likewise invented by Miranda — recruited out of the taverns, the tailor shops, the factories of New York. A ruffle of delight echoed in the martial breast of the Venezuelan as, dressed in full uniform, he reviewed them. Along with the spears and swords, Miranda had brought a printing press, and while still aboard the ship he began to issue proclamations. He had learned from Napoleon that literature was an outstanding weapon of war. The Caribbean, once the sea of slavery, was now to be the new sea of liberty.

As a consequence of his association with so many crowned heads, after having broken bread with so many of the great, Miranda believed himself in a position to organize a European coalition against Spain. And he was successful until he laid before them his idea of making America independent. At that point they all became dubious, hesitant, reluctant. At bottom, none of them were interested in those savage lands of South America. For that reason he quarreled with the French, for that reason ceased his negotiations with Pitt. Even Jefferson, who had just purchased the Louisiana Territory, who sensed the growing international importance of the United States, was not looking for trouble with Spain. When Miranda sailed aboard the Lean-

der, Jefferson wrote a letter to Franklin's newspaper denying that he had given the conspirator any encouragement. Since nobody was willing to give him official support, Miranda had made up his mind that he would have to employ filibuster methods. And so he set out, and here he was, with his two hundred adventurers, on his way to liberate Venezuela. In Santo Domingo he got hold of two more little boats. With these three craft Miranda, the veteran of European wars, the general who with his armies had defeated the best that Germany could put in the field, was on his way to challenge what had been the greatest empire in the world, to dispute its right to govern the colonies it had held for three centuries. This seemed a piece of reckless daring, more fitting a young revolutionary apprentice than a seasoned warrior.

Above the rim of the horizon the ridges of the hills, the profile of his native land, hidden from his eyes for more than thirty years, began to loom up. The flagship displayed, as its battle flag, a white waning moon, and a ruddy sun rising against a blue background; and, in addition, a scarlet pennant bearing the device: "Down with tyranny. Long live liberty."

This time Miranda's dream went up in smoke. The *Leander* had barely got under weigh when an account of the adventure was published throughout the United States. But while some newspapers were acclaiming it as the blessed liberation of the Continent, and handkerchiefs were being sold bearing pictures of Washington and Miranda and the motto "Dawn in South America," the Spanish Minister in Washington, the Marquis of Casa Yrujo, hurriedly sent word to Caracas, Mexico, and Havana to prepare their defenses. When Miranda reached the coastal waters of his native land, the coastguards were waiting for him with loaded cannon, and he had to withdraw. He then landed at Vela del Coro, and after a brief fight overpowered the Spanish garrison and raised his flag. But an army of fifteen hundred Spanish troops was bearing down upon him. With a force of this size, it was not hard to drive out Miranda's handful of filibusters, who spoke only English and had been unable to make contact with the common folk of the region, in whom Miranda had placed his hopes. Miranda was obliged to sail away past the islands, leaving behind him in Venezuela dashed hopes, bewilderment, and his printing press.

Pitt had died, and Miranda returned to London to make another try. He had heated discussions with Sir Arthur Wellesley — the future Duke of Wellington — because England was unwilling to adopt his plan of making war on Spain in America. Meanwhile, the colonies were flooded with copies of *Portrait and Biography of the Traitor Miranda*, and he was burned in effigy in Caracas along with his flag. The kindest terms applied to him were traitor and thief. . . .

Spain's sun was setting. Not the Spain of the people, which, with all the odds against it, had put Napoleon's armies to flight, but the royal Spain, upon whose abject remains the Caesar of France, and even his light-hearted brother, Joseph Bonaparte — whose weakness for liquor had won him the sobriquet of "Pepe Bottles" in Madrid — could proudly strut. Salvador de Madariaga sums up the state of affairs in these words: "Charles IV, because of his imbecility, and Ferdinand VII, because of his cruelty and lack of principle, dishonored the crown when they identified it with their unworthy heads." The storm was brewing in America. The official government organizations proclaimed their loyalty to Ferdinand VII, because he stood as a symbol against Napoleon's ambitions; but, under the surface, Miranda's idea, the old hope of the *comuneros* — independence — was stirring. In the Assembly of Bayonne, Francisco Antonio Zea, the restless New Granadan who was representing Guatemala, emphasized and called attention to the statement of the French Assembly that it would not oppose the independence of the Spanish colonies because it considered it something in the natural order of events. Quito, Mexico, Caracas, Bogotá, Buenos Aires . . . every city of America was a powder keg waiting for the match. Miranda's house in Grafton Street, London, was the meeting place for all the friends of the revolution, conspirators from all parts of Spanish America scurrying about England,

France, Spain visiting the lodges, securing arms. Miranda published a paper, *El Colombiano*. Through his friend Lady Townsend he became acquainted with the Duke of Cumberland and the political leaders of England; he discussed the problems of America with Jeremy Bentham. He received the delegates of Caracas who had come to seek the support of England: López Méndez, Andrés Bello, Simón Bolívar.

Miranda was sixty years old now, Bolívar, twenty-seven. Bolívar viewed the future with the optimism, the faith, the enthusiasm of youth. The painter Gill has left us a portrait of him at this time — not a wrinkle on his brow, his great dark eyes eagerly open, his thick hair waving like a conqueror's black banner, on his full lips the satisfied smile of one who has discovered his true path in life, and on his proud shoulders the elegant cape with its clasp of gold. Miranda's hair was white, and life had stamped his energetic military profile with a fixity of purpose that left no room for smiles. His Don Juan youth had been succeeded by a quiet austerity of habits. Bolívar took passage in the *Sapphire*, and a world in the making, a new page of history, a glory that was just beginning, all of which he carried with him, like his luggage, smiled upon him. A few months later Miranda sailed on the *Avon*. He had with him papers, memoirs, a history that was coming to a close, a life that was near conclusion, a glory that had evaded the grasp of the old dreamer.

The cavalcade reached the city of Caracas. Many of its citizens had traveled to the port of La Guayra to meet Miranda, among them young Simón Bolívar, all eager to clasp the hand of their fellow-countryman whose dramatic career had had five continents as its stage. The crowd pushed closer to see this legendary figure. Who could tell what diabolical ideas this soldier of the French Revolution might have in his head, the leading citizens of the city fretfully wondered. And Miranda, reining in his white horse that pranced along over the cobblestones of the street, looked out over the crowd, the multitude who hailed him as a savior, as the Washington of Spanish America. Perhaps he was recalling the day when Philadelphia had seemed the New Jerusalem. How beautiful the streets of Caracas, all sun and democracy, looked to the revolutionary who had spent a winter in the snowy thoroughfares of New York, seeking the help of the filibusters, who had spent years in fog-shrouded London, fruitlessly attempting to reach an understanding with the cautious, circumspect gentlemen of the City. Miranda went to stay in the home of young Simón Bolívar.

The nation did not, however, put its destiny unconditionally into Miranda's hands. The leading citizens still had their doubts, and the ambition of younger men, anxious to make a name for themselves, was a factor. He barely won a seat in the Congress that was to meet, representing San Juan Bautista de Pao, a settlement in the torrid, remote savannas where the people — rude herders — knew nothing outside their mares, mules, and cattle, and earned their living making cheese. Caracas had not put forward his candidacy. The Congress appointed a triumvirate to govern the country, and Miranda was not included in it; he received only eight votes. But he had his place in this assembly, he made speeches in favor of immediate independence; he was eloquent, and people listened to him. He was appointed one of the commission to design a national flag, and he proposed the three colors — yellow, blue and red — which the members adopted as the country's emblem. Five years before, in the public square of Caracas, the Spanish authorities had burned these colors, his colors. . . .

And when war broke out, it was Miranda who marched at the head of the troops. It was an army not of soldiers but of the people. These were not the trained, seasoned troops with whom he had fought the Germans in Belgium, nor the superb regiments Catherine of Russia had offered him to command; these were herders of the plains, country people, workmen of Caracas. And they met defeat. Bolívar was entrusted with the defense of the stronghold of Puerto Cabello, and he lost it through the treachery of Vinoni. "How can I take up my pen to write you, after losing Puerto Cabello which was put in my hands?" he wrote Miranda. Miranda realized that, for the moment, the war was lost. His experienced eye took in at a glance the full scope of the defeat. He was in his room with four friends when the news of the disaster was brought to him. Pedro Gual came in just then, and seeing them sitting there, silent, bowed, he asked: "What has happened? Good God, what is the matter?" And Miranda, holding out the message, answered: "Venezuela has received a mortal wound!"

An armistice was signed. The patriots evaporated like the dew. The Spaniards grew more overbearing. But if Monteverde, the Spanish commander, kept his word, everything was not lost. In La Guayra, Miranda was preparing to take flight. He would have to seek refuge in the Antilles, in Europe perhaps, waiting for time to deal a new hand. *Paciencia, y barajar.* This was, and would be for several years, the patriots' only possible solution. But in the streets of the port groups of hot-headed, turbulent young men had gathered, muttering that Monteverde would not abide by the terms of the armistice, and that the fault — as always — was Miranda's, that he had been a fool to sign the pact. The most vehement of all was Bolívar. "Let's turn Miranda over to the Spaniards. Don't let him get away."

At three o'clock in the morning there was a knocking at Miranda's door. He got up, opened the door, and was confronted by this group of excited young men, headed by Bolívar, threatening him with arrest. Wearily, without emotion or resistance, Miranda gave himself up, saying as he did so: "Tumults, riots, that's all these people know. . . ."

They handed him over to the Spanish authorities. Before the day had dawned the old man was being led through the streets of La Guayra under the rude insolence of the Spanish soldiery. He was first imprisoned in the fortress of San Carlos, and later put into a cell that had been designed for the punishment of highwaymen, where the water came up to his ankles. He was chained there, and kept on bread and water. But the sight that met Miranda's eyes from his cell window was worse than the prison itself: once more the Spanish flag was fluttering in the breeze, and men were being herded in droves — "the most illustrious and distinguished in station and achievements treated like outlaws, and immured, like myself, in those horrible dungeons."

Six months in the prison of La Guayra. Then six more months in the underground chambers — a living grave — of the fortress of San Felipe in Puerto Cabello, that same fortress where the war was lost when Vinoni betrayed Bolívar and Miranda. Then another six months in the dungeon of the Morro fortress in Puerto Rico, and from there to the Carraca of Cádiz.

In Venezuela, and throughout America, war, that prodigious war of Bolívar's had been resumed, and there had been victories and reverses. Miranda had been in the Carraca for two years when he heard the news that was circulating in the port of Cádiz: over ten thousand troops, fully armed and equipped, were embarking, under the command of General Morillo, to undertake the reconquest of America. Caracas and Santa Marta fell quickly. The patriots in Cartagena withstood a siege of three months, and when Morillo entered the heroic city he found that a third of its inhabitants had perished of hunger. He ordered those leaders who were still living to be shot. He advanced upon Bogotá. Whole households — ailing women, rheumatic old men, infants in arms — left the city in headlong flight, crossing the cold uplands to seek refuge in the hot, remote plains. It was there that Santander and Páez organized their armies of plainsmen and refugees which would in time become the instruments of republican victory. Bolívar took refuge in Jamaica, where he wrote that immortal letter of his.

Time went by, and Bolívar left Jamaica for Haiti. There the Negro Pétion extended a hand to him and offered him help for his plan to undertake the war again in Venezuela. This was little more than a dream, a hope, for Morillo was stronger than ever in the reconquered colonies, and was engaged in signing the death sentences of patriots and in banishing women whose sons or husbands had been in the revolutionary armies. Miranda was dying. He had spent three and a half years in the prison of Cádiz.

It was the 14th of July, 1816, the anniversary of the storming of the Bastille. Pedro José Morán, who had attended Miranda like a faithful dog, wrote this letter to his employers in Cádiz that same day: "This morning, at five minutes past one, my beloved Don Francisco de Miranda yielded up his soul to its Maker. The priests and friars have not allowed me to hold any funeral rites for him, and just as he died, with mattress, sheets, and the rest of the bedclothes, they snatched him up, carried him away, and buried him. Then they returned and took all his clothing and everything that belonged to him to burn it. As soon as I could I have sent you word, and I should like you to tell me what I must do with certain papers that he guarded carefully. . . ."

XXIII

SIMÓN BOLÍVAR'S SEA

The freedom of the New World is the hope of the Universe.
BOLÍVAR

January 19, 1799. A hot wind, redolent of salt, bellied the sails of the *San Ildefonso*, making ready to leave the port of La Guayra. The anchor had been hauled in, the moorings loosed in obedience to the booming order of the captain and the oaths of the sailors. As the ship creaked into motion the frequenters of the waterfront — whites, mulattoes, Negroes — watched from the shore, hardly breathing, following the operation with emotion rather than mere curiosity. Ebony boatmen rowed about the departing ship in their skiffs, canoes, or dugouts.

The *San Ildefonso* was bound for Spain, but January, March, April would go by before it reached the other side of the pond. First it would dawdle about the Caribbean. Its first port of call was Vera Cruz. This pleased the curiosity of the seventeen-year-old passenger who was making his first ocean voyage. His heart beat faster at the thought of the adventures in store for him. The wide world was about to reveal its secrets to him. The boy was rich and handsome but he could barely read and write; Simón Rodríguez, his teacher, following Rousseau's precepts, had brought him up like a savage, climbing mountains, swimming rivers, galloping over the savannas like a centaur. Two years before, he had enlisted in the white battalion of Aragua valley; his finely modeled bronzed face and the bright colors of his uniform had made a great impression on his cousins, the Aristigueta girls. His city residence, his gold mines, his cacao plantation, his stock ranch, the sugar mill of San Mateo gave him an outstanding position among the Creoles of Caracas. Now what might this ocean trip hold in store for him? And what was Simón Bolívar, Simon-

389

cito, thinking of as he stood there on the deck? Of his pretty cousins? Of his possessions and slaves? Of that eccentric, Simón Rodríguez, who when the boy was only fourteen was already expounding to him the most advanced philosophical ideas, and who now was wandering in exile in North America or France for his conspiratorial activities?

The three masts of the *San Ildefonso* rose and fell against the blue of the horizon, amidst the flight of circling gulls. Life aboardship moved as slowly as the shadow across the face of a sun dial. Two weeks elapsed before the coast of Mexico, Vera Cruz, hove into sight. The ship was to make a long stop there. The lad could hardly wait to go ashore and stretch his legs. He hired a horse and made the 270-mile trip from the port to Mexico City as though he were just setting out on a short canter about his own acres. He made the acquaintance of the archbishop and the viceroy, and saw for the first time the splendor of the viceregal court. He spent February and March there, and then returned to Vera Cruz where the *San Ildefonso* was ready to set out again. It stopped for two days in Havana and then set its course for Spain. The ship would enter Spain through a Basque port, that region from which Bolívar's forebears had originally come. They cast anchor in the bay of Santoña and then proceeded up the roadstead of the Nervion to Bilbao. Only a few hours' trip from Bilbao was the village of Bolívar, and the manor house of the Bolívar Jáureguis. This carefree, favored youth now stood upon the continent of the despotic kings and the liberal philosophers that Simón Rodríguez had talked so much about.

July 1802. The people of La Guayra were hurrying down the narrow streets, like ladders of stone, that led to the harbor. The *San Ildefonso* had arrived. It was three and a half years since it had left, carrying Simón Bolívar the boy, and now it was bringing him back, a man, with his bride, María Teresa Toro, the niece of the Marquis of Toro. Simón pointed out to María Teresa the initial profile of his native land: there was the shrine of El Carmen, the belfry of San Juan de Dios, the tower of El

Guamacho encircled by a balcony at the top. And at the very tip of the hill, the Vigía fortress.

This glimpse of his native land was enough to efface from Bolívar's mind the memories of his stay in Europe, where he had really learned to read and had become a fine dancer. The ocean now lay between him and the house of his uncle Esteban Palacios, the man who drew aside the curtain and revealed to him the shamelessness and pettiness of the court, presided over by that licentious Queen María Luisa, toothless but still appetizingly plump, old enough to know better, who "was willing to compromise a kingdom for the sake of favoring her lover," and who was carrying on simultaneous love affairs with the captain of the guard, the Venezuelan Manuel Mallo, and Godoy, the prime minister. There flashed through his mind the recollection of the ambush Godoy had laid for him the day the guard halted in Madrid, in the belief that Bolívar was carrying a message from the Queen for Mallo, and of how he had had to defend himself at the point of his sword. All this, and the image of Napoleon whom he had seen acclaimed by the populace of Paris as the savior of the republic, and of his friend, the Marquis of Estariz, who had introduced him to the French writers — all this no longer meant anything to him. Here was his Venezuela where he intended to pass the happy hours of his honeymoon.

And this was La Guayra, noisy, restless, liberal, surly. It was here that the seeds of the French Revolution brought in by the ships of the Guipuzcoana Company had fallen and borne fruit. Here, five years before, José María España and Manuel Gual had plotted their war of independence. Here, three months after Bolívar sailed for Europe, José María España had fallen into the hands of the Spaniards. In the main square of Caracas they had quartered him, cut off his head, and sent it in a cage as a present to La Guayra.

Simón and María Teresa's cavalcade moved forward to the accompaniment of the congratulations of friends and the cheering of slaves. There was the house of España, the martyr, where the conspirators had foregathered, and where the shocked Spanish officials had found a hundred forbidden books, in French, English, and even Spanish. There was the room where the rebels had taken the oath, had sworn to die, if need be, for the justice of their cause, where the instructions for the rebellion had been drawn up, where they had decided to publish *The Rights of Man* and distribute it throughout the country, where the watchword for the uprising had been given: "Long live the American people!" The slaves were to be freed, and whites and Indians, mulattoes and blacks would all be declared equal. The hateful taxes were to be abolished, a government would be set up, they would have a flag of their own. . . .

As Simón and María Teresa proceeded gaily on their way, all this somber episode was drowned out by the ring of the horses' hoofs on the cobblestones and the noisy merriment of the muleteers. María Teresa barely caught a glimpse of the shriveled skull of José María España in its cage.

June 1803. Once more Simón Bolívar was in the port of La Guayra, once more en route for Europe. He had chartered a boat. Tragedy had spread its dark wing over his brow, had brought his youth to maturity. His brief honeymoon had ended in sorrow, in the horror of that night when the slaves, by flickering torchlight, had borne María Teresa, dying, down from San Mateo, in the nightmare of the day they carried her to her final rest. For the first time the shadow of his destiny could be seen on Simón Bolívar's face. His companions on board ship were the works of Plutarch, Montesquieu, and Rousseau, and a cargo of cacao, indigo, and sugar which would open the routes of the world to him. In true romantic fashion, he was on his way to drown his grief in the vortex of European life.

February 1807. The port of Charleston, South Carolina, on the Atlantic coast of the United States. Aboard the little freighter bound for La Guayra came a man worn out by the frenzied life of Paris. It was Simón Bolívar, who had scattered the gold of his cacao and indigo about the gayest spots of France in search of pleasure. Broken in health, he had been torn away from this life by his old teacher Don Simón Rodríguez, who had taken him on a walking tour through the mountains of Switzerland. Bolívar's purse was light as a result of his gambling proclivities. Walking, walking, they finally reached Italy. Rodríguez had been reciting pages of Rousseau to him. They had talked of liberty. Standing on the Aventine and looking down on the city of Rome, Bolívar took his famous oath: "I swear to free America from the Spaniards." And instead of returning to the Opéra of Paris, to the drawing-rooms, to his love trysts, he spent his time among the Masons, and in contact with the Americans who were plotting. Fanny de Villars, try as she would, could not hold him. He went to Hamburg, and took ship for America. In the United States he visited Philadelphia and Washington, the shrines of independence of that new country. In Boston and New York he heard of the exploits of Miranda, the forerunner.

When he set out for home again his eyes gleamed with the light of a fixed purpose. He had been through the Valley of the Shadow. The ship rounded the Florida keys, sailed past the West Indies, and came in sight of La Guayra. There flashed through Bolívar's mind, as though an electric switch had been suddenly turned on, the recollection of his cousin, José Félix Ribas, that veteran conspirator who attended the secret meetings in Paris wearing the red Cap of Liberty.

June 9, 1810. America was a different place. It seemed a new world. Admiral Cochrane, the governor of Jamaica, had placed a warship at the disposal of the patriot Junta of Caracas, which had seized the government, so it could send delegates to London. And there came aboard the *General Lord Wellington*, here in La Guayra, Simón Bolívar, "Colonel and delegate in chief," López Méndez, vice delegate, and Andrés Bello, secretary of the commission. How had this come about?

In the homes of the Creoles of Caracas, and especially in that of Cousin José Félix Ribas, the friends of freedom gathered to hold secret meetings. As in the days of the *comuneros*, of José María España, of Miranda, the talk was of independence. Any day now there would be a demand for a public assembly. This was revolution. A Chilean priest, Canon Cortés Madariaga, had pronounced a fiery speech urging the seizure of the government. Emparán, the Spanish commissioner, was swept from office by the Junta of patriots. In the market place and streets of Caracas a new ruler was installed: the people. The people made laws, gave orders, carried them out. War was certain to follow, and for this arms and money would be needed. The Creoles turned their eyes toward Washington, visited the English islands of the Antilles. It was then that Cochrane, from Jamaica, suggested that aid might be forthcoming from London. And Bolívar, who had traveled and was rich enough to pay the expenses of the trip, and had the air and bearing the cause needed, was selected to head the mission. The country air of San Mateo had restored his youthful vigor.

December 5, 1810. Not six months had elapsed, and Bolívar was back in La Guayra once more. He had arrived on the *Avon,* an English brigantine. In a few days Miranda, the intellectual father of the revolution, would follow on the *Sapphire.* Bolívar had made his acquaintance in London, at his home in Grafton Street, which was the center to which all the American rebels gravitated to plan their revolutionary undertakings. Miranda introduced Bolívar to the London salons and took him to the studio of Gill, Sir Joshua Reynolds's pupil, who in his portrait of Bolívar painted a medallion on his breast bearing the inscription *Sin libertad no hay patria.* These words, inscribed upon Bolívar's heart, spelled his destiny. He would be the Liberator. He had not been able to secure actual aid in London, but he knew that England would view with satisfaction a war of independence that would destroy the power of Spain in America. He had dragged old Miranda away from London, persuading him to come back and lead the patriot armies. This time as he gazed out on the Caribbean it glistened with the promise of a new light, the war for freedom.

August 27, 1812. This time it was not the gallant man-of-war *General Lord Wellington,* in which he had crossed the Atlantic, nor the graceful *Avon* on which he had taken passage in La Guayra, whose slender keel seemed to be cutting the pathway for his dreams. It was the schooner *Jesús, María y José,* piloted by divine mercy. Seated upon coils of rope Simón Bolívar and his cousin José Félix Ribas were engaged in a wordless dialogue. They were on their way to Curaçao. They were castaways, victims of Miranda's war. Bolívar had lost Puerto Cabello, and with it the war, and the first republic of Venezuela had gone down to failure. The Spaniard, Monteverde, after signing terms of surrender with the patriots, had broken his word and unleashed a campaign of savage reprisals. The prisons of La Guayra were overflowing with white patriots chained to Negroes, thus giving them the opportunity to put into practice, in the ironical gloom of the dungeons, the equality they had preached. Bolívar had gone through the stormiest days of his life. After writing Miranda a letter in which he upbraided himself bitterly for the loss of Puerto Cabello, he had been instrumental in handing over to the Spaniards the first leader in the movement for independence, accusing him of having betrayed the cause. Now he was fleeing Venezuela, with a passport issued by the Spanish commander because he did not consider Bolívar important enough to hold. Bolívar reached Curaçao with ten thousand pesos, which the authorities of the island promptly confiscated. Defeated, all his property in Venezuela impounded by the Spaniards, he had to begin life anew from scratch. He had turned over in his mind desperate solutions — among them, going to Spain to fight alongside Sir Arthur Wellesley against Napoleon.

November 1812. He had been in Curaçao barely two months, and he was embarking again on a brigantine he had chartered with money raised by selling the last of his possessions, a handful of jewels. He was accompanied by José Félix Ribas, and they were on their way to Cartagena. New Granada, too, had raised the standard of independence. The towns were in a state of revolt; the municipal councils had become cores of rebellion, and Cartagena, with its walls of stone, blood, and sun, was in the hands of the patriots. When Bolívar came ashore he said: "Gentlemen, in me you see a son of unhappy Caracas, who miraculously managed to escape from the physical and political defeat of our hopes. I have ever remained loyal to the system of liberty and justice proclaimed by my country, and I have come here to follow the standards of independence that have spread themselves over these states."

The commander of Cartagena assigned him a number of troops. Bolívar was nobody when he reached this city; among its stones he began his meteoric rise to Liberator of America. Embarking these troops in sampans, he ascended the Magdalena River, fell upon the Spanish outposts, thus winning the route that led to the interior of New Granada, and joining the two centers of the Independence — Cartagena, the port, and Bogotá, the capital. His army was a handful of "half-breeds from the dregs of the nation, ruined farmers, or half-savage Indians who volunteered to serve under the discredited banner of the revolution. They were troops without discipline and almost without equipment, barefoot, their only clothing a pair of patched pants, a square of tattered blanket with a hole in the middle for the head, and a broad-brimmed, frayed hat." With these forces he attacked and took by surprise Tenerife, and then Mompox, cleared the mouth of the Magdalena, scaled the peaks of the Andes, driving on through torrid jungles and icy uplands, and descended upon Venezuela. He fought a war to the death, asking and giving no quarter; prisoners were shot or stoned to death, and not even the wounded were spared. With his sword dyed to the hilt in vengeance, he entered Caracas in triumph. The city showered flowers upon his victorious shoulders; the slaves kissed his feet. The Liberator had been born!

September 8, 1814. On board the Italian corsair Bianchi's schooner, the *Arrogante*, fleeing Venezuela once more. No more the conqueror, but Bolívar, the defeated. He was thirty-one years old, and his biographers say he looked forty. In less than two years, from the time he began his breath-taking campaign from Cartagena to Caracas, his fame had sunk from the pinnacle of glory to the abyss of misfortune. His war to the death had been unable to check the barbarous hordes of Boves, whose gruesome fame was to become legendary. Boves was an insignificant Spanish storekeeper of Calabozo, on the plains, who over night became the leader of the Royalist reactionary forces. With his Indian horsemen, who adorned their hats with the ears of their victims, he disputed every one of Bolívar's conquests, until finally not a thing was left the patriots, from the city of Caracas to the humblest village. It is doubtful that history has ever recorded a bloodier struggle. Of Caracas Province's 421,000 inhabitants, 228,651 perished. Bolívar had to leave Caracas, followed by the multitude which fled en masse to the plains — the weak and ill, women with their infants in arms, old men with their white beards — leaving the deserted streets to the will of Boves, the Tiger of the Plains. At Bolívar's ranch, San Mateo, Ricuarte blew up the ammunition stored there in order to hold off with this explosion (in which he himself was killed) the moving hurricane of Boves's red lances. With the defeat of La Puerta and Aragua, Bolívar was completely removed from the theater of war. His own cousin, José Félix Ribas, seized the command, expelled him from the army, accused him of being a thief. Boves — "Pappy" Boves, as the plainsmen called him — died of wounds in battle, but his savage followers avenged his death by cutting off José Félix Ribas's head, frying it in oil, and then putting it on display in Caracas.

This was the situation Bolívar left behind him. But as his faith was unwavering, the *Arrogante* set its sails for Cartagena. The second war and the second republic had been lost in Venezuela; but there was New Granada, where he could once more come back and triumph.

September 6, 1815. This was the city of Kingston in Jamaica. Bolívar had just finished a letter to "a gentleman of the island." Just as Columbus, on this same island, had written the most pathetic of his documents, and had plumbed the depths of misfortune to leave one of the most movingly tragic pages on record, so Bolívar here had just finished the wisest, most far-seeing communication he ever wrote. He talked like the head of a nation, or a dreamer, evaluating the future possibilities of America, prophesying its independence, and outlining the elements of anarchy that would imperil its existence. But his point of departure in analyzing all these factors was the despair of his third defeat. It was a defeat without combats. He who had been the rich Creole of Venezuela, the lion of the Paris salons, the handsome paladin of liberty painted by Gill in London, was now a poor devil, without a cent to his name, talking of suicide, borrowing a hundred dollars from Mr. Hyslop to pay the laundress, the printer, the Frenchwoman in whose boarding-house he was lodged like a common sailor. In New Granada, Bolívar had been unable to make a stand against the Spanish armies. "Providence," he said, "has ordained the ruin of these unfortunate countries." The master of Caracas, who was now laying siege to Cartagena, was no self-appointed guerrilla leader, like Boves, but General Morillo, one of Spain's great generals, who commanded an army of veterans that had defeated Napoleon, and with a will to power that fastened the noose around the throat of every upholder of liberty who fell into his hands.

Bolívar became a journalist, wrote for the *Royal Gazette*, drew up letters, petitions, seeking aid for the cause of independence. "We have no other weapons with which to oppose the enemy," he wrote "than our arms, our breasts, our horses, our lances; the weak need a long struggle to win; the strong can destroy an empire with one battle, as at Waterloo." In his prophetic message, he rose, as he always did in his political writings, above the problems small and large of his own life, and spoke not merely as the leader he had been of the armies of Venezuela and New Granada, but as a man who foresaw his own greatness and failures, who knew what the future of his America would be, and who was drawing up the stark, unvarnished balance of that contradictory, anarchic, dissimilar world, attacking the myth of its unity, which could only be a hope for the distant future.

"The American colonies now fighting for their emancipation will, in the end, be successful; some will constitute themselves into federated or centralized republics; monarchies will almost inevitably be set up in the larger regions, and some of them will be so ill-fated that they will devour their own best elements in the present or in future revolutions. It will not be easy to establish a great monarchy; a great republic would be impossible. . . . It is overambitious to think of forming the whole New World into a single nation with a single power linking its parts to each other and into a whole. It would seem that with their common origin, language, customs, and religion, it should be possible to organize a government that would confederate the various states comprising it; but this cannot be. Climatic differences, geographical differences, conflicting interests, contradictions of character divide America. How beautiful if the Isthmus of Panama could be for us what that of Corinth was for the Greeks! Perhaps some day we shall have the good fortune to set up there an eminent Congress made up of representatives from all the republics, kingdoms, and empires to discuss and decide the great problems of peace and war with the nations of the three other parts of the world. . . ."

Three months after this letter had been written, a servant in Bolívar's hire, a freed slave bribed by God knows whom, on a night as dark as his skin and his soul slipped into the room where Bolívar was sleeping to stab him. He made the attempt, but that night it was not Bolivar who was sleeping in his hammock. A few days later Bolívar was on the Caribbean again, on a trip about the islands. He reached Haiti, which was under the rule of Alexander Pétion, the blacksmith. He had offered to help Bolívar in his mission of liberation and as the son of slaves and the son of white aristocrats of Caracas clasped hands, it marked the beginning of a noble friendship. Bolívar assembled his forces in the Keys of St. Louis. The champions of liberty, who had been awaiting the call in ten islands, gathered at the appointed place. Under the protection of the black republic they laid their plans. Brion, a Dutch ship-builder, and Louis Aury, a French corsair, were among those present. A squadron of boats was assembled — six schooners and a felucca. With these Bolívar and his fellow conspirators set out to sea to reconquer Venezuela for the cause of liberty; to free the slaves, which was all that the president of Haiti had asked in return for his help; to win the support of the plainsmen who no longer rode, lance in hand, with Boves of Spain, but with Páez, the republican tiger; to set up on the banks of the Orinoco, in Angostura, a newspaper, a congress, a capital, a state, from which, supported by an army wearing straw hats and armed with sticks, Bolívar was to address himself to other nations with the bearing of a monarch. And from here the Liberator was to march to Boyacá, Junín, Ayacucho, from the shores of the Caribbean to the frontier of Argentina, setting in motion a human avalanche of Negroes, mulattoes, Indians, half-breeds, and whites, until the Andes had been covered with laurels and the bright flags of the republics flew the length and the breadth of the old viceroyalties.

June 24, 1830. Cartagena. How many wars had been fought in these fifteen years! In another month Bolívar would be forty-seven years old. His sunken chest, his face browned and furrowed by fatigue and disappointments, were mute testimony that he was approaching the Valley of the Shadow. There in the blue bay, glittering in the sun, the black ship waiting for him rode at anchor. On this same Caribbean, on tramp schooners, on men-of-war, on fragile craft, he had dreamed of liberty. Moonlit nights of love, dark days of defeat, pale dawns of new hope: all had been rocked by the waves of this unresting sea. There in the Caribbean lay Curaçao, Jamaica, Haiti — the islands that had been his refuge in days of defeat; and the ports at which he embarked and came ashore with each change of scene of his life. There stood the walls of Cartagena, the cobbled streets of La Guayra, and Puerto Cabello with its diabolical fortresses.

He was now but the shadow of his shadow. From Peru to Venezuela, in every province where he had won a victory for the cause of freedom, the flame of anarchy was spreading. The generals who had supported him in the war of independence now refused to share the fruits of liberty or the rewards of peace. The Great Colombia had split asunder. Only the swift ingenuity of Manuela Sáenz, the woman who had loved him and shared his fortunes to the end, saved his life when a group of plotters burst into his bedroom in Bogotá to kill him on the ground that he was a dictator. It was time to flee once more, to seek a refuge beyond the sea. He was anxious to embark, but what ship's captain would take aboard that frail wreck of the once gallant horseman who galloped over plains and scaled mountains, that graceful dancer who had wooed and won the favors of Fanny Villars in Paris years ago?

In a little cottage at the foot of Popa, Bolívar received the news that was like his own death knell: Sucre, that most faithful of friends, that bravest of generals, had been basely assassinated in a mountain pass.

In the shadow of the walls, quietly, inexorably, the black ship rode at anchor.

But Bolívar did not go aboard the black ship here. The heat of the walled city was smothering him, and he decided instead to travel overland to Baranquilla and take a schooner there. "We'll go to Jamaica," he said. To that island where his English friends lived, Mr. Hyslop, where the treacherous servant had been executed in the public square, where he had written his prophetic letter. The Caribbean was rough, and the schooner was buffeted by the waves. Bolívar was dying. The superstitious sailors, haunted by the silhouette of the black ship, changed their course, and put into Santa Marta, a white city set in a horseshoe of golden sands and green hills on the blue bay. They carried Bolívar off the schooner with delicate care, as though they were taking ashore a handful of bones in which a heart still beat.

December 17, 1830. The house of the Spanish gentleman, Don Joaquín de Mier, on the ranch of San Pedro. The barefoot Negroes move noiselessly along the corridors; in the bedroom the whites stifle their sobs. The Liberator is dying. Ahead of him lies the unquenchable light of his glory; behind him, the words he dictates to the notary with his last breath: "Colombians, you have been witnesses of my efforts to implant liberty where tyranny once reigned. . . . My enemies took advantage of your credulity, and desecrated that which I hold most sacred . . . my love of liberty. My persecutors have brought me to the doors of the tomb; I forgive them. . . . If my death helps to bring to an end party strife and to consolidate union, I shall go down to my grave in peace."

Thus died Simón Bolívar, at Santa Marta, looking out upon the Caribbean, the sea of Liberty.

XXIV

"CUBA LIBRE"

Cuando llegue la luna llena iré a Santiago de Cuba
iré a Santiago,
en un coche de agua negra.
Cantarán los techos de palmera.
Iré a Santiago.
Cuando la palma quiere ser cigüeña,
iré a Santiago.
Y cuando quiere ser Medusa el plátano,
iré a Santiago.

    .   .   .   .   .

Oh Cuba. Oh ritmo de semillas secas!
Iré a Santiago.
Oh cintura caliente y gota de madera.
Iré a Santiago.
Arpa de troncos vivos. Caimán. Flor de tabaco.
Iré a Santiago.
Siempre he dicho que yo iría a Santiago
en un coche de agua negra.
Iré a Santiago.

FEDERICO GARCÍA LORCA

(When the moon is full I shall go to Santiago de Cuba
(I shall go to Santiago
(In a coach of black water.
(The roofs of palm will sing,
(I shall go to Santiago.
(When the palm tree wants to be a stork
(I shall go to Santiago.
(And the banana tree a Medusa
(I shall go to Santiago.

    .   .   .   .   .

(Oh Cuba. Oh, the rhythm of dry seeds!
(I shall go to Santiago.
(Oh, hot waist and click of wood.
(I shall go to Santiago.
(Harp of living trees. Alligator. Tobacco flower.
(I shall go to Santiago.
(I always said I would go to Santiago
(In a coach of black water.
(I shall go to Santiago.)

W ITH the battle of Ayacucho, Spain's domination of the American continent came to an end. The last of the viceroys, governors, generals — such of them as did not leave their bones mouldering in America — had to return to the peninsula to tell their King that America was not a land meant for slavery. America was the living torch of freedom. Every new attempt to reduce it had brought a new disaster, and all that was left of what had once been Spain's vast empire in America was the islands of Puerto Rico and Cuba, the last refuge of those vanquished by Bolívar who clung to them as a shipwrecked man clings to a plank. All the troops returning to Spain passed through Cuba. There were soldiers from Florida, Mexico, Central America, South America. The battlements of Morro fortress in Havana gave them a sense of security, as it stood solidly among the hot waves lapping at its base. Within the city life went its pleasant way. In the valleys the planters cultivated their emerald rows of tobacco, tending it "as though each plant were a delicate lady." On the sugar plantations the slaves, their bare backs glistening with sweat, widened the swathes of cane. Sugar and tobacco — the point counterpoint, to use Don Fernando Ortiz's expression, of Cuba's economy.

Cuba was not the refuge of soldiers only, but of pirates and freebooters. Flying the flags of Colombia or Mexico, these English, French, or North American seafarers swooped out of the island to fall upon some English vessel, or took refuge in its hidden bays and coves.

What was to become of Cuba? The armies of the independence, which had traveled from Caracas to the frontiers of Argentina, had marched from Mexico to Costa Rica, were armies of foot-soldiers or cavalry who considered themselves the masters of the earth, who crossed and recrossed the Andes, but who drew back in fear at the thought of launching themselves on the unstable paths of the waves. The Cubans had been unable to fight the Spaniards single-handed and dislodge them from their island. The refugees were a living testimony to the incompetence of Spain, but the final spark of Spanish hauteur still burned in their breasts.

The planters viewed the Negro republic of Haiti with terror, and trembled in their beds at night thinking that the black beasts of Cuba might be aroused at any moment. The population of the island was more than half colored, and of these four hundred thousand Negroes, two hundred and ninety thousand were slaves. The young men's minds were filled with Bolívar's glorious achievements.

The idea of independence was ever present, but the attempts to achieve it were unimportant, and seemed unlikely to succeed. There were those who longed to see Cuba incorporated into the United States, but President Monroe did not favor the idea. Bolívar and the Mexicans spread rumors to the effect that they were preparing fleets to invade the island, an invasion that would be suspended only if Spain immediately recognized the independence of the continent. It was a political stratagem that kindled the hopes of the Cubans. There were Colombians who were actively engaged in ideological mine-laying from New York to Havana. The Masonic Lodge "Soles y Rayos de Bolívar" was carrying on under-cover activities. The moment came when it seemed as though the separatist movement were about to break out; but when the conspirators, in the course of their preparations, approached Bolívar and Santander, the latter replied that, although they sympathized with the idea, they had no ships to lend them aid. And when the Spaniards executed the two patriots of Camagüey, Francisco Agüero and Manual Andrés Sánchez, in the square at Puerto Principe, it got the people out of the notion of war for a while. The two men had gone from Cuba to Philadelphia, from Philadelphia to Cartagena, from Cartagena to Kingston, from Kingston to Puerto Principe, working everywhere to win support for the revolution. In Cartagena they had been appointed lieutenants of the Colombian navy.

Spain was rushing headlong into the abyss. The Bourbons who succeeded Charles III had retained only the last words of his motto: "Enlightened Despotism." Ferdinand VII had lashed out at the supporters of the constitutional assembly of Cádiz, at the liberals, with all the power his authority and his fanaticism could command. In the processions of rogation for restoring the peace disturbed by Riego's insurrection, many monks were to be seen "wearing a sword girded over their habit, with a crucifix hanging from their girdle, and tucked into it a dagger and a pair of pistols." The conflict was grim in Spain, and at the "holocausts of piety" rather than ruling a Christian kingdom it seemed as though the King were presiding over some savage pagan spectacle where the executions were counted not by dozens or hundreds, but by thousands. Three representatives of Cuba, who had secured a vote in favor of the island's autonomy in the assembly of Cádiz, saved their skins only by fleeing to Gibraltar, and thence to the United States.

Fortunately, Cuba lay far enough from Madrid to be out of the reach of Ferdinand's vengeful arm. Many Spanish liberals had taken refuge in the island and had become enamored of its charms.

The truth was that the government of Spain had learned very little in the wars of America. The ties of blood between families of Spain and those of Cuba were increasing; many Spaniards had crossed the ocean to settle in the Pearl of the Antilles. Yet nowhere else in all their possessions did the Spanish sovereigns rule with such blind and blundering ineptness. It was Castelar who remarked that the kings who were constitutional in Spain were absolute in Cuba, that ministers who were responsible in Spain could proceed as they liked in matters affecting Cuba. The representatives elected by Cuba to the Spanish Congress had to return without being able to carry out their missions, because, as Cuba had been promised special legislation, until these laws were passed the Cubans had no voice in Spain. It was sixty years before the laws were passed. Those in power in Spain had only one thought in mind: the slave trade. The governors of the island had but one ambition: to amass a fortune through their share in the profits of slave-running. In ten years, from 1821 to 1831, the slave-traders brought in three hundred illicit cargoes,

which England was unable to halt, adding sixty thousand slaves
to those already in the island. The governors could allege in
their defense that they were in good company, for the Duchess
of Riansares, the widow of Ferdinand VII, was a shareholder in
the companies engaged in this black traffic.

Out of these circumstances, as a reaction to them, came rebellion, that dream of poets and adventurers. All the Cubans
who had dreamed and were to dream of freedom were, without
exception, poets. Every ten, every twenty years someone took it
upon himself to launch a revolutionary movement. And it was
always a dreamer who paid for his audacity on the scaffold or
on the field of battle. From Plácido to José Martí this was fated
to be Cuba's destiny.

Plácido was the first to fall, in 1844, and it is fitting that it
should have been he because he was the most symbolic figure
of all; in addition to being a poet, he had Negro blood. A confession was torn from him by the lash, and along with the Negro
Pimienta, the musician, and his other companions, he represented the group of emancipated Negroes who died to procure
the freedom of the Negro slaves. After them came Narciso López, an adventurer who suffered in 1851 the penalty of garroting;
and then Céspedes and Figueredo, who launched the proclamation of Yara, which may be considered the beginning of Cuban
independence.

Céspedes embarked upon the struggle armed "with a gold-
handled tortoise-shell cane." He was a lawyer of an old and distinguished family, a poet who wrote love poems and sonnets describing the beauties of his native Bayamo, which were for years
the favorite choice of young ladies given to recitation. One day
he started a war. For ten years such a bitter contest was carried
on in Cuba that the casualties amounted to over two hundred
thousand. Spain promised the Cubans a generous peace, but
once it was signed she flouted it with royal treachery. There
were unforgettable moments in this tragic struggle, like the day
in 1874 when Céspedes ordered his horse Telemaco saddled
and set off for the village of San Lorenzo to give the children

their lesson in reading and writing. Céspedes had been obliged to abandon his command and take refuge in the hills, but he was still the great gentleman as he rode along on his spirited horse, in his velvet waistcoat and with his six-shooter. The Spaniards surprised him and fired upon him. Céspedes defended himself as he retired along the edge of a ravine, firing his bullets one by one and saving the last for himself. He had said on one occasion: "I pray that God will give me the courage to die with the dignity befitting a Cuban, though I do not think the occasion will arise, for my revolver has six shots, five for the Spaniards and one for myself." But he did not have time to use it. Brigido Verdecia's bullet pierced his heart, and Céspedes' body rolled down the ravine. When they recovered it there was still one shot in his revolver.

Figueredo, like Céspedes, was from Bayamo, and like him, rich, well-born, romantic. In intimate gatherings, at lodge meetings, Perucho Figueredo was always talking about the revolution. In his country home, as he sat at the piano composing melodies that would be on everyone's lips, he dreamed of seeing his Cuba free. He wrote poetry, his biting caricatures being drawn with great skill. His life would soon have as its accompaniment a martial strain, a song which he had composed and cherished as his own *Marseillaise*, and which, without grasping its intention, everybody was playing or whistling in the streets; the slaves hummed it as they bent to their work on the plantations. *Perucho's March*, people called it. The governor himself sang his baby to sleep with it, little knowing that it was to become the cradle song of liberty. Revolution flamed up once more. On "Perucho's" plantation, Las Mangas, people worked day and night as in a war plant, making bullets, trying to set up a powder mill. The division he had organized, La Bayamesa, drilled on his estate. Through the streets of his native city of Bayamo, in broad daylight, he galloped on his fine horse, distributing the proclamation that called the people to arms. Before the governor knew what was happening, the subversive paper had done its work, and Perucho was on his way back to Las Mangas to organize the attack on Bayamo. *Perucho's March* was ringing in

the heart of every patriot, and there was a note of defiance in it.
At the "big house," men and women were preparing a flag of
the same colors as that Narciso López had raised. And when it
was ready, the flag of free Cuba, all of them — men and women,
Negroes and whites — swore to lay down their lives for it. The
slaves were declared free, and they went mad with joy and rum,
leaping, shouting African words, whistling *Perucho's March.*
Bayamo was encircled. The slaughter was appalling, but it was
a quick victory. Soon the church bells were ringing out wildly, and
salvos of cannon celebrated the triumph. Perucho shouted in the
town square: "Long live Free Cuba!" and thousands of voices began to hum *Perucho's March.* "Write the words," cried the
crowd, so right there on the pommel of his saddle, as he reined in
his pawing horse, he improvised the stanzas. The great gathering
of people stood silent, reverent, as though at Sunday mass. They
were awaiting in silence the birth of the song of Free Cuba, the
song of Bayamo. Perucho wrote nervously, and then began to
sing:

> *Bayamese, rush to arms!*
> *Your country looks on in pride.*
> *Fear not a glorious death —*
> *Who dies for his country lives. . . .*

The dead were now forgotten. Through the streets swept the
revolutionists with their new song. Perucho rode at their head,
and beside him his standard-bearer — his daughter Candelaria,
sixteen years old.

After this first triumph came the long war, reverses, flight.
Perucho lived the life of an outlaw, sick, alone, with one faithful servant, harried by the bands closing in on him. He defended
himself to his last bullet, and when he saw that the end had
come, he tried to commit suicide by throwing himself on his
sword. But his own weakness betrayed him, and they took him
alive. From the death cell on the night before his execution he
wrote his wife: "Dearest Isabel: I arrived here yesterday after
an uneventful trip, and I pray to God that you and our children
are in the best of health. A court martial was held today to try

me, and, as there can be no doubt that their verdict will be carried out, I am writing you at once to urge you to accept this with the most Christian resignation. . . ."

In the homes of Cuban refugees in Florida, New York, Mexico, Guatemala, Bogotá, Caracas, the flame of hope was kept alive. The first war had been lost, but the determination to liberate Cuba was firmer than ever. In the Havana theater, when *El Perro Huevero* was played, and the actors, following their lines, said: "Long live the land where the cane grows," a shout from the gallery would answer: "Long live Cuba!" Those in the orchestra seats would reply: "Long live Spain!" — and chairs, broken bottles, and revolver shots flew through the air. When the volunteers who had enlisted with the Spanish army marched through the streets, they were greeted with contemptuous smiles by girls and students from the house windows, which so infuriated the volunteers that they rushed into the homes and dragged the irreverent spectators off to prison. One volunteer received a note from three of his fellow students asking him: "Do you know how apostasy was punished in olden times?" The insulted youth took the note to the authorities, and the next day the three signers were in prison and the author of the message was sentenced to six years at hard labor in the stone quarries. This was José Martí, who was little more than a child. Many a hardened criminal had died at this work, breaking rock from morning till night, in the blazing heat of the tropical sun. Like Plácido, like Céspedes, like Perucho Figueredo, Martí was a poet, one of the greatest of Spanish America. A few hours before being taken to the military prison, he wrote a poem which is reminiscent of *Perucho's March*:

> *My country sends me there. Even death at her*
> *Hands is still sweet.*

One day a compassionate Spaniard with influence in official circles procured Martí's release from prison, and he was exiled to Spain. There this poet and orator talked in the café, on the street-corner, wherever he could find two Spaniards willing to argue — that is to say, everywhere. His imprisonment had left the stamp of suffering on his pale young face, but there was a dynamic quality in him that won him friends and admirers wherever he went. He seemed the last romantic. In Havana the Spaniards were continuing to make the students the target of their vengefulness. On some insignificant pretext eight medical students were shot and thirty-five sent to prison. Martí knew them; they were friends of his. From that moment the purpose and decision that was to shape the rest of his life became irrevocable. He spoke at Masonic meetings, he wrote articles for the newspapers, he published a report of what he had seen and suffered entitled *Political Imprisonment in Cuba*. . . . And in spite of his boyish air, this pale young man with the broad forehead and shining eyes was applauded and respected wherever he spoke. He was called The Apostle.

From Spain to Mexico, to Guatemala, to New York. . . . This was the itinerary of his life, always the same burning devotion to the cause of Cuba, always the speeches that lifted up the hearts of all who heard them, and, with all this, his poetry. But none of it was enough; what was needed was action. It seems incredible, but this poet, this orator, managed to assemble three ships loaded with arms in New York Harbor. The officers who were to be in charge of the uprising heeded his counsel; in Cuba they were waiting for him. But, as might have been expected, there was a traitor, and the American government learned about the poet's three ships and confiscated them. The police were on Martí's trail, but he managed to elude them, galloping on horseback along the roads, slipping like a ghost through the cities, and always maintaining contact with the conspirators, who never lost heart. Penny by penny he collected new funds for the revolution, and revived the enthusiasm of the military leaders. In Cuba the news was spread that The Apostle was on his way. War broke out. Martí was feverishly happy. "For me my native land will never be triumph, but suffering and duty. . . . My one desire is to die there, without a word, beside the last tree, the humblest soldier. . . ."

From the deck of the fruit ship returning him to his country, he saw, in the afternoon sun, the mountains of Cuba. The sea was the Caribbean, and the coast lay three miles away. A little boat carrying six men was put over the side. In this fragile shell, which the waves alternately tossed into the air and sucked into their trough, rode Martí, burning with impatience to set foot on his sacred soil.

At last Free Cuba was about to be born, before his eyes. Fording rivers, crossing swamps and mountains, Martí pushed on to join the soldiers of freedom. His place was beside them, he wanted to share their dangers, to be one in the fight with white man and Negro, student and seasoned soldier, with all those who loved liberty. And in the hour of battle, on April 19, 1895, reckless, foolhardy, for the head was unable to check the galloping heart which was no longer marking the hours of life but rushing to meet death, he charged forward, in the vanguard, and enemy bullets cut him down and left him lying on the field, wrapped in the crimson flag of his own blood.

When the Spaniards brought back to Havana in a cheap wooden coffin this trophy of a battle that would have no effect on the final outcome of the war, they had no idea that this dying for country which is living was Martí's triumph. It was his path to eternal glory. The island was now a huge boat, spattered with blood, as the boats of the Antilles had always been, beneath a canopy of song: the undying poems of José Martí.

There is no wise lesson of experience to be learned from the great drama of the Cuban War, says Don Angel Ossorio; all that has remained is the operetta *Gigantes y Cabezudos*. The war came because it was inevitable. The government of Spain had paid no heed to Maura or Pi Margall, who insisted that Cuba must be given her independence just like the other former colonies. The gentlemen of Madrid laughed at them, as did the generals. Meanwhile the United States was moving toward the inevitable solution which held a possible threat to the sovereignty of the new republic. In 1896–97 Valeriano Weyler, the general in whose hands Spain entrusted the fate of her troops, turned Cuba into a series of concentration camps where men, women, and children, suspected of a love of liberty, were herded like cattle. Hundreds of them died of hunger and fever every day. The American consul informed his government and the world at large that there were four hundred thousand persons shut up in these living graveyards. Over half the population of the province of Havana was in them.

These were the terms on which the Spanish government planted the question of Cuba. For this reason it was decided as it was. The United States intervened, and Spain lost Cuba, Puerto Rico, and the Philippines. Cuba was to go on fighting for her liberation.

XXV

PRELUDE TO THE PANAMA CANAL

The land there grows very narrow, and the two oceans come close together, no more than seven leagues apart; for, although the distance from Portobello to Panama is eighteen leagues, this is because the road is winding. There has been talk of cutting through this short distance because of the difficulties of travel over those eighteen leagues; some argue against it, saying the land would be flooded because one ocean is at a lower level than the other, but the wiser think this is nonsense.

ANTONIO DE HERRERA
(*Décadas*)

From that day when Balboa first gazed upon the Pacific, the idea of a canal linking the two new seas was to become a dream that obsessed the minds of men for four centuries. It is not too far-fetched to say that this bold conquistador, this son of the people, carried upon his shoulders the first ships that crossed the Isthmus. He wanted to explore the new sea, his sea. With his men he cut the straightest trees in the forest for masts, and managed to saw out boards. Loading everything on the shoulders of Indians and his fellow-explorers — planks, spars, sails, and nails — he crossed the mountains to a river where he assembled his ships and descended its waters to the sea. What he saw, what his comrades saw, in the bits and pieces they carried as they trudged along the mountain defiles was the ship. Each one — in hands that clasped the ax, on shoulders that bore the timbers, on backs that bent under the weight of the cables — was carrying a piece of the ship. The slopes of the hills were a dense, steaming mass of vegetation, and the branches with their shining green leaves — laurels, fittingly enough — which afforded shade against the sun and protection from the tropical rains, seemed, as they parted before the advancing men, the waves of a vegetable sea; over these waves, rocked by the imagination of the conquistadors, the ship advanced. Four centuries

413

later, engineers had leveled the hills and joined the two oceans, and great power-driven liners passed through the Canal. But this marvel of our days in no wise detracts from the grandeur of that first vision, barbarous, sweaty, panting, in which the violence of these rude, rustic adventurers was tempered by the ingenuousness of their dreams.

After Balboa, the search for the strait, for the direct passage, engaged the efforts of navigators, geographers, and engineers of all the world. Their names came to form the most complete roster of will-o'-the-wisp followers in the remarkable record of the discoveries.

There are many points of similarity with the Suez Canal. Both canals represent man's efforts to conquer the seas. Once more the Mediterranean and the Caribbean reflect each other in the mirrors of their waters. And in the name of Ferdinand de Lesseps the two are linked to the life of a man who fluctuated between the heights of glory and the depths of human misery.

It is almost impossible to say when the history of Suez began. The need for a canal, in the Old as in the New World, made itself felt from the moment man first approached the regions of Suez and Panama. On the maps of the world, those three gigantic land masses which are Africa, Asia, and Europe appear joined only by that little link of land lying between the Red Sea and the Mediterranean. In the world of man's activities, these bonds of the earth were nothing but a nuisance; getting rid of them would mean being able to move freely and independently. The Egyptians, the Greeks, and the Asiatic peoples all felt the same way. On the ruins of the Temple of Karnak there is an inscription mentioning the existence of a canal in 1380 b.c. This canal passed into oblivion, and Pharaoh Necho tried to build a new one; one hundred and twenty thousand men died in the attempt. At different times in remote epochs ships were able to pass from the Red Sea to the Nile, and thence to the Mediterranean, with cargoes of camphor, pearls, pepper, and eunuchs.

To come to more recent times: In the fifteenth century the

Venetians tried to make arrangements with Egypt to cut a canal. Leibnitz, in the seventeenth century, recommended such a plan to Louis XIV. At the end of the eighteenth, Napoleon wanted to do it, and ordered the plans drawn up. At the beginning of the nineteenth century, the French followers of Saint-Simon envisaged the opening of the two canals, those of Suez and of Panama, as part of their plan to regenerate the world. At the opportune moment some years later Ferdinand de Lesseps aroused the interest of all, high and low, in the enterprise, and built the Suez Canal. When it was finished, Disraeli, with the vision of a genius, laid hands on it so deftly and so quickly that for this alone, if for no other reason, his name will live forever in the annals of the British Empire.

At the beginning of the history of America, all the discoveries revolved about the same problem. A continent was unfolding before the astonished eyes of navigators seeking, not a continent, but a direct passage to India. It was a piece of good fortune for America that there was this little obstacle to halt the eager rush. . . . When in course of time it was realized that there were no straits, but only an isthmus, men began to conceive plans to correct this geographical oversight. Until the last day of their domination, the Spaniards were mulling over the problem; it was one of the reasons for the voyage to America of Jorge Juan and Antonio Ulloa, the two geographers. To Spain the project did not seem unfeasible. Not far from Panama a canal many leagues long had been built to connect Cartagena with the Magdalena River. This was the Dique Canal, on which tens of thousands of slaves labored, digging through sand and dredging the swamps until at last easy communication by water had been established between the great port and the interior of the viceroyalty. And one person had even attempted and accomplished the interocean communication on his own. Antonio Cerezo, a priest of Novita, dug a small canal joining the San Juan River to a tributary of the Atrato; in 1788 canoes passed through it from ocean to ocean. Like the Suez, the Panama Canal has its prehistoric antecedents.

The first problem was to know where the canal should be cut. La Condamine had proposed to the Academy of Sciences of Paris a passage through Nicaragua. Francisco Miranda had interested Pitt in the matter, and a study of the Panama route was undertaken. In 1814, the Spanish Cortes had advanced the idea of building a canal across the Isthmus of Tehuantepec. Humboldt pointed out nine possible routes, five of which were located at various points between Colombia and Mexico. But there was no clear-cut plan. As Humboldt had remarked, though this was a basic problem for world trade, no investigation had been made that could afford a basis for any scientific conclusion. Everyone had his own ideas. At times, the men coming closest to the solution were those least qualified. In the eighteenth century a French peasant of Provence, who had been sentenced to the galleys for some offense, Convict No. 1336, addressed to Benjamin Franklin a plan for enduring peace. Franklin was greatly impressed, and published it. The prisoner had a clear idea of navigation on the seven seas, probably acquired over long years of meditation while plying the oar of his punishment. "There is the Isthmus of Panama in America," he wrote, "and that of Suez between Asia and Africa, which prevent the union of the four oceans and oblige those who must sail around the world to take three years in the process, besides risking their lives on the stormy and often icy seas. These two isthmuses must be cut by two canals, some sixty feet wide, thirty feet deep, and about forty leagues long. In this way it will be possible to circumnavigate the globe. . . ."

The great Goethe's ideas on the subject were not so clear as those of Convict No. 1336, but in certain respects he showed keen intuition and perception. "Humboldt," said Goethe, "with his thorough knowledge of the problem, has indicated several places that might perhaps be better than Panama, utilizing the currents of the Gulf of Mexico. But I ask myself whether the United States will let this opportunity slip through their fingers. It is absolutely indispensable for them to have a means of passage from the Gulf of Mexico to the Pacific Ocean, and I feel sure that they will secure it. . . ."

Up to this point this is history. Now the projects begin. Where to build the canal? Through Panama? Through Nicaragua? Through Tehuantepec? And it was not the problem of the route alone. Even where the isthmuses were narrowest, there were still hills. It was an age of great constructions and machinery, and men's minds were heated with engineering dreams. Captain James Buchanan Eads proposed a Gargantuan railroad across the Isthmus of Tehuantepec which would receive the ships on the Atlantic side and transport them to the Pacific on huge rolling platforms "just as a mother carries her babe in her arms." The captain's platforms carrying the ocean liners appear in the plans moving over six rails and drawn by three pairs of engines. The plan was enthusiastically received, and the drawings can still be seen as one of the most delightful pictures of those times. Others proposed digging a tunnel, since a canal at sea-level seemed out of the question; those belonging to the school of mechanics talked of locks; those of the school of engineering, of tunnels. A Frenchman, Airiau, drew up a plan for a canal in Darien, addressed to the president of Colombia; the first thing that strikes the reader on opening the book is the colored plate of the proposed capital of Darien — the largest city in the world: from the center of an octagonal square bisected by the canal, the avenues radiate like the spokes of a wheel; there are beautiful streets and gardens on all sides, and around the city run the boulevards of Antioquia, Cauca, Boyacá, Cundinamarca, Santander, and Panama.

Little by little the fantasies fell by the wayside, and the general opinion hovered between two possible choices: Panama and Nicaragua. Concessions for the Nicaragua route had been obtained successively by a French company, by Monsignor Viteri, Bishop of Salvador, and by a firm of businessmen of New York and New Orleans. None of these made an inch of progress. In Central America, as in all the former Spanish colonies — as, perhaps, in all the world — all hope was centered on France. France was the home of scientists. Daring inspirations came from France. Central America was full of romantics, and the romantics dreamed of setting Louis Napoleon free from the fortress of Ham, where Louis-Philippe was holding him prisoner, bringing him to Central America, and putting him at the head of the greatest undertaking of the century, the interocean canal, the "Napoleon Canal." The Minister of Central America in Paris invented some kind of excuse to visit the prisoner and laid the plan before him. Later Louis Napoleon made his escape to England; he had taken the project very seriously, and he published a pamphlet urging friends of progress to help carry it out. But then came the Revolution of 1848. Louis Napoleon returned to France, became president, then had himself crowned emperor as Napoleon III, and forgot about Nicaragua. His thoughts turned to Mexico, where he made his ill-fated attempt to install Maximilian as emperor.

At about the same time that Louis Napoleon was campaigning for the French presidency, on this side of the Atlantic an event had taken place that was to bring about a complete change in the life of America: the discovery of gold in California. Before this, the canal had had no special meaning for America. It was thought of as a means of getting from one ocean to another, always with the idea that the world had only two centers of interest: Europe and Asia. For centuries Europe's greatest concern was to procure products of the Orient. To open up trade routes with Asia the Italian merchants joined the Crusades; to find other new channels, Columbus discovered the new world. Even Humboldt, La Condamine, Miranda, and Convict No. 1336 were thinking of the canal only as a means of linking the two quantities of the ever-present equation: Europe, Asia. And yet the facts of the matter in the nineteenth century were very different. Pepper was no longer worth what it had brought in the fifteenth century. The passage from one ocean to the other would now be, first and foremost, America's gain. It may be that one day the Pacific will acquire that value as a link between Europe and Asia which the savants of the sixteenth century ascribed to it. But for the moment its conquest, its ease of access, had a different significance, that of giving movement to the life of America. Europe had been looking on America as a way station for a long time; three and a half centuries had not been enough to make her understand that this was a New World.

With the discovery in 1848 of gold in California came the mad Gold Rush toward the Pacific. The frontier of North America, which for three hundred years had advanced at a snail's pace, which in 1800 stopped at the Mississippi, leaving half the continent as a stamping ground for the buffalo and the Indian, now moved forward at a dizzy speed. Covered wagons went bouncing along over the waving grass plains through a cloud of dust, the eager seekers for gold lashing on the horses. But how wide the plains were! There seemed to be no end to them. And as the days went by, the feverish imagination of the weary passengers of the wagon trains was tormented by the thought that others might get there first. How could the trip be speeded up? By the sea route. By taking a steamboat in New York or New Orleans that would carry them to Panama or Nicaragua, then overland across the Isthmus, and by another ship to the Pacific.

The first steamship line for Pacific navigation happened to have been organized on the eve of the discovery of the gold mines. The first ship was making its maiden voyage and, having rounded Cape Horn, had put in at the port of Callao just as the news of the discovery electrified the world. To the surprise and dismay of the captain, a hundred Peruvians came aboard. When they reached Panama, there were five hundred Americans waiting on the dock. The boat's capacity was one hundred and fifty passengers. The Americans were prepared to kick the Peruvians off the boat. The company's officials found themselves surrounded by a swarm of belligerent would-be passengers. None of them could reconcile himself to missing the first boat for San Francisco. To make sure of holding their reservations, the Peruvians, though they were sizzling under the Panama sun, refused to go ashore even for a minute. Finally — on cots in the passageways, crowded into staterooms, piled up on deck — three hundred and seventy-five managed to get aboard. There was not food enough for them, no water to wash with. The ship's fuel gave out; chairs, doors, and tables were stuffed into the firebox to keep up the steam in the boilers. Even so, it was impossible to make port. They had to hoist sail. But they did move ahead. At last they saw the mouth of the bay. San Francisco! A minute after docking there was not a soul aboard the boat. Even the cooks were over the side, like deer, on their way to the mines, to riches.

And the other journeys by boat were not very different. Clusters of human beings crowded together moving slowly ahead to the noisy churning of the paddle wheels, whiling away the tedious days in gaming, swearing, challenging one another to duels, always hovering on the brink of a human storm that cleared away as though by magic the minute the ship entered the Golden Gate.

At the time when the route across Panama was one steady stream of adventurers, similar scenes were taking place in Nicaragua. An American company that had obtained a concession to dig a canal there saw what was happening in Panama, and put aside the idea of a canal. Commodore Vanderbilt, the head of the company, prepared with all speed to enter the competition. He soon had boats — they were called floating pigsties — running from New York to the port of San Juan del Norte. There the passengers changed to little river boats that sailed down the San Juan River to San Carlos fort, across the lake, and then by muleback to the Atlantic, or in the company's new omnibuses, painted blue and white, Nicaragua's national colors.

The Americans arriving in Panama found the place more abandoned than in the days of Drake. Then it had been the trade route for merchants as far away even as Argentina, for in three hundred years only once had the port of Buenos Aires been opened to commerce by the Spaniards. But with the Independence, Panama ceased to be the port of entry for the Continent. The grass sprang up between the stones of the road the mule-trains so long traveled.

The government in Bogotá kept up a languid, fitful communication with the Isthmus. It was not easy to reach moribund

Panama, with its yellow fever and its snakes. The French had obtained a concession to build a railroad, but the railroad made no headway. The first waves of Americans that crossed the Isthmus by mule or canoe, crowding into the wayside inns, seemed to be moving along a battle front or through a gypsy camp rather than along highways or through cities. To the inhabitants of Panama it seemed as if the inmates of some insane asylum had descended upon them. While the new arrivals waited for their boat, they gambled, drank, fought, and got into scrapes. It was the same sight to be seen on the frontier that was moving westward from the Mississippi to California in the north.

A group of Americans undertook the building of a railroad. With a dozen Indians armed with machetes, they started to cut a clearing through the jungle. The heat, the mosquitoes, the fevers killed the laborers like flies. The ties rotted. The company was on the point of throwing in its hand several times. It imported laborers from everywhere, even China. The Chinese brought opium and tea with them. The whites died of fever, the coolies of homesickness. Many committed suicide. But finally the job was finished. The terminus on the Atlantic, which Colombia wanted to call "Colón," was named "Aspinwall" by the company, for the president of the Pacific Mail. To implement its view, the government of Colombia ordered the post office to return all correspondence addressed to Aspinwall, marked "destination unknown." This railroad carried all the gold sent from California to New York. It became a highly profitable enterprise, paying dividends as high as forty-four percent. Between 1856 and 1904 it made a profit of $37,800,000.

One day in April, 1856, nine hundred and fifty passengers were waiting in Panama to take passage on the Pacific Mail boat. The boat was waiting for high tide, and it notified passengers that it would not sail until eleven that night. The footloose men were loafing about taverns and cheap hotels, drinking to kill time. Women and children were wearily waiting in the station waiting-room. Jack Oliver was drunk; he went to a stand where a Negro was selling watermelons, took a slice, and walked away. "Hey, Mister," said the Negro, "that costs ten cents." The Mister did not even look at the Negro. "Ten cents, Mister!" The Mister laughed, but still made no move to pay, because he did not feel like it and because it was funny to see the Negro crying and carrying on. The Negro ran after Oliver. Shouts and screams. The Negro pulled out a knife, another Mister threw him a coin — but it was too late. The trouble had started. The natives took the Negro's part; the Americans, the white man's. The affair turned into a battle; the Americans took shelter in the station; fifteen of the passengers and two Panamanians were left dead on the field. Thirteen Panamanians and sixteen Americans had been wounded.

The American agent investigating the case decided that Jack Oliver had drawn his pistol against the Negro, but that some-one else had fired the first shot. The governor of Panama maintained that the aggression had been started by the Americans, and the consuls of Great Britain, France, and Ecuador were of the same opinion. The American agent advised his government to occupy the Isthmus at once from ocean to ocean unless Colombia could guarantee the Americans absolute protection. As a result, two warships steamed into port and troops disembarked. Nothing happened, not a shot was fired, the troops returned to their ships, and the ships sailed off.

In Washington the news of the little war over the slice of watermelon was received at the time when President Pierce, the youngest head of the Union so far, was developing his policy of aggressive expansion. It was the "manifest destiny" of the United States to extend its control over the Caribbean zone. Pierce's attitude toward the Negroes was that of an out-and-out supporter of slavery. He had looked favorably on Walker's activities in Nicaragua and had recognized the government Walker had set up. In Ostend, three of his ministers had signed the "Cuban Manifesto" asking for the annexation of Cuba. Now the President was about to put the screws on Colombia.

Pierce ordered the American Minister in Bogotá and Mr. Isaac E. Morse to present a "reclamation." Colombia was asked to declare Colón and Panama free cities, cede the United States the islands in Panama Bay as naval bases, transfer to the United States its rights in the railroad, and pay an indemnity for the lives of the Americans killed.

Colombia received the demands with indignation. A long controversy followed, and conferences, and letters. The Americans placed the value of the dead Americans at $400,000. After long altercation, Colombia was obliged to sign an agreement promising to pay $195,410 for the Americans who had been killed, $65,070 for supplementary claims, $9,277 for "expenses of the commission," and $142,637 for interest. This was the fashion in which the great powers collected their claims against Latin America in such cases.

A similar incident took place in Nicaragua. The captain of the *Routh*, sailing down Lake Nicaragua to the port of San Juan del Norte, fired on a boatman and killed him. One of the passengers, a typical "Mister," denied all rights of the local authorities to take action against a North American citizen, and made the Negroes return to their places and leave their "dead dog" behind. But that night the Negroes started a riot, and the Mister who had done the talking was hit in the face with a bottle. A reclamation followed. The Secretary of State in Washington ordered the United States consul to demand satisfaction from the government of Nicaragua, and $24,000 damages for the bottle blow. He was also instructed, if the negotiations were not successful, to order San Juan del Norte bombarded immediately. The consul carried out the orders to the letter. The city was bombarded and such of it as was not blown up was fired. That was how such things were ordered in President Pierce's day. When Pierce's term of office expired, and the figure of Lincoln began to loom up on the horizon, the Negroes of Cuba sang this song:

> Onward, Lincoln, onward,
> Our hope looks up to thee!

XXVI

THE HUMAN GEOGRAPHY
OF THE CANAL

The pity of it was that Roosevelt could not be patient enough to do it honestly.

JAMES TRUSLOW ADAMS

Speak softly and carry a big stick.

THEODORE ROOSEVELT

YELLOW fever, mosquitoes, poor Negroes, drunken white men, red-light houses, gambling tables — that was a picture of Colón or Panama in those days. It was said that every tie laid on the railroad had cost the life of a workingman. Scorpions dropped from the roofs of the houses, snakes crawled under the beds, and alligators waddled through the market place. Exaggerations, imagination. The fact was that the gold from California was shipped by this railroad, and that the eyes of the world began to turn toward the Isthmus. What Bolívar had said about its being the crossroads of the world was coming true. And for this reason it was a danger zone. In Colombia people were saying Jack Oliver's slice of watermelon had cost the country $400,000. The romantic radicals who had assembled to give the nation a new constitution proposed moving the capital from Bogotá to Panama. In Panama, they said, lies the future of the world. One of the group, astute and cynical, remarked: "Please notice that Colombia is shaped like a rooster, and Panama is the neck. If we move the capital to Panama the day they cut off our neck, we will have lost everything." The suggestion was dropped.

Across the Atlantic the Suez Canal had just been inaugurated. De Lesseps, who delighted in great exhibitions, shows, inaugurations, organized the historic ceremony in November 1869. It was majestically presided over by the Khedive of Egypt. Sixty-eight ships flying the flags of all nations passed from the Red Sea into the Mediterranean. They were led by the "royal cruiser," bearing Empress Eugénie, the Emperor of Austria, the Prince of Wales, the Crown Prince of Prussia. . . . Lesseps's fame was world-wide; there was no room for more decorations on his chest. Gambetta christened him "the great Frenchman." Victor Hugo coined the phrase: "Lesseps has astonished the world by showing it what can be accomplished without war." Europe professed only one religion: that of Progress.

Five hundred ships passed through the Suez Canal each year. In Paris a congress of scientists gathered under the auspices of the Geographical Society to study the possibility of communication between the Atlantic and Pacific by means of a canal across Central America. Lesseps explained what he had done at Suez, the scientists agreed that the undertaking was possible, the Société Civile Internationale du Canal Interocéanique du Darien agreed to underwrite the cost of the preliminary studies, and a commissioner was sent to Bogotá to secure an option to survey the field. Lieutenant Lucien-Napoleon-Bonaparte Wyse, at the head of a group of experts, went out to Panama.

Once more the name of the Napoleons appeared on the map of the Caribbean. This young man was the illegitimate son of Princess Letitia Bonaparte, Napoleon's niece, and the lover she had taken; she was separated from her husband, the Irish writer Thomas Wyse. The son, who was a Bonaparte and not a Wyse, was clever, hard-working, and ambitious. In a few days he had investigated the technical problems of the work, examined all the possibilities. He hastened to Bogotá on muleback, crossing the three spurs of the Andes that separate the port of Buenaventura from the capital. His plan was to secure the final concession, and in two months of feverish activity he obtained the government's permission, the congress's approval, and the president's sanction. He returned to Panama, drew up the plans, prepared a tentative budget, and, drawing on his imagination, outlined the necessary technical details. Then he began his return journey to Paris, stopping en route at Nicaragua and Washington. He offered four possible solutions: a deep canal at sealevel, a canal with locks, a canal with a tunnel ten miles long, and another that would require a tunnel only three and a half miles long, though this tunnel could be eliminated at an additional cost of $3,000,000. Doing away with the tunnel, he said, would make the crossing easier for timid people, but was it worth while taking them into account?

Wyse tried to interest people in Washington and New York in his plans, and invited them to attend the congress of scientists scheduled to meet in Paris. He talked with President Hayes and the members of his cabinet. Only Secretary Evarts showed himself dubious and cautious. "My interview with him was difficult, because he believed he discerned the hand of the French government behind the undertaking; he fails to realize that, owing to my relations with the imperial family, I have to proceed cautiously with the government of the Republic."

The International Congress held in Paris in 1879 was one of the most impressive and spectacular gatherings that could be imagined. One hundred and thirty-six scientists, bankers, and politicians from twenty-three nations were assembled on the platform of the Geographical Society on the Boulevard Saint-Germain. The hall was crowded with ladies. There were speeches, great enthusiasm, committee meetings, and banquets, many banquets. For fifteen days this congress held the spotlight in France. Napoleon-Bonaparte Wyse was putting over his ideas and plans with such success that there were some who said the congress had been convoked just for him. This was not quite true. The cynosure of all eyes was old Lesseps, who, for all his seventy-four years, was as robust as an oak, and he lent the congress a pleasant note with his cordial air, his smile, and his gallantry to the ladies. He radiated the satisfaction that comes from a long, successful, and well-spent life.

At the final plenary session Lesseps arose and moved that the congress should pass a resolution to the effect that an interocean canal at sea-level was feasible, and that it was to begin at the Gulf of Limón in Panama Bay. The voting was public, and when Lesseps's turn came he got to his feet and, in a voice that echoed through the hall and reverberated in the souls of his hearers, answered: "I vote in the affirmative, and I have agreed to direct the enterprise." The applause was deafening. The name of Lesseps, and with it that of France, would be linked to the two great canals of the world.

Lesseps's biography is fascinating. He was a man of the world, who knew the secrets of good food, elegant living, society balls, and the right clubs. He had been a great swimmer, a great horseman, a great hunter, a great dancer. He had begun his career as consul in Tunis, Alexandria, Barcelona, and Madrid. He had been French Minister in Rome. A friendship had sprung up between him and Mohammed Saïd, the son of Abbas Pasha, and when the latter died Mohammed invited Lesseps to his coronation. The two horsemen made the trip together from Alexandria to Cairo across the desert. Lesseps had read the report of Le Père, the engineer in charge of the expedition Napoleon sent out to study the canal project, and it occurred to him to try to interest the Pasha. Carefully choosing his words and the moment, Lesseps laid his ideas before him as they rode along. It seemed to the Pasha that luck was tapping him on the shoulder: his name would be associated with one of mankind's most stupendous undertakings, and he would revive a tradition that had persisted in Egypt for two thousand years, that of restoring the communication between the two oceans. At his inaugural banquet, the Pasha arose and announced, as he offered a toast, that his friend Lesseps was going to build the canal.

A series of struggles followed: to overcome England's tortuous opposition, to hold out against the bankers who demanded a five-percent commission for selling stock in the undertaking, and to persuade the simple folk of France to invest their savings in the project. Lesseps surmounted all these obstacles. He had an irresistible power of attraction for the lowly, and he could hold his own among the tycoons. The four hundred thousand shares were taken up by the Ottoman Empire, Mohammed, and the working people of France. Of these shares, 207,111 were bought by the waiters, sewing girls, and shoemakers of Paris, Bordeaux, Nantes, Cherbourg. One night when Lesseps was getting out of a cab, as he went to pay the driver he noticed that the other was smiling at him under his bristling mustache in a manner at once friendly and ironical. "Do you know me?" "Certainly, M. de Lesseps — I am one of the stockholders in your company." So, Lesseps calculated, these plain people who had built Suez would now build the Panama Canal.

Charles de Lesseps, his son, was not so optimistic as his father about the Panama project. In his opinion, Napoleon-Bonaparte Wyse was a charlatan, not qualified to draw up the plan. The elder Lesseps was old, he was not an engineer, he knew Panama only by hearsay. "One can work only one miracle in a lifetime," he told his father affectionately. "Don't worry, son," was the reply; "there are going to be two in mine." And Charles, who did not believe in the undertaking, from then on followed his father's lead blindly, unwilling to abandon him. And with this devotion he followed him even to prison, for the enterprise eventually developed into one of the scandals of the century, wrecking much of France's prestige in the New World.

Although Lesseps was a great promoter, he had overlooked one detail: the press. As the newspapers had not received their accustomed gratuities, they turned on the scheme. Panama was described as a death-hole. Lesseps decided upon a theatrical gesture: he would go there with his wife and three of his children to inaugurate the work. One of the attractions for strollers in the Bois de Boulogne was to see Lesseps with his wife and his nine youngest children out walking on Sunday. It was a demonstration of paternal devotion and inexhaustible virility such as Frenchmen knew how to appreciate at their true value, and they greeted M. Ferdinand reverently and smiled fondly upon his numerous progeny.

As he had publicly announced, M. Ferdinand set out for Panama. The city made ready to receive him, sparing nothing in the way of fireworks and illumination. And in the year 1880, on New Year's Day, Lesseps, his wife and children, a group of public officials, the bishop, the engineers, and the journalists, went aboard the *Taboguilla,* a rickety little boat to attend the formal ceremony of starting the work. Considerable time was lost in lunches, visits, and polite nothings, and night had come and they were still far from the spot where Tototte de Lesseps, with all the charm of her seven years, was to turn the first shovelful of dirt that would launch the undertaking. As the act was symbolic, it was decided that Tototte could put her shovel into a box of sand on the deck of the *Taboguilla*, and the bishop would pronounce his blessing. Thus the Panama Canal was begun.

Lesseps then went to the United States. He visited New York, rode on the Elevated, admired the railroad stations, the Equitable Life Building with its six elevators. Banquets, speeches, receptions. Twisting the points of his mustache, he contemplated with delight the manifestations of progress. And he rectified an initial error: his neglect of the press. This time he spared no efforts. The undertaking was converted into a canal of paper. Money was spent like water on publicity. The banks received $50,000 a year just for lending their name to the enterprise. Lesseps was no longer the man who, to save the commission demanded by the Rothschilds for selling stock in the Suez Canal, broke with business tradition and sold the stock directly to the public. Now he was throwing money around with senile carelessness. The purchasing committee organized in New York was paid $1,200,000 for services it never rendered. The Paris cabbies' centimes were going down a rat hole, and meanwhile, in Panama, after Tototte's first shovelful, the shovels were moving slowly.

Lesseps' fundamental mistake was deciding to build the canal at sea-level. For seven years the work was done on this basis, and millions of francs were spent without any return. With the floating of each new loan, Lesseps arranged to make speeches all over France. He and his son went from one theater to another. Charles did the speaking; Ferdinand, seated on the platform, smiled and nodded approval. It was the beginning of the tragedy. The press became friendly; it apologized for its earlier attacks. There was not a newspaper that was not receiving money from the company. The government lent its support; it, too, was getting its share. But the years went by, and even a gold mine would not have been able to keep up with the expenditures, and the Canal was making no progress. When it was too late, the plan of locks was decided upon, and Gustave Eiffel, for whom the tower in Paris is named, was to build them.

In eight years the company had spent almost 13,000,000 francs to win the support of two thousand, five hundred and seventy-five newspapers. The day finally came when only one solution seemed possible: to secure a law from the Chamber of Deputies authorizing it to suspend payments. The law was not passed, and in December 1888 the company went into bankruptcy. Lesseps and his partners were brought to trial. Out of consideration for the fact that he was an officer of the Legion of Honor, the case was tried before the First Appellate Court of Paris. Lesseps was now eighty-three years old. A newspaper, *La Libre Parole*, came out with the statement that twenty senators and deputies had received bribes to put the measure authorizing the last loans through; it mentioned by name those who had negotiated the bribery: Baron de Reinach and Messrs. Cottu, Blane, and Arton. The Minister of Justice took action to speed up the investigation, and with every new step the dimensions of a scandal involving many persons in high circles became more shocking. Reinach, Herz, and Arton were Jews of German origin. The French people, enraged at this evidence of how their savings had been poured down the drain, gave vent to a storm of anti-Semitic hatred that reached its peak a few years later in the Dreyfus Case. Reinach testified regarding the three million francs he had handled for publicity purposes and, after clasping the hand of his friend, Georges Clemenceau, went to his apartment, where he died, apparently the victim of poison. Arton, whom Reinach had indicated as the person in actual charge of the business, fled to England. After a sensational hunt, during which detectives trailed him over half of Europe, a journalist found him. He went to jail after he had testified, simply and cynically, before the judges as to how he had distributed the 2,000,000 francs given him by Baron Reinach. He concluded: "I did not 'buy' anybody; I handed out checks for ten, twenty, fifty, a hundred thousand francs the same way you send a box of cigars to a person who has done you a favor." Herz, the cleverest of the lot, fled, and from a watering place in England looked on in amusement at the futile efforts of the French authorities to obtain his extradition.

These men had acted as bankers for the sake of their commission. The money had been paid out of the company funds by Charles de Lesseps. Charles had been obsessed by the idea of putting the Canal through, not only by blasting rocks in Panama but by digging in the slime of Paris. He confessed his guilt, alleging in his defense that he had been the victim of the insatiable and inescapable greed of French politicians.

The account of the scandal occupies volumes. Among those best informed there are two schools of thought: one claims that a hundred and fifty deputies accepted bribes; the other puts the figure at a hundred and four. Floquet, the Premier, was said to have received 250,000 francs. Lesseps testified that he had been obliged to pay the Minister of the Interior, Baïhaut, 375,000 francs, and Baïhaut finally made this pathetic confession: "I am guilty. For fifteen years I served France loyally as deputy and minister, and my conduct was irreproachable. Even now I am unable to explain how I fell into this temptation. . . ."

The scandal rocked the whole country. One day the deputy Déroulède bravely came out and said: "Gentlemen, there is a name that is on all your lips, but that no one of you dares pronounce for fear of three things: the man's sword, his pistol, and his tongue. Well, I am going to defy these three things and name him: he is M. Clemenceau! . . ." It was true. Clemenceau, it was brought out among other things, had received money from Herz for his paper, La Justice. A duel followed. Shots were exchanged, but this time M. Clemenceau failed to hit his target.

Let us go back for a moment to take up another thread of this history. At the Polytechnic Institute of Paris there was an ambitious boy who was fated to live a novel, for his soul was that of an adventurer. One day, reading a newspaper account of the opening of the Suez Canal, he said to his mother: "How unlucky I am not to have been able to be associated with that

431

undertaking!" "Don't you worry, son," his mother replied. "Suez is finished, but there is another canal to be built in Panama. You can do it." One of his classmates was a boy who was to pay dearly for his Jewish blood: Alfred Dreyfus.

Then came the preparations for the Panama Canal. Once more Lesseps was the man of the hour, and the boy, who had just received his degree in engineering at the school of bridges and highways, wanted to take part in this last great adventure of the century. But the Panama Canal was a private enterprise, and by the school rules, the youth had to spend five years on State works. He was sent first to Africa, then to the highway being built between Paris and Cherbourg, until finally his dream was within his grasp: he went to Panama. Through a series of fortuitous circumstances he became chief engineer there. He was twenty-six years old. He studied carefully the canal plan calling for locks, and, though it was too late, persuaded the French company to adopt it. At the same time, he was initiated into two basic aspects of life in Panama: the fevers and the people. As a result of the fevers he had to return to France. There he made a number of business connections and, when he saw that the Lesseps company was going under, he began to cherish the hope that fate might have reserved for him what Lesseps was unable to accomplish. This engineer, a mixture of d'Artagnan and businessman — shrewd, ambitious, eloquent, scheming — was Philippe Bunau-Varilla. In the course of a few years, after giving up his post as State engineer and taking part in a number of financial ventures, he worked at the building of the railroad in the Belgian Congo and on flood control on the rivers in Rumania; he became president of the Madrid-Cáceres-Portugal railroad, one of the principal stockholders in the newspaper *Le Matin* of Paris, and editorial-writer; he ran for deputy with the idea of spurring France on to the idea of undertaking the building of the Canal once more, was defeated, and then published a book: *Panama — Past, Present and Future*.

On a train trip, Bunau-Varilla made the acquaintance of the Russian, Count Serge Witte, talked to him about Panama, and tried to show him that the future of the great Russian empire lay in Panama. Just as the Suez Canal, he explained, was the backbone of the Anglo-Saxon world and the continuation of the railroads that traverse the American continent, so the Panama Canal would be the natural extension of the Trans-Siberian railway. The Count was fascinated and convinced. Without hesitating he promised Bunau-Varilla that as soon as he reached St. Petersburg he would lay the matter before the Czar.

Not to put all his eggs in one basket, Bunau-Varilla next approached the English, and repeated to them what he had said to the Count, but in reverse: it was the glory of the British Empire he was interested in, he assured them.

But as things in England moved slowly, Bunau-Varilla turned his eyes to the United States, since, in the opinion of the silver-tongued engineer, the future of the United States lay in the Panama Canal. . . .

Bunau-Varilla explained his interest in finding capital to back his ideas by his ardent desire to save the glory of France. But it would be well to bear one fact in mind. After Lesseps's crash France's only solution for salvaging what she could from the wreckage was to form a new company, and Bunau-Varilla had invested in this speculation a good part of his fortune, which was considerable. The option granted by Colombia was about to expire, and if Russia, England, or the United States did not decide upon some step, and if the government of Colombia were not willing to grant an extension, the engineer stood to lose his money.

The first thing to do in the United States was to convince the government and Congress that Nicaragua was not the place for the Canal. So the two men most interested in the affair at the moment, Bunau-Varilla and a New York lawyer by the name of Cromwell, began their work in the lobbies of Congress, in newspapers, in clubs, at dinners. The need for the Canal had been impressed upon the public by the circumstances of the Spanish-American War. The battleship *Oregon*, for instance, which was at San Francisco, had had to proceed under forced draught through the Strait of Magellan to take part in the Battle of Santiago de Cuba in July 1898. It had broken all records, making the thirteen-thousand-mile trip in sixty-eight days. But it was plain to everyone that as long as this situation existed, the United States was at the mercy of her enemies. Bunau-Varilla published a pamphlet in which he belabored two points: America's imperative need for a canal and the inadvisability of building it in Nicaragua, where the work would take much longer and where there was always the risk of volcanic disturbances. According to the Frenchman's map, all Central America except Panama was a hotbed of volcanoes. His argument could not have been better timed. Mt. Pelée had just erupted in Martinique — in May 1902 — and the city of St. Pierre lay in ruins. The people of North America, always impressionable, were profoundly affected by the spectacular publicity given to this news. The Frenchman took advantage of the circumstance to point up the situation: "Take warning, you who favor the idea of the canal in Nicaragua. Momotombo is waiting for you there. So unknown are earthquakes in Panama that the arch of the church of Santo Domingo, which was one of the few buildings that escaped the fires started by Morgan when he raided the city, is still standing. It has remained intact because Panama is solid ground."

So intense was this earthquake propaganda that the government of Nicaragua felt called upon to protest. There have been no earthquakes or shocks in Nicaragua since 1835, an official communication stated. The Frenchman tore this communication to shreds. In 1902 — he pointed out — Momotombo had erupted. To mark the occasion, the government of Nicaragua had issued a stamp showing a volcano that looked like Vesuvius in the background, and the lake and railroad in the foreground. Bunau-Varilla went about to stamp-dealers, bought up as many of these stamps as he could find, and, pasting them on sheets of writing paper, he saw that one reached the desk of every Senator in Washington, marked "Official testimony regarding volcanic activity in Nicaragua."

434

Another party to all that was going on, an interested though practically mute spectator, was Colombia. Panama belonged to her, and she knew that it contained the key to her future. This arm of land, golden between two blue seas, forms the base of the nation's coat-of-arms; above it are the Phrygian Cap of Liberty and, at the top, two horns of plenty. Rather than a coat-of-arms, it looks like a vignette of all Colombia's history — the history of a people that three hundred, four hundred years before, starting at this isthmus, had begun to dream of the day when they should achieve liberty and plenty. But Colombia, like all the other Spanish American republics, had been rent by civil wars and in the course of its creation and organization had gone through the romantic, heroic anarchy of the nineteenth century. Even now a bitter struggle was being waged. The Conservatives had deposed the president they had put into office, a man of over eighty, and had replaced him with the vice-president, who was about the same age. The new executive, skeptical and vacillating, had reached that stage of life where he knew that, even if he failed to find peace in his political career, he would find it when he laid his head to rest on a stone pillow, and that the day was not too distant.

From the far-off window of Bogotá, perched so high that it was sometimes above the clouds, the panorama was a confused one. France, which had been passionately venerated as the abode of intelligence, the cradle of liberty, the mother of progress — to a superlative degree as befitted a romantic age — was now rocked by scandal. Thanks to the activities of Lesseps the name of Panama had become a stench in the nostrils. Tragedy seemed to be approaching Colombia as in a nightmare — and Colombia was unable to move. Railroads could not be built through the passes of the Andes wth the ease with which rails were laid across the plains of the Mississippi, and travel was still by mule. Panama was closer to New York by steamer than to Bogotá by bridle path.

A combination of dreamers, scoundrels, businessmen, and friends of progress were making plans in France and the United States for an undertaking that was to be carried out in territory

435

belonging to Colombia. In Washington an agreement was being reached for transferring the interests of the French company to the American government, according to a plan worked out by Bunau-Varilla. The U. S. Secretary of State and the Minister of Colombia had reached an agreement on a treaty to be submitted to the consideration of the Senates in Washington and Bogotá. The Minister had done his utmost to secure favorable terms, but the final text — which was largely the work of Cromwell, the lawyer of the French company — did not satisfy the Colombians. The treaty, following the lines of the agreement submitted by Bunau-Varilla, gave pre-eminence to the French company's interests, as was only natural. The United States had agreed to pay it $40,000,000, a good price for a corpse. The French had asked for $109,141,150. But the most serious part of the affair was not this; it was the terms of the treaty. Colombia realized that these terms would reduce her sovereignty in the Isthmus, and felt herself to be in the same situation as the United States when Secretary Hay signed a treaty with the English ambassador Pauncefote, which the Senate had refused to ratify for analogous reasons. The man who had led a vigorous campaign against its acceptance was Theodore Roosevelt.

Now this same Roosevelt, as President, had persuaded the Senate in Washington to approve the treaty drawn up with Colombia, and expected the legislature of Colombia to do the same, from duress rather than conviction. The President was a man of boundless energy, a big-game hunter, a rancher, who believed it was the manifest destiny of the United States to control the Caribbean, and who regarded the neighboring lands of the South as contemptible mice. One day England, Italy, and Germany blockaded the coast of Venezuela and fired on two fortresses by way of collecting some outstanding debts. For the moment, Roosevelt forgot about the Monroe Doctrine because it seemed to him a fine thing to "give Venezuela a kick in the pants" to teach her to fulfill her obligations. The President radiated an atmosphere of insolent optimism because his country was making its weight felt throughout the world by reason of its astounding progress. England had declared that it would view with favor the assumption of a guardianship by the United States over Latin America to avoid embroilments and to have a responsible power with which to deal.

In Bogotá, the old president, in his carpet slippers and skull cap, surrounded by conspirators and malcontent army leaders as advisers, was no match for Roosevelt. His ascent to power had been bad; getting out was going to be worse.

When the treaty was presented to the Colombian Congress it was evident that it would not be ratified. The patriotically minded used the argument of lost sovereignty in their attacks. The more prudent pointed out that the indemnity offered Colombia was totally inadequate. And all objected to the fact that Washington "was not asking — it was telling." The Minister of the United States in Bogotá transmitted to his government a suggestion he had received to the effect that of the $40,000,000 offered the French Company, Colombia should be paid $10,-000,000, and that instead of $10,000,000 for the concession, she should receive $15,000,000. These were questions of dollars and cents, but they made a deep impression on a country that had seen the railroad company of the Isthmus earn $50,000,000 in a few years, and was mortified that it should be treated with less regard than the French Company, which was like the illegitimate child of a woman responsible for the whole mess. Roosevelt flatly refused to modify the terms. "Although the President is favorably inclined toward the Panama project," said Miles P. DuVal, "there is the United States Senate to be taken into account, and elections are coming in November."

Roosevelt, who had pressed the United States Senate to reject the Hay-Pauncefote Treaty, refused to recognize the rights of the Colombian Senate to act as a deliberative body. Through the columns of the North American press the Colombian Senate received this notification: "President Roosevelt is determined to have the Panama canal route. He has no intention of beginning negotiations for the Nicaraguan route. . . . Advices received here daily indicate great opposition to the canal treaty at

Bogotá. . . . Information also has reached this city that the State of Panama stands ready to secede from Colombia and enter into a canal treaty with the United States. . . . A republican form of government will be organized. . . . The President of the United States would promptly recognize the new government. . . ." In his turn, John Hay, the Secretary of State, tele-graphed the American Minister in Bogotá: "If Colombia should now reject the treaty or unduly delay its ratification, the friendly understanding between the two countries would be so seriously compromised that action might be taken by the Congress next winter which every friend of Colombia would regret. . . ." And Bunau-Varilla, who was not going to play second fiddle to anybody, cabled the President of Colombia: "Failure to ratify the treaty will leave two choices open: the building of the canal through Nicaragua . . . or its construction through Panama after the Isthmus has seceded and declared its independence under the protection of the United States, as took place with Cuba. . . ."

The debating in Bogotá grew more impassioned. The note of the Secretary of State had come like a bombshell. Roosevelt was growing impatient and, in his unmistakable style he informed the Secretary of State: "Make it as strong as you can to Beaupré [Minister of the United States in Bogotá]. These contemptible little creatures in Bogotá ought to understand how much they are jeopardizing things and imperiling our future." Beaupré, following these instructions, wrote to the Minister of Foreign Affairs of Colombia while the treaty was being debated: "If Colombia really desires to maintain the present friendly relations existing between the two countries . . . the pending treaty should be ratified exactly in its present form, without any modifications whatever."

In Colombia the Senate refused to ratify the treaty.

Roosevelt's reaction is clear from these words of a personal letter to the Secretary of State: "Dear John: I fear we may have to give a lesson to those jack-rabbits." To his friend Professor Schurman he wrote: "If Congress will give me a certain amount of freedom and a certain amount of time, I believe I can do much better than by any action taken out of hand. But, of course, what Congress will do I don't know." And five days later he wrote to the Secretary of State: "At present I feel that there are two alternatives: (1) to take up Nicaragua; (2) in some shape or way to interfere when it becomes necessary so as to secure the Panama route without further dealing with the foolish and homicidal corruptionists in Bogotá. I am not inclined to have any further dealings whatever with those Bogotá people."

It must be borne in mind that this was the temperament of the President and the language of the period. When certain North American newspapers suggested a possible estrangement between the President and his Secretary of State, the President wrote his "Dear John" a letter in which he said: "Of course, do not give a thought to the newspapers and other swine who delight to invent tales about our relations." Senator Hanna wrote Roosevelt: "We must make *allowances* for the political situation in Colombia and the nature of the Animals we are dealing with. . . ." And Roosevelt answered: "I am not as sure as you are that the only virtue we need to exercise is patience. I think it well worth considering whether we had not better warn these jack-rabbits that great though our patience has been, it can be exhausted. . . ."

Some time before signing the treaty under study by the legislatures of the two nations, Roosevelt had already taken certain steps. Two American officers who were in Venezuela received orders to proceed to Panama in civilian dress, concealing their identity and acting as though they were on private business. The officers returned to Washington and informed the President that the belief current in Panama was that a secession revolt was soon going to break out. Bunau-Varilla wrote an editorial in *Le Matin* announcing that there would be a revolution in Panama, that the country would declare itself independent of Colombia, and that Roosevelt would immediately negotiate a treaty with the new republic — because the rights of nations like Colombia, said the writer, have a limit, and that limit is the good of mankind. And Roosevelt, he added, will base his action on this principle. Bunau-Varilla sent a copy of his article to the President, and then went to the United States where he stopped in Room 1162 of the Waldorf-Astoria. A group of Friends of Independence had been organized in Panama, and one of its leaders, Dr. Amador, went to New York, where he talked with Bunau-Varilla in Room 1162. There Bunau-Varilla outlined a complete plan: Bunau would act as intermediary to procure them such funds as they needed, and Washington would order its warships to stand off Panama so that Colombia could not send troops ashore to put down the revolution; Panama was to name Bunau-Varilla as its Minister Plenipotentiary to Washington, and he would arrange to have the treaty for the building of the Canal signed at once. The plan was accepted *in toto*.

Bunau-Varilla proceeded to Washington, talked with Roosevelt, and came away with the impression that Roosevelt would not neglect any opportunity that presented itself. Roosevelt has left his impression of this interview in a letter to a friend: "Privately, I would say that I should be delighted if Panama were an independent state, or if it made itself so at this moment, but for me to say so publicly would amount to an instigation for a revolt, and therefore I cannot say it. . . ."

Bunau-Varilla did not let the grass grow under his feet. He drew up a constitution and a declaration of independence. He designed a national flag, which his wife embroidered. He twisted his bushy French mustache and mused: "I am making a republic." In Panama, although they did not realize it, they were all relying on his promises with regard to money, recognition, and military support. Although no one had actually told him so, he knew that Washington would send the warships, and he could so assure the Panamanians. No man was ever more adept at reading between the lines, or had a keener ear for the unspoken word.

Certain Colombian troops reached Colón. It was purely a routine move. There was no sign of revolution. The troops were to proceed from Colón to Panama, and from there probably to the Costa Rican frontier. Mr. Shaler, the manager of the railroad in Colón, received the officers, entertained them in his private car, and ordered the engine to proceed. "But where are the troops?" "They'll be coming on the next train." The officers reached Panama. There was a solemn reception at the government house. The officers were flattered, but that was not what they had come for. They had the governor himself ask the railroad to have the troops brought. The railroad replied: "We cannot give them transportation unless their fares are paid in advance." The officers answered: "The fare will be paid at once, but send the troops." The governor told them not to worry, that the troops would soon be there; but they never arrived. Thus Mr. Shaler did his part to see that the revolution was effected without bloodshed. The revolution had not yet broken out.

Francis B. Loomis, Assistant Secretary of State and Bunau-Varilla's friend, sent an anxious telegram from Washington to the American consul in Panama: "Uprising on the Isthmus reported. Keep department promptly and fully informed." The consul replied: "No uprising yet. Reported will be in the night. Situation critical."

And in November 1903 the revolution broke out. A tiny Colombian gunboat managed to get within gun range and fired the six shots it had. Not a life was lost, unless one counts a Chinese killed and a donkey wounded in the streets of the city. In keeping with the plan drawn up, the American cruiser *Nashville* and the gunboat *Dixie* stood at the entrance to the harbor to prevent the landing of Colombian troops. On November 6 — one day, seventeen hours, and forty-one minutes after Washington had been informed by the American consul of the revolution — the Secretary of State issued a statement: "The people of Panama, in what would seem to be a unanimous move, has severed its political connections with the republic of Colombia and has assumed its independence." And then he at once instructed the Minister in Colombia to notify the government that the United States had recognized the new republic, and that the best plan would be for Colombia to enter into relations with the new state.

Without a moment's delay Bunau-Varilla was named envoy extraordinary and minister plenipotentiary of the Republic of Panama to the United States. On November 13, President Roosevelt received him officially at the White House. On the 15th, Sunday, he received from Secretary Hay the outline of the treaty. On the 16th, by ten at night, Bunau-Varilla had drawn up the complete and final version, which he returned to the Secretary of State on the 17th. A commission of lawyers was sent by Panama to examine the text of the treaty on which her future depended, and when they reached New York Bunau-Varilla telegraphed them: "Stay where you are and don't say why you have come." On the 18th the treaty was signed with great solemnity by Secretary Hay and Bunau-Varilla for the two governments. They used the inkwell that had belonged to Lincoln, and Hay offered a choice of two rings as seals: the one worn by Lord Byron when he died and that bearing the coat-of-arms of the Hay family. Bunau-Varilla used the Hay signet; Hay, that of Lord Byron. The lawyer who assisted Bunau-Varilla in the revision of the treaty text that Sunday night received $10,000. On the 24th the treaty was sent to Panama by a boat that left New York for Colón. The ship reached Colón on December 1. On the 2nd the government of Panama ratified it and returned it with all the official seals. On the 7th, Roosevelt, in his report to Congress on the state of the nation, gave an account of what had taken place. Although the Panama affair had once more become a major scandal, and the Senate was even asked to investigate Bunau-Varilla's activities, the treaty was ratified, and the investigation was never held. After all, Bunau was the official representative of a friendly nation!

Roosevelt commented on the situation in a letter to the editor of *Out West*, a Los Angeles periodical, as follows: ". . . But about this Colombian business, my feeling is that, if anything, I did not go far enough. No more cruel despotism outside of Turkey exists than that of the so-called Colombian Republic under its present political and ecclesiastical managements. . . . To the worst characteristics of 17th century Spain, and of Spain at its worst under Philip II, Colombia has added a squalid savagery of its own, and it has combined with exquisite nicety the worst forms of despotism and of anarchy, of violence and of fatuous weakness, of dismal ignorance, cruelty, treachery, greed and utter vanity. I cannot feel much respect for such a country. . . ." The reason for these discreet utterances by President Roosevelt was that the Congress of Colombia had refused to ratify a treaty it considered unfair.

Three months and twenty days after Panama's declaration of independence, the Senate in Washington approved the Bunau-Varilla treaty without any changes by a vote of 66 to 14. On the 25th the treaty was signed by both parties. Bunau-Varilla wrote: "I have defended the work of the genius of France; I have avenged her honor; I have served France." In his heart he was thinking that *he* was the genius of France. Two months later the United States Treasury Department made out a check for $40,000,000 to the French Company. "The great unsolved mystery," writes Samuel Flagg Bemis, "is who got the forty million." Bunau-Varilla resigned from his post as minister and gave up his diplomatic career. His mission had been fulfilled. He claimed that all he had received was a little better than $100,000, which represented the value of his shares. France made him a chevalier of the Legion of Honor.

In 1906 Stockholm awarded President Roosevelt the Nobel Peace Prize. In 1911 at the University of California, Roosevelt, his academic gown slipping from his broad shoulders, spoke before the students assembled in the Greek theater of the university's beautiful campus. The construction of the Canal was almost completed, and the two oceans would soon be linked together. Roosevelt, in ringing tones and sarcastic words said, amidst the laughter and applause of his listeners: "Fortunately the crisis came at a period when I could act unhampered. Accordingly I took the Canal Zone, started the Canal, and then left the Congress not to debate the Canal, but to debate me."

The tempestuous days of imperialism were over. After President Taft took office, Roosevelt went to explore the jungles of Brazil, to kill snakes and alligators. Then Woodrow Wilson was elected President, and it was he who in 1914 pressed the electric button in Washington that set off the charge that shattered the last rock and allowed the waters of the two oceans to flow together. But his policy in international affairs was one of rectification. He condemned imperialism in his speeches, and acknowledged that in the case of Colombia Roosevelt had used high-handed methods. A treaty was drawn up which began with a clause in which the government of the United States expressed its sincere regret for what had occurred. When Roosevelt, on his return from the jungle, learned of the new state of affairs, he lashed out in these words: "The proposed treaty is a crime against the United States. It is an attack upon the honor of the United States which, if justified, would convict the United States of infamy. . . . The payment can only be justified upon the ground that this nation has played the part of a thief or of a receiver of stolen goods."

The United States Senate did not ratify this treaty until 1922, three years after Roosevelt's death.

The Canal was a magnificent achievement. France paid dear for her experience, Colombia "got it in the neck," Gorgas killed the mosquitoes, the locks were built, and the ships sailed through. It is a marvelous sight, like a thing of magic, to see from the distance how the huge ocean liners are raised in the locks and then pass from the Atlantic to the Pacific, from the Pacific to the Atlantic, drawn by mechanical mules. As seen from the highways of the Canal Zone, they look like elephants being dragged along on chains by little dogs. James Truslow Adams, the American historian, deplored the fact that Roosevelt had lacked the patience to do the job honestly. And Bemis observed: "The intervention of 1903 is really the blot on the Latin American policy of the United States, and it is a big one." Nothing was done in Nicaragua, but from Nicaragua came the poetical expression of Spanish America's condemnation of Roosevelt. The poetry of Rubén Darío, the author of the *Ode to Roosevelt*, represents to that America what Walt Whitman's poems stand for in North America:

THE AGE OF LIBERTY

You would have to be, O Roosevelt,
God's Own mighty hunter and dread rifleman
To hold us in your clutching iron claws.

.   .   .   .   .   .

And even though you count on everything,
You still lack one thing: God.

RUBÉN DARÍO
(Ode to Roosevelt)

EPILOGUE TO THIS HISTORY,

PROLOGUE TO A NEW LIFE

Tʜᴇ twentieth century is in its forty-fifth year. This is a goodly age for a century, especially for a century in which life has moved at such a dizzying pace. Nevertheless, the place of the twentieth century in history is still an enigma. Wars have achieved new proportions; they are now global, they are fought on the seven seas, on the five continents, in the depths of the oceans, and in the air. Why do men fight? What are they seeking? Man cannot live in peace, he cannot remain static, he must fight for something. If there is to be peace, it will have to be an active peace, the motives of conflict will have to be kept alive, though transformed, to provide an outlet for man's ambition, his inventiveness, his restless spirit.

What is the balance that remains from these tales of the life of the New World? A series of bandits' exploits, some will say. In this world of ours, peoples do not behave like choirs of angels, and in the course of the struggle human passions have stained more than one page of their annals with blood and even with mud. But beneath the murky, confused currents of American life that have been flowing for four hundred years, there runs a living stream of the noblest aspirations. The history of the ideals of America is the history of its people. Sometimes the people have found generous leaders; sometimes their captains have been bandits; sometimes their champions have been, at one and the same time, a purifying and a consuming fire. But out of all these contradictory elements the New World has arisen as the hope of free men.

The people have passed through a series of phases in the course of their forward march. In the sixteenth century their ambition was to conquer a world; in the seventeenth, to mingle their blood with that of the conquered world; in the eighteenth, to achieve their liberty; in the nineteenth, to affirm their independence. These are all parts of a single concept — democracy — which persists as a goal to be aimed at, a hope, an ideal yet to be won. There will be complete democracy only when there is justice for the lowly; when there is respect — not mere "tolerance" — for one's neighbor, and the possibility of working and living together in a community of men of all sorts.

The Caribbean has been the tempestuous sea over which all the hurricanes have swept. This will hold true in the future. The manifest destiny of America is not the imperialistic ambitions of one country, but the extension of democratic ideals throughout the hemisphere. This is how it is understood by all who inhabit the lands that stretch from Alaska to Patagonia. As they reflect on the legends of their heroes, the black, the brown, the white people of islands still sing:

> Onward, Lincoln, onward,
> Our hope looks up to thee.

And the ships with their gay-colored flags that set out upon this stormy sea sail under the protection of those words that Bolívar gave his warriors as their shield and buckler when they went into battle: "The liberty of America is the hope of mankind."

Free Cuba; democratic Costa Rica; redeemed Venezuela; indomitable Mexico; noisy Martinique; the all-powerful United States; Panama, heart of the mariner's compass; Guatemala, which stretches back to the earliest dreams of the Indians; Colombia, nurtured on the love of her republic; musical Haiti; Ponce de Leon's Puerto Rico; Columbus's Santo Domingo; Rubén Darío's Nicaragua; Honduras, oppressed again and again — tiny islands, great continents, little republics — all gaze out upon these waters and entrust their hopes to them.

The islands, the republics, are sown with dictators, with barbarous leaders who are the last survivors of the nineteenth century. They will not endure. One by one, they will topple before the surge of the people. Many of them can already be seen tottering, in their beribboned, theatrical uniforms, with their tin swords, above the rising tide of the masses. The twentieth century has not yet spoken its last word. Just as out of the mature waters of the Mediterranean we saw the divine form of the Renaissance Venus emerge, so in the warm breezes of the Caribbean the flags of democracy will fly symbolizing the hope of the nations of America, the fulfillment of the promise of Bolívar: "The liberty of America is the hope of the universe."

449

BIBLIOGRAPHY

CHAPTER I

EMIL LUDWIG: *The Mediterranean: Saga of a Sea*. New York and London: Whittlesey House, McGraw-Hill Book Co.; 1942.

WILHELM VON BODE: *Sandro Botticelli*. New York: Charles Scribner's Sons; 1925.

F. A. VARNHAGEN: *Amerigo Vespucci, son caractère, ses écrits, sa vie et ses navigations*. Lima, 1865.

STEFAN ZWEIG: *Amerigo, a comedy of errors in history*. New York: Viking Press; 1942.

M. FERNÁNDEZ DE NAVARRETE: *Colección de viajes y descubrimientos*. Madrid, 1829.

EDWARD GIBBON: *The Decline and Fall of the Roman Empire*. New York: Modern Library; 1933.

C. F. YOUNG: *The Medici*. New York: Modern Library; 1933.

CHAPTER II

M. FERNÁNDEZ DE NAVARRETE, op. cit.

FERNANDO COLÓN: *Historia del Almirante don Cristóbal Colón*. Madrid, 1892.

ANDRÉS BERNÁLDEZ: *Historia de los Reyes Católicos*. Sevilla, 1870.

BARON VON HUMBOLDT: *Colón y el descubrimiento de América*. Madrid: Biblioteca Clásica; 1926.

SAMUEL ELIOT MORISON: *Admiral of the Ocean Sea*. Boston: Little, Brown & Co.; 1942.

SALVADOR DE MADARIAGA: *El Muy Magnífico don Cristóbal Colón*. Buenos Aires, 1940.

DUQUESA DE BERWICK Y DE ALBA: *Nuevos Autógrafos de Cristóbal Colón*. Madrid, 1902.

M. SERRANO Y SANZ: *Orígenes de la dominación española*. Madrid: Bailly-Baillière; 1918.

WILLIAM H. PRESCOTT: *History of the Reign of Fernando and Isabella*. London: Richard Bentley & Son; 1849.

CHAPTER III

WILLIAM H. PRESCOTT, op. cit.

PRUDENCIO DE SANDOVAL: *Historia de la vida y hechos del Emperador Carlos V*. Pamplona, 1634.

450

BIBLIOGRAPHY

Gonzalo Fernández de Oviedo: *Historia general y natural de Indias.* Madrid, 1853.

M. Fernández de Navarrete, op. cit.

Fray Bartolomé de las Casas: *Historia de las Indias.* Madrid, 1875.

M. Serrano y Sanz, op. cit.

CHAPTER IV

José Toribio Medina: *El Descubrimiento del Océano Pacífico.* Santiago de Chile, 1914.

Ángel de Altolaguirre: *Vasco Núñez de Balboa.* Madrid, 1914.

M. Serrano y Sanz, op. cit.

M. Fernández de Navarrete, op. cit.

Pietro Martire: *De orbe novo.* Sevilla, 1511.

Gonzalo Fernández de Oviedo, op. cit.

Fray Bartolomé de las Casas, op. cit.

Manuel José Quintana: *Vidas de españoles.* Paris, 1845.

CHAPTER V

Alonso de Santa Cruz: *Crónica del Emperador Carlos V.* Madrid, 1920–2.

Prudencio de Sandoval, op. cit.

Francisco Cervantes de Salazar: *Crónica de la Nueva España.* Madrid, 1914.

Bernal Díaz del Castillo: *Conquista de la Nueva España.* Madrid, 1853.

Hernán Cortés: *Relaciones y Cartas.* Madrid, 1852.

Francisco López de Gómara: *Conquista de México.* Madrid, 1852.

William H. Prescott: *History of the Conquest of Mexico.* London, 1849.

Miguel M. Lerdo de Tejada: *Apuntes históricos de la heroica ciudad de Vera Cruz.* Mexico: I. Cumplido; 1850–8. 3 vols.

CHAPTER VI

Gonzalo Fernández de Oviedo, op. cit.

Alvar Núñez Cabeza de Vaca: *Naufragios y relación de la jornada que hizo a la Florida.* Madrid, 1922.

Inca Garcilaso de la Vega: *La Florida: Historia del Adelantado Hernando de Soto.* Lisboa, 1605.

The Elvas account of De Soto from the beginning of his enterprise to his arrival and encampment in Florida; in Shipp, Barnard: *The History of Hernando de Soto and Florida*. Philadelphia, 1881.

JOSEPH ACOSTA: *Historia natural de las Indias*. Sevilla, 1590.

LEONARD OLSCHKI: "Ponce de Leon's Fountain of Youth"; in the *Hispanic American Historical Review*, August 1941.

GERMÁN ARCINIEGAS: *The Knight of El Dorado*. New York: Viking Press; 1942.

CHAPTER VII

M. MIGNET: *Rivalité de François I et Charles Quint*. Paris, 1875.

HENRY M. BAIRD: *The Rise of the Huguenots of France*. New York, 1879.

ALONSO DE SANTA CRUZ, op. cit.

FRANCISCO LÓPEZ DE GÓMARA: *"Anales del Emperador Carlos V"; Boletín de la Real Academia de la historia*. Madrid, 1913, Vol. LXII, pp. 323–7.

A. F. POLLARD: *Henry VIII*. London: Longmans, Green & Co.; 1934.

J. C. BREVOORT: *Verrazano the Navigator*. New York, 1874.

HENRY LEMONNIER: *Histoire de France*, Vol. V (Ernest Lavisse, éditeur).

INCA GARCILASO DE LA VEGA, op. cit.

W. ADOLPHE ROBERTS: *The French in the West Indies*. Indianapolis: Bobbs-Merrill Co.; 1942.

FRANÇOIS RABELAIS: *Gargantua et Pantagruel*. (*Œuvres complètes*, Paris, 1929, 5 vols., Vols. I and II.)

LEONARDO OLSCHKI: "The Columbian Nomenclature of the Lesser Antilles," in the *Geographical Review*, November 1943.

GERMÁN ARCINIEGAS: *Germans in the Conquest of America*. New York: The Macmillan Co.; 1943.

CHAPTER VIII

J. E. NEALE: *Queen Elizabeth*. New York: Harcourt, Brace & Co.; 1934.

FRANCIS HACKETT: *Henry the Eighth*. New York: Horace Liveright; 1929.

R. A. J. WALLING: *A Sea-Dog of Devon: A Life of Sir John Hawkins*. London, 1907.

GEOFFREY CALLENDER: *The Naval Side of British History*. London: Christophers; [1924].

JOAN SUÁREZ DE PERALTA: *Tratado del descubrimiento de Yndias y su conquista*. Madrid: Hernández; 1878.

JAMES ANTHONY FROUDE: *English Seamen of the XVI Century*. London: Longmans, Green & Co.; 1923.

JULIAN S. CORBETT: *Drake and the Tudor Navy*. London, 1898.

ZELIA NUTTALL: *New Light on Drake*. London: Hakluyt Society; 1914.

BIBLIOGRAPHY

JUAN DE CASTELLANOS: *Discurso del Capitán Draque.* (Con prólogo, notas y documentos de Ángel González Palencia.) Madrid, 1921.

LADY ELLIOTT-DRAKE: *The Family and Heirs of Sir Francis Drake.* London: Smith, Elder & Co.; 1922. 2 vols.

JOHN SPARKE and JOHN HAWKINS: *Narratives.* London: Hakluyt Collection; 1893.

LOPE DE VEGA: *La Dragontea.* Madrid, 1598.

PEDRO HENRÍQUEZ UREÑA: *La cultura y las letras coloniales en Santo Domingo.* Buenos Aires, 1936.

FRAY PEDRO SIMÓN: *Noticias historiales de las conquistas de Tierra Firme.* Bogotá, 1882.

A. E. W. MASON: *The Life of Francis Drake.* New York: Doubleday, Doran & Co.; 1942.

SIR FRANCIS DRAKE: *The World Encompassed.* London: Hakluyt Collection; 1893.

Documentos del Archivo de Indias. (*Boletín de Historia y Antigüedades,* Bogotá, 1933, Vol. XX.)

CHAPTER IX

FRAY PEDRO SIMÓN, op. cit.

FRAY ANTONIO CAULÍN: *Historia corográphica de la Nueva Andalucía.* Madrid, 1779.

FLÓREZ DE OCARIZ: *Genealogías del Nuevo Reino de Granada.* Madrid, 1674.

JOSEPH GUMILLA: *El Orinoco ilustrado.* Madrid, 1741.

LYTTON STRACHEY: *Elizabeth and Essex.* New York: Harcourt, Brace & Co.; 1928.

J. E. NEALE, op. cit.

IRVIN ANTHONY: *Raleigh and His World.* New York: Charles Scribner's Sons; 1934.

THOMAS WRIGHT: *The History of Ireland.* London and New York [1854], 3 vols.

SIR WALTER RALEIGH: *The Discovery of Guiana.* (Foreword and documents by Sir Robert H. Schomburgk.) London Hakluyt Society; 1848.

——: *The History of the World* (*with the Life and Tryal of the Author*). London, 1687.

——: "His Last Speech"; in *The World's Best Orations,* David J. Brewer, editor.

J. A. VAN HEUVEL: *El Dorado.* New York, 1844.

CHAPTER X

W. ADOLPHE ROBERTS: *The French in the West Indies.* Indianapolis: Bobbs-Merrill Co.; 1942.

JOHN FISKE: *The Dutch and Quaker Colonies in America.* Boston: Riverside Pocket edition, Houghton Mifflin Co.; 1915.

JOHN LOTHROP MOTLEY and WILLIAM ELLIOT GRIFFIS: *The Dutch Republic.* London, 1899.

LENIS BLANCHE: *Histoire de la Guadaloupe.* Paris, 1938.

ARTHUR PERCIVAL NEWTON: *The Colonizing Activities of the English Puritans.* London, 1914.

JAMES BURNEY: *History of the Buccaneers of America.* London, 1816.

PHILIP AINSWORTH MEANS: *The Spanish Main.* New York: Charles Scribner's Sons; 1935.

JOHN EXQUEMELING: *The Buccaneers of America.* London, 1684.

E. A. CRUIKSHANK: *The Life of Henry Morgan.* Toronto: The Macmillan Co.; 1935.

CHAPTER XI

EDWARD LONG: *History of Jamaica.* London, 1774.

THOMAS GAGE: *A New Survey of the West Indies.* London, 1655.

W. ADOLPHE ROBERTS: *The Caribbean.* Indianapolis: Bobbs-Merrill Co.; 1940.

VINCENT T. HARLOW: *A History of Barbados.* Oxford, 1926.

C. S. S. HIGHAM: *The Development of the Leeward Islands under the Restoration.* Cambridge: University Press; 1921.

E. A. CRUICKSHANK, op. cit.

JOHN EXQUEMELING, op. cit.

JAMES BURNEY, op. cit.

CHAPTER XII

JEAN BAPTISTE LABAT: *Nouveau Voyage aux isles de l'Amérique.* La Haye, 1724.

JEAN BAPTISTE DU TERTRE: *Histoire général des Antilles habitées par les Français.* Paris, 1667–71.

SIEUR PONTIS: *Account of the Taking of Carthagena.* London, 1740.

NELLIS M. CROUSE: *The French Struggle for the West Indies.* New York: Columbia University Press; 1943.

W. ADOLPHE ROBERTS: *The French in the West Indies.* Indianapolis: Bobbs-Merrill Co.; 1942.

BIBLIOGRAPHY

JERÓNIMO BECKER and JOSÉ MARÍA RIVAS GROOT: *El Nuevo Reino de Granada en el siglo XVIII*. Madrid, 1921.

JOHN FISKE, op. cit

CHAPTER XIII

WALDEMAR WESTERGAARD: *The Danish West Indies under Company Rule*. New York: The Macmillan Co., 1917.

GEORGE PRATT INSH: *The Company of Scotland Trading to Africa and the Indies*. New York: Charles Scribner's Sons; 1932.

FRANCIS RUSSELL HART: *The Disaster of Darien*. Boston: Houghton Mifflin Co.; 1929.

JAMES SAMUEL BARBOUR: *William Paterson and the Darien Company: Original Letters and Official Documents*. London, 1907.

GRAHAM BALFOUR: *The Life of Robert Louis Stevenson*. London, 1918.

FRANK CUNDALL: *The Darien Venture*. New York: Hispanic Society of America; 1926.

EDWARD LONG: *History of Jamaica*. London, 1774. 3 vols.

WILLIAM LEE: *Daniel Defoe*. London: J. C. Hollen; 1869. 3 vols.

GERSTLE MACK: *The Land Divided*. New York: Alfred A. Knopf; 1944.

CHAPTER XIV

CHARLES GAYARRÉ: *History of Louisiana*. New Orleans, 1885.

W. ADOLPHE ROBERTS: *The French in the West Indies*. Indianapolis: Bobbs-Merrill Co.; 1942.

HODDING CARTER: *The Lower Mississippi*. New York: Farrar & Rinehart; 1942.

CHAPTER XV

ANTONIO FERRER DEL RÍO: *Historia del reinado de Carlos III*. Madrid, 1856.

ANTONIO CÁNOVAS DEL CASTILLO: *Bosquejo histórico de la casa de Austria en España*. Madrid, 1911.

RAMÓN DE BASTERRA: *Una empresa del siglo XVIII: los navíos de la Ilustración*. Caracas, 1925.

JACOBO DE PEZUELA: *Historia de la isla de Cuba*. Madrid, 1868–78.

PEDRO HENRÍQUEZ UREÑA, op. cit.

CHAPTER XVI

JOSÉ MANUEL GROOT: *Historia eclesiástica y civil de la Nueva Granada*. Bogotá, 1869.

BIBLIOGRAPHY

EDWARD VERNON: *An Account of the Expedition to Carthagena in 1740.* London, reprinted Edinburgh, 1743.

MODESTO LAFUENTE: *Historia general de España.* Madrid, 1850.

A Journal of the Expedition to Carthagena. London: J. Roberts; 1744.

LEANDER MCCORMICK GOODHEART: "Admiral Vernon, His Marylanders and His Medals"; in *Maryland Historical Magazine*, September 1905.

CLAYTON C. HALL: "Maryland's Part in the Expedition against Carthagena"; in the *Hispanic American Historical Review*, May 1943.

FRANCIS RUSSELL HART: *Ataques del Almirante Vernon al Continente Americano. (Boletín de Historia y Antigüedades*, Bogotá, July 1917.)

CHAPTER XVII

EDMOND and JULES GONCOURT: *Madame Pompadour.* Paris, 1860.

CHARLES GAYARRÉ, op. cit.

JACOBO DE LA PEZUELA, op. cit.

ANTONIO FERRER DEL RÍO, op. cit.

JUAN F. YELA UTRILLA: *España ante la guerra de independencia de los Estados Unidos.* Lérida, 1925. 2 vols.

HERBERT ASBURY: *The French Quarter.* New York: Alfred A. Knopf; 1936.

ARTHUR P. WHITAKER: "Antonio de Ulloa"; in the *Hispanic American Historical Review*, May 1935.

CHAPTERS XVIII & XIX

C. L. R. JAMES: *The Black Jacobins.* New York: Dial Press; 1938.

PERCY WAXMAN: *The Black Napoleon.* New York: Harcourt, Brace & Co.; 1931.

THOMAS MADIOU: *Histoire de Haïti.* Port-au-Prince, Haiti, 1922.

ADOLPHE CABON: *Histoire de Haïti.* Port-au-Prince, Haiti [192?–37], 4 vols.

DANTES BELLEGARDE: *Haïti et ses problémes.* Montreal: Editions B. Valiquette; 1941.

JOSEPH TURQUAN: *L'Impératrice Josephine.* Paris, 1895–6.

BARON DE MENEVAL: *L'Impératrice Josephine.* Paris, 1910.

ARTHUR RAMOS: *As culturas negras no novo mundo.* Rio de Janeiro, 1937.

H. P. DAVIS: *Black Democracy.* New York: Dial Press; 1928.

CHAPTER XX

The Pirates' Own Book, or Authentic Narratives of the Lives, Exploits and Executions of the Most Celebrated Robbers. Boston, 1924.

BIBLIOGRAPHY

CAPTAIN CHARLES JOHNSON: *A General History of the Robberies and Murders of the Most Notorious Pirates.* London, 1724.

LYLE SAXON: *Lafitte, the Pirate.* New York: Appleton-Century Co.; 1939.

HERBERT ASBURY, op. cit.

CONSTANCE ROURKE: *Audubon.* New York: Harcourt, Brace & Co.; 1936.

CHAPTER XXI

ALEJANDRO MARURE: *Bosquejo histórico de las revoluciones en Centro América.* Guatemala, 1877–8. 2 vols.

ROBUSTIANO VERA: *Apuntes para la historia de Honduras.* Santiago de Chile, 1899.

LORENZO MONTÚFAR: *Walker en Centro América.* Guatemala, 1887.

WILLIAM WALKER: *The War in Nicaragua.* Mobile, 1860.

CHAPTER XXII

WILLIAM SPENCE ROBERTSON: *La Vida de Miranda.* Buenos Aires, 1938.

JOSÉ NUCETE SARDI: *Aventura y tragedia de Don Francisco Miranda.* Caracas, 1935.

RICARDO BECERRA: *Vida de Don Francisco Miranda.* Caracas, 1896.

SALVADOR DE MADARIAGA: *España.* Buenos Aires, 1942.

Archivo del General Miranda. Caracas, 1929–38. 15 vols.

R. BOTERO SALDARRIAGA: *"Los Afrancesados"*; in *Revista de las Indias,* Bogotá, April 1939.

CHAPTER XXIII

JULES MANCINI: *Bolívar.* Paris, 1930.

VICENTE LECUNA: *Proclamas y discursos del Libertador.* Caracas, 1939.

RIVAS VICUÑA: *Las Guerras de Bolívar.* Bogotá, 1934–8.

CASTO FULGENCIO LÓPEZ: *La Guaira.* Caracas, 1941.

LUIS BERMÚDEZ DE CASTRO: *Boves.* Madrid, 1934.

THOMAS ROURKE: *Man of Glory, Simón Bolívar.* New York: William Morrow & Co.; 1941.

TOMÁS CIPRIANO DE MOSQUERA: *Memorias sobre la vida del Libertador.* Bogotá, 1940.

CHAPTER XXIV

RAMIRO GUERRA SÁNCHEZ: *Manuel de Historia de Cuba.* Havana, 1938.

ÁNGEL OSSORIO Y GALLARDO: *Orígenes próximos de la España actual.* Buenos Aires, 1940.

457

H. Portell Vilá: *Céspedes*. Madrid, 1931.

Fernando Figueredo Socarrás: *Pedro Figueredo*. Cabu, 1924.

Jorge Mañach: *Martí el Apóstol*. Buenos Aires, 1936.

Fernando Ortiz: *Contrapunteo del tabaco y el azúcar*. Havana, 1940.

Salvador de Madariaga: *España*. Buenos Aires, 1942.

CHAPTERS XXV & XXVI

Gerstle Mack: op. cit.

André Siegfried: *Suez and Panama*. New York: Harcourt, Brace & Co.; [1940].

Miles P. Duval: *Cádiz to Cathay*. Stanford University Press, 1940.

Samuel Flagg Bemis: *The Latin American Policy of the United States*. New York: Harcourt, Brace & Co.; 1943.

Allan Nevins and Henry Steele Commager: *America, the History of a Free People*. Boston: Little, Brown & Co.; 1943.

BIBLIOGRAPHICAL UPDATE
FOR THE 2003 EDITION

Among numerous books published on Caribbean history since 1946, the following provide a good introduction and bibliographical data for further research.

GENERAL CARIBBEAN HISTORY

Benítez-Rojo, Antonio. *The Repeating Island: The Caribbean and the Postmodern Perspective*, translated by James Maranisse. Durham: Duke University Press, 1992.

Bolland, O. Nigel. *Struggles for Freedom: Essays on Slavery, Colonialism, and Culture in the Caribbean and Central America*. Belize: The Angelus Press; Kingston, Jamaica: Ian Randle Publishers, 1997.

Knight, Franklin. *The Caribbean: The Genesis of a Fractured Nationalism*. 2d ed. New York: Oxford University Press, 1990.

Lewis, Gordon K. *Main Currents in Caribbean Thought: The Historical Evolution of Caribbean Society in Its Ideological Aspects, 1492–1900*. Baltimore: Johns Hopkins University Press, 1983.

Martínez-Fernández, Luis. *Torn Between Empires: Economy, Society, and Patterns of Political Thought in the Hispanic Caribbean, 1840–1878*. Athens: University of Georgia Press, 1994.

Mintz, Sidney W. *Caribbean Transformations*. New York: Columbia University Press, 1989.

Mintz, Sidney, and Sally Price, eds. *Caribbean Contours*. Baltimore: Johns Hopkins University Press, 1985.

Richardson, Bonham C. *The Caribbean in the Wider World, 1492–1992: A Regional Geography*. Cambridge and New York: Cambridge University Press, 1992.

Rogozínski, Jan. *A Brief History of the Caribbean: From the Arawak and Caribes to the Present*. New York: Penguin, 1999.

Williams, Eric. *From Columbus to Castro: The History of the Caribbean 1492–1969*. London: Andre Deutsch, 1970.

THE MEDITERRANEAN SEA

The intellectual successors to Ludwig's *The Mediterranean* are the writings of Fernand Braudel, especially *The Mediterranean and the Mediterranean World in the Age of Philip II*, translated by Sian Reynolds. 2 vols. New York: Harper & Row, 1972–73.

PRE-COLUMBIAN CULTURE
AND CHRISTOPHER COLUMBUS

Cohen, J. M., editor and translator. *The Four Voyages of Christopher Columbus; being his own log-book, letters and dispatches with connecting narrative drawn from the Life of the Admiral by his son Hernando Colon and other contemporary historians*. Harmondsworth: Penguin, 1969.

Fernández de Oviedo y Valés, Gonzalo. *Natural History of the West Indies*, edited and translated by Sterling Stoudemire. Chapel Hill: University of North Carolina Press, 1959.

Phillips, William D., Jr., and Carla Rahn Phillips. *The World of Christopher Columbus*. New York: Cambridge University Press, 1992.

West, Robert, and John Augellis. *Middle America: Its Lands and People*. Englewood Cliffs, N.J.: Prentice Hall, 1989.

THE EUROPEAN EXPANSION

Allen, Hubert R. *Buccaneer: Admiral Sir Henry Morgan*. London: Barker, 1976.

Boxer, Charles R. *The Dutch Seaborne Empire, 1600–1800*. New York: Knopf, 1965.

Domínguez Ortiz, Antonio. *The Golden Age of Spain, 1515–1659*, translated by James Casey. London: Weidenfeld and Nicolson, 1971.

Duffy, Michael. *The British Expeditions to the West Indies and the War against Revolutionary France*. Oxford: Oxford University Press, 1987.

Fick, Carolyn. *The Making of Haiti: The Saint Domingue Revolution from Below*. Knoxville: University of Tennessee Press, 1990.

Johnson, H. B., Jr., ed. *From Conquest to Empire: The Iberian Back-*

around of Latin American History. New York: Knopf, 1970.

Lane, Kris E. *Blood and Silver: A History of Piracy in the Caribbean and Central America.* Kingston: Ian Randle Publishers, 1999.

McNeill, William H. *The Rise of the West.* Chicago: University of Chicago Press, 1963.

Parry, John H. *The Spanish Seaborne Empire.* New York: Knopf, 1966.

————. *The Age of Reconnaissance.* Berkeley: University of California Press, 1981.

Rankin, Hugh F. *The Golden Age of Piracy.* Williamsburg, Va.: Colonial Williamsburg; New York: Holt, Rinehart & Winston, 1969.

Ros, Martin. *Night of Fire: The Black Napoleon and the Battle for Haiti,* translated by Karin Ford-Treep. New York: Sarpedon, 1994.

Sugden, John. *Sir Francis Drake.* New York: Henry Holt, 1990.

SLAVERY AND PLANTATION

Curtin, Philip. *The Atlantic Slave Trade.* Madison: University of Wisconsin Press, 1969.

Curtin, Philip. *The Rise and Fall of the Plantation Complex: Essays in Atlantic History.* 2nd ed. Cambridge: Cambridge University Press, 1998.

Mintz, Sidney W. *Sweetness and Power: The Place of Sugar in Modern History.* New York: Viking, 1985.

Mintz, Sidney, and Richard Price. *The Birth of African-American Culture: An Anthropological Perspective.* Boston: Beacon Press, 1992.

Shepherd, Verene, and Hilary McD. Beckles, eds. *Caribbean Slavery in the Atlantic World.* Princeton: Markus Wiener Publishers, 2000.

LATIN AMERICAN REVOLUTION

Bushnell, David, ed. *El Libertador: Writings of Simón Bolívar,* translated by F. H. Forndoff. New York: Oxford University Press, 2003.

Harvey, Robert. *Latin American Struggle for Independence*. Woodstock: Overlook Press, 2000.

Racine, Karen. *Francisco de Miranda: A Transatlantic Life in the Age of Revolution*. Wilmington, Del.: SR Books, 2003.

Trend, J.B. *Bolivar and the Independence of Spanish America*. New York: Harper & Row, 1968.

NATIONAL HISTORIES

Cuba

Humboldt, Alexander von. *The Island of Cuba*, translated by J.S. Thrasher and Shelley Frisch. With a new introduction by Luis Martínez-Fernández. Princeton: Markus Wiener, 2001.

Perez, Louis A., Jr. *Cuba: Between Reform and Revolution*. New York: Oxford University Press, 1999.

Thomas, Hugh. *Cuba, or, the Pursuit of Freedom*. New York: Da Capo, 1998.

Puerto Rico

Wagenheim, Olga Jiménez de. *Puerto Rico: An Interpretive History from Pre-Columbian Times to 1900*. Princeton: Markus Wiener, 1998.

The Dominican Republic

Moya Pons, Frank. *The Dominican Republic: A National History*. Princeton: Markus Wiener, 1998.

Sagás, Ernesto, and Orlando Inoa, eds. *The Dominican People: A Documentary History*. Princeton: Markus Wiener, 2003.

Haiti

Arthur, Charles, and Michael Dash, eds. *Libète: A Haiti Anthology*. Princeton: Markus Wiener, 1999.

Heinl, Michael, Robert Debs Heinl, Jr., and Nancy Gordon Heinl. *Written in Blood: The Story of the Haitian People, 1492–1995*. Lanham, Md.: University Press of America, 1996.

James, C. L. R. *The Black Jacobins: Toussaint L'Ouverture and the San Domingo Revolution*, with introduction and notes by James Walvin. London; New York: Penguin, 2001.

Nicholls, David. *From Dessalines to Duvalier: Race, Colour and National Independence in Haiti*. New Brunswick, N.J.: Rutgers University Press, 1996.

Barbados

Hilary McD. Beckles. *History of Barbados*. New York: Cambridge University Press, 1999.

Panama

LaFeber, Walter. *The Panama Canal: The Crisis in Historical Perspective*. New York: Oxford University Press, 1989 (updated edition).

Nicaragua

Rosset, Peter, and John Vandermeer, eds. *The Nicaragua Reader: Documents of a Revolution under Fire*. New York: Grove Press, 1983.

Jamaica

Sherlock, Philip, and Hazel Bennett, *The Story of the Jamaican People*. Princeton: Markus Wiener, 1998.

CHRONOLOGY

1451 Birth of Columbus in Genoa
1454 Birth of Vespucci in Florence
1475 Simonetta Vespucci chosen Queen of Beauty in Florence
1476 Death of Simonetta Vespucci
1485 Henry VII crowned King of England

1492 Discovery of America

1492 Granada falls to Their Catholic Majesties
1492 Death of Lorenzo de' Medici
1493 Pope Alexander VI issues bull dividing new discoveries between Spain and Portugal

1493-6 Second voyage of Columbus

1494 Birth of Francis Drake
1497 Vasco da Gama rounds Cape of Good Hope

1497 First voyage of John Cabot

1498-1500 Third voyage of Columbus
1499 Voyage of Sebastian Cabot
1500 Cabral discovers Brazil
1502-4 Fourth voyage of Columbus

1504 Death of Queen Isabella of Spain
1505 Death of Pope Alexander VI
1506 Death of Columbus
1506 Philip the Fair enters Spain and dies same year
1509 Death of Henry VII of England. Succeeded by Henry VIII (b.1491)

1510 First Negro slaves brought into the Antilles
1513 Balboa discovers the Pacific
1513 Ponce de León discovers Florida

1515 Francis I (b.1494) crowned King of France
1516 Death of Ferdinand the Catholic. Beginning of regency of Cisneros
1517 Charles V (b.1500) crowned King of Castile

1519 Charles V of Spain elected Holy Roman Emperor

1519–22 Voyage of Magellan

1519–22 Conquest of Mexico by Cortés

1519–21 War of the *comuneros* in Spain

1519 English corsairs appear

1523 Verrazano captures ship carrying treasure sent to Spain by Cortés

1525 Francis I taken prisoner at Pavia

1527 Pánfilo de Narváez's expedition to Florida

1528 William Hawkins's voyage to Brazil

1521 Conquest of Peru by Pizarro

1534 Rabelais publishes *Gargantua*

1536–8 Conquest of New Granada by Jiménez de Quesada

1538 First university in America founded in Santo Domingo

1539 Hernando de Soto's expedition to Florida

1539 First book published in Mexico

1547 Death of Henry VIII of England. Succeeded by Edward VI

1547 Death of Francis I of France. Succeeded by Henry II

1547 Death in Seville of Hernán Cortés

1551 University of Mexico founded

1553 Death of Edward VI of England. Succeeded by Mary Tudor

1556 Charles V abdicates in favor of Philip II

1558 Elizabeth ascends throne of England

1562 First voyage of John Hawkins

1564 Second voyage of John Hawkins

1567 Third voyage of Hawkins and his defeat at San Juan de Ulua

1572 Drake raids Panama

1577 Drake sails around the world

1585 Ralegh founds Virginia colony

1586 Drake raids Santo Domingo and Cartagena

1587 Drake raids Cádiz

1588 Defeat of the Spanish Armada

1595 First voyage of Ralegh to Guiana

1595 Final voyage of Hawkins and Drake, and their deaths

1598 Death of Philip II. Succeeded by Philip III

1600 East India Company founded in England

1603 Death of Queen Elizabeth of England. Succeeded by James I

1605 Publication of *Don Quixote*

1610 Assassination of Henry IV of France

1612 Voyage of La Ravardière to the Amazon

1617 Final expedition of Ralegh to Guiana

1618 Ralegh beheaded

1620 García Girón de Loaisa of Cartagena drives off corsairs

1625 Dutch pirates attack Puerto Rico

1635 *Compagnie des Isles de l'Amérique* organized under auspices of Richelieu

1635 Birth of Henry Morgan

1648–61 Spain loses Low Countries

1655 Occupation of Jamaica by Penn and Venables

1658 Birth of William Paterson

1664 *Compagnie de la France Equinoctiale* founded under auspices of Colbert

1665 St. Eustatius, Saba, and Tobago occupied by the English

1665 Charles II crowned King of Spain

1666 Antigua, Monserrat, and

467

San Cristobal occupied by the French

1666   Guiana occupied by the Dutch

1667   Peace of Breda

1668   Morgan captures Portobello
1671   The Danes occupy St. Thomas
1671   Morgan takes Panama

1671   Danish West India Company founded

1678   Esquemeling's book published
1685   Louis XIV issues Negro Code

1688   Death of Morgan
1695   Ducasse attacks Cartagena

1695   Foundation of the Company of Scotland Trading to Africa and the Indies

1698   Paterson occupies Darien

1700   Death of Charles II of Spain and end of Hapsburg dynasty. Crown passes to Philip V, first of the Bourbon kings of Spain
1702–13   War of the Spanish Succession
1704   English occupy Gibraltar

1707   First book printed in Havana

1713   Treaty of Utrecht. England granted monopoly of slave trade
1717   Mississippi Company founded in France

1718   New Orleans founded

1719   *Robinson Crusoe* published

1721   University of Caracas founded
1721   University of Havana founded
1722   First number of newspaper *Hoja Volante* appears in Mexico

1728   Guipuzcoana Company organized

1729   *Gaceta de Guatemala* published
1739   Vernon takes Puerto Cabello
1741   Vernon withdraws from siege of Cartagena

1762 English occupy Havana

1763 France cedes Florida, Canada, San Vicente, Tobago, Dominica, Grenada, to England

1767 Expulsion of Jesuits from Spanish America

1795 Toussaint L'Ouverture sets up his government in Haiti

1801 Haiti declares its complete independence

1802 Le Clerc arrests Toussaint L'Ouverture

1803 Purchase of Louisiana by United States

1803 French withdraw from Haiti

1806 Miranda lands in Venezuela

1809 Martinique and Guadalupe occupied by English

1810–24 Spanish American Wars of Independence

1810 Freebooter Jean Lafitte heads smugglers of Barataria

1746 Death of Philip V of Spain. Succeeded by Ferdinand VI

1746–1804 Societies of Friends of the Country founded in Spain

1759 Death of Ferdinand VI of Spain. Succeeded by Charles III

1759–72 Publication of the *Encyclopédie* in France

1761 Signing of Family Pact: France and Spain against England

1763 Treaty of Paris

1767 Expulsion of the Jesuits from Spain

1788 Death of Charles III of Spain. Succeeded by Charles IV

1789 French Revolution opens

1796 Napoleon marries Joséphine

1808 Riot in Aranjuez in favor of Ferdinand VII

1808 Ferdinand VII and Charles IV abdicate in Bayonne. Joseph Bonaparte made King of Spain

1808–14 War of Spanish people against Napoleon

1812 Constitution of Cádiz

1814 Ferdinand VII returns to Spain and abrogates Constitution of Cadiz

1822 Iturbide crowned Emperor
of Mexico
1823 Proclamation of Monroe
Doctrine
1830 Death of Simón Bolívar

1836 Spain recognizes independence of South American republics

1855 William Walker president
of Nicaragua
1857 Walker leaves Central
America
1860 Walker executed in Honduras
1863 Troops of Napoleon III occupy Mexico
1867 Emperor Maximilian of
Mexico executed
1868–78 First war of Cuban independence

1869 Suez Canal inaugurated

1879 Meeting in Paris of *Congrés
International d'Etudes du Canal
Interocéanique*
1880 Lesseps begins work on
Panama Canal

1895 Second war of Cuban independence. Death of Martí
1898 Spain loses Cuba and Puerto
Rico
1902 Cuba declared independent
1903 Roosevelt decides to build
canal in Panama
1903 Panama secedes from
Colombia

INDEX

ABOUT THE AUTHOR

Germán Arciniegas, who had a distinguished career as a historian, statesman, diplomat, and public intellectual, with over seventy books and thousands of essays to his credit, was born in Bogotá on December 6, 1900. While a law student at the prestigious National University in Bogotá, Arciniegas became a radical student leader, organizing a nationwide federation to protest government policies. He contributed articles to newspapers and magazines, founded the review *Universidad* in Bogotá in 1928, and became editor of the newspaper *El Tiempo* in 1939. He served several terms as a congressman, and held the post of Colombian minister of education.

His first book, *The Student at the Round Table,* roundly criticized the military and dictatorships in Latin America. Many of his later books were banned, and as a result he was forced into exile in the United States in the early 1950s.

Arciniegas taught at several universities in the United States, including the University of California at Berkeley, the University of Chicago, and Columbia University. He was known as an outspoken critic of the State Department's conciliatory policies towards repressive regimes. *Caribbean: Sea of the New World* and *Latin America: A Cultural History* introduced an international audience to Arciniegas' panoramic view of his continent. Other books that appeared in English include *America in Europe: A History of the New World in Reverse* and *The Knight of El Dorado.*

In 1953, and again in 1954 and 1957, Arciniegas was detained for "security questioning" in New York when he returned from trips abroad. He had been falsely denounced as a Communist by the Colombian dictatorship then in power. He was held at Ellis Island and released after a media campaign led by the *New York Times.* Soon after, Arciniegas turned to a diplomatic career, and in 1959 was appointed Colombian ambassador to Italy; he later served in Israel, Venezuela, and the Vatican.

Even when he was in his nineties, Arciniegas continued to

arouse controversy in his native Colombia by clashing with pre-eminent politicians, drug traffickers, and Marxist guerrillas, and in the United States he attacked restrictive immigration policies.

When Arciniegas died in 1999, President Andres Pastrana of Colombia decreed three days of mourning for this prolific and outspoken public figure, who has been described as "one of the continent's most important writers."

SOURCES

Obituary, "Germán Arciniegas, 98, Critic of Latin American Dictators," *The New York Times* (5 December 1999)

The Perucho Figueredo Page, <http://figueredo.freeservers.com/main.html>.

CPSIA information can be obtained at www.ICGtesting.com
Printed in the USA
BVOW020942041012

302118BV00001B/16/P